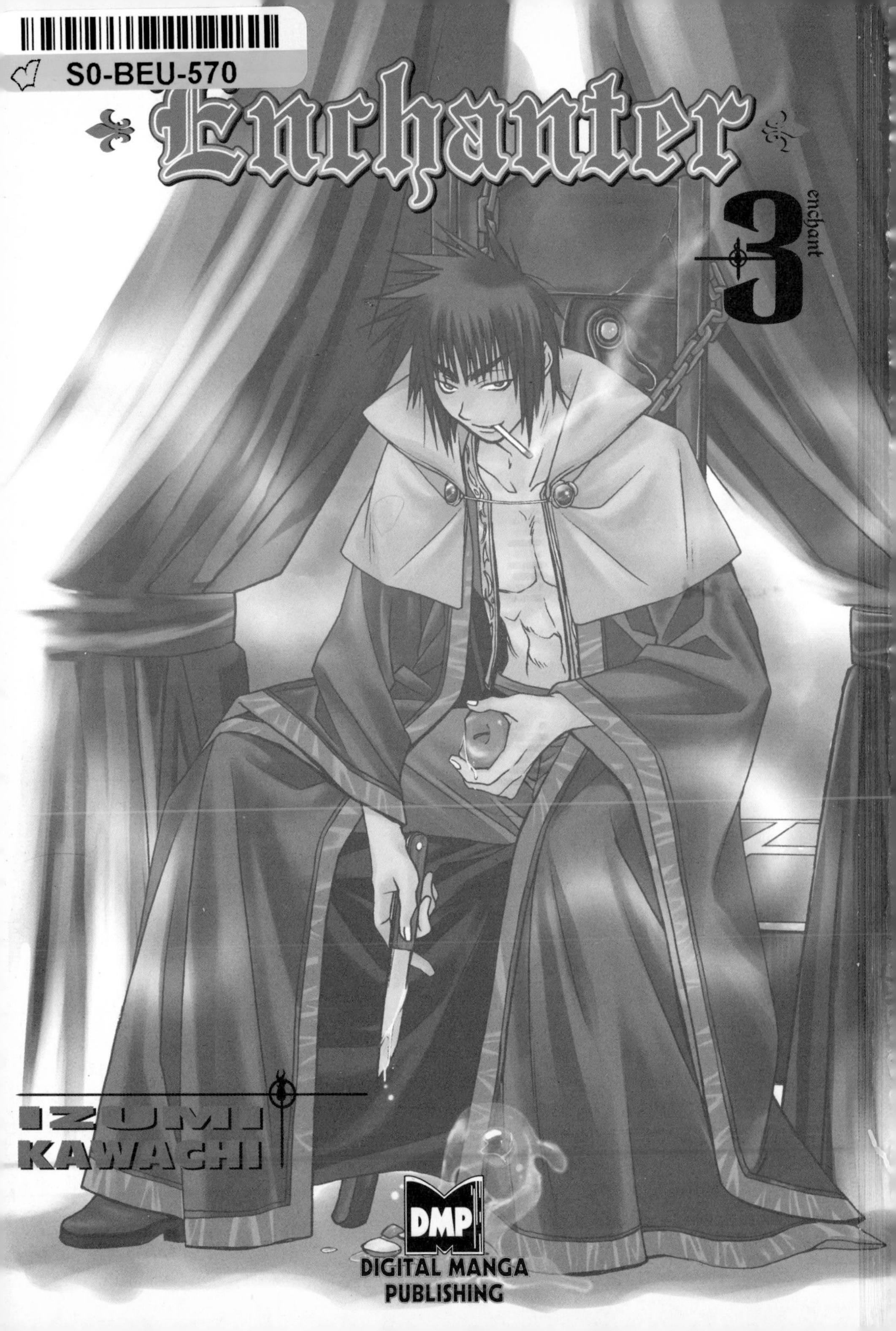
Enchanter
3
enchant
IZUMI
KAWACHI
DMP
DIGITAL MANGA
PUBLISHING

Enchanter 3

enchant

CONTENTS

Translation	Sachiko Sato
Lettering	IHL
Graphic Design	Fred Lui / Wendy Lee
Editing	Stephanie Donnelly
Editor in Chief	Fred Lui
Publisher	Hikaru Sasahara

English Edition Published by
DIGITAL MANGA PUBLISHING
A division of DIGITAL MANGA, Inc.
1487 W 178th Street, Suite 300
Gardena, CA 90248

www.dmpbooks.com

First Edition: February 2007
ISBN-10: 1-56970-864-9
ISBN-13: 978-1-56970-864-4

1 3 5 7 9 10 8 6 4 2

Printed in China

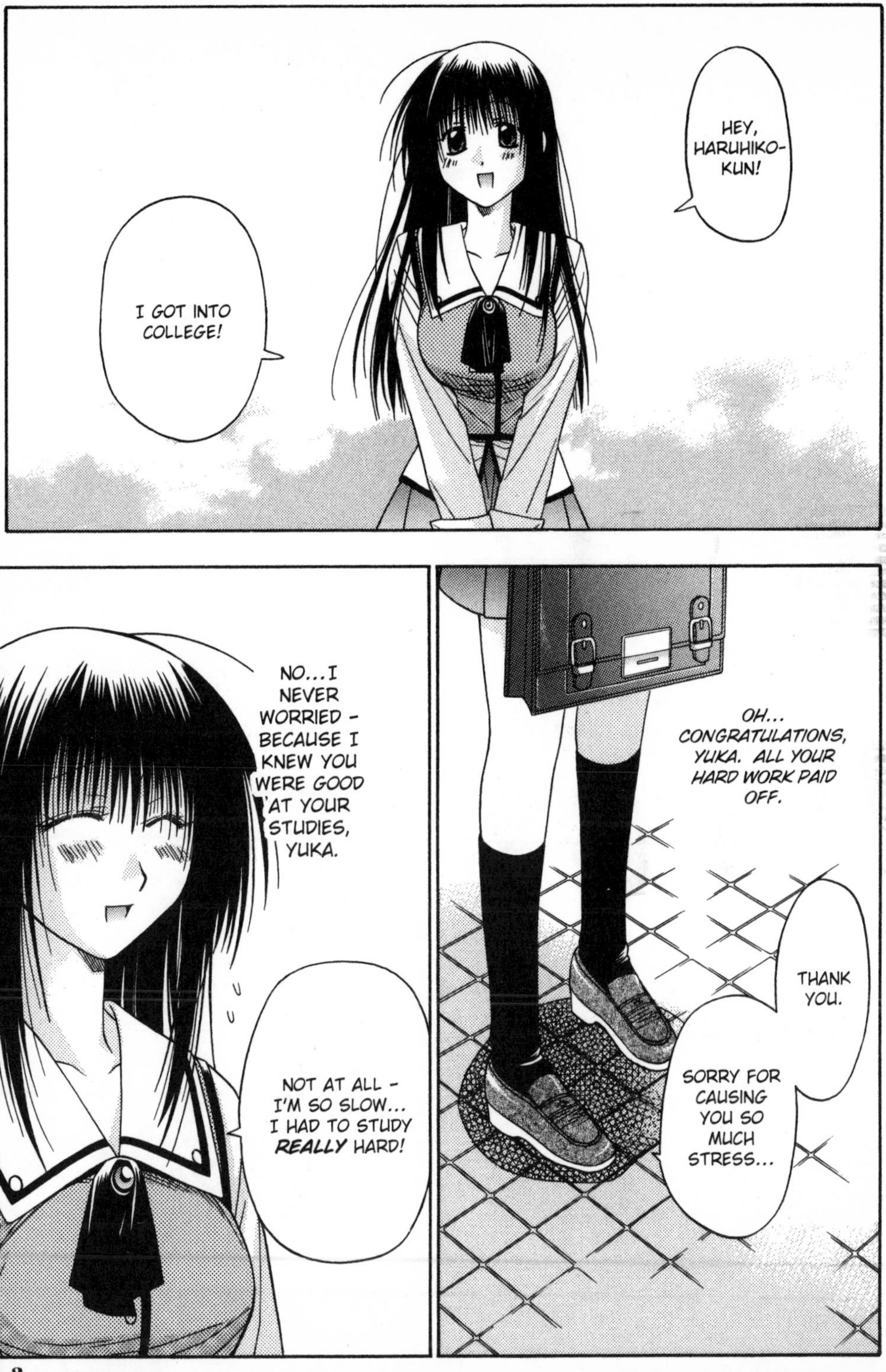
HEY, HARUHIKO-KUN!
I GOT INTO COLLEGE!
OH... CONGRATULATIONS, YUKA. ALL YOUR HARD WORK PAID OFF.
THANK YOU.
SORRY FOR CAUSING YOU SO MUCH STRESS...
NO...I NEVER WORRIED - BECAUSE I KNEW YOU WERE GOOD AT YOUR STUDIES, YUKA.
NOT AT ALL - I'M SO SLOW... I HAD TO STUDY *REALLY* HARD!

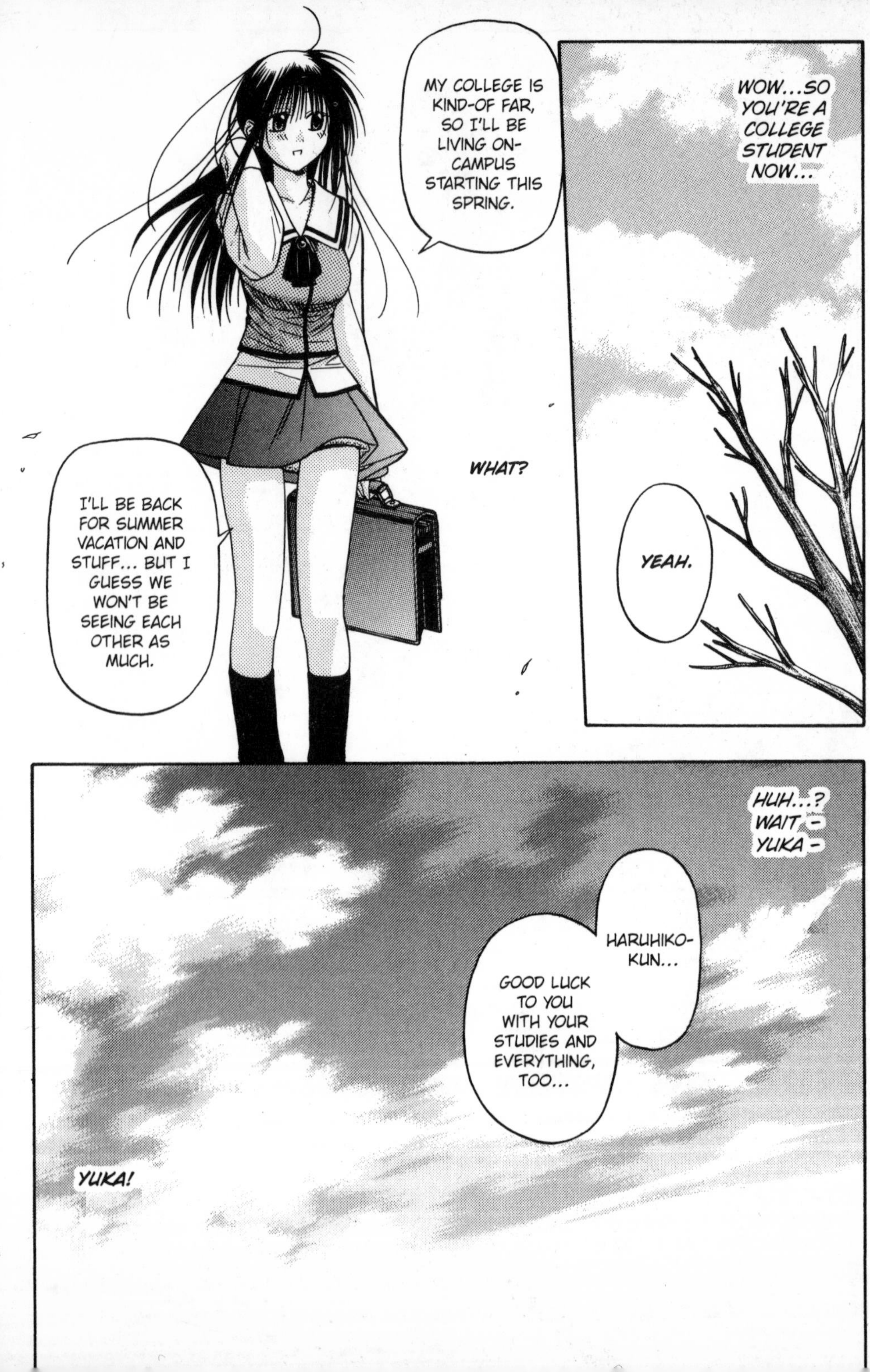
WOW...SO YOU'RE A COLLEGE STUDENT NOW...
YEAH.
MY COLLEGE IS KIND-OF FAR, SO I'LL BE LIVING ON-CAMPUS STARTING THIS SPRING.
WHAT?
I'LL BE BACK FOR SUMMER VACATION AND STUFF... BUT I GUESS WE WON'T BE SEEING EACH OTHER AS MUCH.
HUH...? WAIT - YUKA -
HARUHIKO-KUN...
GOOD LUCK TO YOU WITH YOUR STUDIES AND EVERYTHING, TOO...
YUKA!

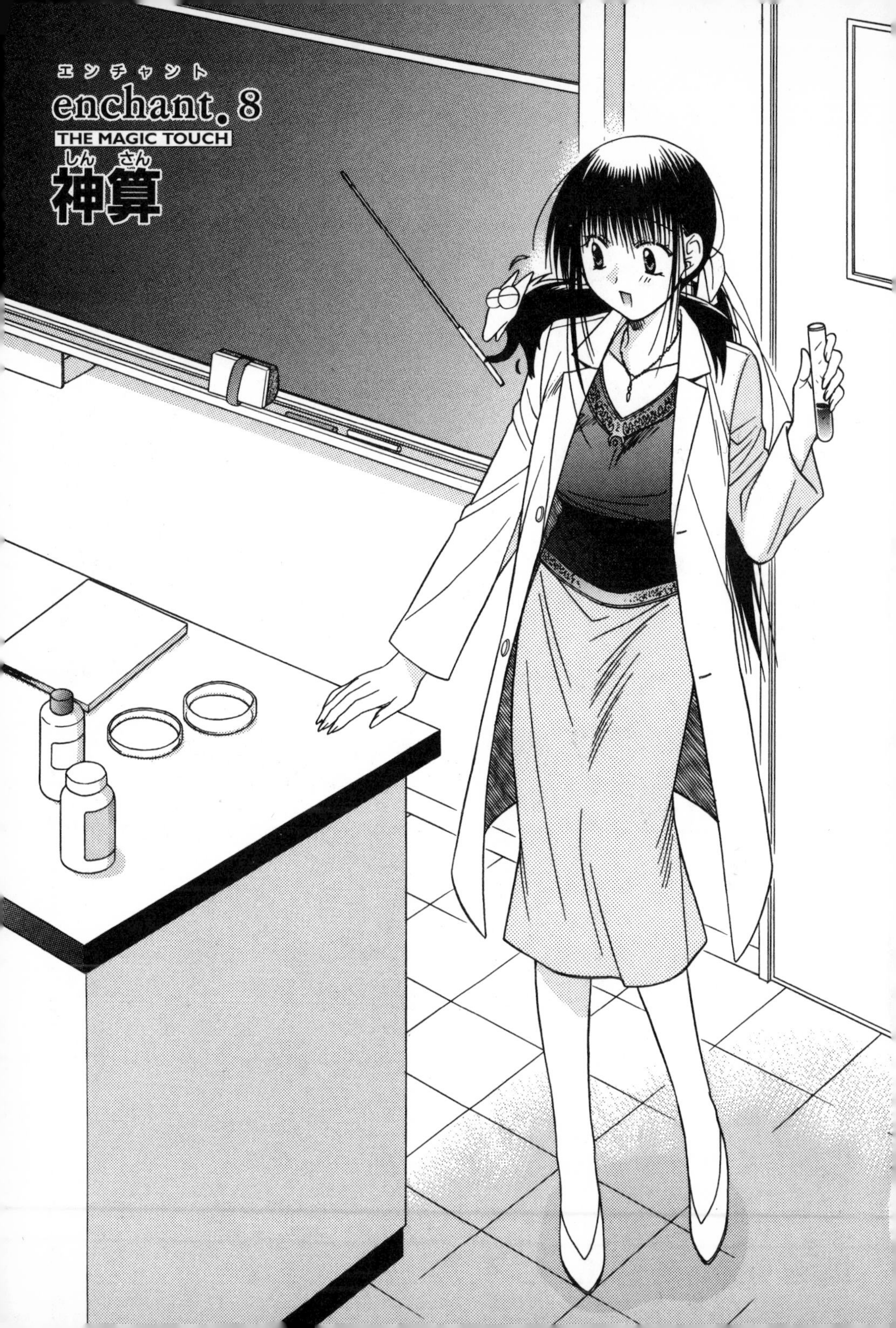
エンチャント
enchant. 8
THE MAGIC TOUCH
しんさん
神算

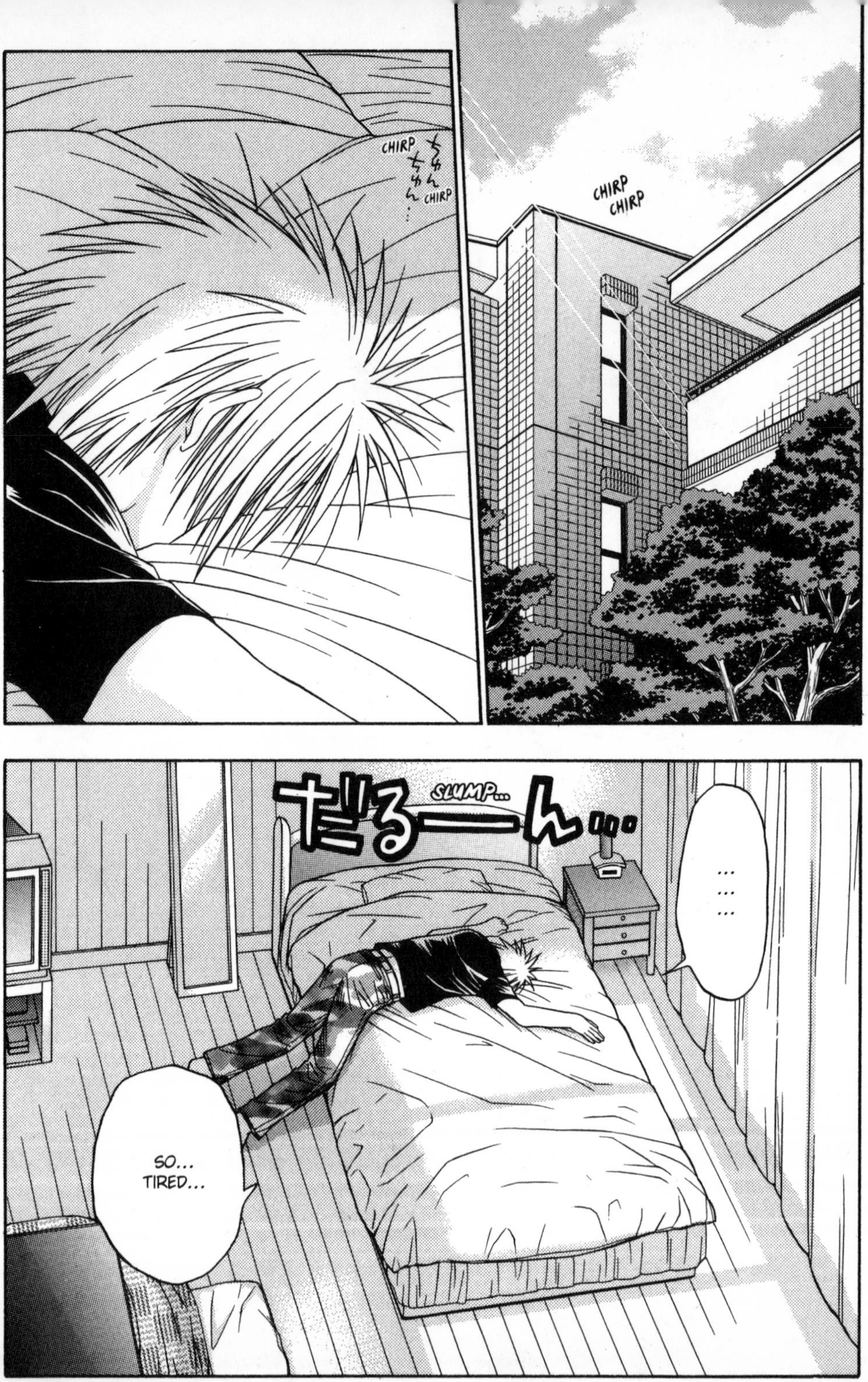
CHIRP
CHIRP
CHIRP
ちゅん ちゅん…
CHIRP
…
…
…
だるーーん…
SLUMP…
SO… TIRED…

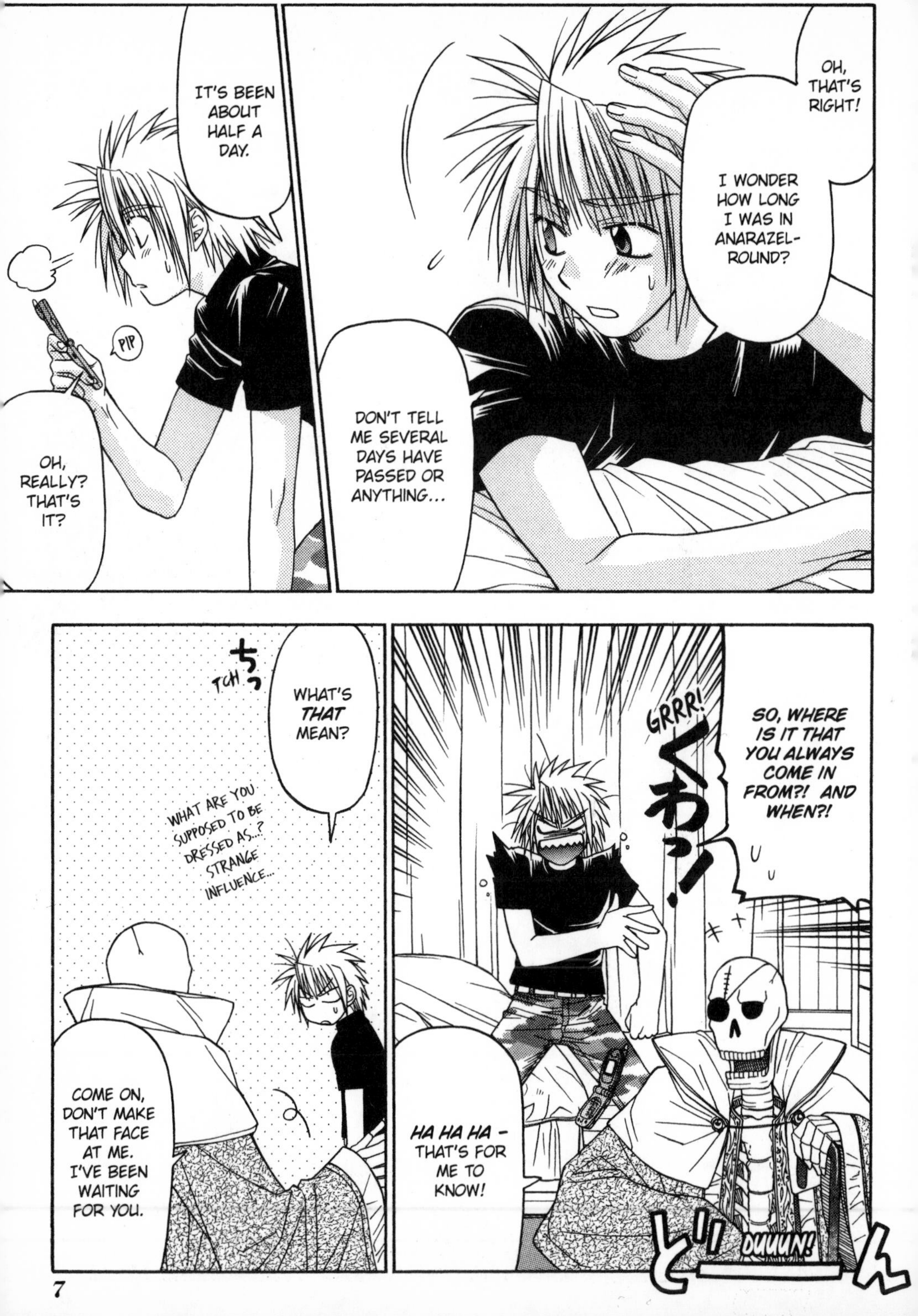

OH, THAT'S RIGHT!
I WONDER HOW LONG I WAS IN ANARAZEL-ROUND?
DON'T TELL ME SEVERAL DAYS HAVE PASSED OR ANYTHING...
IT'S BEEN ABOUT HALF A DAY.
PIP
OH, REALLY? THAT'S IT?
GRRR!
SO, WHERE IS IT THAT YOU ALWAYS COME IN FROM?! AND WHEN?!
HA HA HA - THAT'S FOR ME TO KNOW!
DUUUN!
WHAT'S THAT MEAN?
TCH
WHAT ARE YOU SUPPOSED TO BE DRESSED AS...? STRANGE INFLUENCE...
COME ON, DON'T MAKE THAT FACE AT ME. I'VE BEEN WAITING FOR YOU.

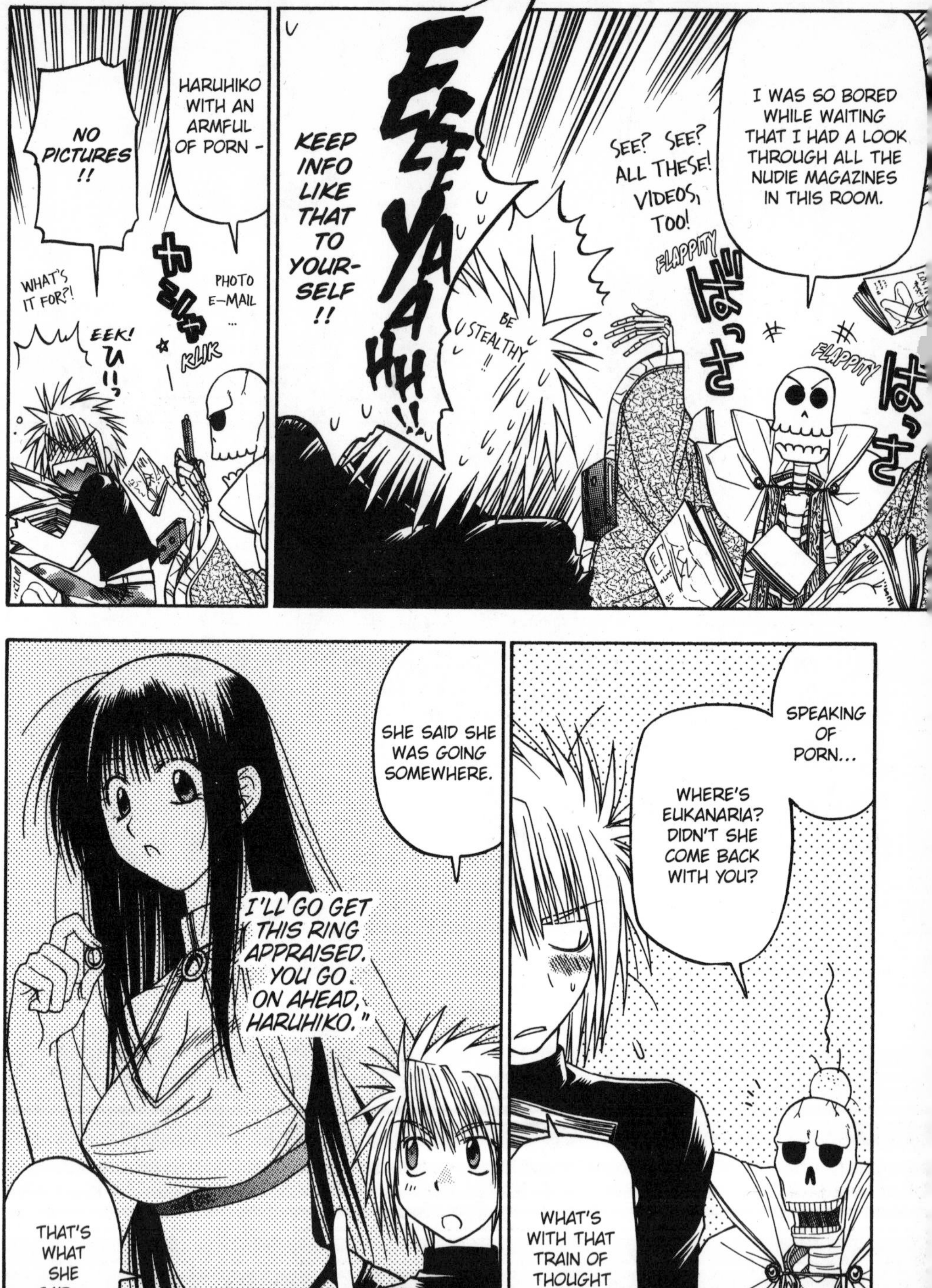
I WAS SO BORED WHILE WAITING THAT I HAD A LOOK THROUGH ALL THE NUDIE MAGAZINES IN THIS ROOM.
SEE? SEE? ALL THESE! VIDEOS, TOO!
FLAPPITY
ばっさ
FLAPPITY
はっさ
EEEYAAHH!!
KEEP INFO LIKE THAT TO YOURSELF!!
BE STEALTHY!!
HARUHIKO WITH AN ARMFUL OF PORN -
PHOTO E-MAIL ...
KLIK
NO PICTURES!!
WHAT'S IT FOR?!
EEK! ひぃっ
SPEAKING OF PORN...
WHERE'S EUKANARIA? DIDN'T SHE COME BACK WITH YOU?
WHAT'S WITH THAT TRAIN OF THOUGHT ...?
SHE SAID SHE WAS GOING SOMEWHERE.
"I'LL GO GET THIS RING APPRAISED. YOU GO ON AHEAD, HARUHIKO."
THAT'S WHAT SHE SAID...

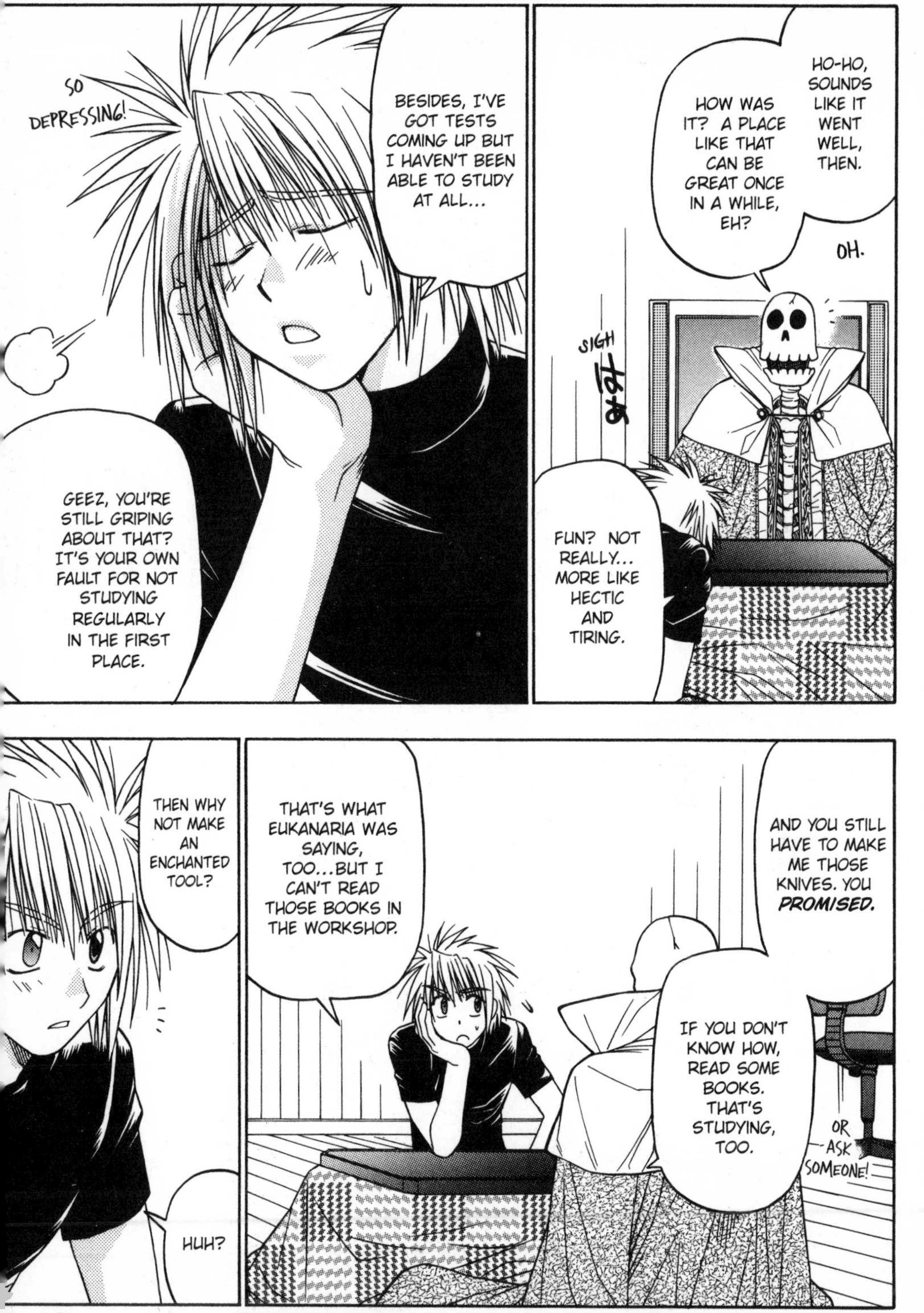

OH.
HOW WAS IT? A PLACE LIKE THAT CAN BE GREAT ONCE IN A WHILE, EH?
HO-HO, SOUNDS LIKE IT WENT WELL, THEN.
SIGH はあ
FUN? NOT REALLY... MORE LIKE HECTIC AND TIRING.
BESIDES, I'VE GOT TESTS COMING UP BUT I HAVEN'T BEEN ABLE TO STUDY AT ALL...
SO DEPRESSING!
GEEZ, YOU'RE STILL GRIPING ABOUT THAT? IT'S YOUR OWN FAULT FOR NOT STUDYING REGULARLY IN THE FIRST PLACE.
AND YOU STILL HAVE TO MAKE ME THOSE KNIVES. YOU **PROMISED.**
IF YOU DON'T KNOW HOW, READ SOME BOOKS. THAT'S STUDYING, TOO.
OR ASK SOMEONE!
THAT'S WHAT EUKANARIA WAS SAYING, TOO...BUT I CAN'T READ THOSE BOOKS IN THE WORKSHOP.
THEN WHY NOT MAKE AN ENCHANTED TOOL?
HUH?

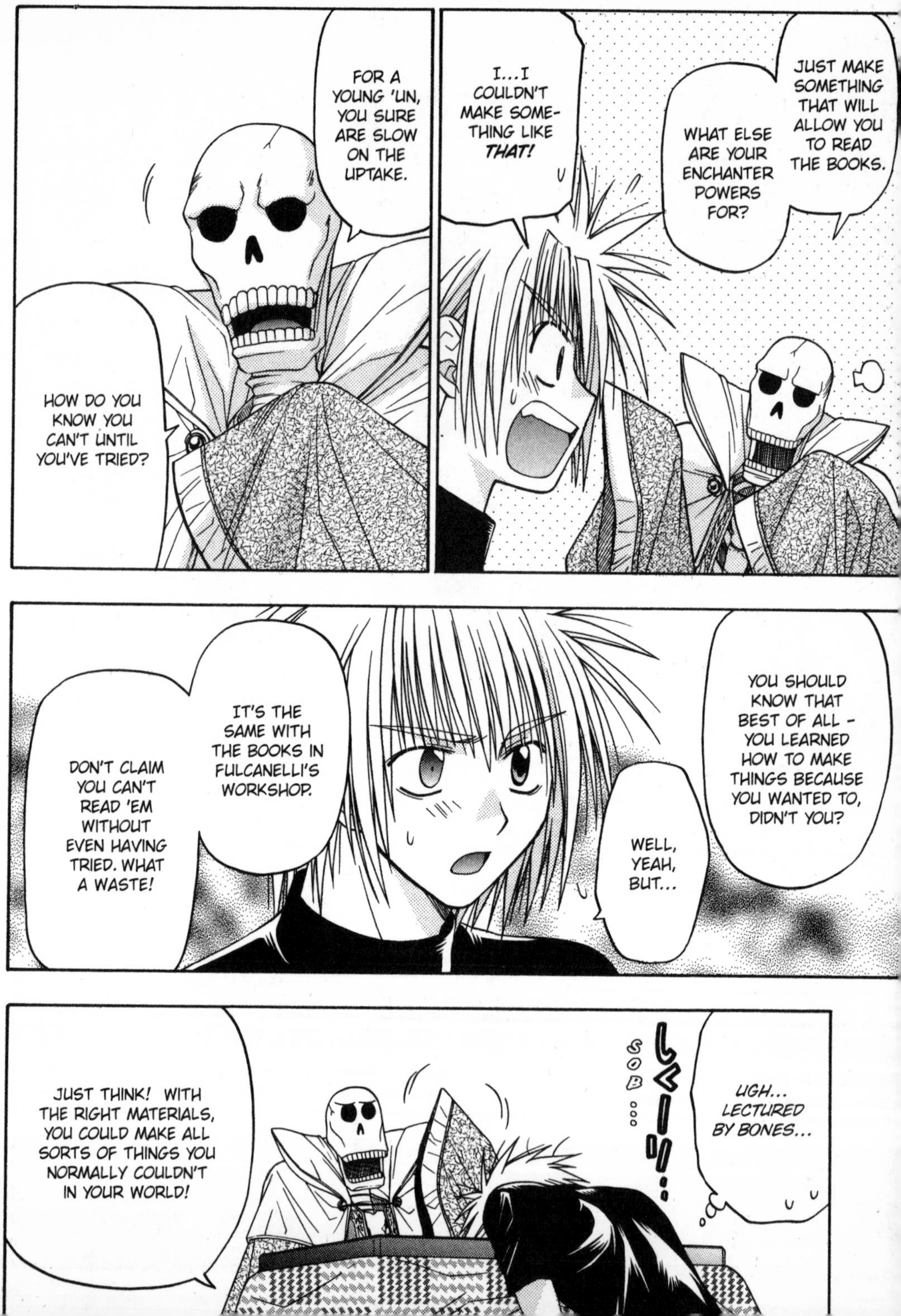
JUST MAKE SOMETHING THAT WILL ALLOW YOU TO READ THE BOOKS.
WHAT ELSE ARE YOUR ENCHANTER POWERS FOR?
I...I COULDN'T MAKE SOME-THING LIKE *THAT!*
FOR A YOUNG 'UN, YOU SURE ARE SLOW ON THE UPTAKE.
HOW DO YOU KNOW YOU CAN'T UNTIL YOU'VE TRIED?
YOU SHOULD KNOW THAT BEST OF ALL - YOU LEARNED HOW TO MAKE THINGS BECAUSE YOU WANTED TO, DIDN'T YOU?
WELL, YEAH, BUT...
IT'S THE SAME WITH THE BOOKS IN FULCANELLI'S WORKSHOP.
DON'T CLAIM YOU CAN'T READ 'EM WITHOUT EVEN HAVING TRIED. WHAT A WASTE!
UGH... LECTURED BY BONES...
SOB...
JUST THINK! WITH THE RIGHT MATERIALS, YOU COULD MAKE ALL SORTS OF THINGS YOU NORMALLY COULDN'T IN YOUR WORLD!

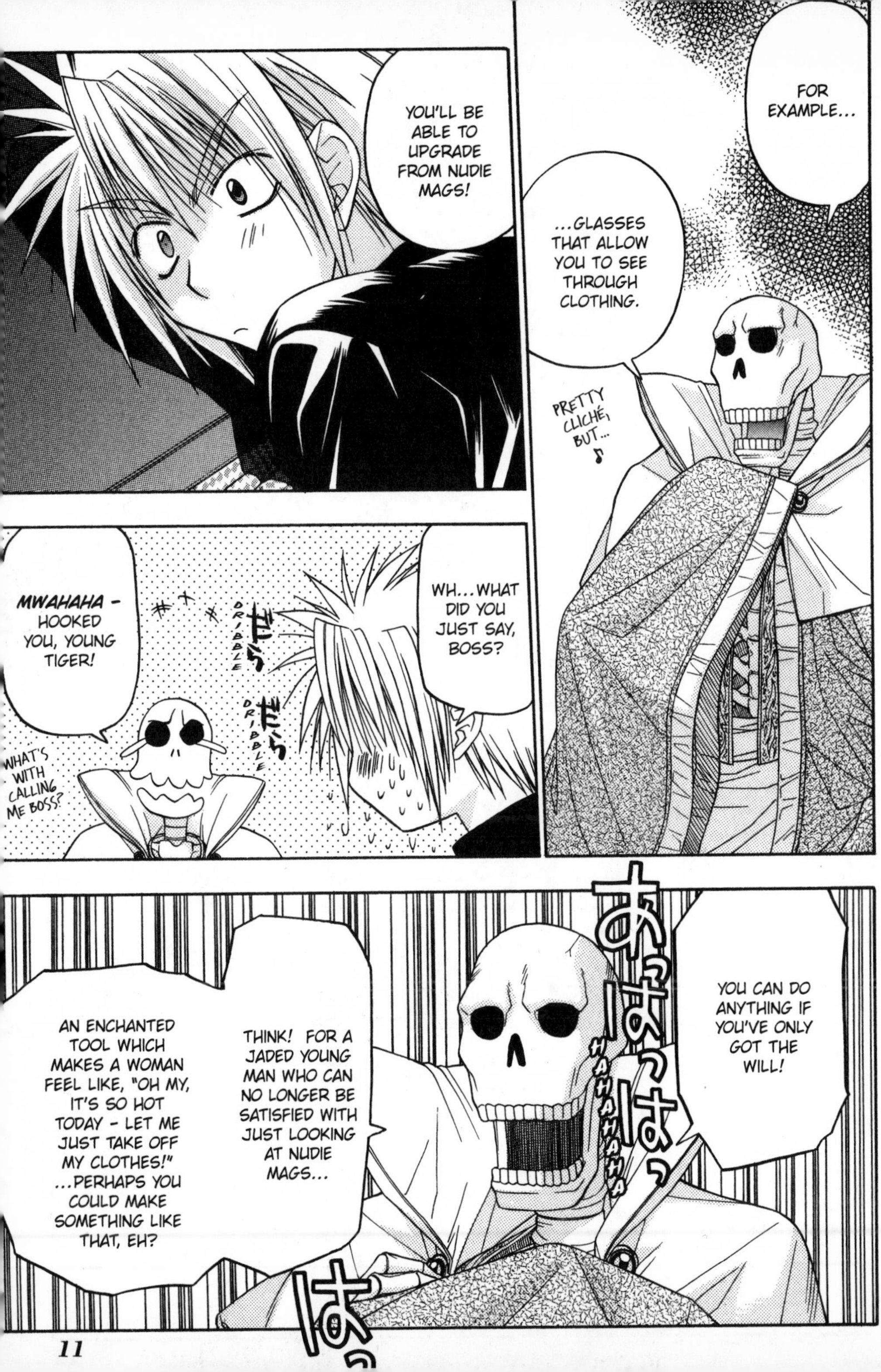
FOR EXAMPLE...
...GLASSES THAT ALLOW YOU TO SEE THROUGH CLOTHING.
PRETTY CLICHÉ, BUT... ♪
YOU'LL BE ABLE TO UPGRADE FROM NUDIE MAGS!
WH...WHAT DID YOU JUST SAY, BOSS?
だら DRIBBLE
だら DRIBBLE
MWAHAHA - HOOKED YOU, YOUNG TIGER!
WHAT'S WITH CALLING ME BOSS?
YOU CAN DO ANYTHING IF YOU'VE ONLY GOT THE WILL!
あっはっはっ
HAHAHAHA
はっ
THINK! FOR A JADED YOUNG MAN WHO CAN NO LONGER BE SATISFIED WITH JUST LOOKING AT NUDIE MAGS...
AN ENCHANTED TOOL WHICH MAKES A WOMAN FEEL LIKE, "OH MY, IT'S SO HOT TODAY - LET ME JUST TAKE OFF MY CLOTHES!" ...PERHAPS YOU COULD MAKE SOMETHING LIKE THAT, EH?

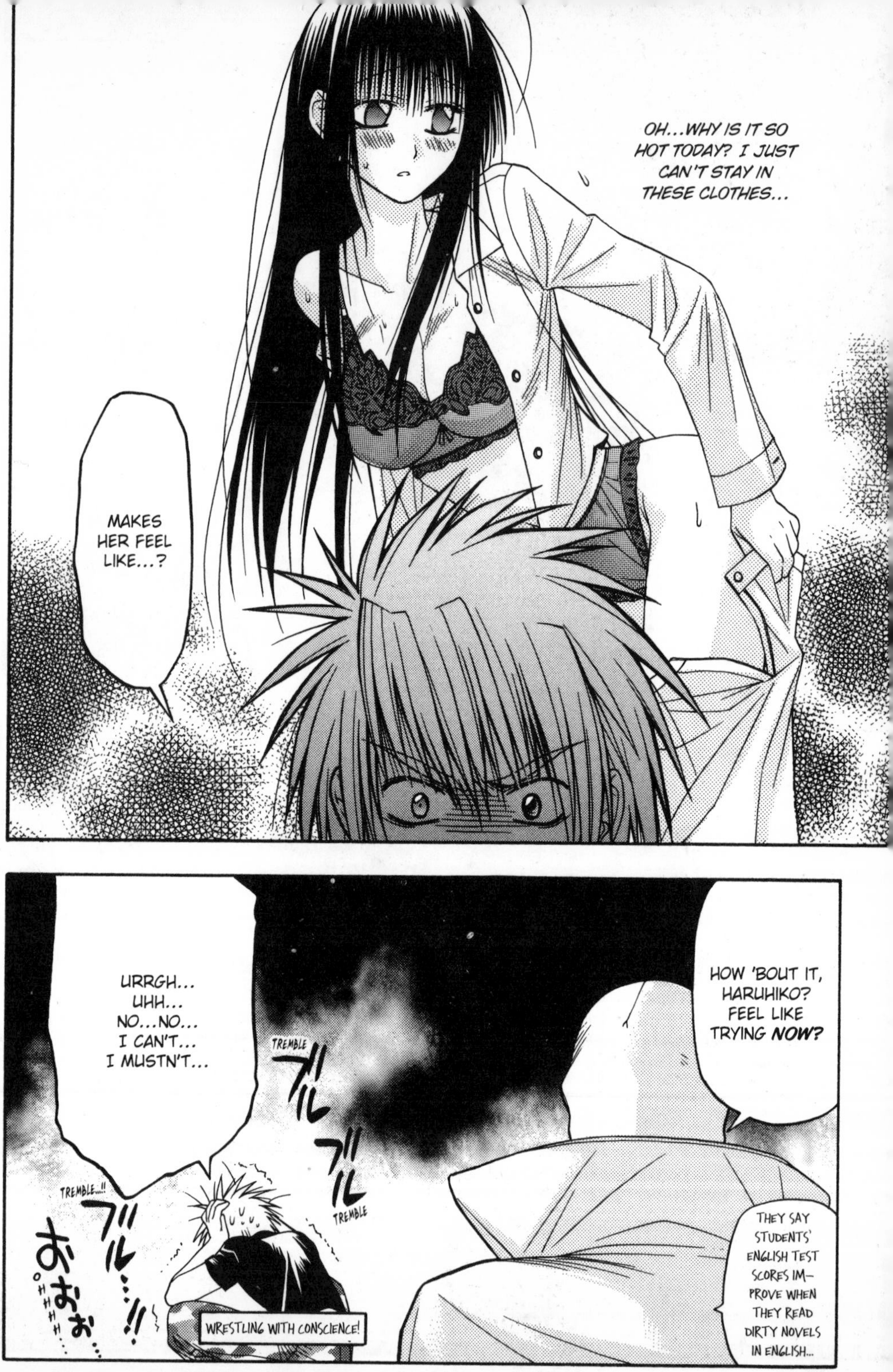
OH...WHY IS IT SO HOT TODAY? I JUST CAN'T STAY IN THESE CLOTHES...
MAKES HER FEEL LIKE...?
HOW 'BOUT IT, HARUHIKO? FEEL LIKE TRYING **NOW?**
THEY SAY STUDENTS' ENGLISH TEST SCORES IM-PROVE WHEN THEY READ DIRTY NOVELS IN ENGLISH...
URRGH... UHH... NO...NO... I CAN'T... I MUSTN'T...
TREMBLE
ブル
ブル
TREMBLE
TREMBLE...!!
ブル...!!
おおぉ
OHHHH...
WRESTLING WITH CONSCIENCE!

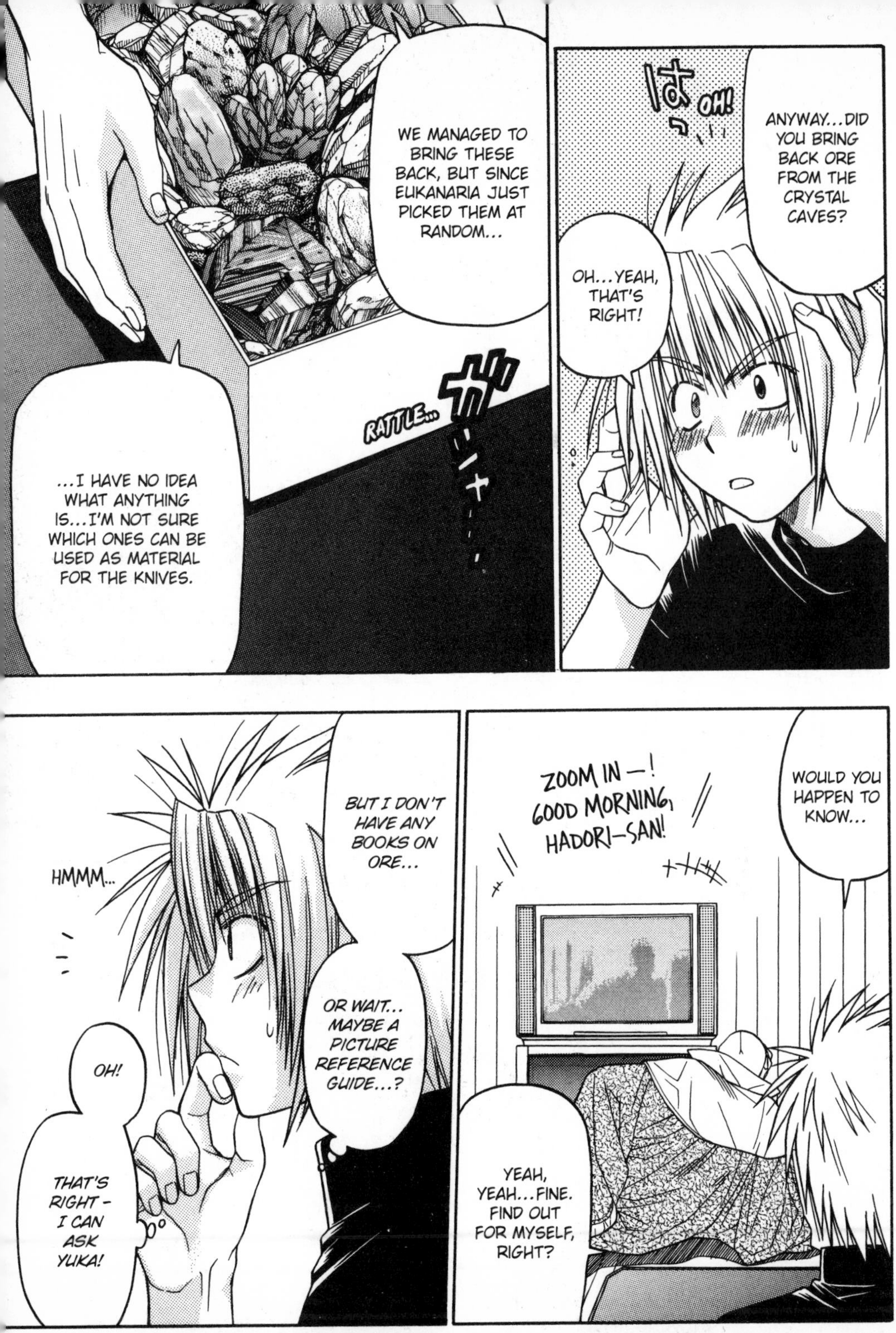
ANYWAY...DID YOU BRING BACK ORE FROM THE CRYSTAL CAVES?
OH!
OH...YEAH, THAT'S RIGHT!
WE MANAGED TO BRING THESE BACK, BUT SINCE EUKANARIA JUST PICKED THEM AT RANDOM...
RATTLE...
...I HAVE NO IDEA WHAT ANYTHING IS...I'M NOT SURE WHICH ONES CAN BE USED AS MATERIAL FOR THE KNIVES.
WOULD YOU HAPPEN TO KNOW...
ZOOM IN—! GOOD MORNING, HADORI-SAN!
YEAH, YEAH...FINE. FIND OUT FOR MYSELF, RIGHT?
BUT I DON'T HAVE ANY BOOKS ON ORE...
HMMM...
OR WAIT... MAYBE A PICTURE REFERENCE GUIDE...?
OH!
THAT'S RIGHT - I CAN ASK YUKA!

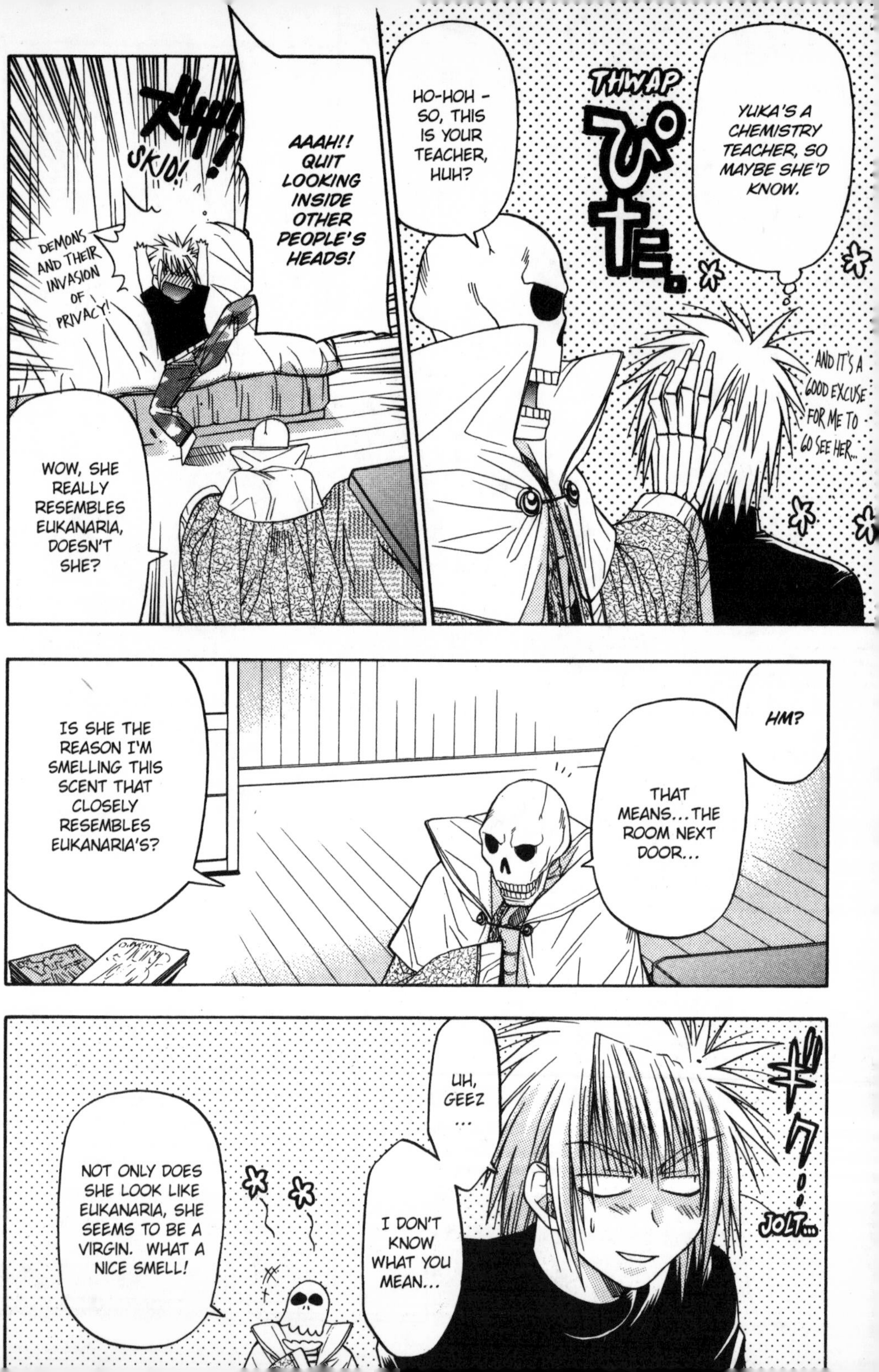

YUKA'S A CHEMISTRY TEACHER, SO MAYBE SHE'D KNOW.
THWAP
AND IT'S A GOOD EXCUSE FOR ME TO GO SEE HER...
HO-HOH - SO, THIS IS YOUR TEACHER, HUH?
AAAH!! QUIT LOOKING INSIDE OTHER PEOPLE'S HEADS!
SKID!
DEMONS AND THEIR INVASION OF PRIVACY!
WOW, SHE REALLY RESEMBLES EUKANARIA, DOESN'T SHE?
HM?
THAT MEANS...THE ROOM NEXT DOOR...
IS SHE THE REASON I'M SMELLING THIS SCENT THAT CLOSELY RESEMBLES EUKANARIA'S?
JOLT...
UH, GEEZ...
I DON'T KNOW WHAT YOU MEAN...
NOT ONLY DOES SHE LOOK LIKE EUKANARIA, SHE SEEMS TO BE A VIRGIN. WHAT A NICE SMELL!

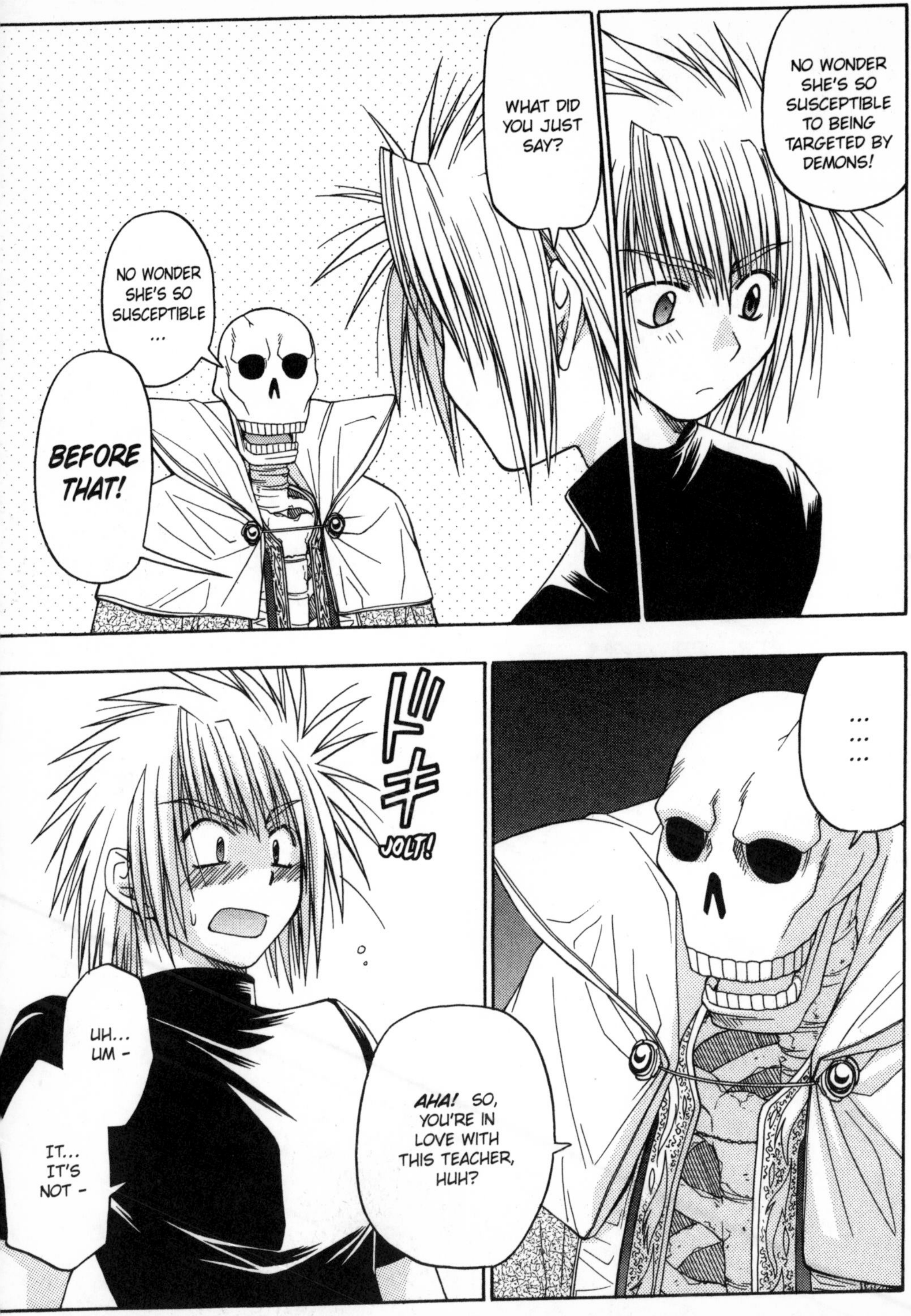
NO WONDER SHE'S SO SUSCEPTIBLE TO BEING TARGETED BY DEMONS!
WHAT DID YOU JUST SAY?
NO WONDER SHE'S SO SUSCEPTIBLE ...
BEFORE THAT!
... ...
AHA! SO, YOU'RE IN LOVE WITH THIS TEACHER, HUH?
ドキ
JOLT!
UH... UM -
IT... IT'S NOT -

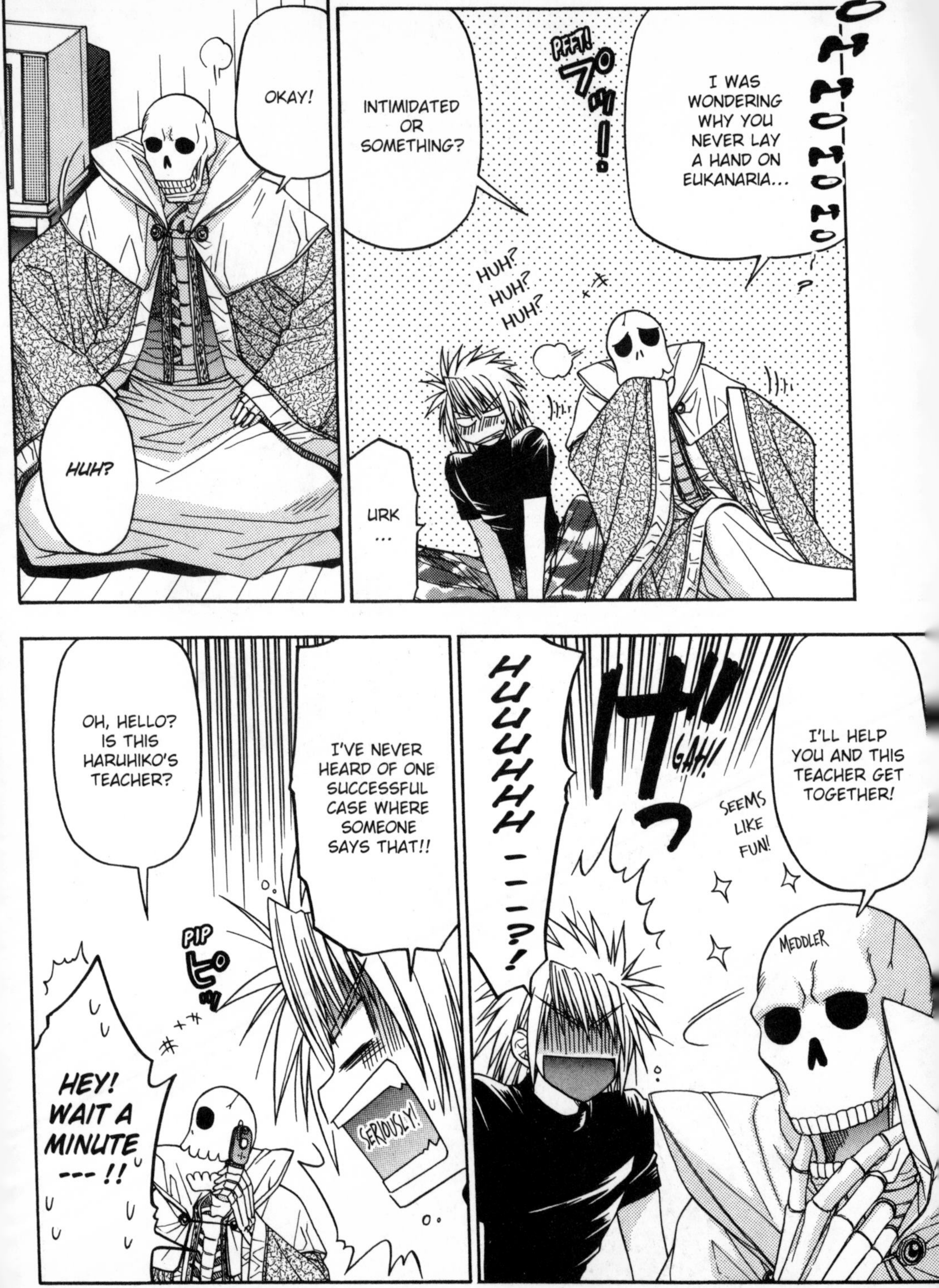
OHHOHOHO~?
I WAS WONDERING WHY YOU NEVER LAY A HAND ON EUKANARIA...
PFFT! プッ!!
INTIMIDATED OR SOMETHING?
HUH? HUH? HUH?
URK ...
OKAY!
HUH?
I'LL HELP YOU AND THIS TEACHER GET TOGETHER!
SEEMS LIKE FUN!
MEDDLER
ゲッ GAH!
HUUUHHHH---?!
I'VE NEVER HEARD OF ONE SUCCESSFUL CASE WHERE SOMEONE SAYS THAT!!
SERIOUSLY!
OH, HELLO? IS THIS HARUHIKO'S TEACHER?
PIP ピッ
HEY! WAIT A MINUTE---!!

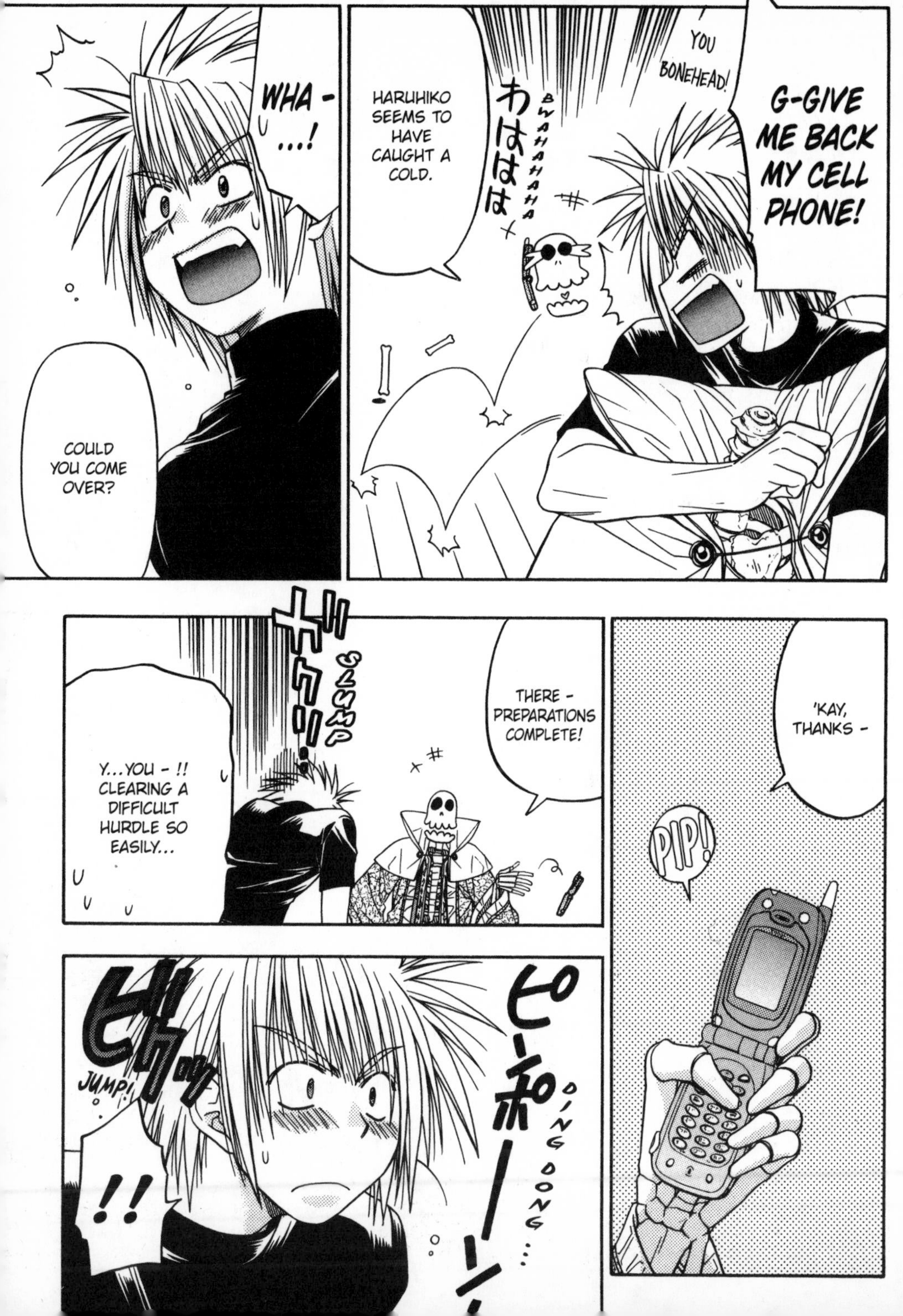
G-GIVE ME BACK MY CELL PHONE!
YOU BONEHEAD!
わははは
BWAHAHAHAHA
HARUHIKO SEEMS TO HAVE CAUGHT A COLD.
WHA - ...!
COULD YOU COME OVER?
'KAY, THANKS -
PIP!
THERE - PREPARATIONS COMPLETE!
ガクッ!!
SLUMP
Y...YOU - !! CLEARING A DIFFICULT HURDLE SO EASILY...
ピンポーン
DING DONG...
ビクッ
JUMP!
!!

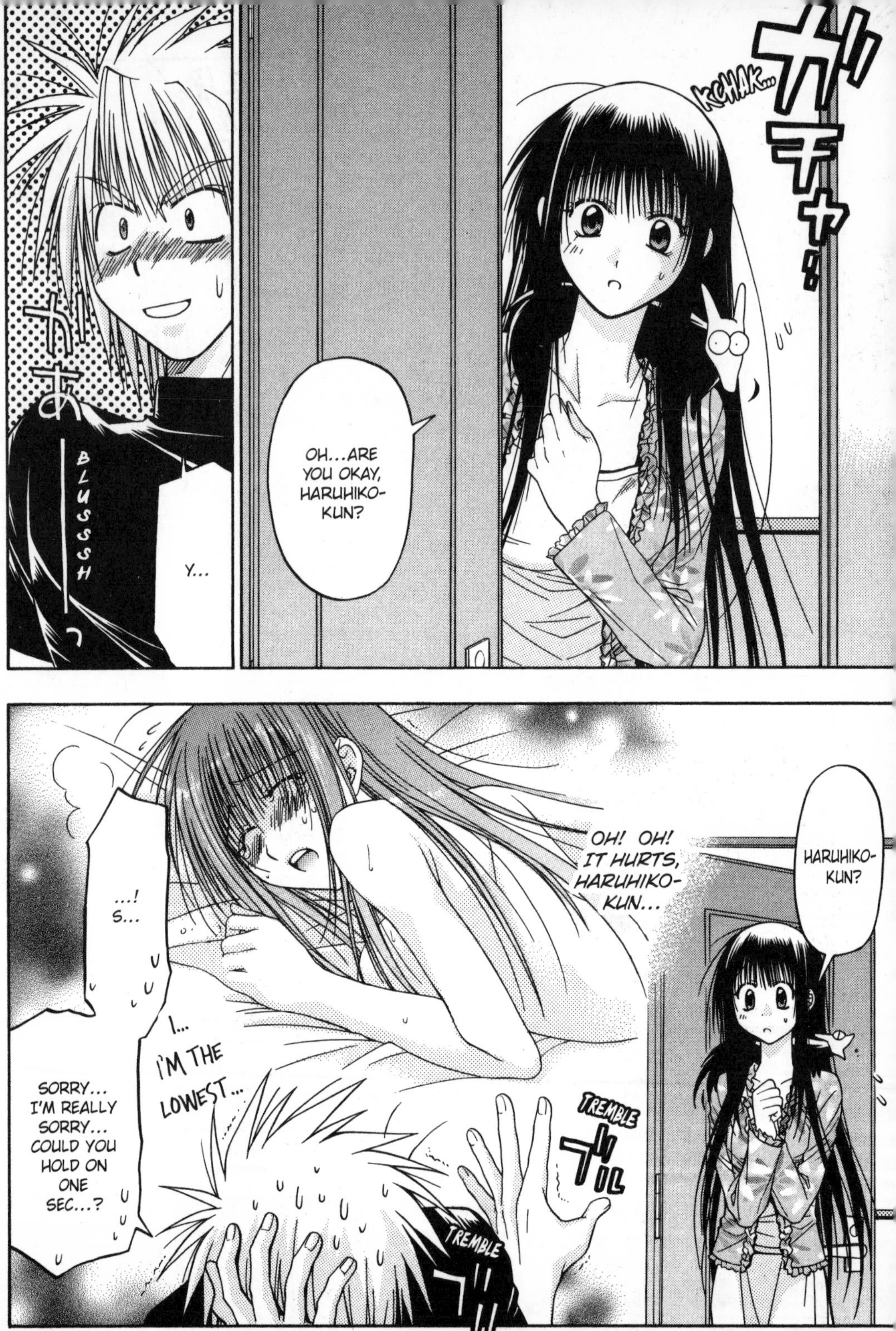
KCHAK...
ガチャ!
OH...ARE YOU OKAY, HARUHIKO-KUN?
BLUSSSH
かぁーっ
Y...
HARUHIKO-KUN?
OH! OH! IT HURTS, HARUHIKO-KUN...
TREMBLE
ブル
I... I'M THE LOWEST...
...! S...
SORRY... I'M REALLY SORRY... COULD YOU HOLD ON ONE SEC...?
TREMBLE
ブル

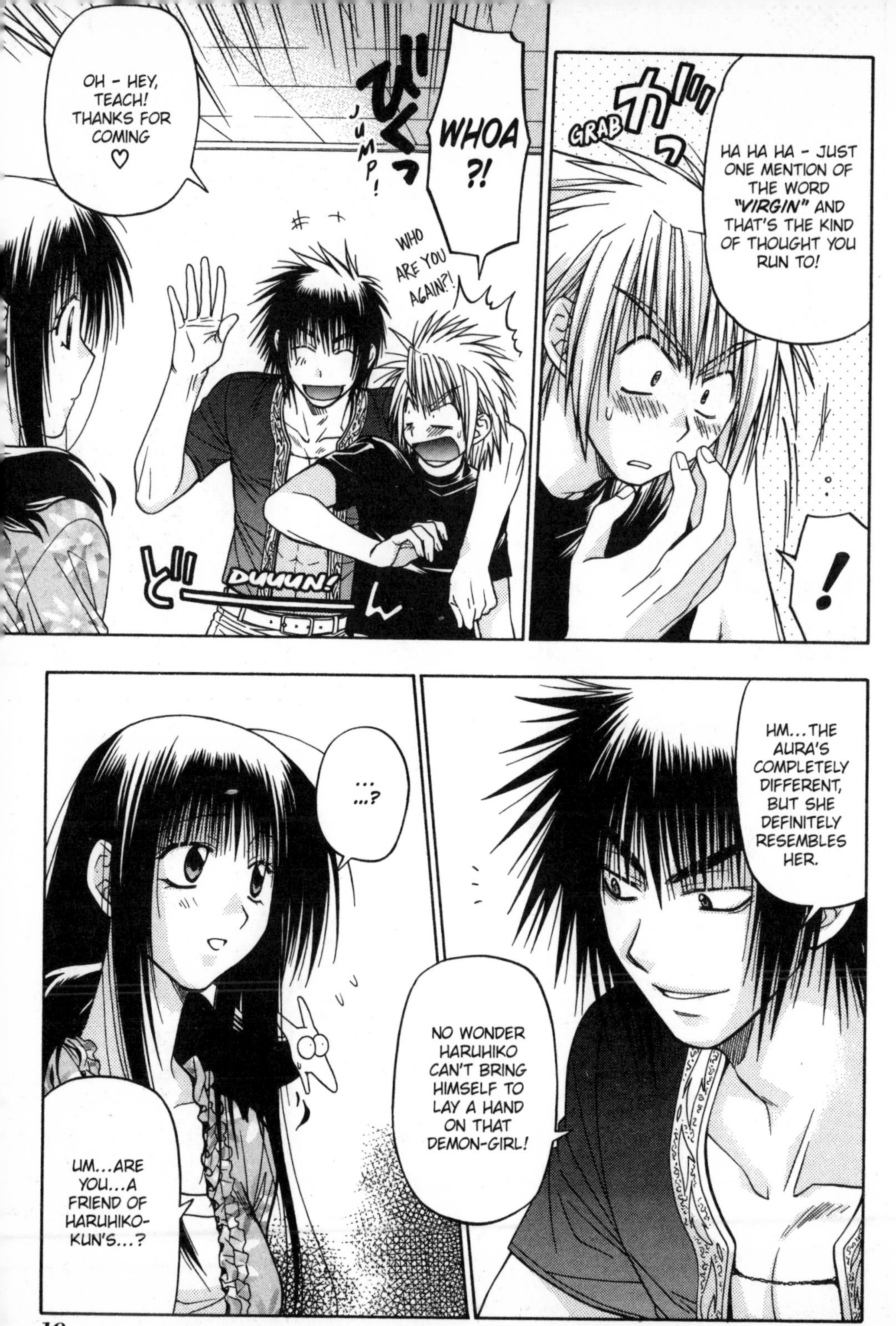
GRAB
HA HA HA - JUST ONE MENTION OF THE WORD "VIRGIN" AND THAT'S THE KIND OF THOUGHT YOU RUN TO!
!
WHOA ?!
JUMP!
OH - HEY, TEACH! THANKS FOR COMING ♡
WHO ARE YOU AGAIN?!
DUUUN!
HM...THE AURA'S COMPLETELY DIFFERENT, BUT SHE DEFINITELY RESEMBLES HER.
NO WONDER HARUHIKO CAN'T BRING HIMSELF TO LAY A HAND ON THAT DEMON-GIRL!
... ...?
UM...ARE YOU...A FRIEND OF HARUHIKO-KUN'S...?

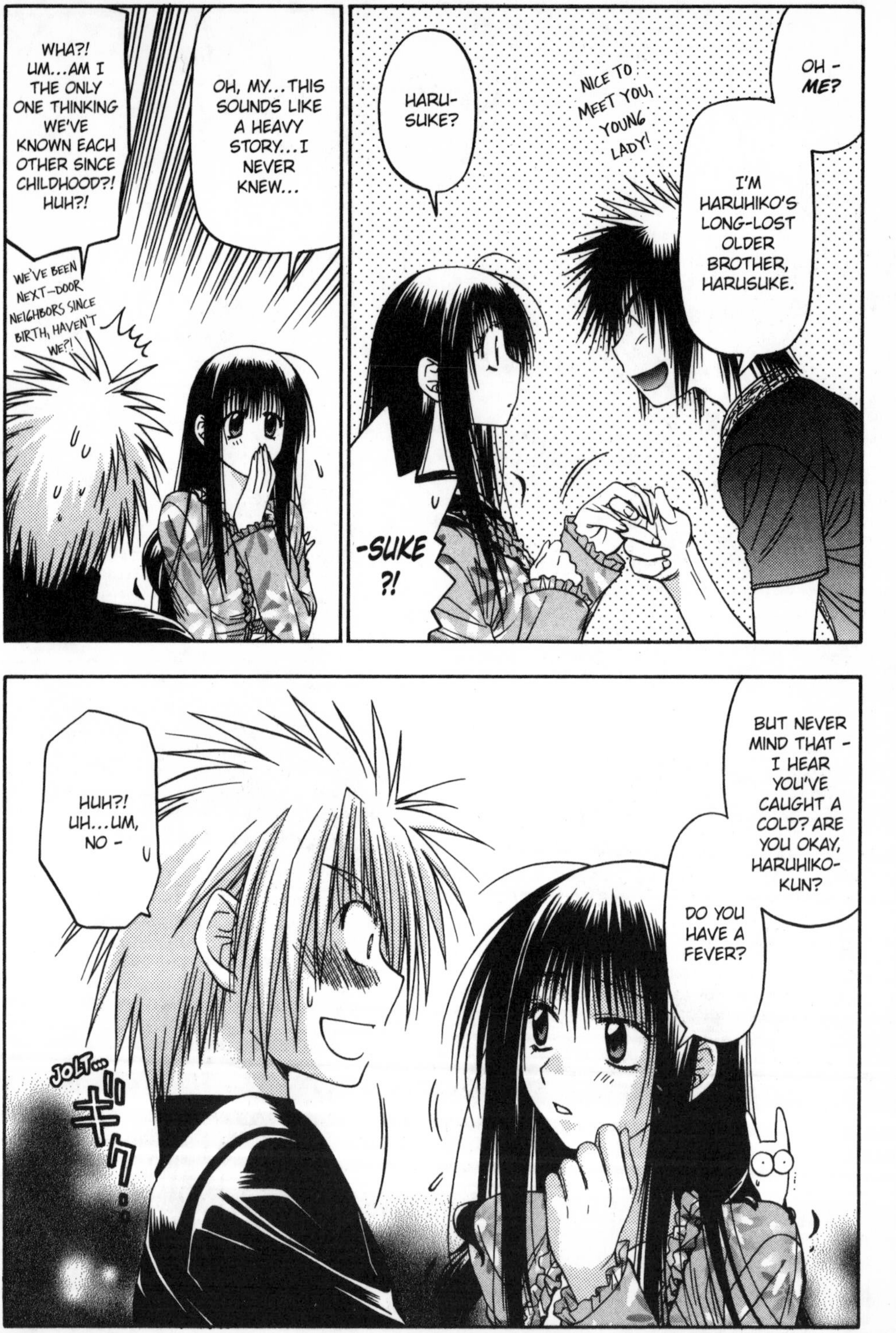
OH - ME?
I'M HARUHIKO'S LONG-LOST OLDER BROTHER, HARUSUKE.
NICE TO MEET YOU, YOUNG LADY!
HARU-SUKE?
-SUKE ?!
OH, MY...THIS SOUNDS LIKE A HEAVY STORY...I NEVER KNEW...
WHA?! UM...AM I THE ONLY ONE THINKING WE'VE KNOWN EACH OTHER SINCE CHILDHOOD?! HUH?!
WE'VE BEEN NEXT-DOOR NEIGHBORS SINCE BIRTH, HAVEN'T WE?!
BUT NEVER MIND THAT - I HEAR YOU'VE CAUGHT A COLD? ARE YOU OKAY, HARUHIKO-KUN?
DO YOU HAVE A FEVER?
HUH?! UH...UM, NO -
JOLT...
ギク...

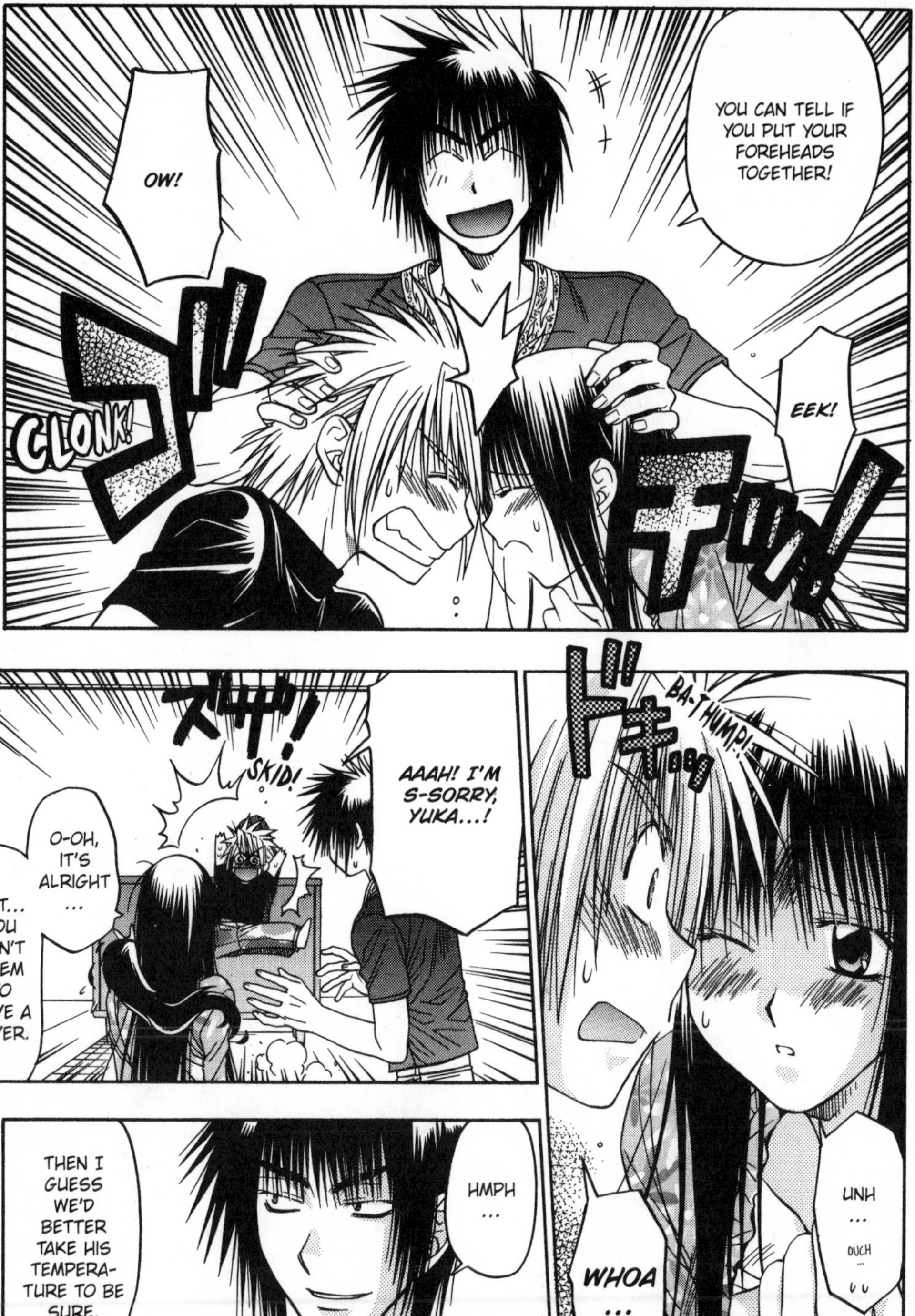
YOU CAN TELL IF YOU PUT YOUR FOREHEADS TOGETHER!
EEK!
CLONK!
OW!
BA-THUMP!
UNH ...
OUCH ...
WHOA ...
SKID!
AAAH! I'M S-SORRY, YUKA...!
O-OH, IT'S ALRIGHT ...
BUT... YOU DON'T SEEM TO HAVE A FEVER.
HMPH ...
THEN I GUESS WE'D BETTER TAKE HIS TEMPERATURE TO BE SURE.

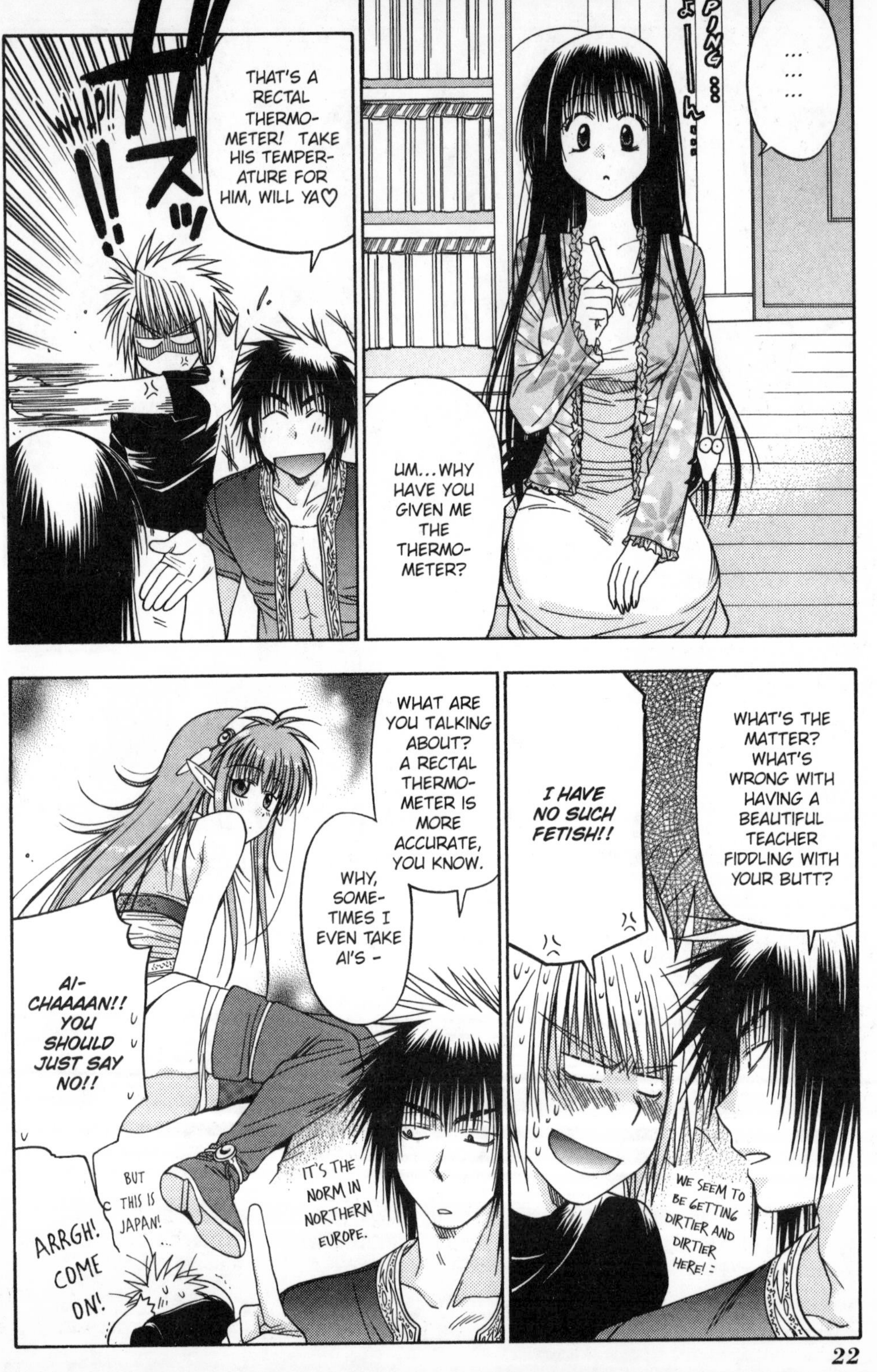
......
PING...
ぴょーーん…
UM...WHY HAVE YOU GIVEN ME THE THERMOMETER?
THAT'S A RECTAL THERMOMETER! TAKE HIS TEMPERATURE FOR HIM, WILL YA♡
WHAP!!
ガスッ!!
WHAT'S THE MATTER? WHAT'S WRONG WITH HAVING A BEAUTIFUL TEACHER FIDDLING WITH YOUR BUTT?
I HAVE NO SUCH FETISH!!
WE SEEM TO BE GETTING DIRTIER AND DIRTIER HERE!
WHAT ARE YOU TALKING ABOUT? A RECTAL THERMOMETER IS MORE ACCURATE, YOU KNOW.
WHY, SOMETIMES I EVEN TAKE AI'S -
AI-CHAAAAN!! YOU SHOULD JUST SAY NO!!
IT'S THE NORM IN NORTHERN EUROPE.
BUT THIS IS JAPAN!
ARRGH! COME ON!

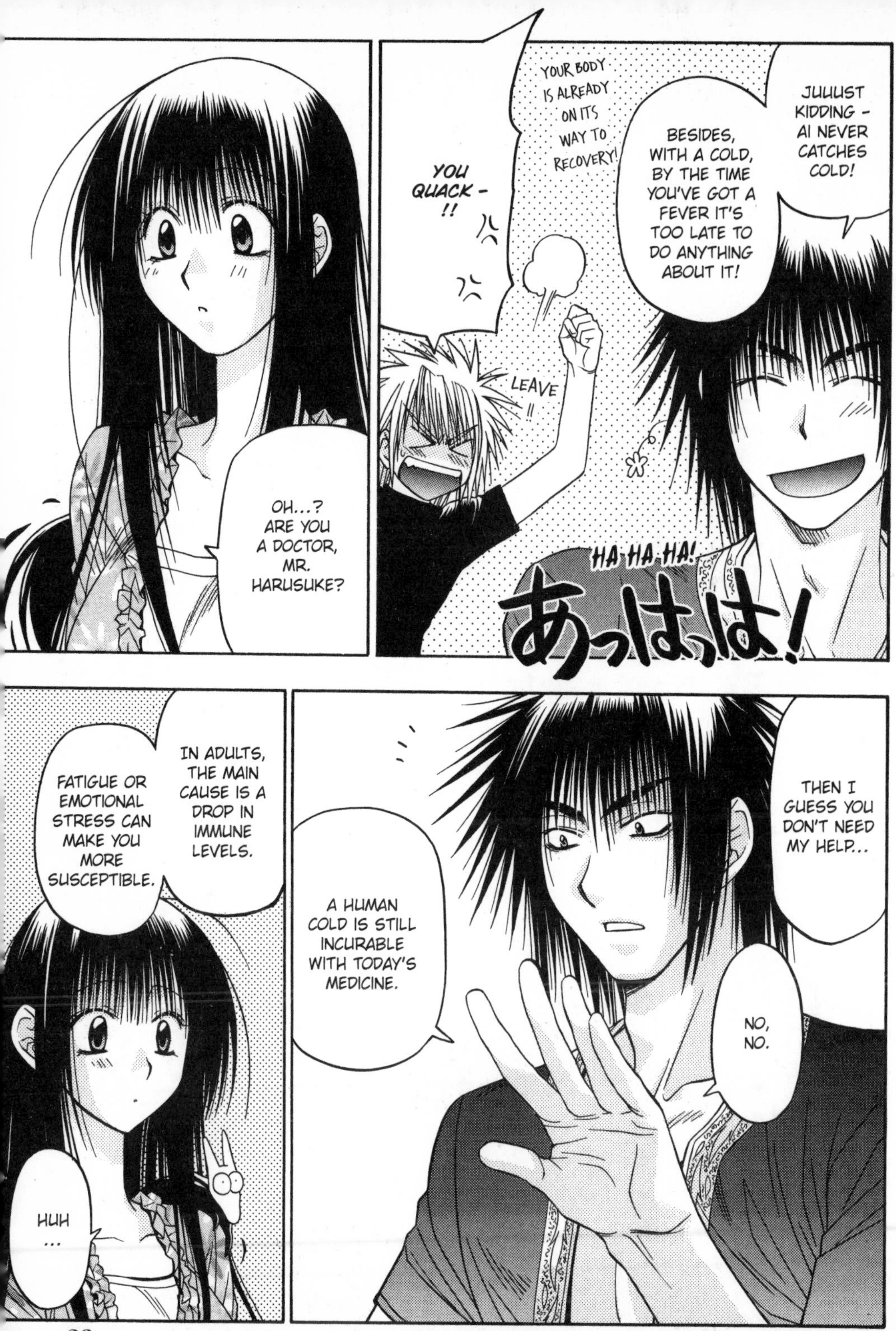
JUUUST KIDDING - AI NEVER CATCHES COLD!
BESIDES, WITH A COLD, BY THE TIME YOU'VE GOT A FEVER IT'S TOO LATE TO DO ANYTHING ABOUT IT!
YOUR BODY IS ALREADY ON ITS WAY TO RECOVERY!
YOU QUACK - !!
LEAVE !!
HA HA HA!
あっはっは!
OH...? ARE YOU A DOCTOR, MR. HARUSUKE?
THEN I GUESS YOU DON'T NEED MY HELP...
NO, NO.
A HUMAN COLD IS STILL INCURABLE WITH TODAY'S MEDICINE.
IN ADULTS, THE MAIN CAUSE IS A DROP IN IMMUNE LEVELS.
FATIGUE OR EMOTIONAL STRESS CAN MAKE YOU MORE SUSCEPTIBLE.
HUH ...

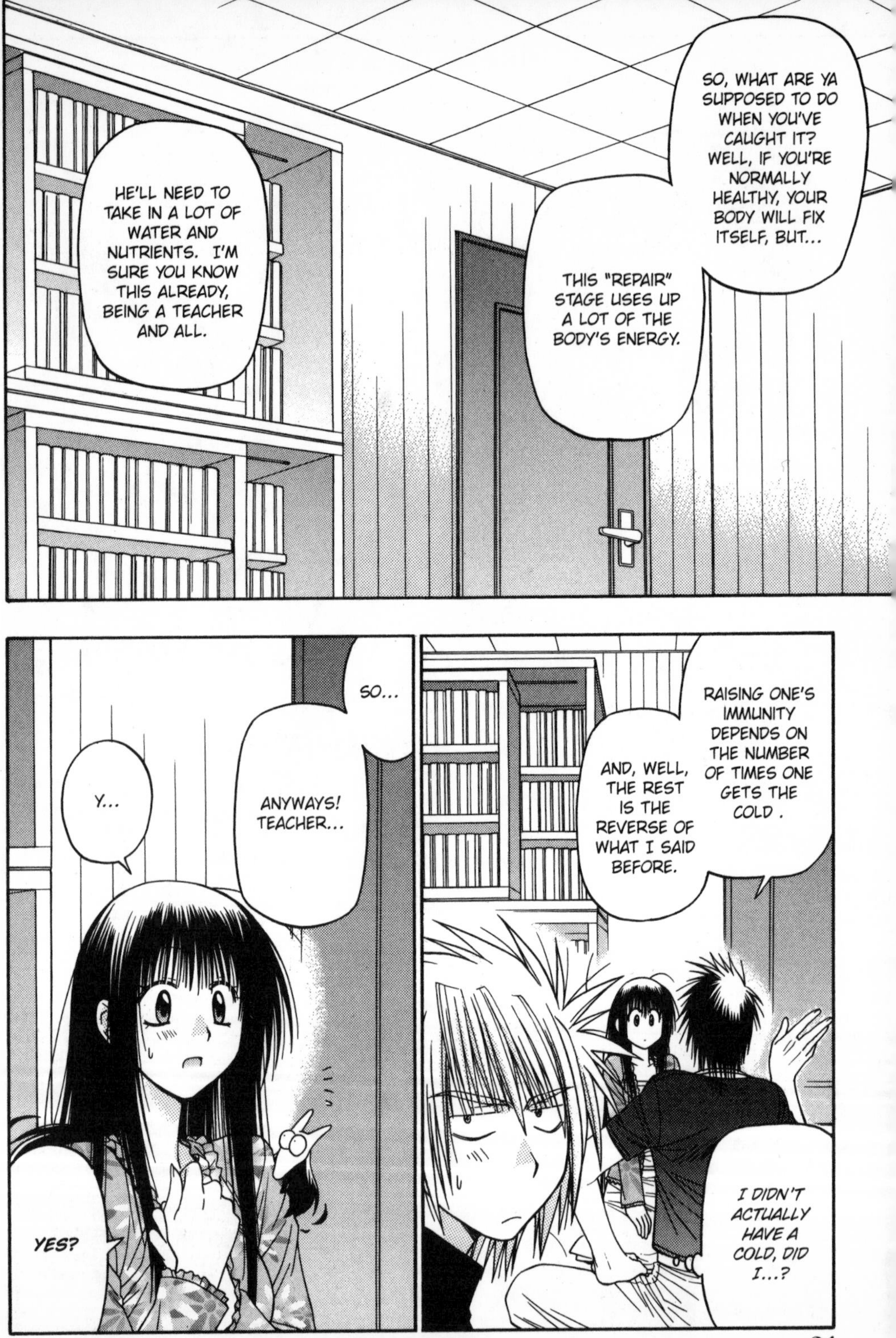
SO, WHAT ARE YA SUPPOSED TO DO WHEN YOU'VE CAUGHT IT? WELL, IF YOU'RE NORMALLY HEALTHY, YOUR BODY WILL FIX ITSELF, BUT...
THIS "REPAIR" STAGE USES UP A LOT OF THE BODY'S ENERGY.
HE'LL NEED TO TAKE IN A LOT OF WATER AND NUTRIENTS. I'M SURE YOU KNOW THIS ALREADY, BEING A TEACHER AND ALL.
RAISING ONE'S IMMUNITY DEPENDS ON THE NUMBER OF TIMES ONE GETS THE COLD .
AND, WELL, THE REST IS THE REVERSE OF WHAT I SAID BEFORE.
I DIDN'T ACTUALLY HAVE A COLD, DID I...?
SO...
ANYWAYS! TEACHER...
Y...
YES?

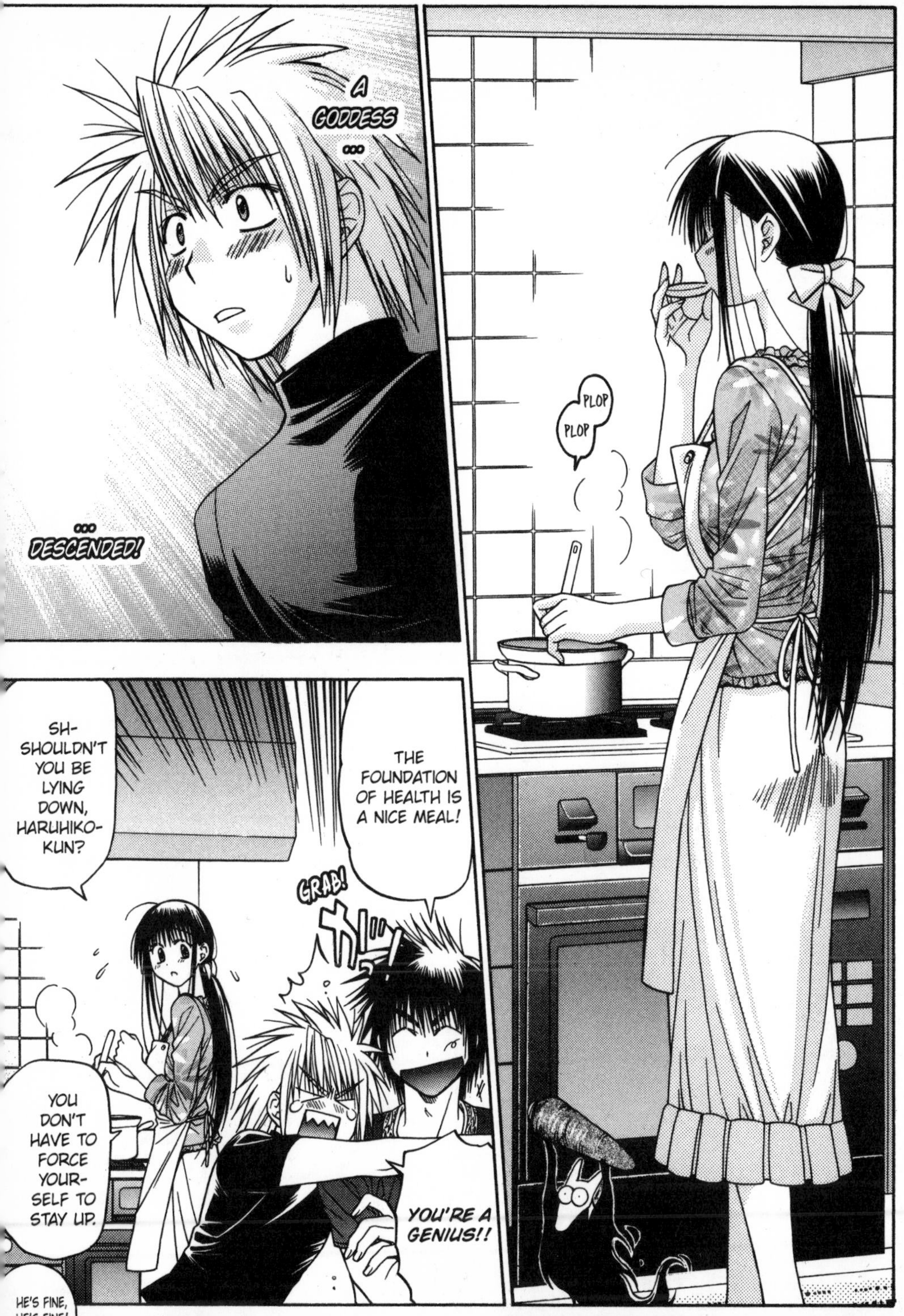
PLOP
PLOP
A GODDESS...
...DESCENDED!
THE FOUNDATION OF HEALTH IS A NICE MEAL!
SH-SHOULDN'T YOU BE LYING DOWN, HARUHIKO-KUN?
GRAB!
YOU'RE A GENIUS!!
YOU DON'T HAVE TO FORCE YOURSELF TO STAY UP.

HE'S FINE, HE'S FINE!
—SUKE

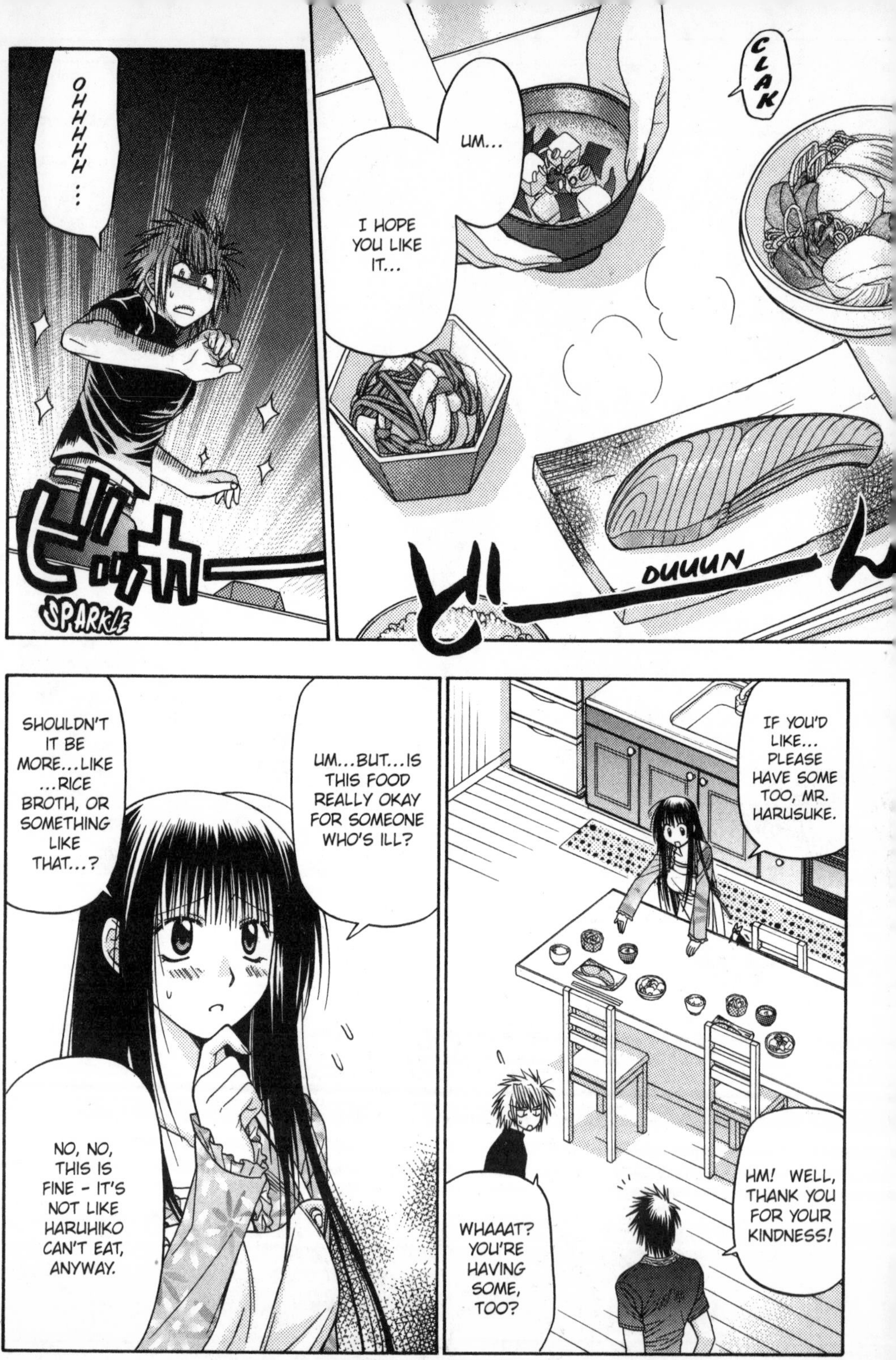
CLAK
UM...
I HOPE YOU LIKE IT...
DUUUN
OHHHHH...
SPARKLE
IF YOU'D LIKE... PLEASE HAVE SOME TOO, MR. HARUSUKE.
HM! WELL, THANK YOU FOR YOUR KINDNESS!
WHAAAT? YOU'RE HAVING SOME, TOO?
UM...BUT...IS THIS FOOD REALLY OKAY FOR SOMEONE WHO'S ILL?
SHOULDN'T IT BE MORE...LIKE ...RICE BROTH, OR SOMETHING LIKE THAT...?
NO, NO, THIS IS FINE - IT'S NOT LIKE HARUHIKO CAN'T EAT, ANYWAY.

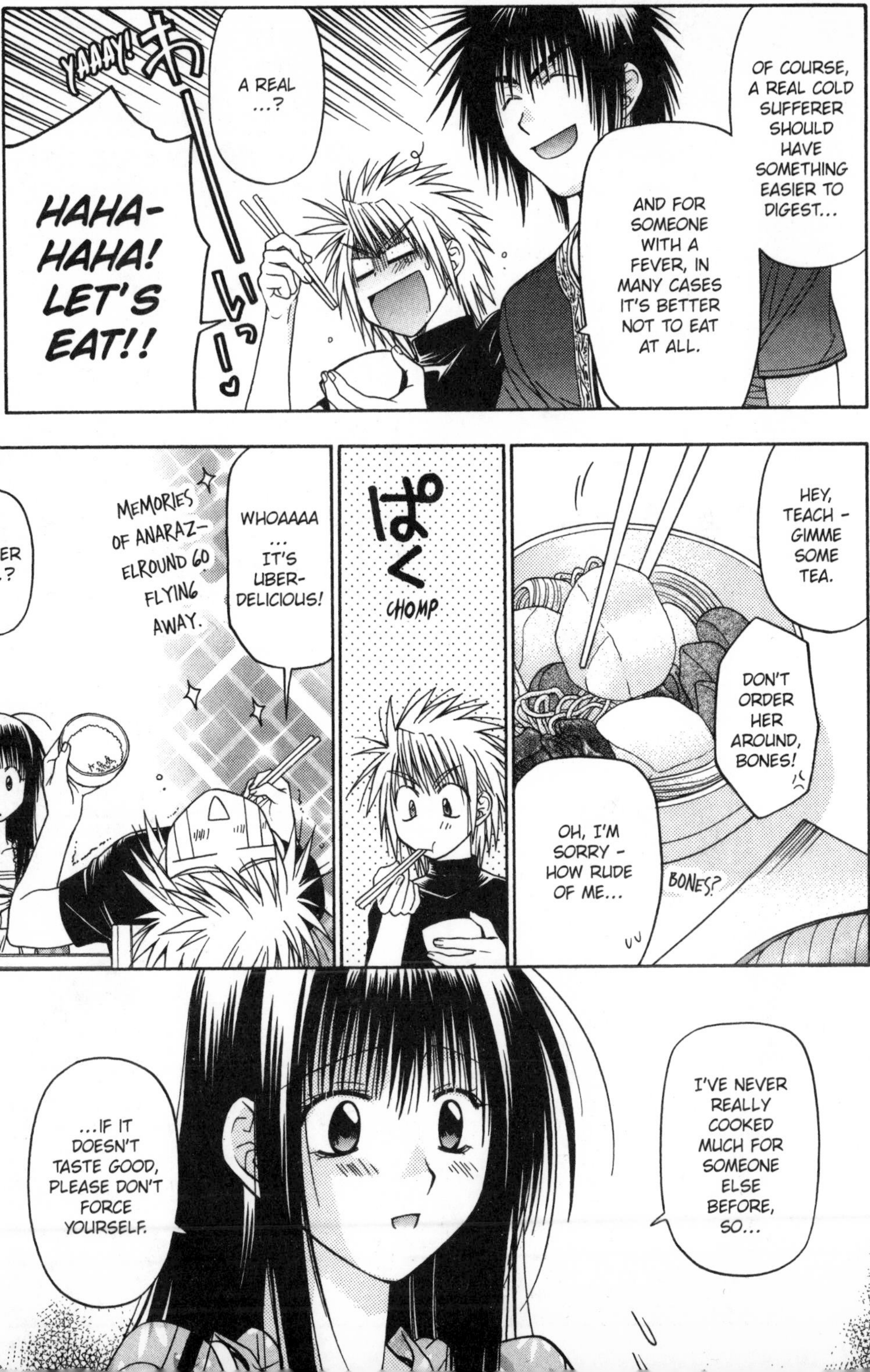
OF COURSE, A REAL COLD SUFFERER SHOULD HAVE SOMETHING EASIER TO DIGEST...
AND FOR SOMEONE WITH A FEVER, IN MANY CASES IT'S BETTER NOT TO EAT AT ALL.
A REAL ...?
YAAAY! わーいっ
HAHA-HAHA! LET'S EAT!!
HEY, TEACH - GIMME SOME TEA.
DON'T ORDER HER AROUND, BONES!
BONES?
OH, I'M SORRY - HOW RUDE OF ME...
ぱく
CHOMP
WHOAAAA ... IT'S UBER-DELICIOUS!
MEMORIES OF ANARAZ-ELROUND 60 FLYING AWAY.
UBER ...?
I'VE NEVER REALLY COOKED MUCH FOR SOMEONE ELSE BEFORE, SO...
...IF IT DOESN'T TASTE GOOD, PLEASE DON'T FORCE YOURSELF.

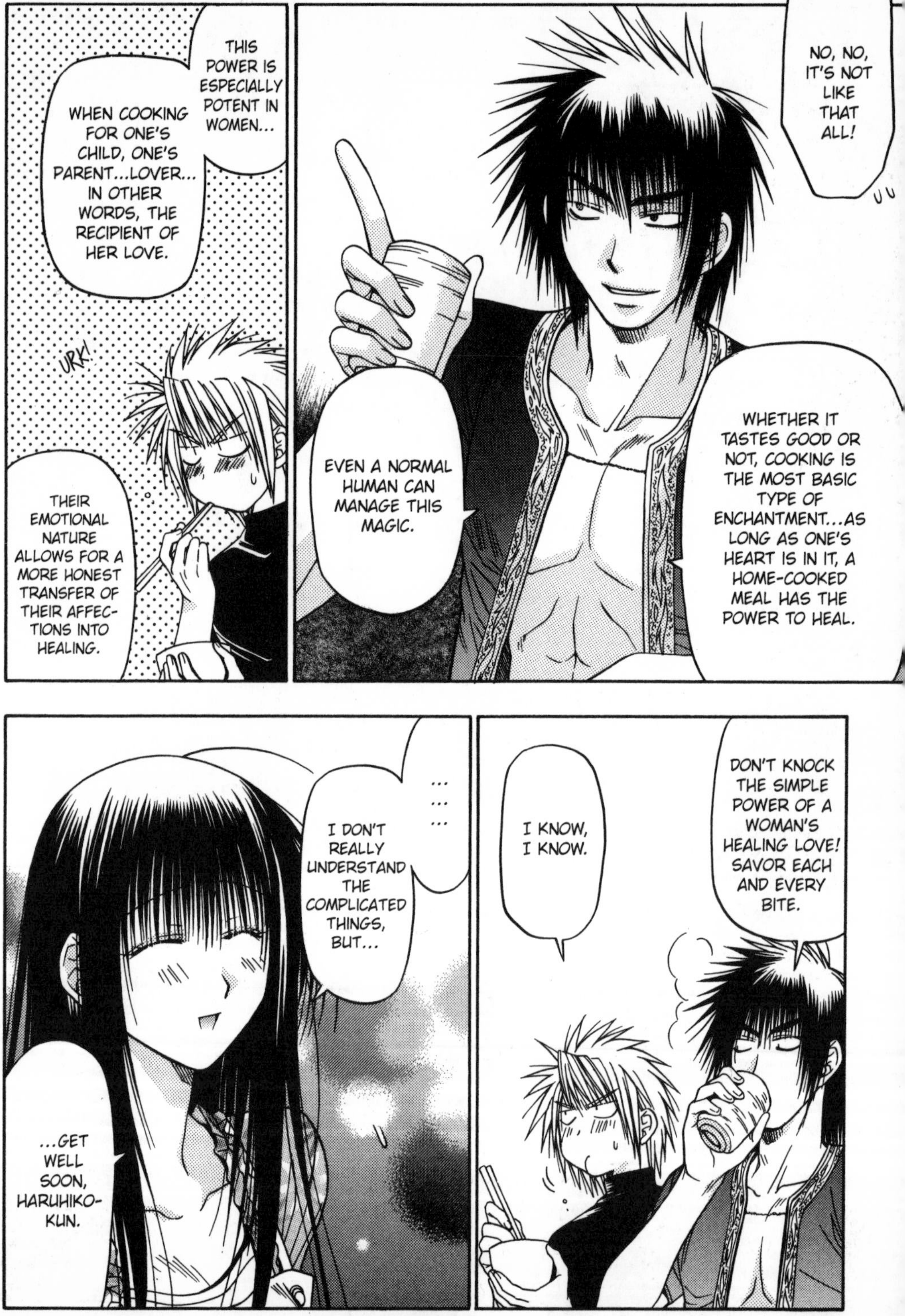
NO, NO, IT'S NOT LIKE THAT ALL!
WHETHER IT TASTES GOOD OR NOT, COOKING IS THE MOST BASIC TYPE OF ENCHANTMENT...AS LONG AS ONE'S HEART IS IN IT, A HOME-COOKED MEAL HAS THE POWER TO HEAL.
EVEN A NORMAL HUMAN CAN MANAGE THIS MAGIC.
THIS POWER IS ESPECIALLY POTENT IN WOMEN...
WHEN COOKING FOR ONE'S CHILD, ONE'S PARENT...LOVER... IN OTHER WORDS, THE RECIPIENT OF HER LOVE.
URK!
THEIR EMOTIONAL NATURE ALLOWS FOR A MORE HONEST TRANSFER OF THEIR AFFEC-TIONS INTO HEALING.
DON'T KNOCK THE SIMPLE POWER OF A WOMAN'S HEALING LOVE! SAVOR EACH AND EVERY BITE.
I KNOW, I KNOW.
... ...
I DON'T REALLY UNDERSTAND THE COMPLICATED THINGS, BUT...
...GET WELL SOON, HARUHIKO-KUN.

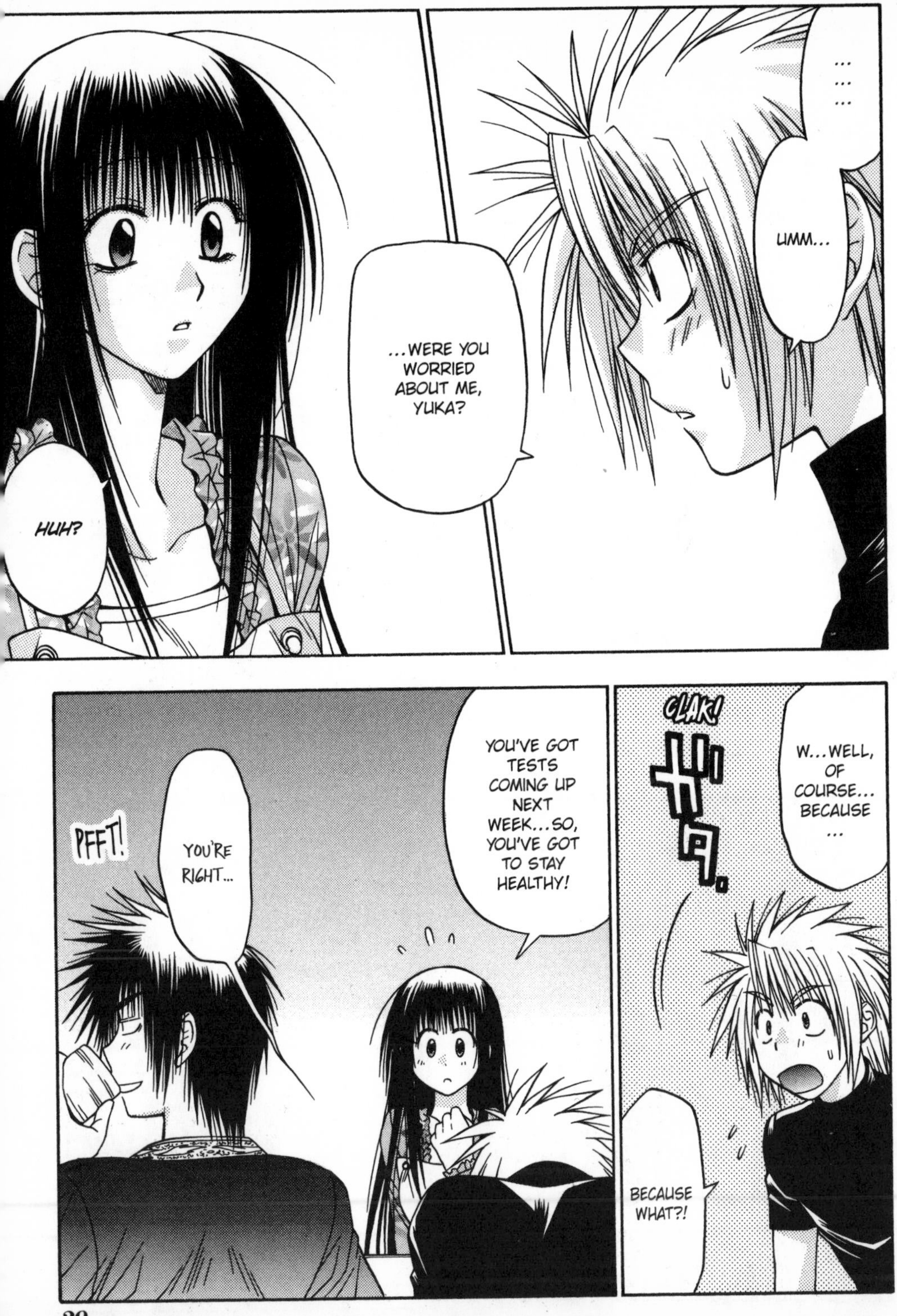
...
...
...
UMM...
...WERE YOU WORRIED ABOUT ME, YUKA?
HUH?
CLAK!
W...WELL, OF COURSE... BECAUSE ...
BECAUSE WHAT?!
YOU'VE GOT TESTS COMING UP NEXT WEEK...SO, YOU'VE GOT TO STAY HEALTHY!
YOU'RE RIGHT...
PFFT!

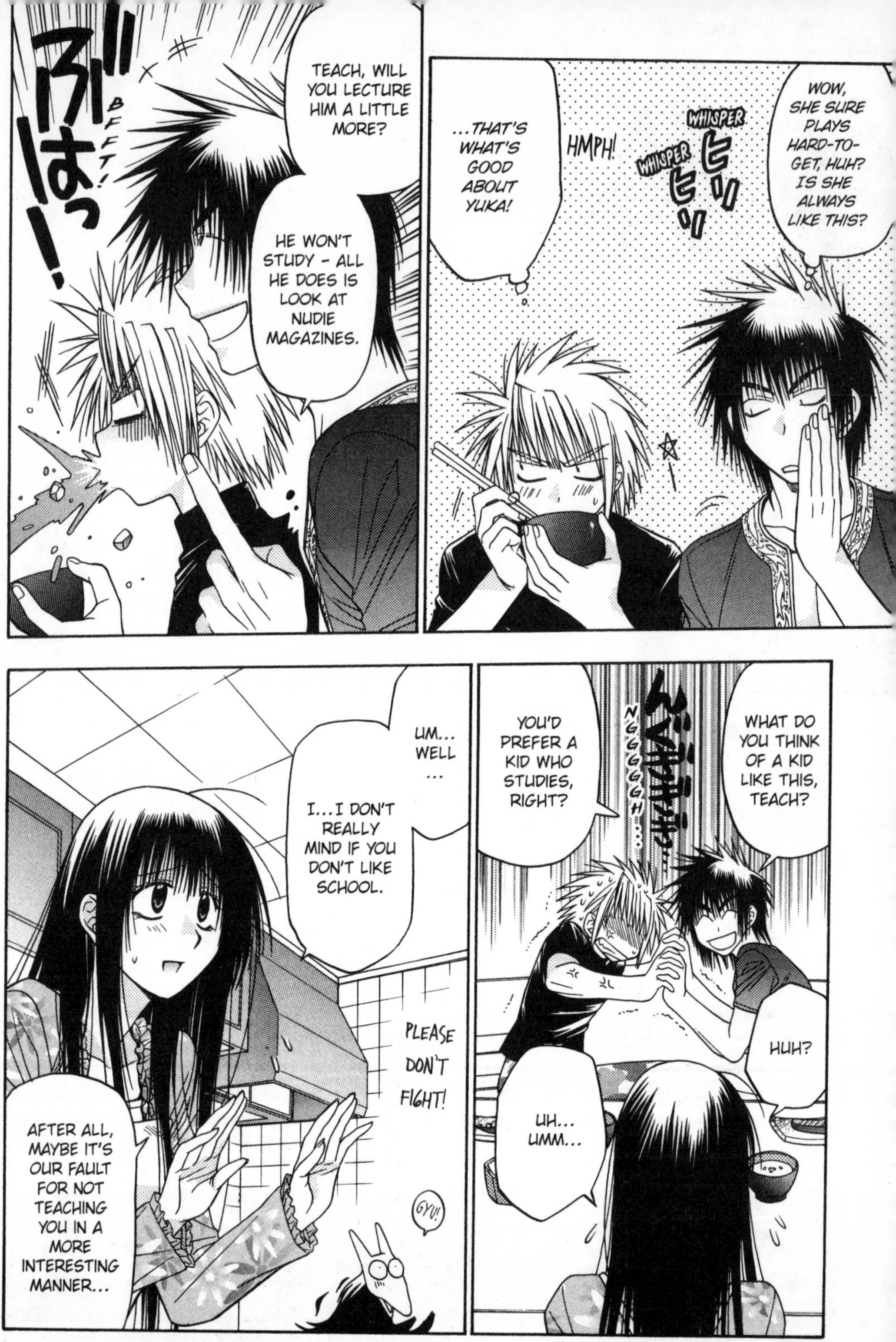
WOW, SHE SURE PLAYS HARD-TO-GET, HUH? IS SHE ALWAYS LIKE THIS?
WHISPER
WHISPER
HMPH!
...THAT'S WHAT'S GOOD ABOUT YUKA!
TEACH, WILL YOU LECTURE HIM A LITTLE MORE?
HE WON'T STUDY - ALL HE DOES IS LOOK AT NUDIE MAGAZINES.
ぶはっ!!
BFFT!
WHAT DO YOU THINK OF A KID LIKE THIS, TEACH?
YOU'D PREFER A KID WHO STUDIES, RIGHT?
NGGGGGH...
HUH?
UH... UMM...
UM... WELL...
I...I DON'T REALLY MIND IF YOU DON'T LIKE SCHOOL.
PLEASE DON'T FIGHT!
AFTER ALL, MAYBE IT'S OUR FAULT FOR NOT TEACHING YOU IN A MORE INTERESTING MANNER...
GYU!

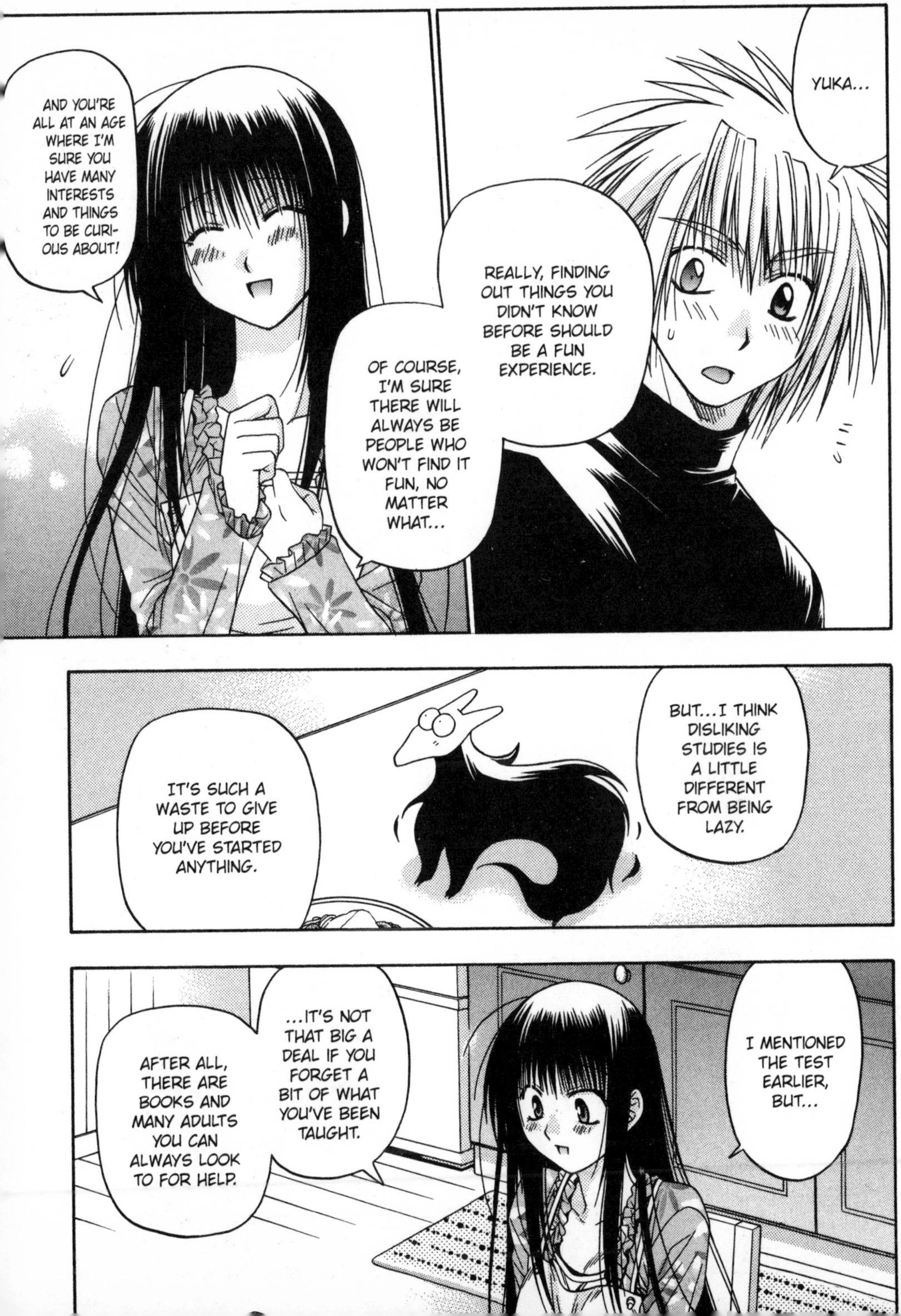
YUKA...
REALLY, FINDING OUT THINGS YOU DIDN'T KNOW BEFORE SHOULD BE A FUN EXPERIENCE.
OF COURSE, I'M SURE THERE WILL ALWAYS BE PEOPLE WHO WON'T FIND IT FUN, NO MATTER WHAT...
AND YOU'RE ALL AT AN AGE WHERE I'M SURE YOU HAVE MANY INTERESTS AND THINGS TO BE CURIOUS ABOUT!
BUT...I THINK DISLIKING STUDIES IS A LITTLE DIFFERENT FROM BEING LAZY.
IT'S SUCH A WASTE TO GIVE UP BEFORE YOU'VE STARTED ANYTHING.
I MENTIONED THE TEST EARLIER, BUT...
...IT'S NOT THAT BIG A DEAL IF YOU FORGET A BIT OF WHAT YOU'VE BEEN TAUGHT.
AFTER ALL, THERE ARE BOOKS AND MANY ADULTS YOU CAN ALWAYS LOOK TO FOR HELP.

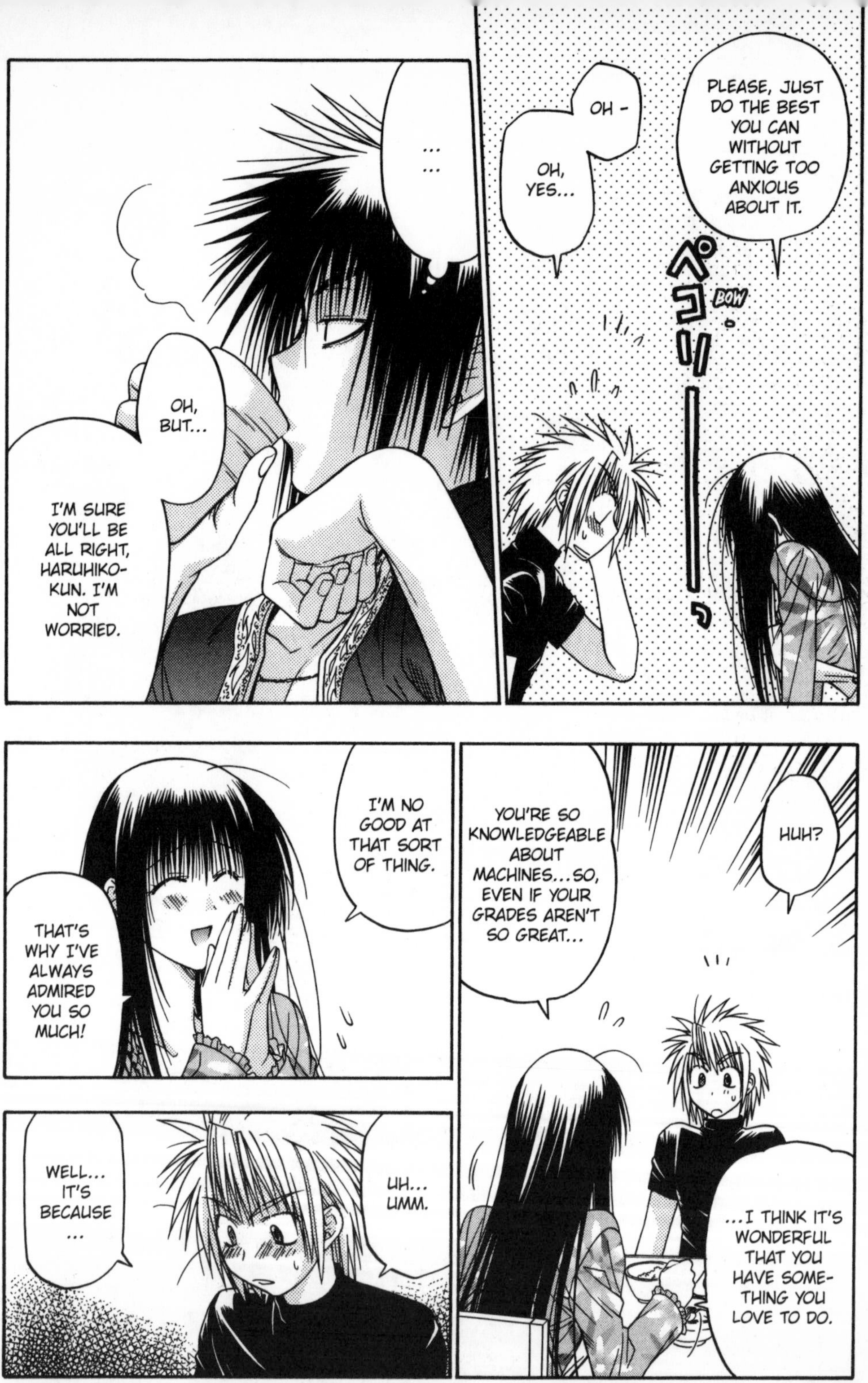

PLEASE, JUST DO THE BEST YOU CAN WITHOUT GETTING TOO ANXIOUS ABOUT IT.
OH -
OH, YES...
ペコリーッ
BOW
......
OH, BUT...
I'M SURE YOU'LL BE ALL RIGHT, HARUHIKO-KUN. I'M NOT WORRIED.
HUH?
YOU'RE SO KNOWLEDGEABLE ABOUT MACHINES...SO, EVEN IF YOUR GRADES AREN'T SO GREAT...
...I THINK IT'S WONDERFUL THAT YOU HAVE SOME-THING YOU LOVE TO DO.
I'M NO GOOD AT THAT SORT OF THING.
THAT'S WHY I'VE ALWAYS ADMIRED YOU SO MUCH!
UH... UMM.
WELL... IT'S BECAUSE ...

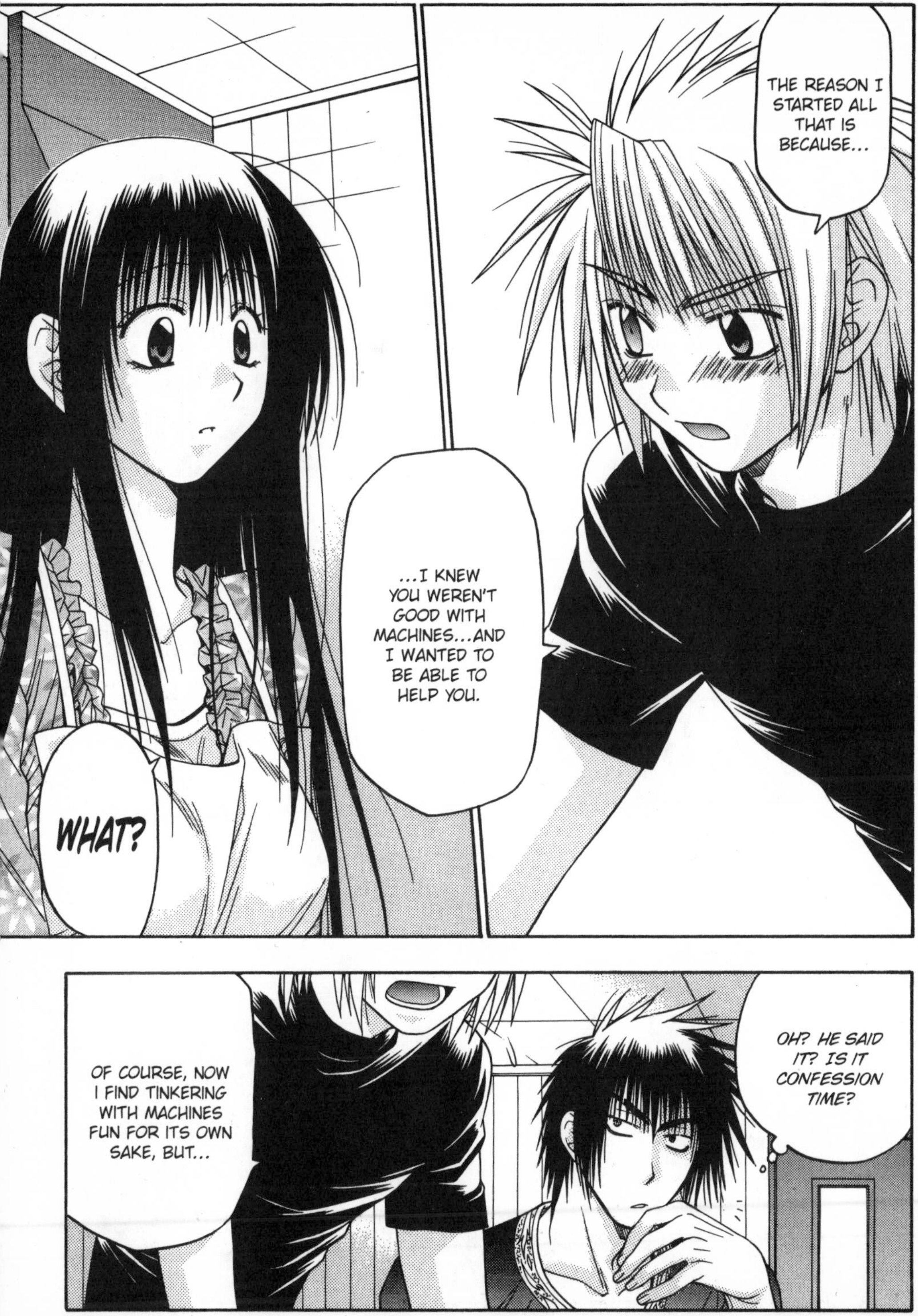
THE REASON I STARTED ALL THAT IS BECAUSE...
...I KNEW YOU WEREN'T GOOD WITH MACHINES...AND I WANTED TO BE ABLE TO HELP YOU.
WHAT?
OH? HE SAID IT? IS IT CONFESSION TIME?
OF COURSE, NOW I FIND TINKERING WITH MACHINES FUN FOR ITS OWN SAKE, BUT...

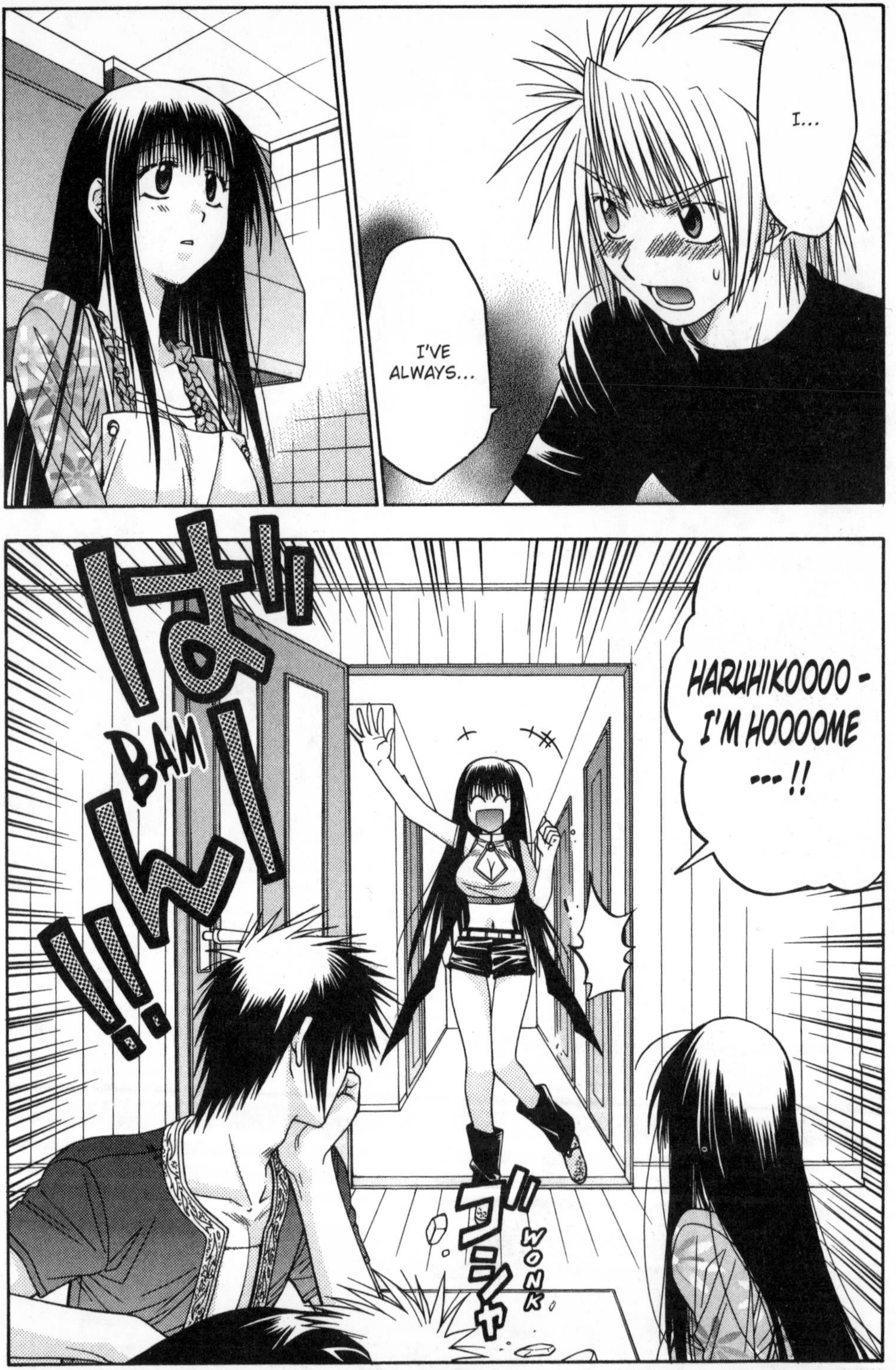
I...
I'VE ALWAYS...
HARUHIKOOOO - I'M HOOOOME ---!!
BAM
WONK

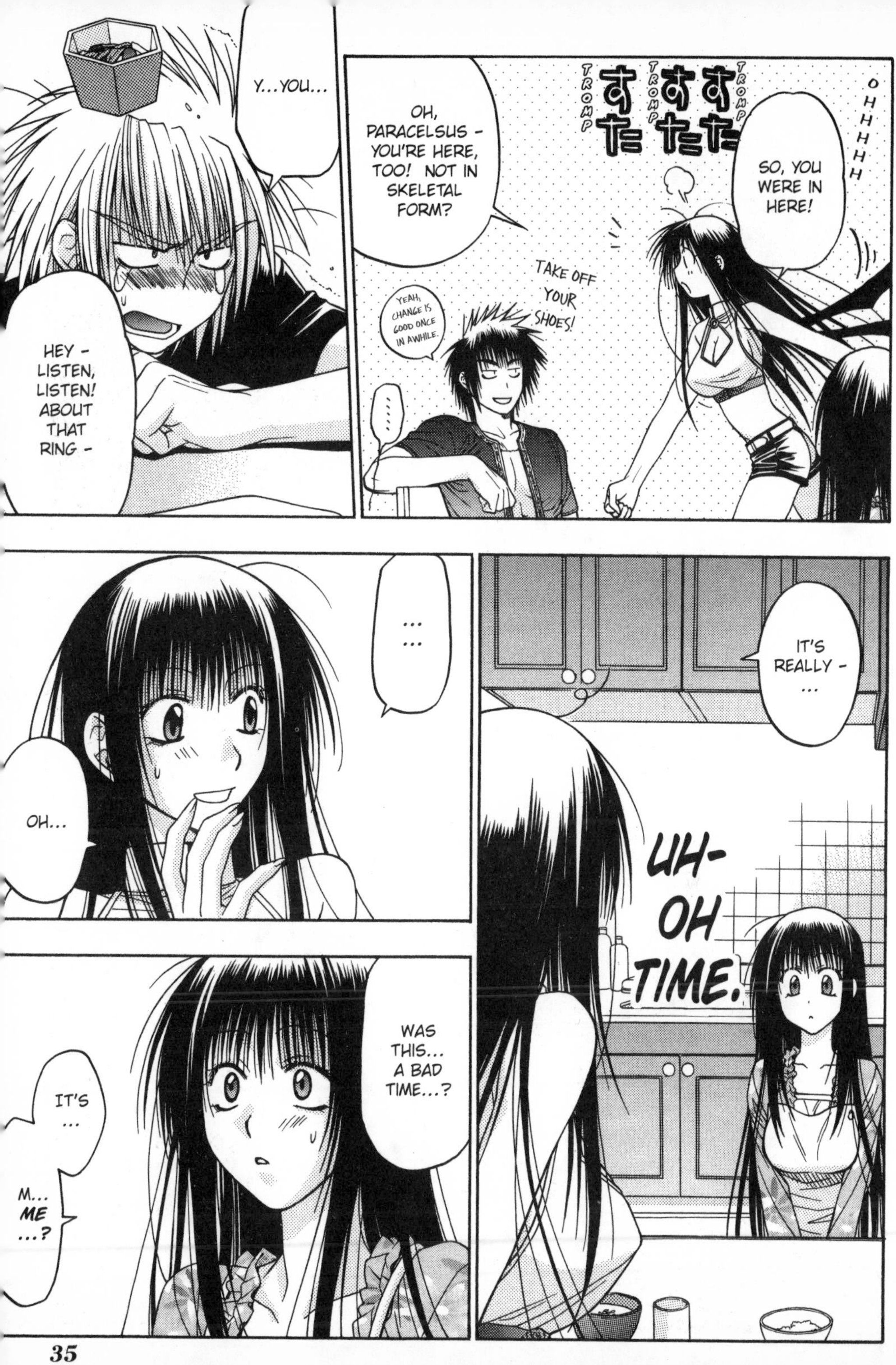

OHHHHHH
すた すたすた
TROMP TROMP TROMP
SO, YOU WERE IN HERE!
OH, PARACELSUS - YOU'RE HERE, TOO! NOT IN SKELETAL FORM?
TAKE OFF YOUR SHOES!
YEAH, CHANGE IS GOOD ONCE IN AWHILE.
......
Y...YOU...
HEY - LISTEN, LISTEN! ABOUT THAT RING -
IT'S REALLY - ...
UH-OH TIME.
... ...
OH...
WAS THIS... A BAD TIME...?
IT'S ...
M... ME ...?

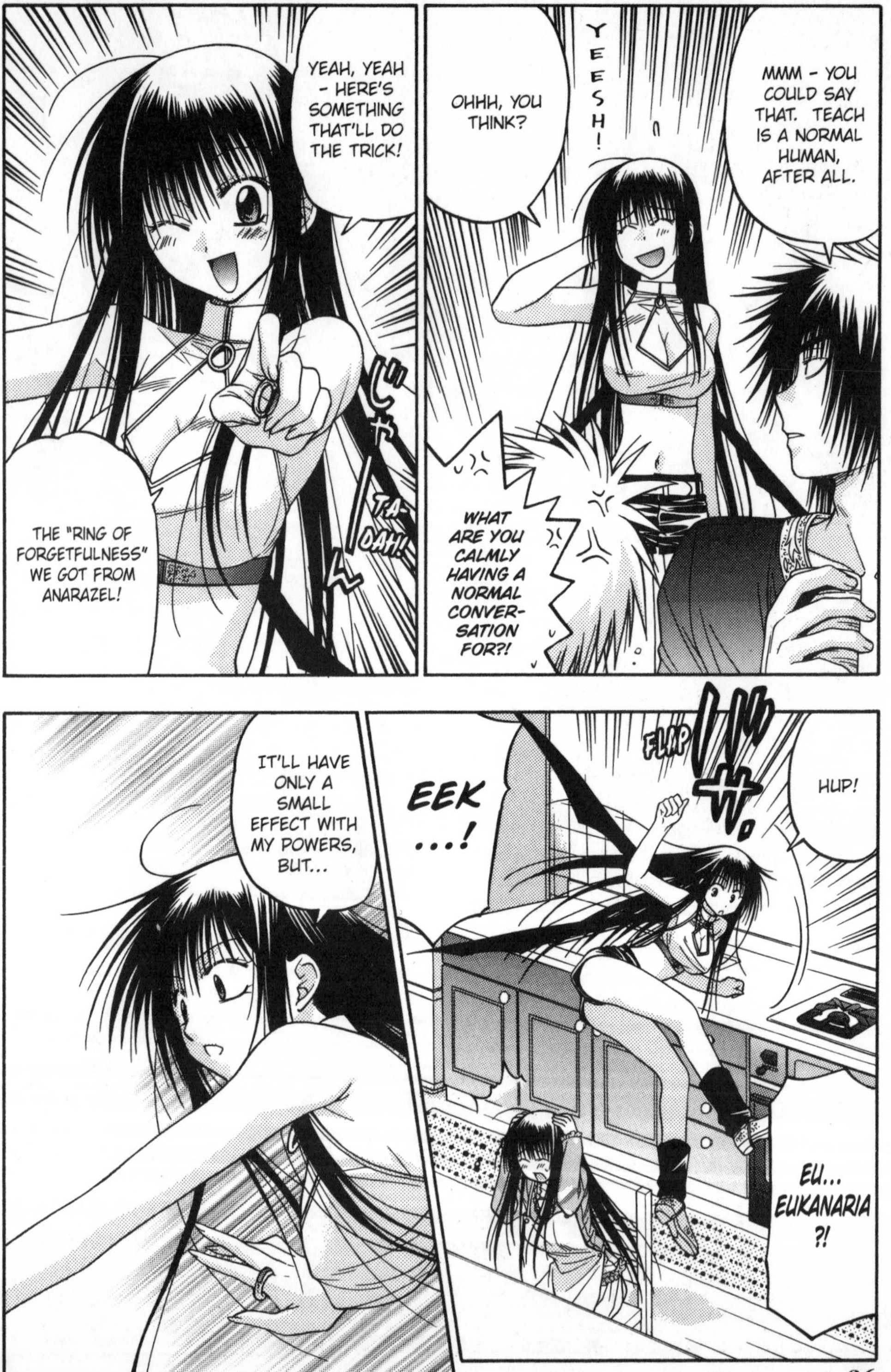
MMM - YOU COULD SAY THAT. TEACH IS A NORMAL HUMAN, AFTER ALL.
YEESH!
OHHH, YOU THINK?
WHAT ARE YOU CALMLY HAVING A NORMAL CONVER-SATION FOR?!
YEAH, YEAH - HERE'S SOMETHING THAT'LL DO THE TRICK!
TA-DAH!
THE "RING OF FORGETFULNESS" WE GOT FROM ANARAZEL!
HUP!
FLAP
EEK ...!
EU... EUKANARIA ?!
IT'LL HAVE ONLY A SMALL EFFECT WITH MY POWERS, BUT...

VWOOSH

SSSH!!

JUST A -

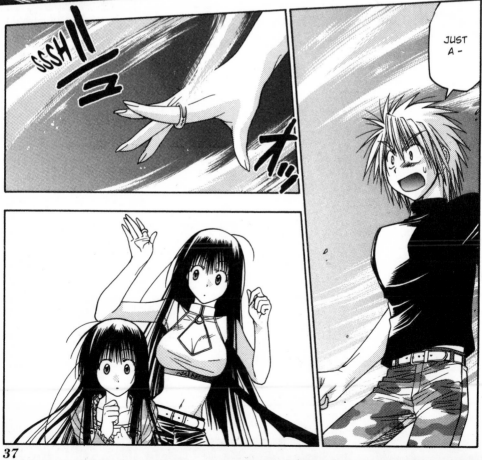

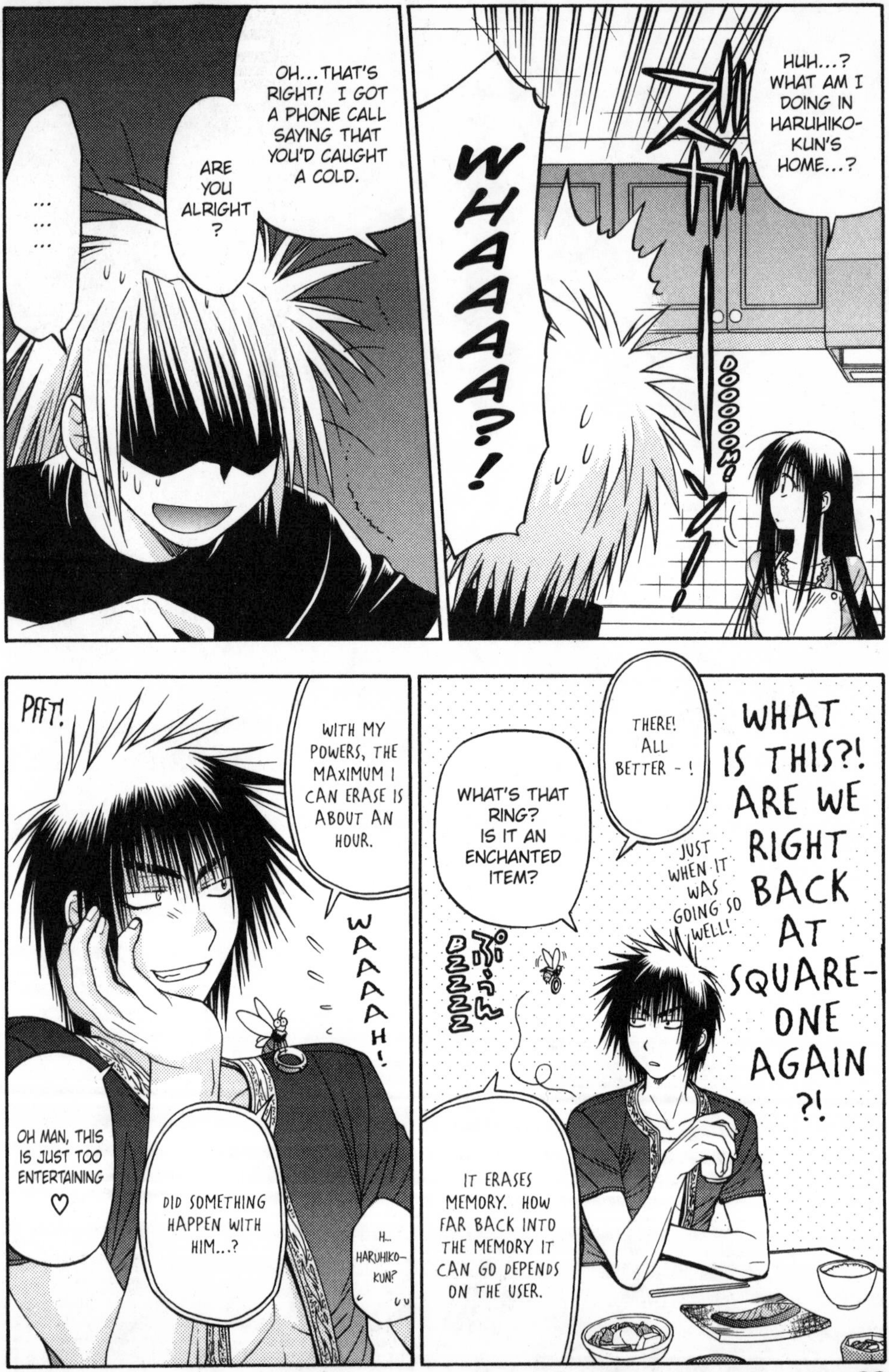
HUH...? WHAT AM I DOING IN HARUHIKO-KUN'S HOME...?
WHAAAAAA?!
DOOOOOOM
OH...THAT'S RIGHT! I GOT A PHONE CALL SAYING THAT YOU'D CAUGHT A COLD.
ARE YOU ALRIGHT?
....
WHAT IS THIS?! ARE WE RIGHT BACK AT SQUARE-ONE AGAIN?!
JUST WHEN IT WAS GOING SO WELL!
THERE! ALL BETTER -!
WHAT'S THAT RING? IS IT AN ENCHANTED ITEM?
ぷ〜ん
BZZZZ
IT ERASES MEMORY. HOW FAR BACK INTO THE MEMORY IT CAN GO DEPENDS ON THE USER.
PFFT!
WITH MY POWERS, THE MAXIMUM I CAN ERASE IS ABOUT AN HOUR.
WAAAAAH!
OH MAN, THIS IS JUST TOO ENTERTAINING ♡
DID SOMETHING HAPPEN WITH HIM...?
H... HARUHIKO-KUN?

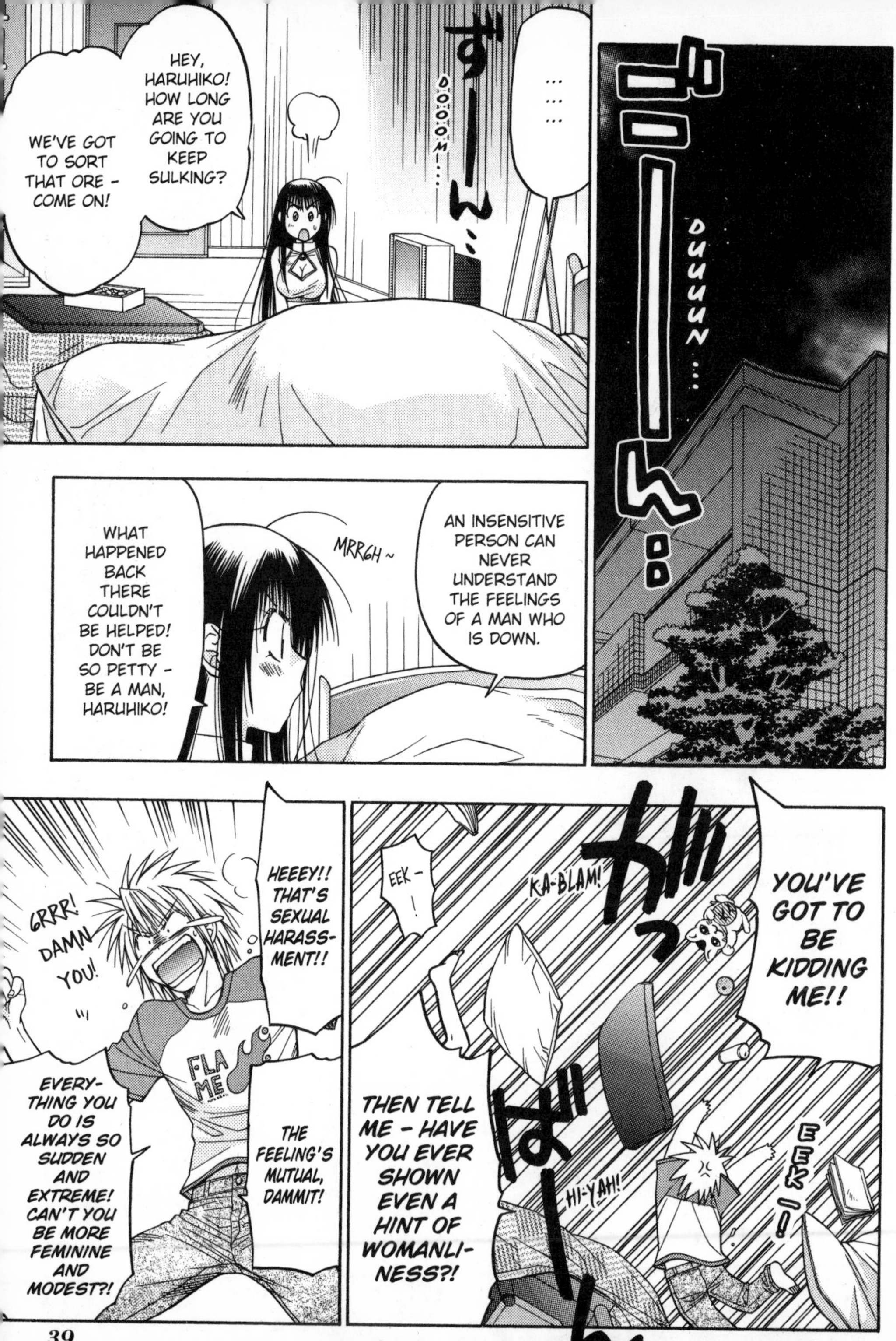
DUUUUN...
...
...
...
D-O-O-O-M...
HEY, HARUHIKO! HOW LONG ARE YOU GOING TO KEEP SULKING?
WE'VE GOT TO SORT THAT ORE - COME ON!
AN INSENSITIVE PERSON CAN NEVER UNDERSTAND THE FEELINGS OF A MAN WHO IS DOWN.
MRRGH~
WHAT HAPPENED BACK THERE COULDN'T BE HELPED! DON'T BE SO PETTY - BE A MAN, HARUHIKO!
YOU'VE GOT TO BE KIDDING ME!!
KA-BLAM!
EEK - !
THEN TELL ME - HAVE YOU EVER SHOWN EVEN A HINT OF WOMANLI-NESS?!
HI-YAH!
EEK - !
HEEEY!! THAT'S SEXUAL HARASS-MENT!!
GRRR! DAMN YOU!
THE FEELING'S MUTUAL, DAMMIT!
EVERY-THING YOU DO IS ALWAYS SO SUDDEN AND EXTREME! CAN'T YOU BE MORE FEMININE AND MODEST?!

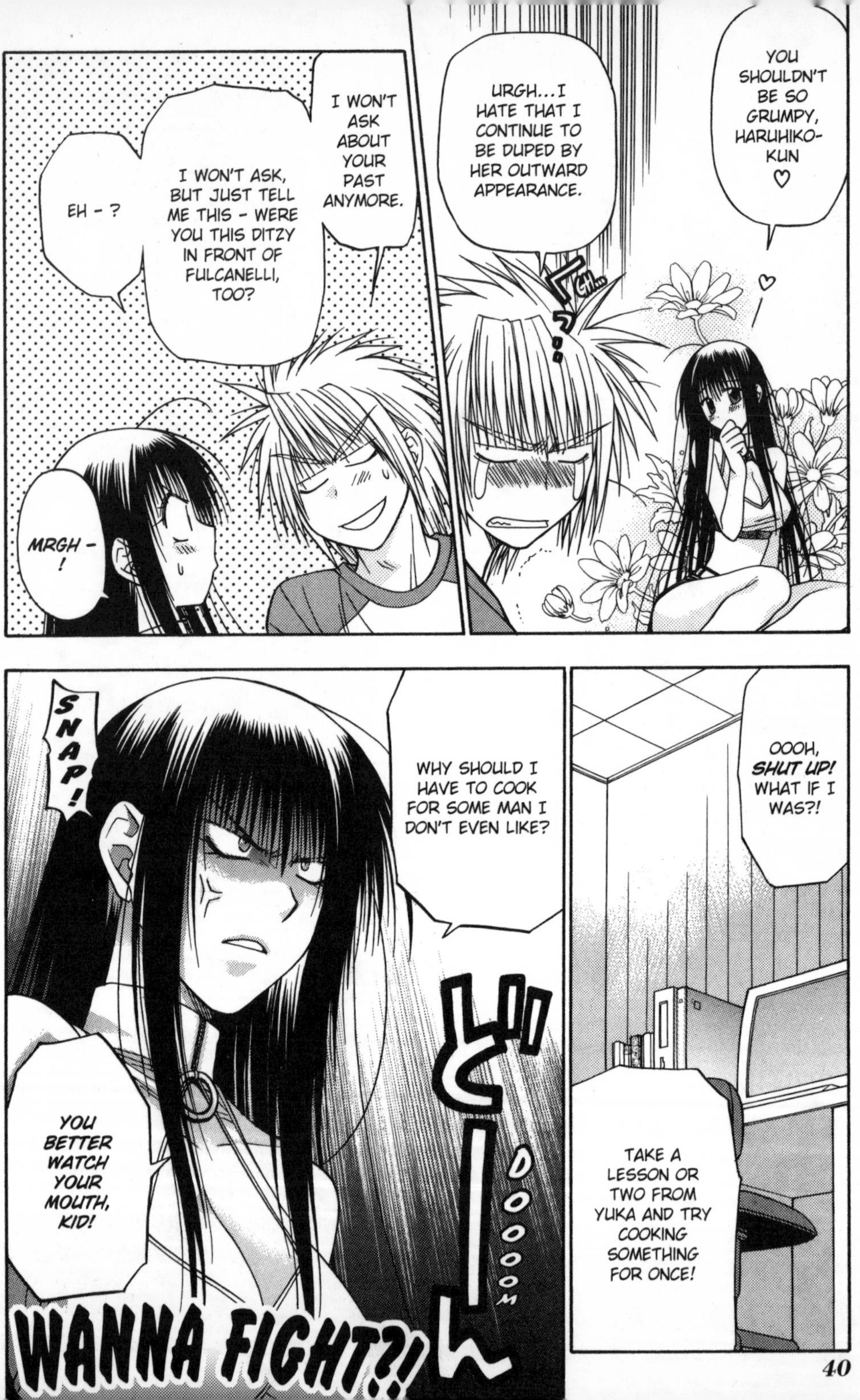

YOU SHOULDN'T BE SO GRUMPY, HARUHIKO-KUN ♡
URGH...I HATE THAT I CONTINUE TO BE DUPED BY HER OUTWARD APPEARANCE.
I WON'T ASK ABOUT YOUR PAST ANYMORE.
I WON'T ASK, BUT JUST TELL ME THIS - WERE YOU THIS DITZY IN FRONT OF FULCANELLI, TOO?
EH - ?
MRGH - !
OOOH, SHUT UP! WHAT IF I WAS?!
TAKE A LESSON OR TWO FROM YUKA AND TRY COOKING SOMETHING FOR ONCE!
SNAP!
WHY SHOULD I HAVE TO COOK FOR SOME MAN I DON'T EVEN LIKE?
YOU BETTER WATCH YOUR MOUTH, KID!
DOOOOOM
WANNA FIGHT?!

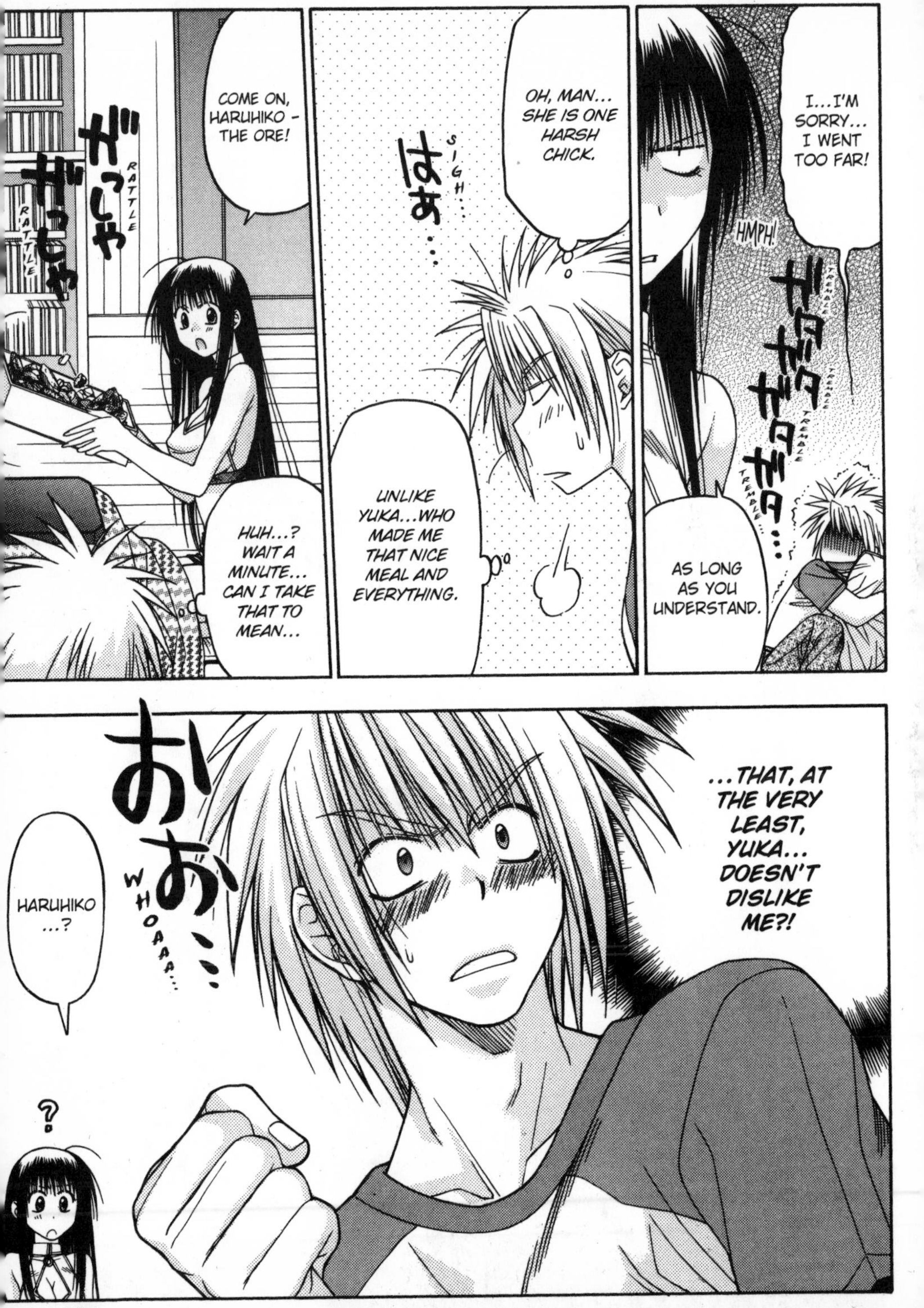
I...I'M SORRY... I WENT TOO FAR!
HMPH!
ガタガタガタガタ...
TREMBLE TREMBLE TREMBLE TREMBLE
AS LONG AS YOU UNDERSTAND.
OH, MAN... SHE IS ONE HARSH CHICK.
はぁ...
SIGH...
UNLIKE YUKA...WHO MADE ME THAT NICE MEAL AND EVERYTHING.
COME ON, HARUHIKO - THE ORE!
ガっしゃ ガっしゃ
RATTLE RATTLE
HUH...? WAIT A MINUTE... CAN I TAKE THAT TO MEAN...
...THAT, AT THE VERY LEAST, YUKA... DOESN'T DISLIKE ME?!
おおぉ
WHOAAA...
HARUHIKO ...?
?

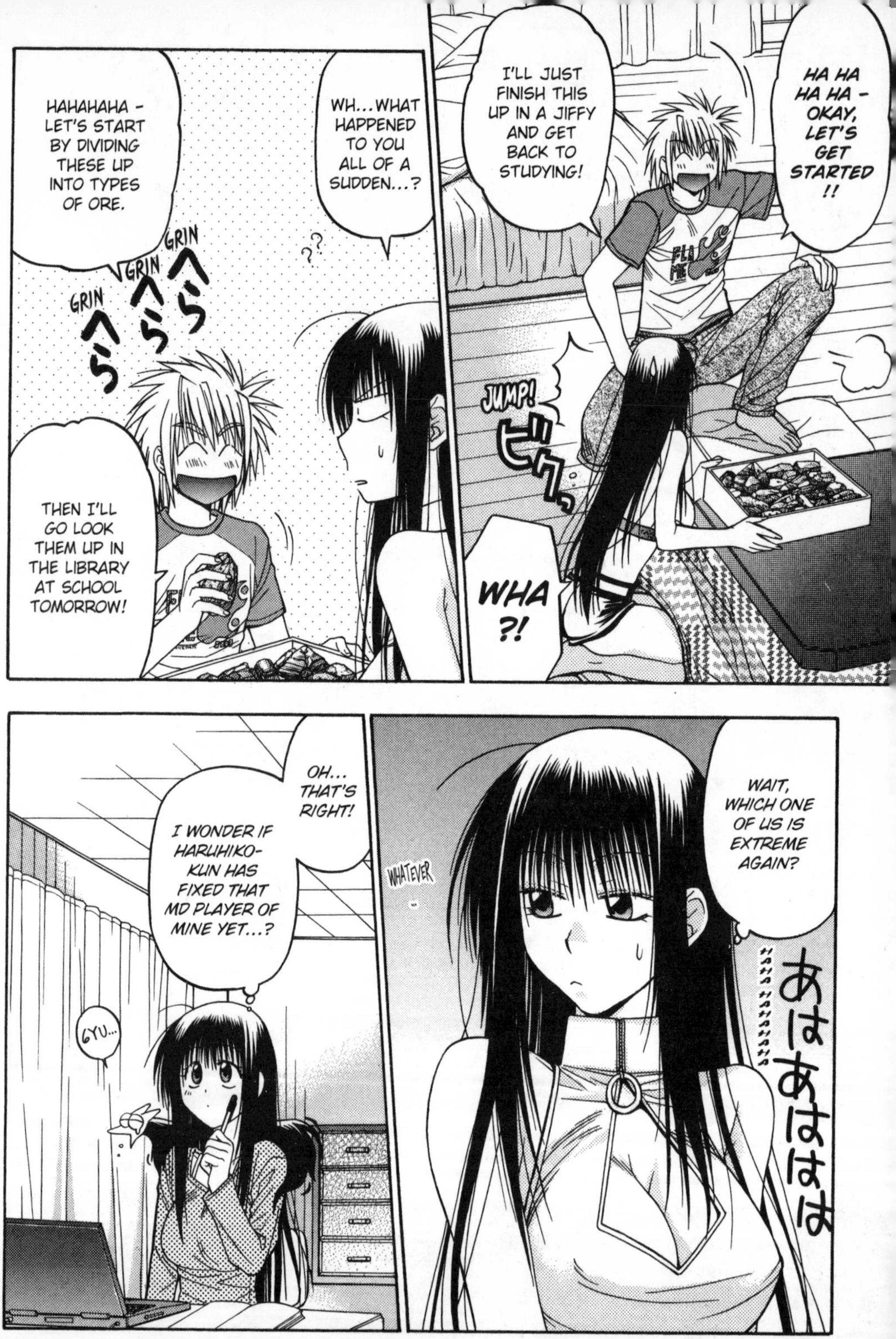
HA HA HA HA - OKAY, LET'S GET STARTED !!
I'LL JUST FINISH THIS UP IN A JIFFY AND GET BACK TO STUDYING!
JUMP! ビク
WHA ?!
WH...WHAT HAPPENED TO YOU ALL OF A SUDDEN...?
HAHAHAHA - LET'S START BY DIVIDING THESE UP INTO TYPES OF ORE.
GRIN へら
GRIN へら
GRIN へら
THEN I'LL GO LOOK THEM UP IN THE LIBRARY AT SCHOOL TOMORROW!
WAIT, WHICH ONE OF US IS EXTREME AGAIN?
WHATEVER
HAHAHAHAHA あははは
OH... THAT'S RIGHT!
I WONDER IF HARUHIKO-KUN HAS FIXED THAT MD PLAYER OF MINE YET...?
GYU...

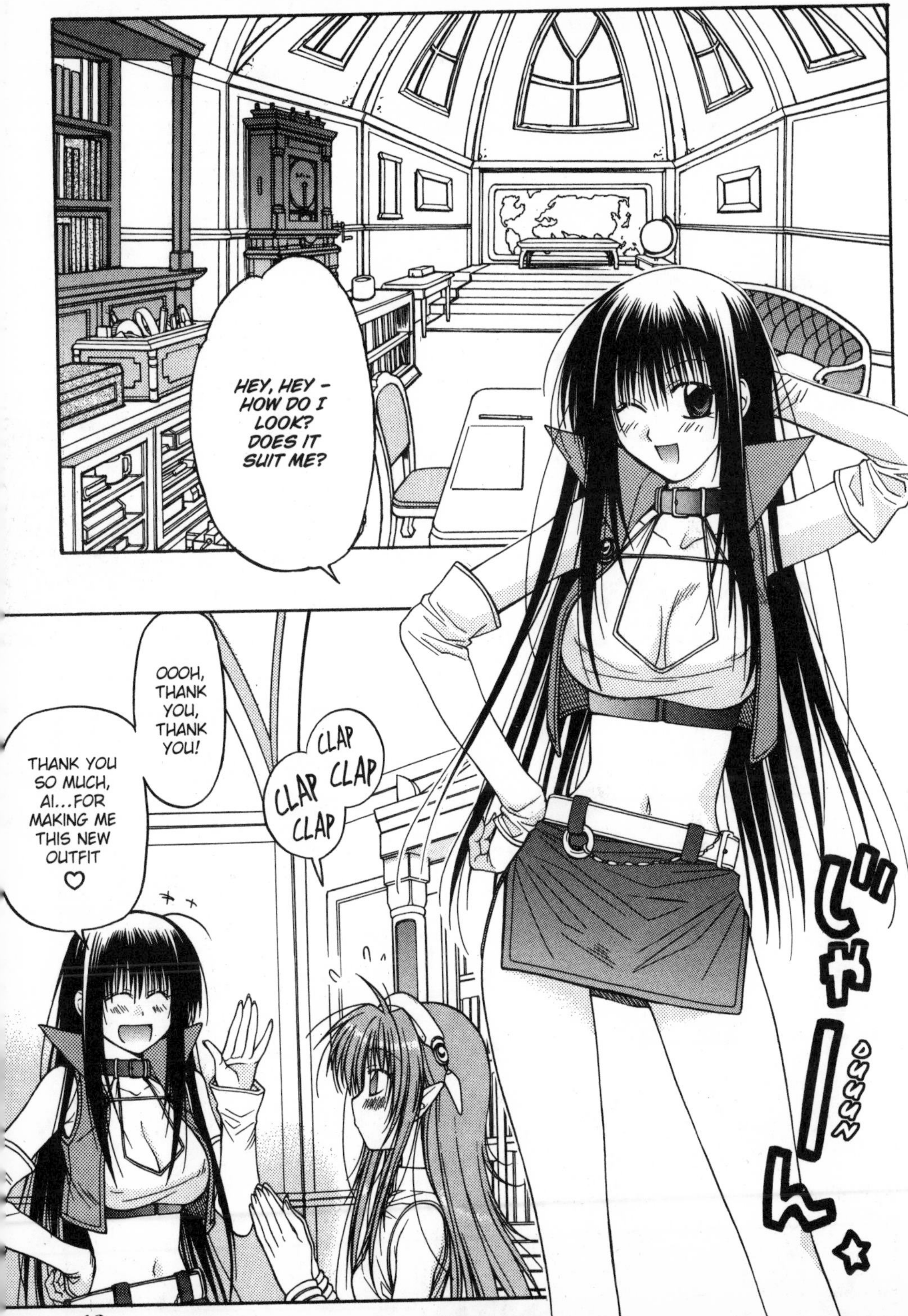
HEY, HEY - HOW DO I LOOK? DOES IT SUIT ME?
じゃーーん☆
DUUUN
CLAP CLAP CLAP CLAP
OOOH, THANK YOU, THANK YOU!
THANK YOU SO MUCH, AI...FOR MAKING ME THIS NEW OUTFIT ♡

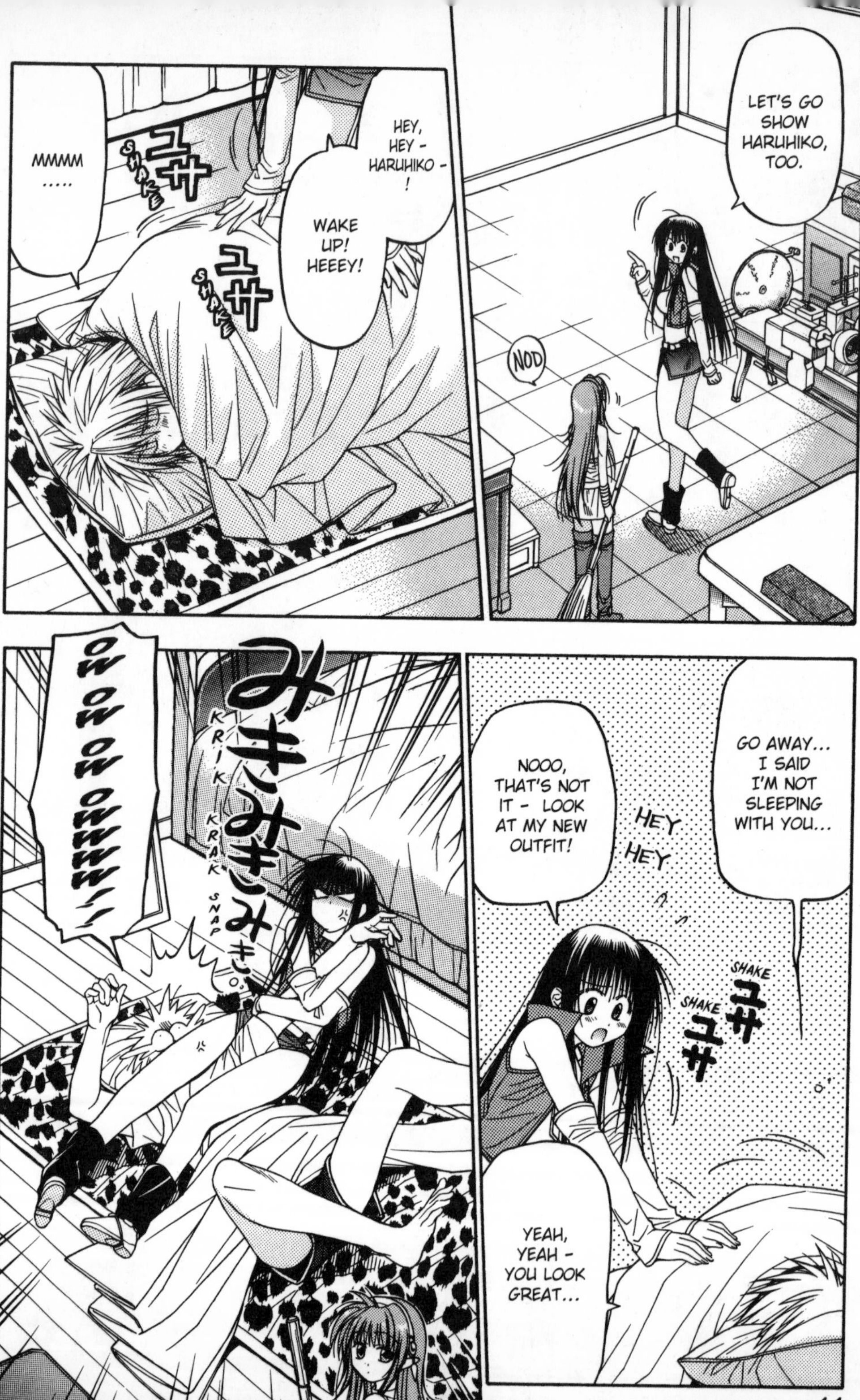
LET'S GO SHOW HARUHIKO, TOO.
NOD
HEY, HEY - HARUHIKO -!
WAKE UP! HEEEY!
ユサ SHAKE
ユサ SHAKE
MMMM .....
GO AWAY... I SAID I'M NOT SLEEPING WITH YOU...
NOOO, THAT'S NOT IT - LOOK AT MY NEW OUTFIT!
HEY HEY
SHAKE ユサ
SHAKE ユサ
YEAH, YEAH - YOU LOOK GREAT...
KRIK KRAK SNAP
OW OW OW OW OWWWW!!

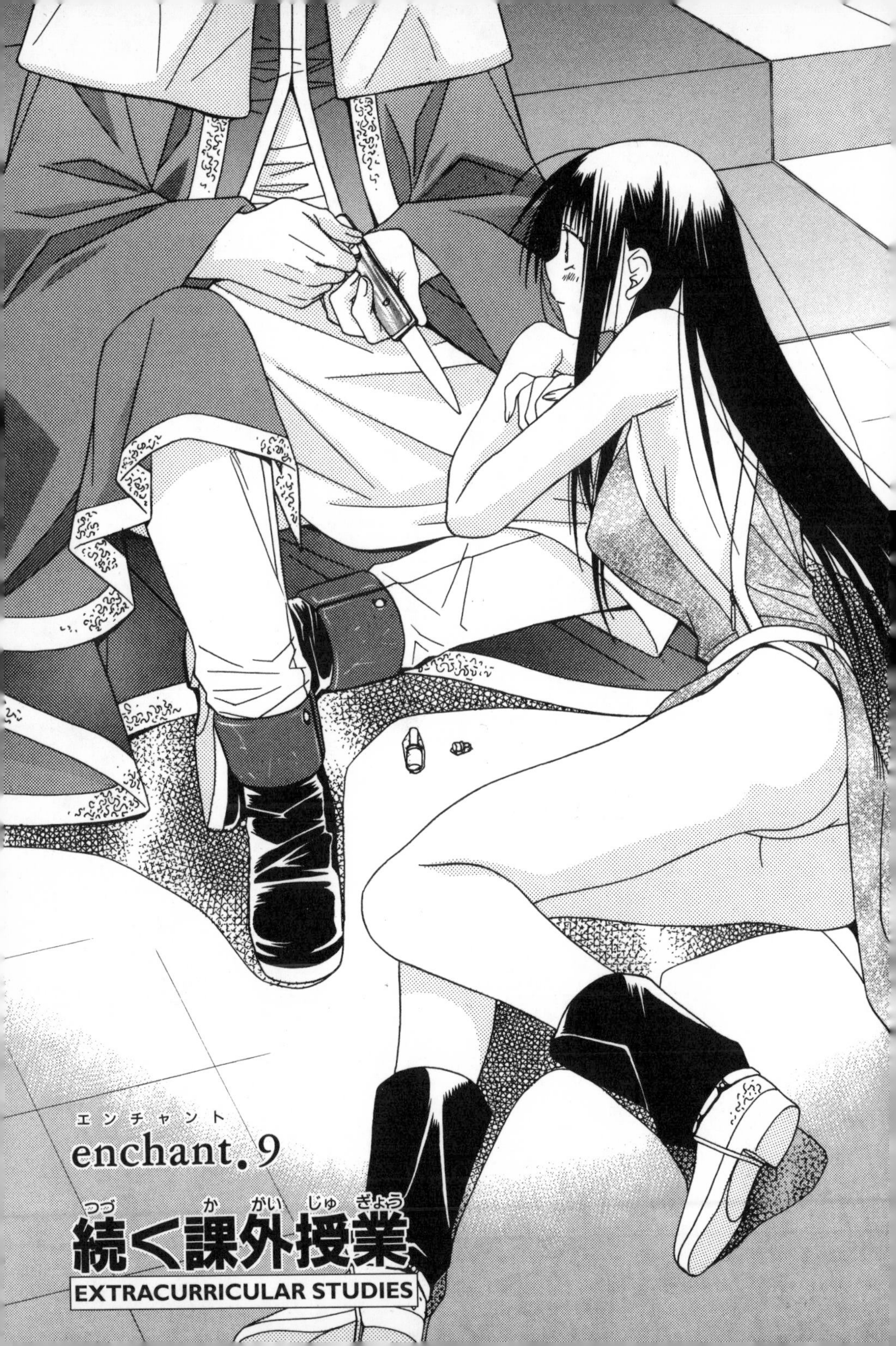
エンチャント
enchant. 9
続く課外授業
EXTRACURRICULAR STUDIES

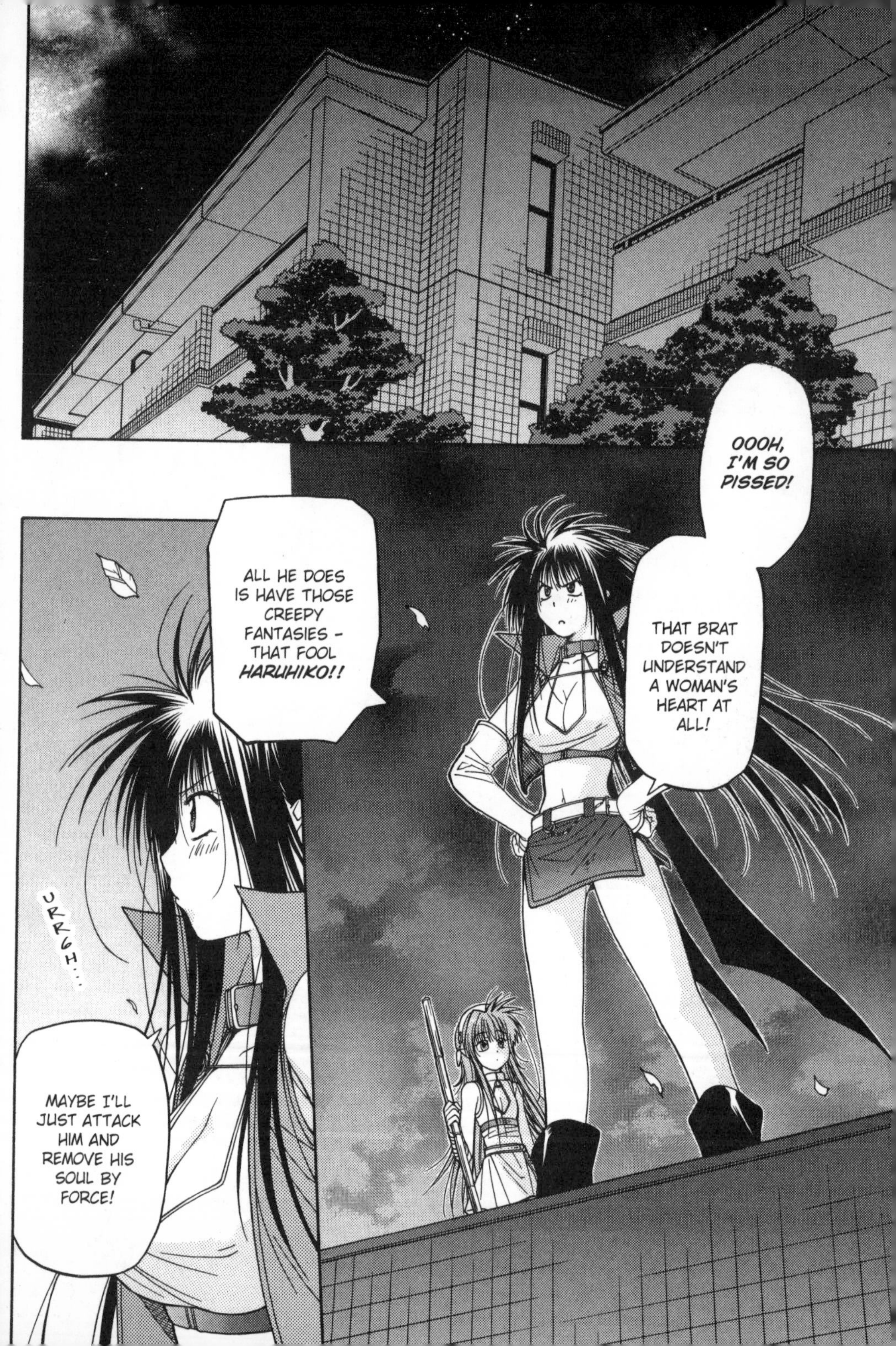
OOOH, I'M SO PISSED!
THAT BRAT DOESN'T UNDERSTAND A WOMAN'S HEART AT ALL!
ALL HE DOES IS HAVE THOSE CREEPY FANTASIES - THAT FOOL HARUHIKO!!
URRGH...
MAYBE I'LL JUST ATTACK HIM AND REMOVE HIS SOUL BY FORCE!

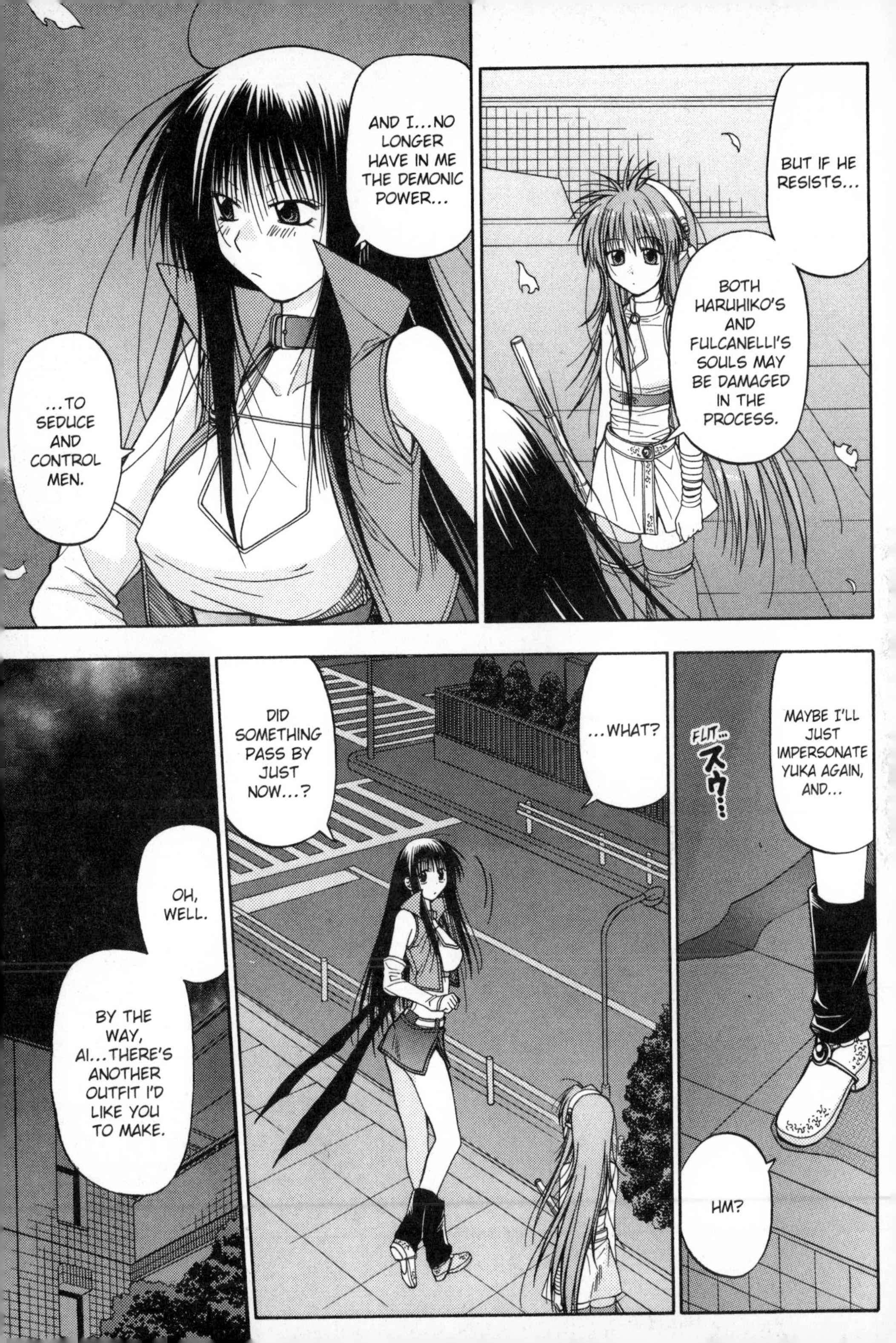
BUT IF HE RESISTS...
BOTH HARUHIKO'S AND FULCANELLI'S SOULS MAY BE DAMAGED IN THE PROCESS.
AND I...NO LONGER HAVE IN ME THE DEMONIC POWER...
...TO SEDUCE AND CONTROL MEN.
MAYBE I'LL JUST IMPERSONATE YUKA AGAIN, AND...
FLIT... スゥ...
HM?
...WHAT?
DID SOMETHING PASS BY JUST NOW...?
OH, WELL.
BY THE WAY, AI...THERE'S ANOTHER OUTFIT I'D LIKE YOU TO MAKE.

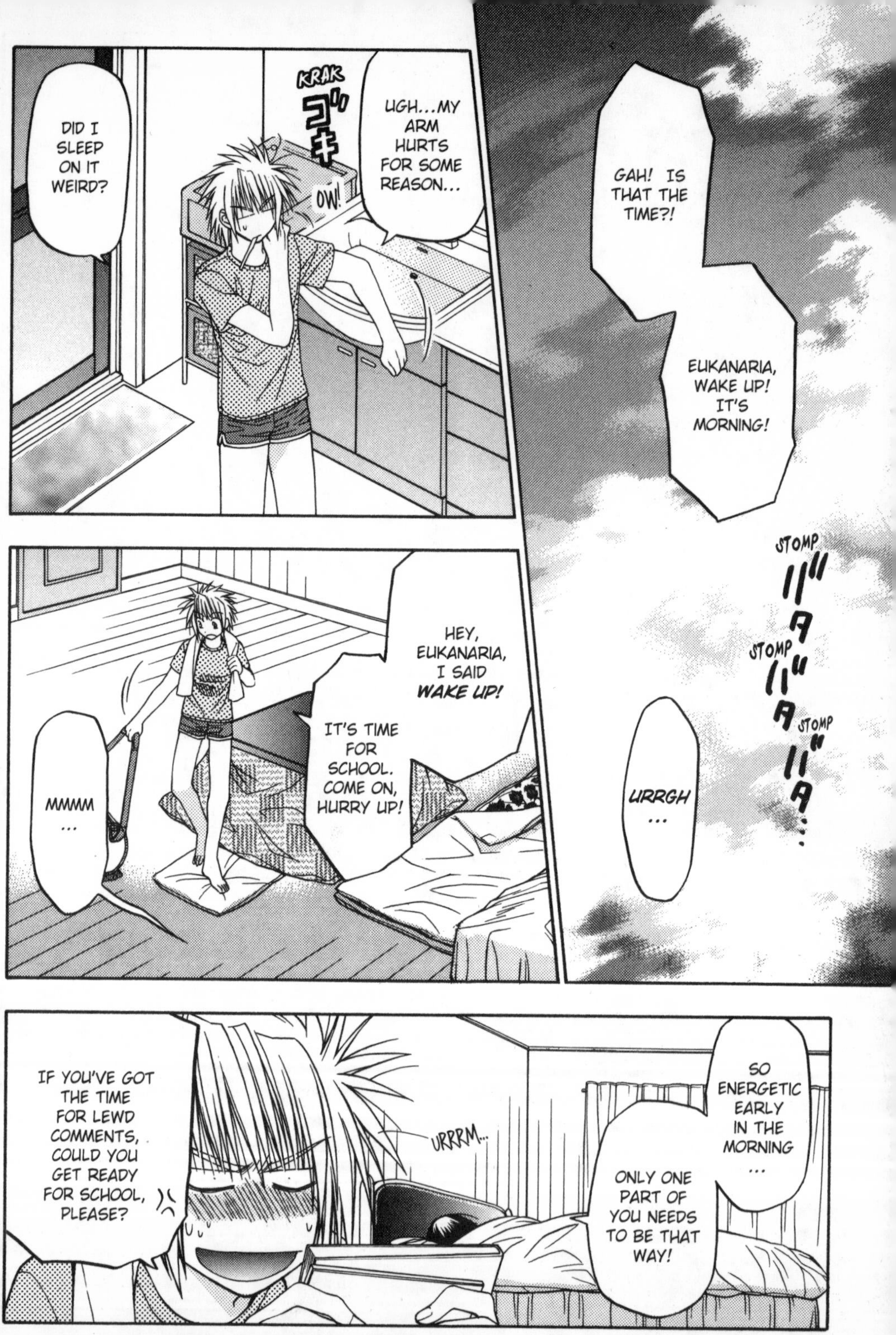
GAH! IS THAT THE TIME?!
EUKANARIA, WAKE UP! IT'S MORNING!
STOMP
STOMP
STOMP
URRGH ...
UGH...MY ARM HURTS FOR SOME REASON...
KRAK
OW!
DID I SLEEP ON IT WEIRD?
HEY, EUKANARIA, I SAID *WAKE UP!*
IT'S TIME FOR SCHOOL. COME ON, HURRY UP!
MMMM ...
SO ENERGETIC EARLY IN THE MORNING ...
ONLY ONE PART OF YOU NEEDS TO BE THAT WAY!
URRRM...
IF YOU'VE GOT THE TIME FOR LEWD COMMENTS, COULD YOU GET READY FOR SCHOOL, PLEASE?

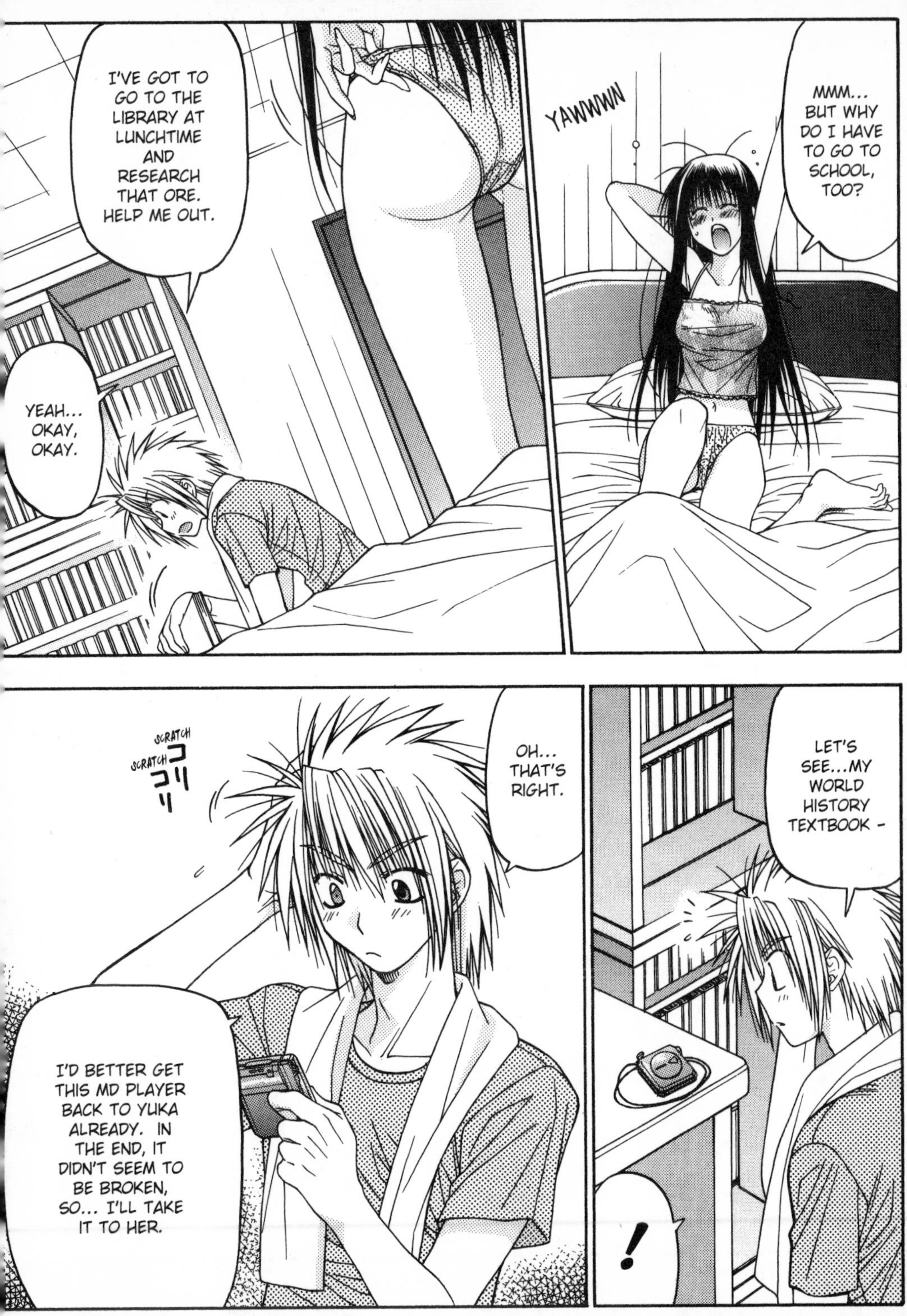
YAWWWN
MMM... BUT WHY DO I HAVE TO GO TO SCHOOL, TOO?
I'VE GOT TO GO TO THE LIBRARY AT LUNCHTIME AND RESEARCH THAT ORE. HELP ME OUT.
YEAH... OKAY, OKAY.
LET'S SEE...MY WORLD HISTORY TEXTBOOK -
!
OH... THAT'S RIGHT.
SCRATCH SCRATCH
I'D BETTER GET THIS MD PLAYER BACK TO YUKA ALREADY. IN THE END, IT DIDN'T SEEM TO BE BROKEN, SO... I'LL TAKE IT TO HER.

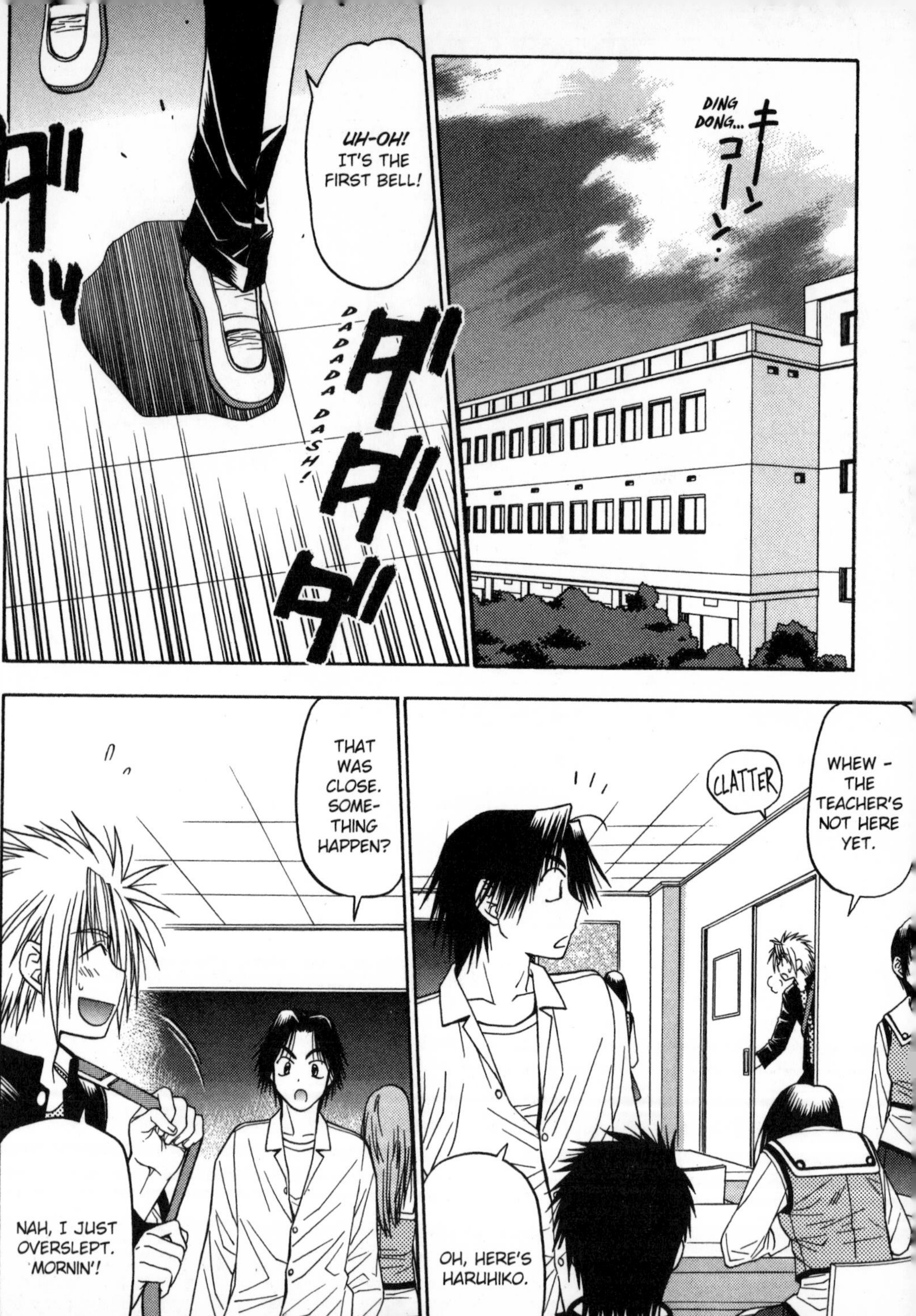
DING DONG...
キーンコーン…
UH-OH! IT'S THE FIRST BELL!
ダッ
DADADA DASH!
ダダダ
WHEW - THE TEACHER'S NOT HERE YET.
CLATTER
OH, HERE'S HARUHIKO.
THAT WAS CLOSE. SOME-THING HAPPEN?
NAH, I JUST OVERSLEPT. 'MORNIN'!

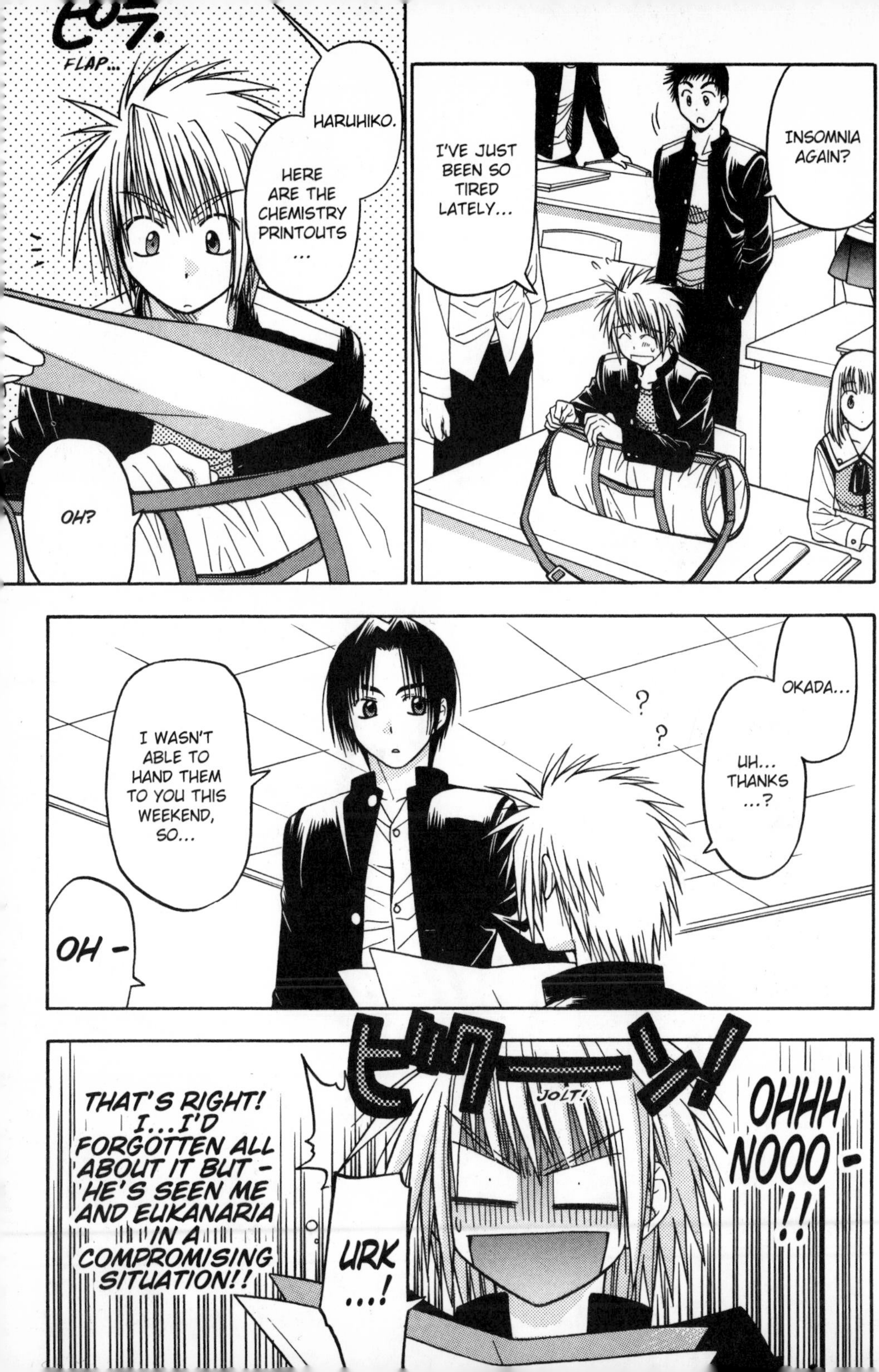
INSOMNIA AGAIN?
I'VE JUST BEEN SO TIRED LATELY...
FLAP...
HARUHIKO.
HERE ARE THE CHEMISTRY PRINTOUTS ...
OH?
OKADA...
UH... THANKS ...?
? ?
I WASN'T ABLE TO HAND THEM TO YOU THIS WEEKEND, SO...
OH -
JOLT!
OHHH NOOO - !!
URK ...!
THAT'S RIGHT! I...I'D FORGOTTEN ALL ABOUT IT BUT - HE'S SEEN ME AND EUKANARIA IN A COMPROMISING SITUATION!!

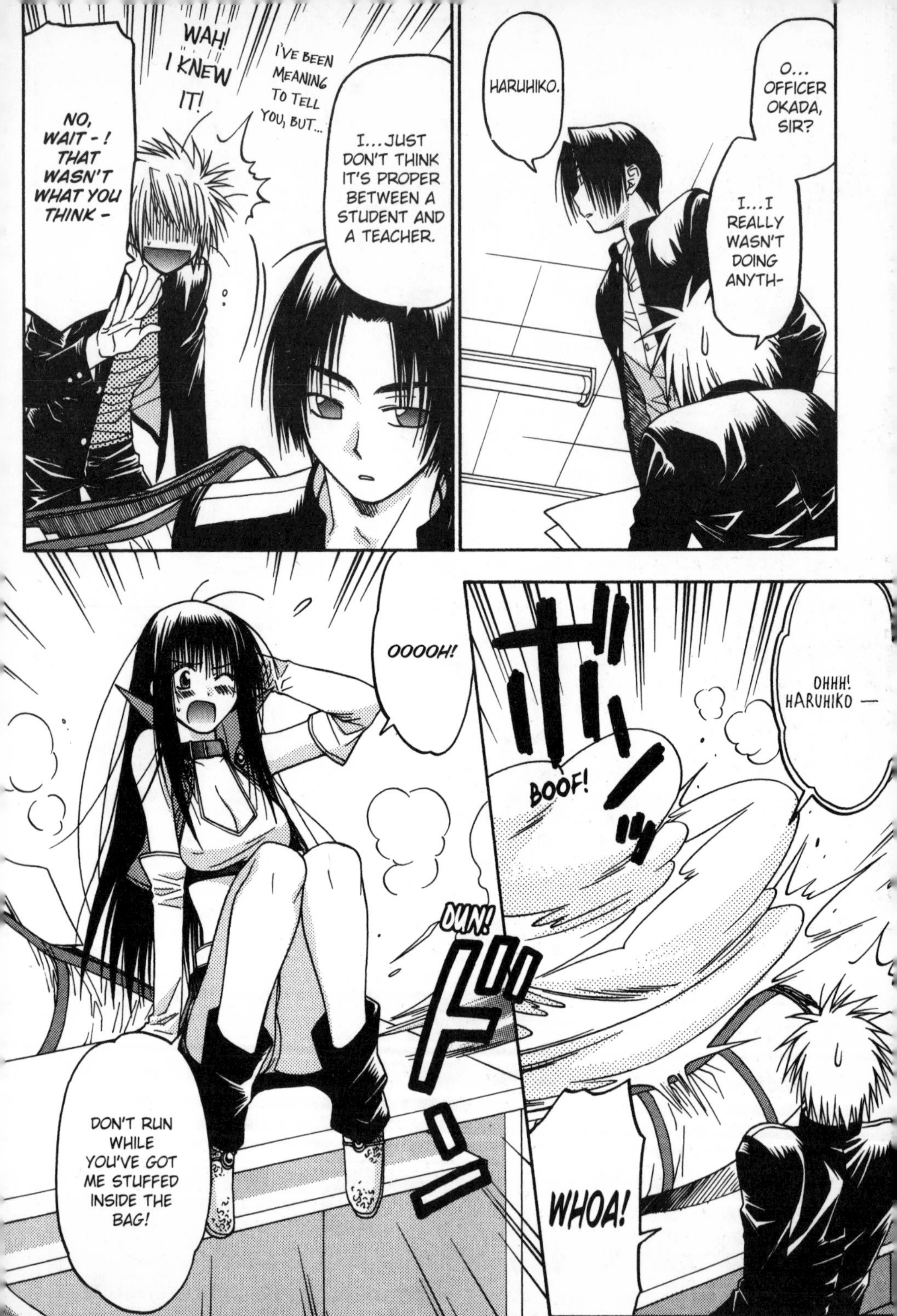
O... OFFICER OKADA, SIR?
HARUHIKO.
I...I REALLY WASN'T DOING ANYTH-
I'VE BEEN MEANING TO TELL YOU, BUT...
I...JUST DON'T THINK IT'S PROPER BETWEEN A STUDENT AND A TEACHER.
WAH! I KNEW IT!
NO, WAIT-! THAT WASN'T WHAT YOU THINK-
OHHH! HARUHIKO —
BOOF!
WHOA!
OOOOH!
DUN!
DON'T RUN WHILE YOU'VE GOT ME STUFFED INSIDE THE BAG!

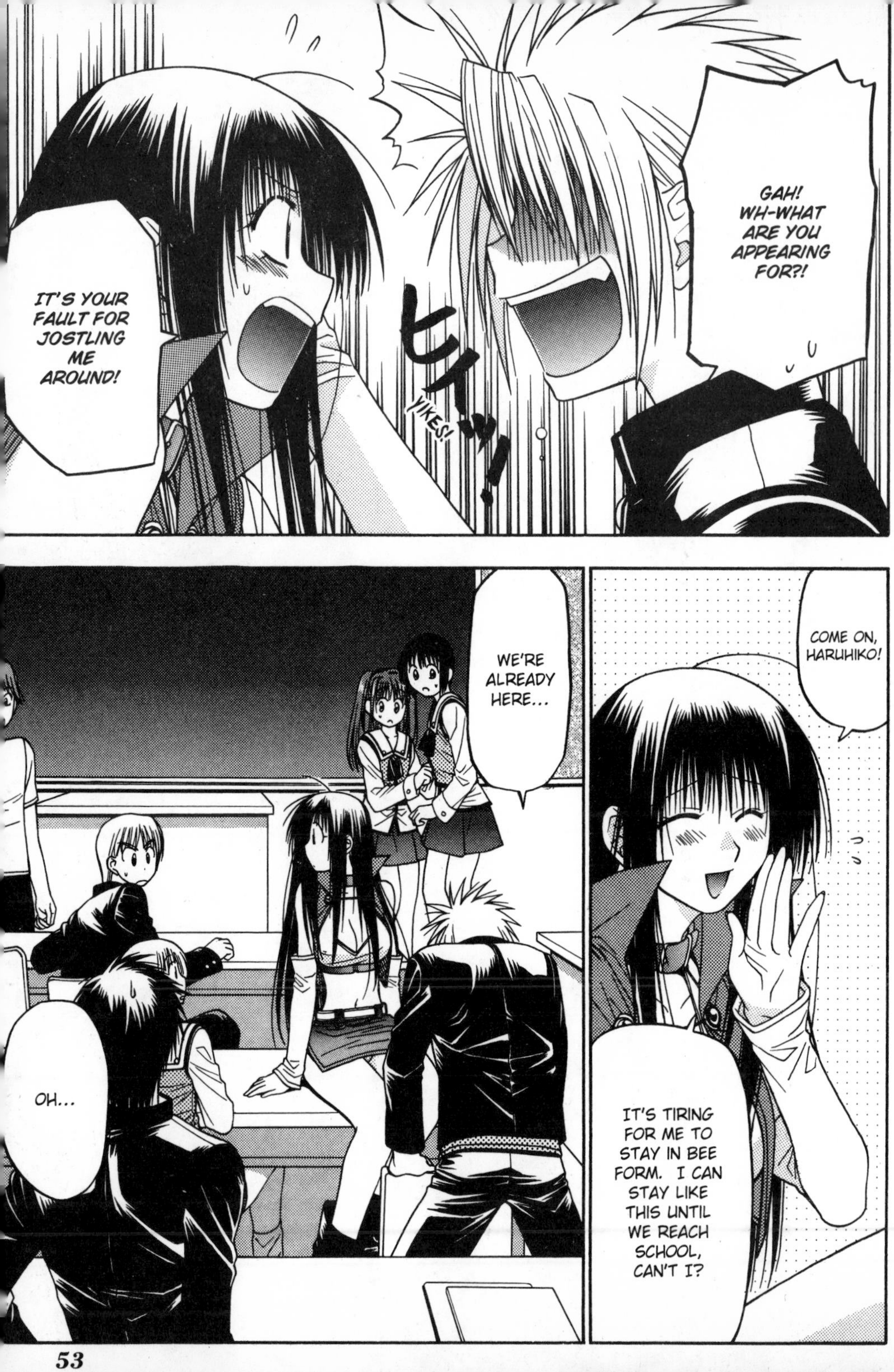
GAH! WH-WHAT ARE YOU APPEARING FOR?!
ヒィーッ!
YIKES!
IT'S YOUR FAULT FOR JOSTLING ME AROUND!
COME ON, HARUHIKO!
IT'S TIRING FOR ME TO STAY IN BEE FORM. I CAN STAY LIKE THIS UNTIL WE REACH SCHOOL, CAN'T I?
WE'RE ALREADY HERE...
OH...

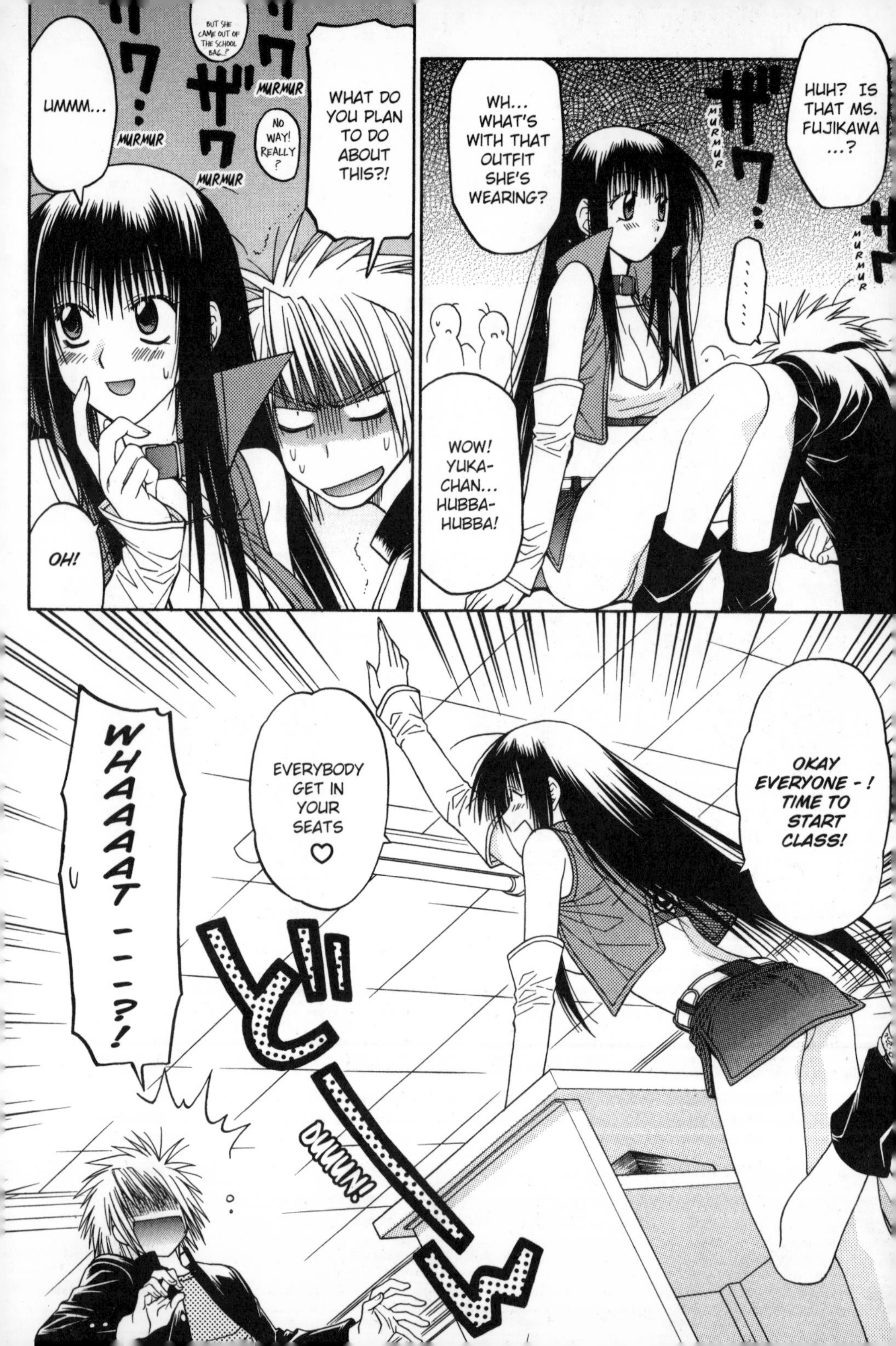
HUH? IS THAT MS. FUJIKAWA ...?
MURMUR
......
WH... WHAT'S WITH THAT OUTFIT SHE'S WEARING?
MURMUR
WOW! YUKA-CHAN... HUBBA-HUBBA!
BUT SHE CAME OUT OF THE SCHOOL BAG..?
MURMUR
WHAT DO YOU PLAN TO DO ABOUT THIS?!
NO WAY! REALLY ?
MURMUR
UMMM...
MURMUR
OH!
OKAY EVERYONE - ! TIME TO START CLASS!
EVERYBODY GET IN YOUR SEATS ♥
WHAAAAT ---?!
DUMUN!

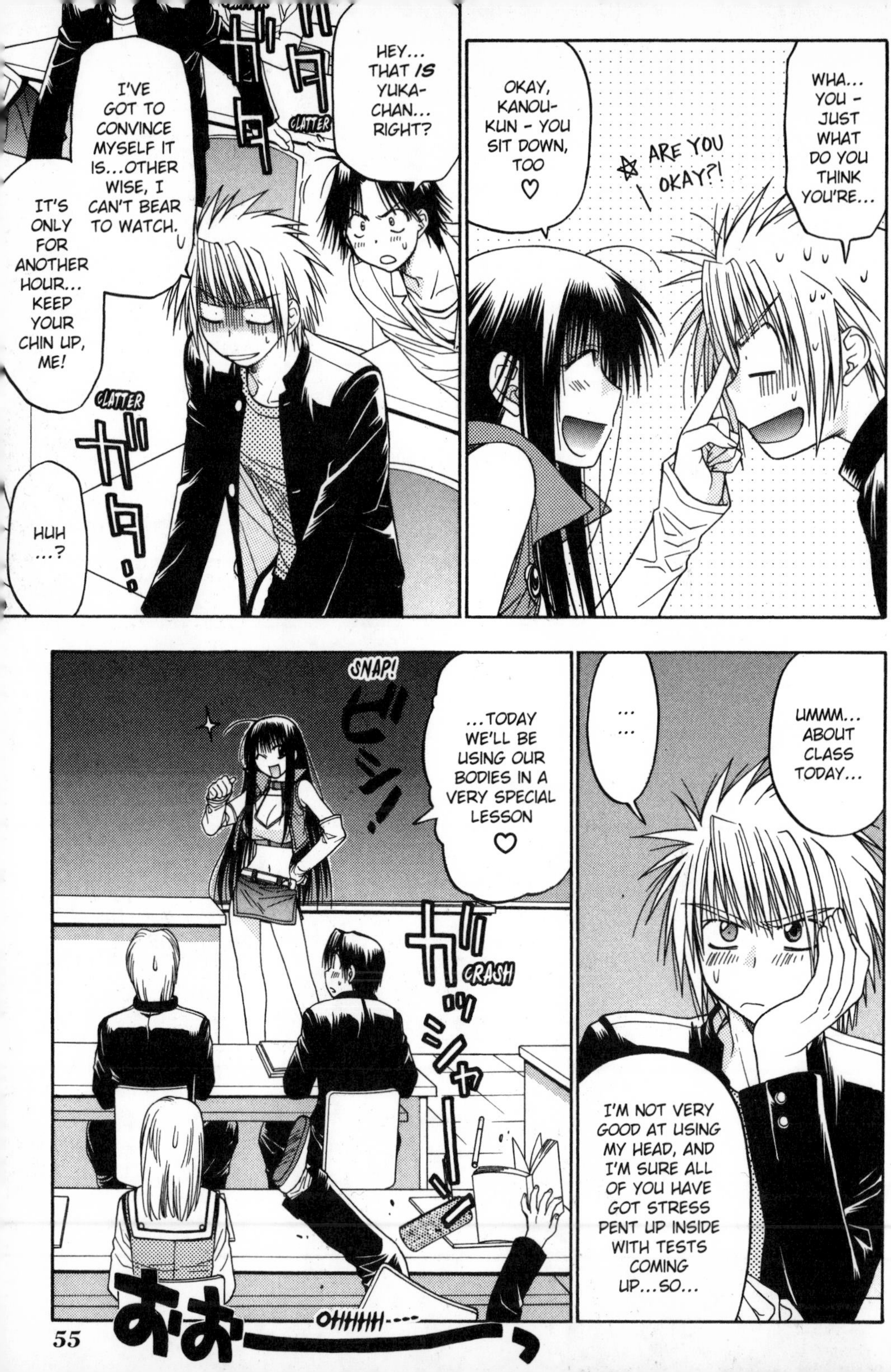
WHA... YOU - JUST WHAT DO YOU THINK YOU'RE...
ARE YOU OKAY?!
OKAY, KANOU-KUN - YOU SIT DOWN, TOO ♡
HEY... THAT IS YUKA-CHAN... RIGHT?
CLATTER
I'VE GOT TO CONVINCE MYSELF IT IS...OTHER WISE, I CAN'T BEAR TO WATCH.
IT'S ONLY FOR ANOTHER HOUR... KEEP YOUR CHIN UP, ME!
CLATTER
HUH ...?
UMMM... ABOUT CLASS TODAY...
... ...
I'M NOT VERY GOOD AT USING MY HEAD, AND I'M SURE ALL OF YOU HAVE GOT STRESS PENT UP INSIDE WITH TESTS COMING UP...SO...
...TODAY WE'LL BE USING OUR BODIES IN A VERY SPECIAL LESSON ♡
SNAP!
CRASH
OHHHHH----

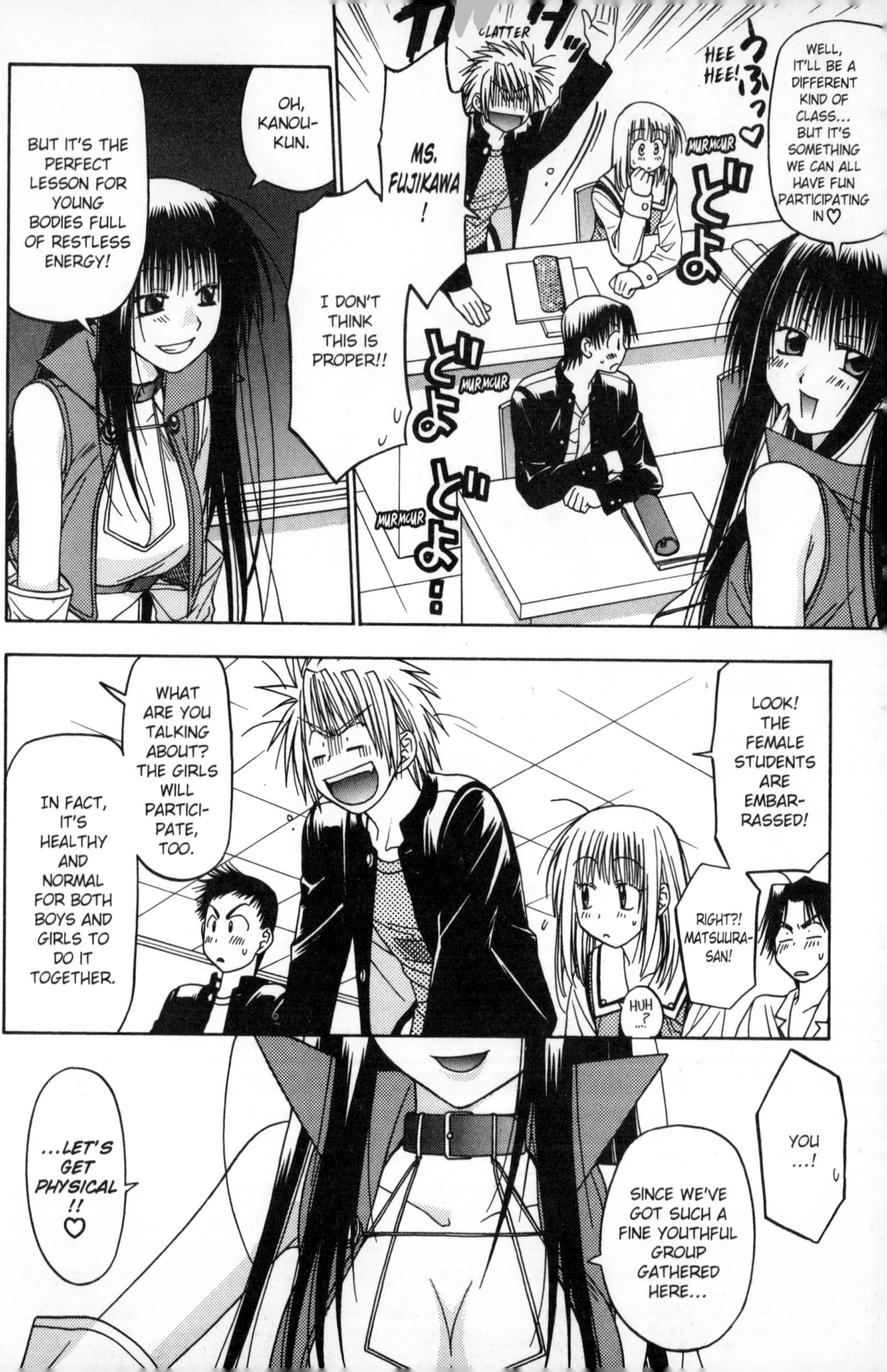

WELL, IT'LL BE A DIFFERENT KIND OF CLASS... BUT IT'S SOMETHING WE CAN ALL HAVE FUN PARTICIPATING IN♡
うふっ♡
HEE HEE!
どよ
MURMUR
CLATTER
MS. FUJIKAWA!
I DON'T THINK THIS IS PROPER!!
どよ
MURMUR
どよどよっ
MURMUR
OH, KANOU-KUN.
BUT IT'S THE PERFECT LESSON FOR YOUNG BODIES FULL OF RESTLESS ENERGY!
LOOK! THE FEMALE STUDENTS ARE EMBARRASSED!
RIGHT?! MATSUURA-SAN!
HUH ...?
WHAT ARE YOU TALKING ABOUT? THE GIRLS WILL PARTICI-PATE, TOO.
IN FACT, IT'S HEALTHY AND NORMAL FOR BOTH BOYS AND GIRLS TO DO IT TOGETHER.
YOU ...!
SINCE WE'VE GOT SUCH A FINE YOUTHFUL GROUP GATHERED HERE...
...LET'S GET PHYSICAL!! ♡

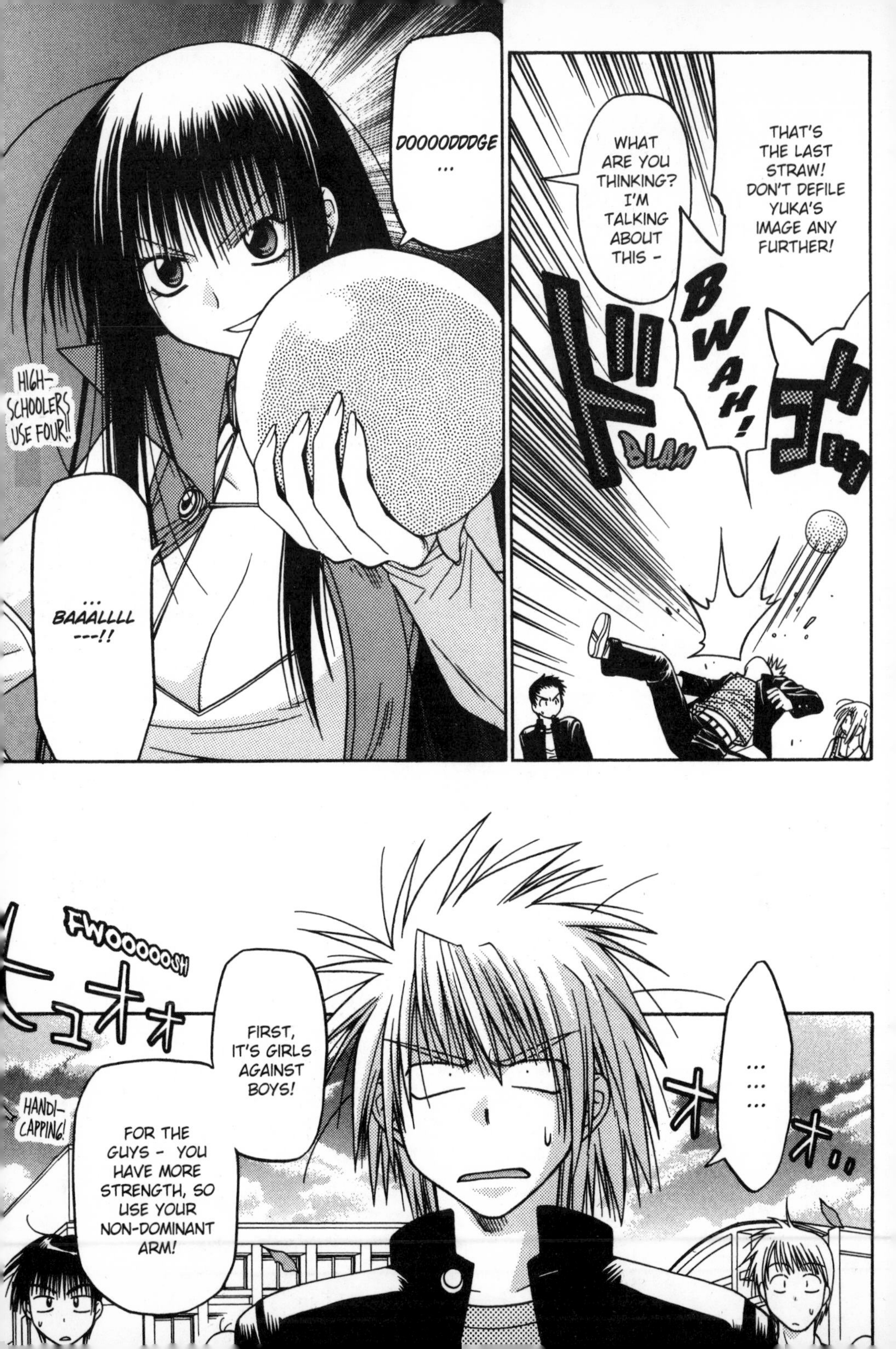
THAT'S THE LAST STRAW! DON'T DEFILE YUKA'S IMAGE ANY FURTHER!
WHAT ARE YOU THINKING? I'M TALKING ABOUT THIS -
BWAH!
BLAM
DOOOODDDGE ...
HIGH-SCHOOLERS USE FOUR!!
... BAAALLLL ---!!
... ...
FWOOOOOOSH
FIRST, IT'S GIRLS AGAINST BOYS!
FOR THE GUYS - YOU HAVE MORE STRENGTH, SO USE YOUR NON-DOMINANT ARM!
HANDI-CAPPING!

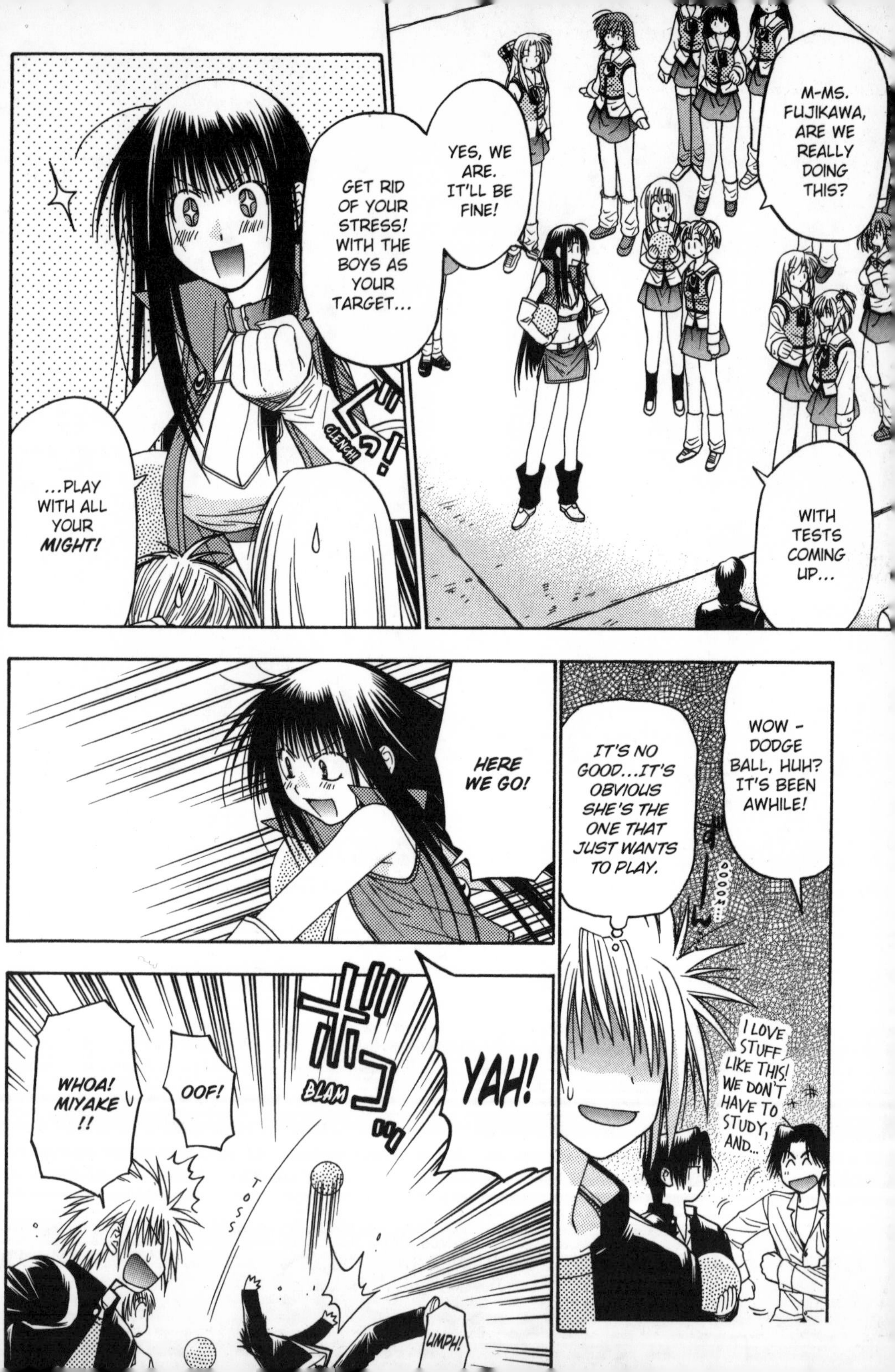
M-MS. FUJIKAWA, ARE WE REALLY DOING THIS?
WITH TESTS COMING UP...
YES, WE ARE. IT'LL BE FINE!
GET RID OF YOUR STRESS! WITH THE BOYS AS YOUR TARGET...
CLENCH!
...PLAY WITH ALL YOUR MIGHT!
WOW - DODGE BALL, HUH? IT'S BEEN AWHILE!
IT'S NO GOOD...IT'S OBVIOUS SHE'S THE ONE THAT JUST WANTS TO PLAY.
DOOOOM...
I LOVE STUFF LIKE THIS! WE DON'T HAVE TO STUDY, AND...
HERE WE GO!
YAH!
BLAM
OOF!
WHOA! MIYAKE !!
TOSS
UMPH!

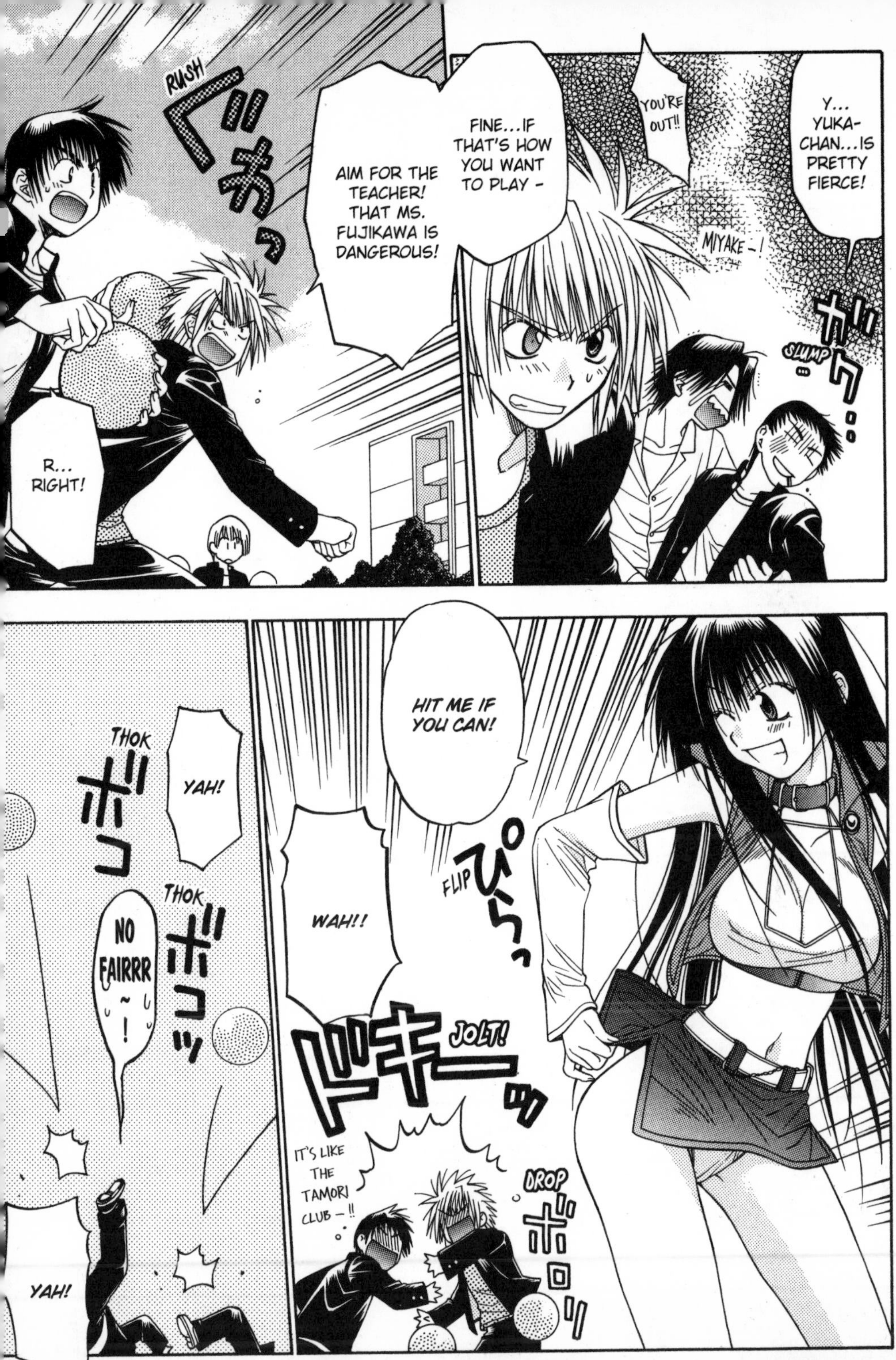
Y... YUKA-CHAN...IS PRETTY FIERCE!
YOU'RE OUT!!
MIYAKE –!
SLUMP
FINE...IF THAT'S HOW YOU WANT TO PLAY –
AIM FOR THE TEACHER! THAT MS. FUJIKAWA IS DANGEROUS!
RUSH
R... RIGHT!
HIT ME IF YOU CAN!
FLIP
WAH!!
JOLT!
DROP
IT'S LIKE THE TAMORI CLUB –!!
THOK
YAH!
THOK
NO FAIRRR ~!
YAH!

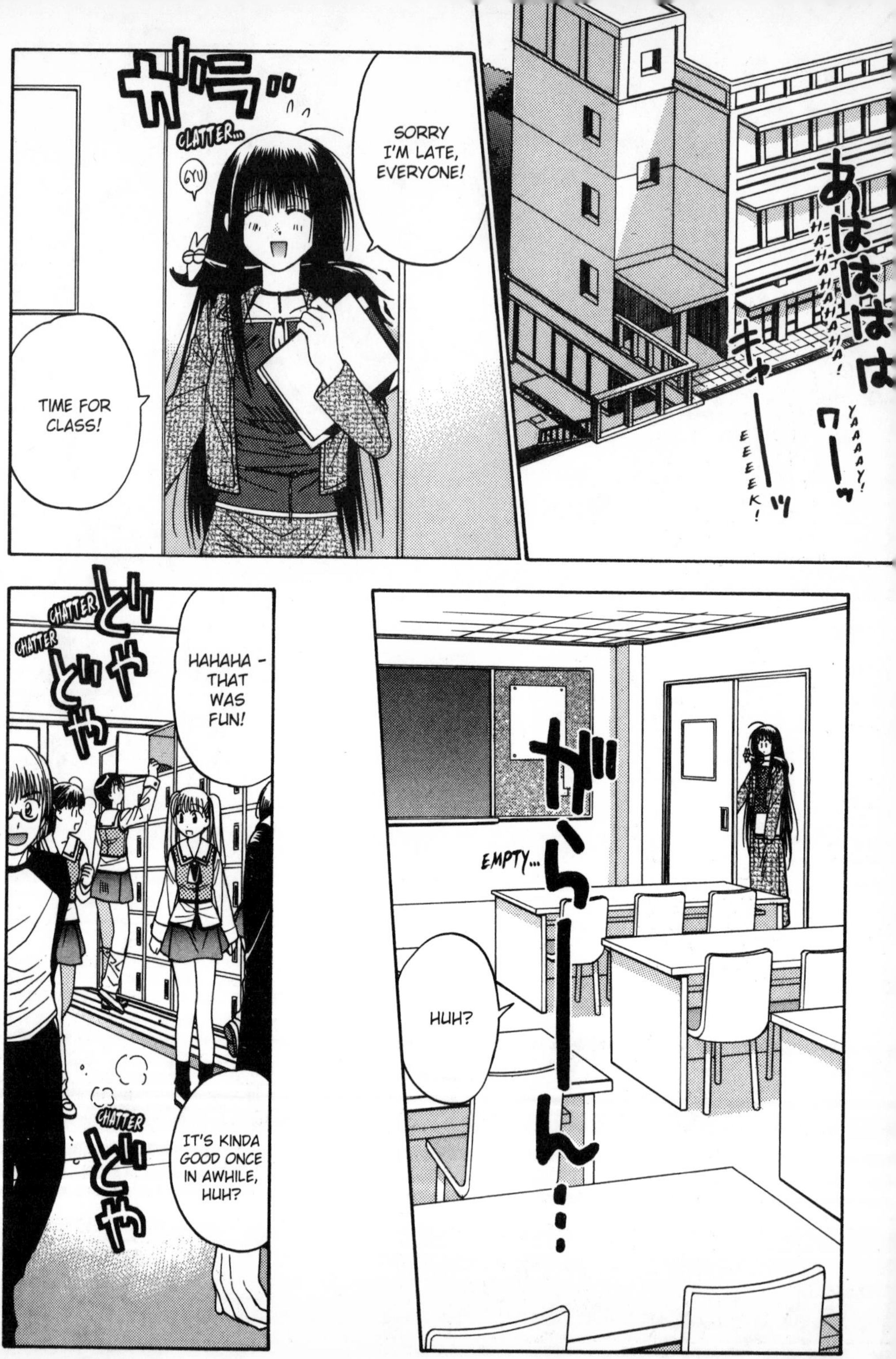
あははは
HAHAHAHAHA!
ワーッ
YAAAAY!
キャーッ
EEEEEK!
ガラッ
CLATTER...
GYU
SORRY I'M LATE, EVERYONE!
TIME FOR CLASS!
がら〜ん…
EMPTY...
HUH?
どやどや
CHATTER
CHATTER
HAHAHA - THAT WAS FUN!
どや
CHATTER
IT'S KINDA GOOD ONCE IN AWHILE, HUH?

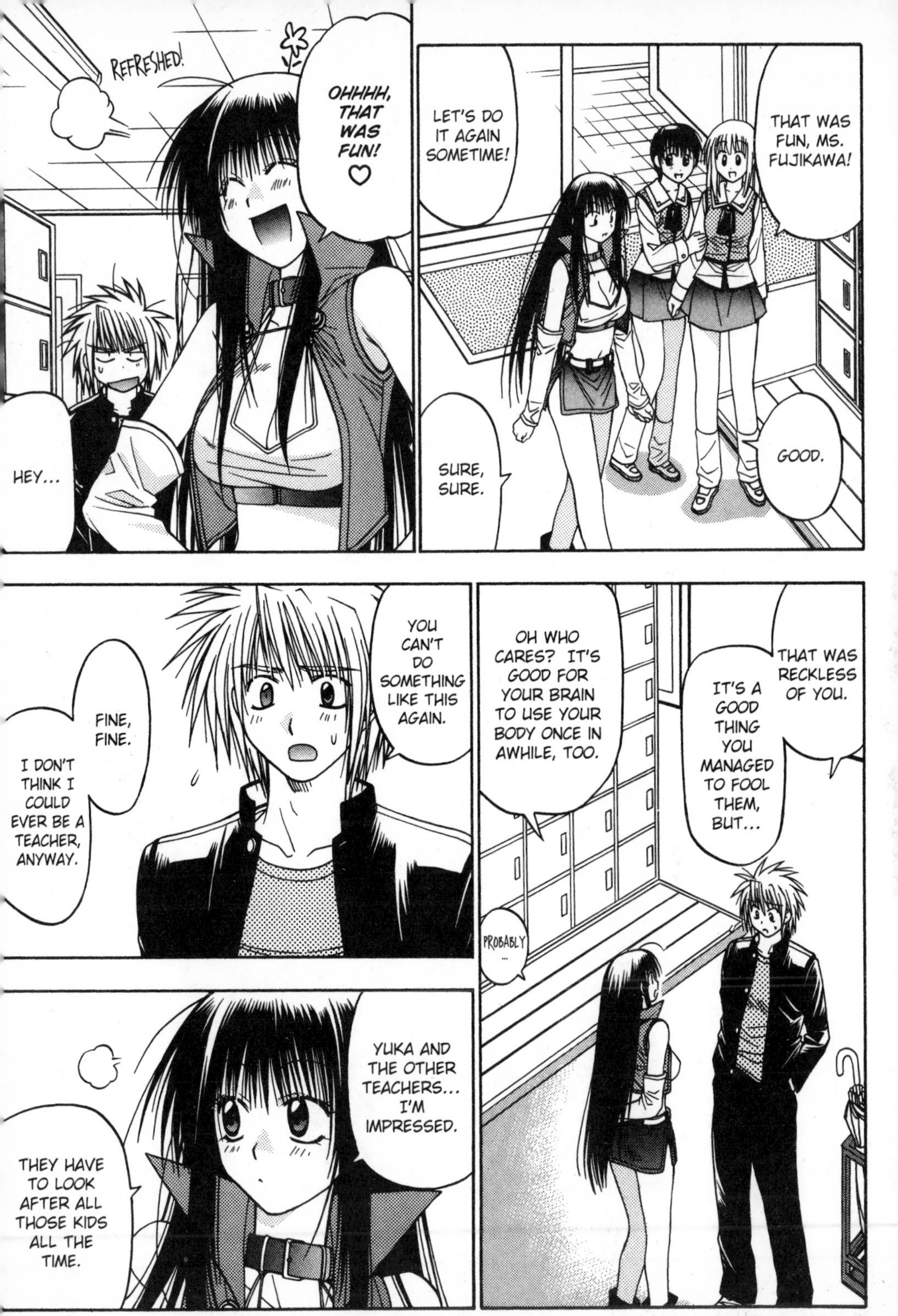
THAT WAS FUN, MS. FUJIKAWA!
LET'S DO IT AGAIN SOMETIME!
GOOD.
SURE, SURE.
OHHHH, THAT WAS FUN! ♡
REFRESHED!
HEY...
THAT WAS RECKLESS OF YOU.
IT'S A GOOD THING YOU MANAGED TO FOOL THEM, BUT...
OH WHO CARES? IT'S GOOD FOR YOUR BRAIN TO USE YOUR BODY ONCE IN AWHILE, TOO.
PROBABLY...
YOU CAN'T DO SOMETHING LIKE THIS AGAIN.
FINE, FINE.
I DON'T THINK I COULD EVER BE A TEACHER, ANYWAY.
YUKA AND THE OTHER TEACHERS... I'M IMPRESSED.
THEY HAVE TO LOOK AFTER ALL THOSE KIDS ALL THE TIME.

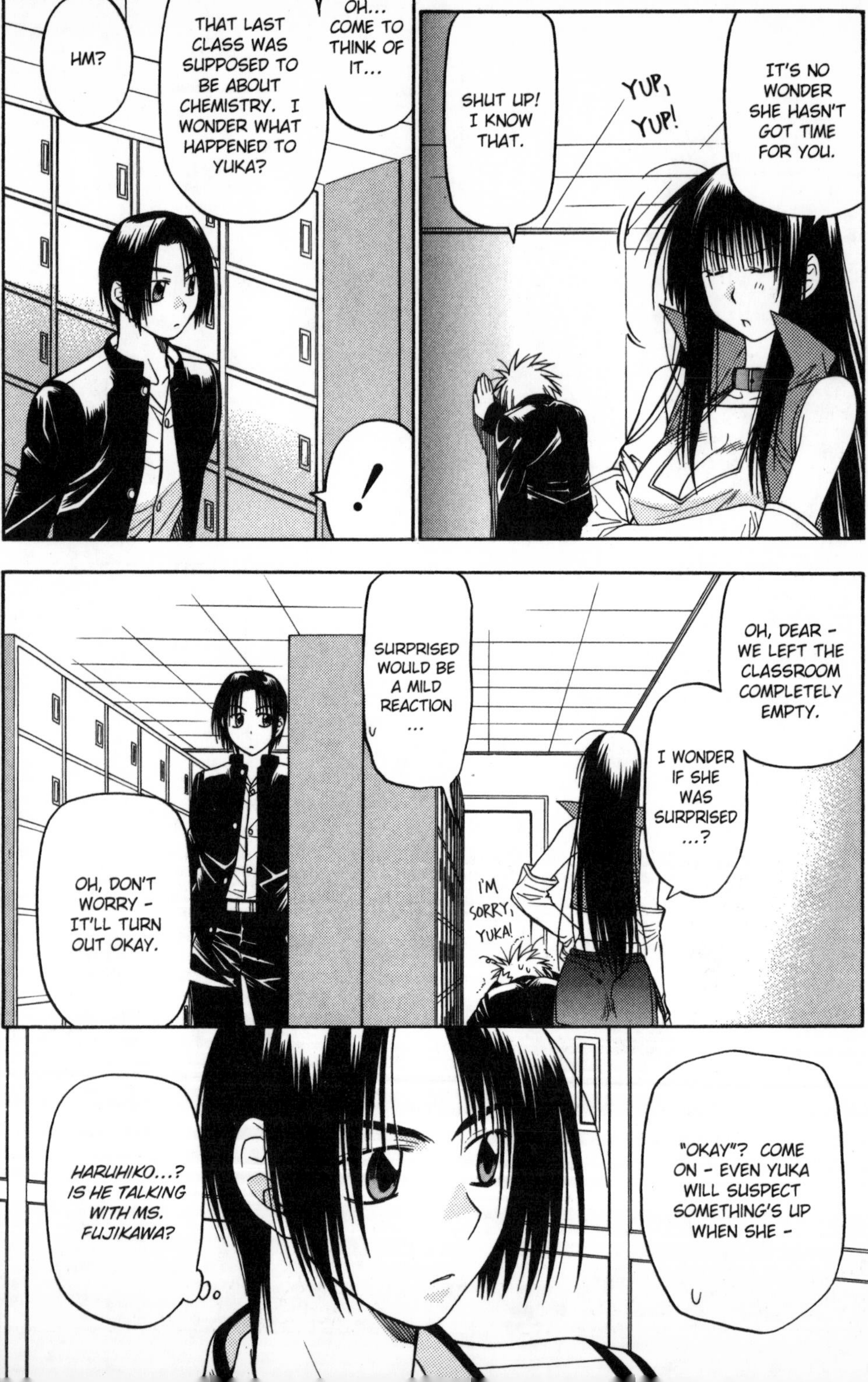

IT'S NO WONDER SHE HASN'T GOT TIME FOR YOU.
YUP, YUP!
SHUT UP! I KNOW THAT.
OH... COME TO THINK OF IT...
THAT LAST CLASS WAS SUPPOSED TO BE ABOUT CHEMISTRY. I WONDER WHAT HAPPENED TO YUKA?
HM?
!
OH, DEAR - WE LEFT THE CLASSROOM COMPLETELY EMPTY.
I WONDER IF SHE WAS SURPRISED ...?
SURPRISED WOULD BE A MILD REACTION ...
I'M SORRY, YUKA!
OH, DON'T WORRY - IT'LL TURN OUT OKAY.
"OKAY"? COME ON - EVEN YUKA WILL SUSPECT SOMETHING'S UP WHEN SHE -
HARUHIKO...? IS HE TALKING WITH MS. FUJIKAWA?

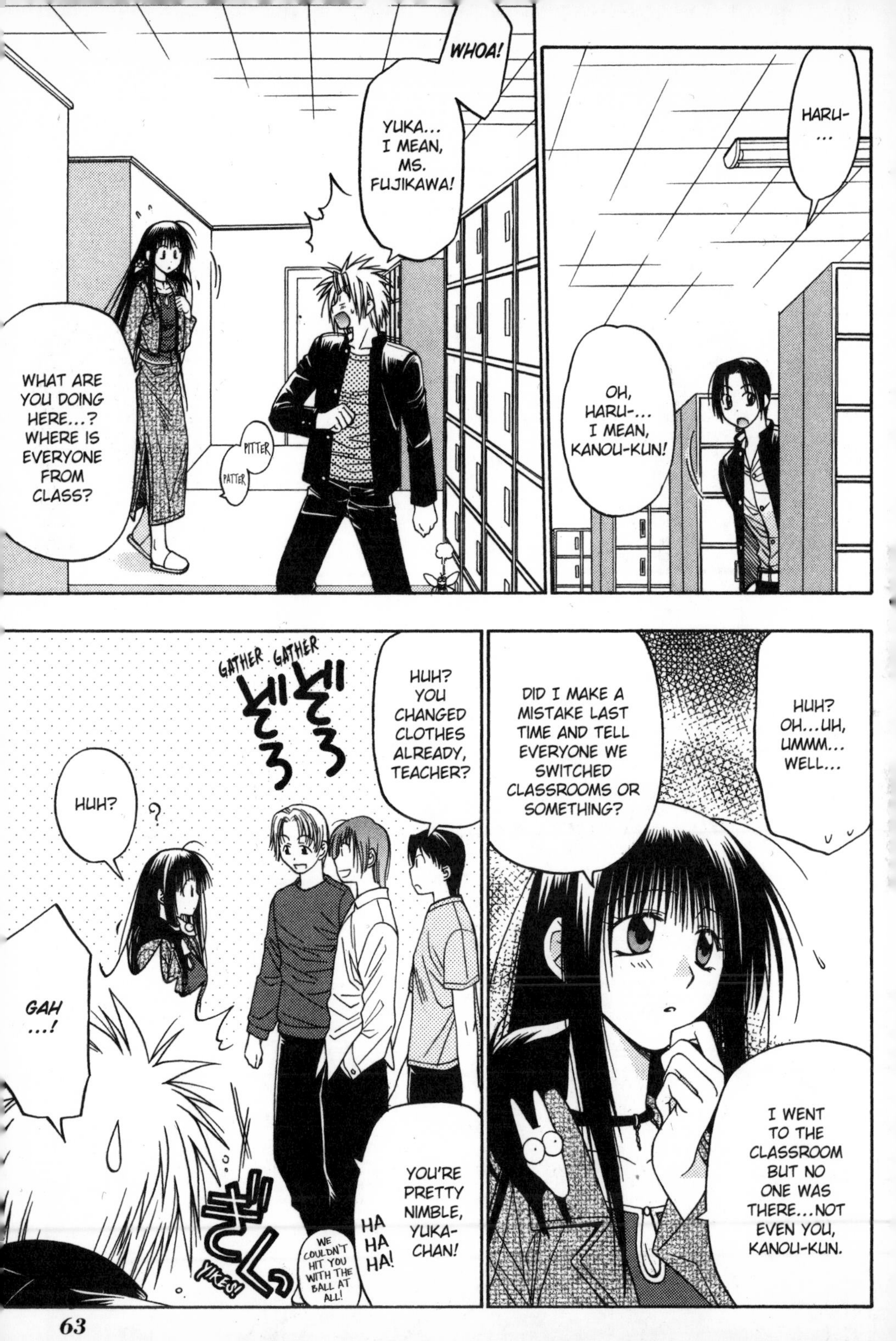
HARU-...
OH, HARU-... I MEAN, KANOU-KUN!
WHOA!
YUKA... I MEAN, MS. FUJIKAWA!
WHAT ARE YOU DOING HERE...? WHERE IS EVERYONE FROM CLASS?
PITTER
PATTER
HUH? OH...UH, UMMM... WELL...
DID I MAKE A MISTAKE LAST TIME AND TELL EVERYONE WE SWITCHED CLASSROOMS OR SOMETHING?
I WENT TO THE CLASSROOM BUT NO ONE WAS THERE...NOT EVEN YOU, KANOU-KUN.
HUH? YOU CHANGED CLOTHES ALREADY, TEACHER?
GATHER GATHER
HUH?
GAH ...!
YOU'RE PRETTY NIMBLE, YUKA-CHAN!
HA HA HA!
WE COULDN'T HIT YOU WITH THE BALL AT ALL!
YIKES!

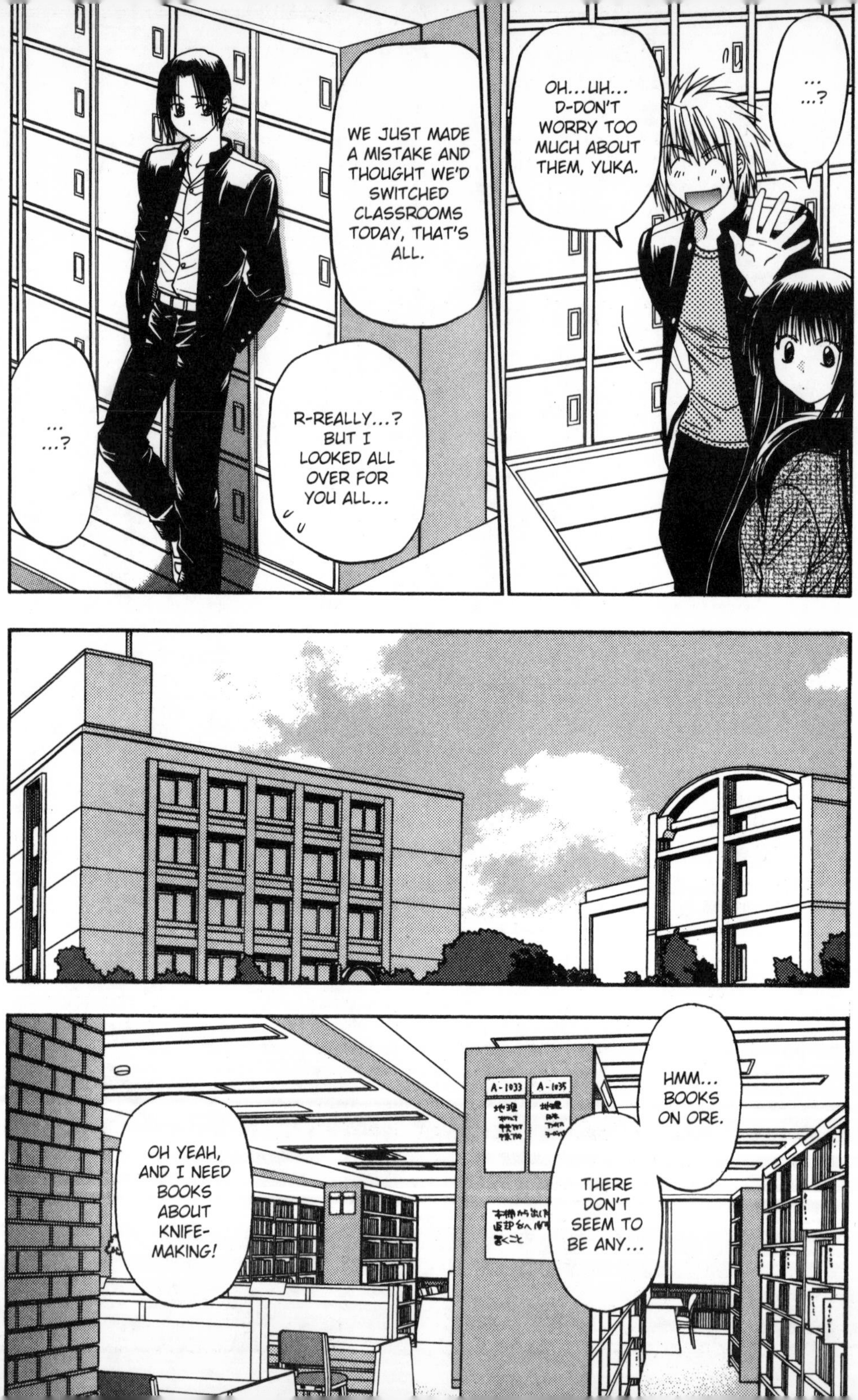

... ...?
OH...UH... D-DON'T WORRY TOO MUCH ABOUT THEM, YUKA.
WE JUST MADE A MISTAKE AND THOUGHT WE'D SWITCHED CLASSROOMS TODAY, THAT'S ALL.
R-REALLY...? BUT I LOOKED ALL OVER FOR YOU ALL...
... ...?
A-1033
A-1035
HMM... BOOKS ON ORE.
THERE DON'T SEEM TO BE ANY...
OH YEAH, AND I NEED BOOKS ABOUT KNIFE-MAKING!

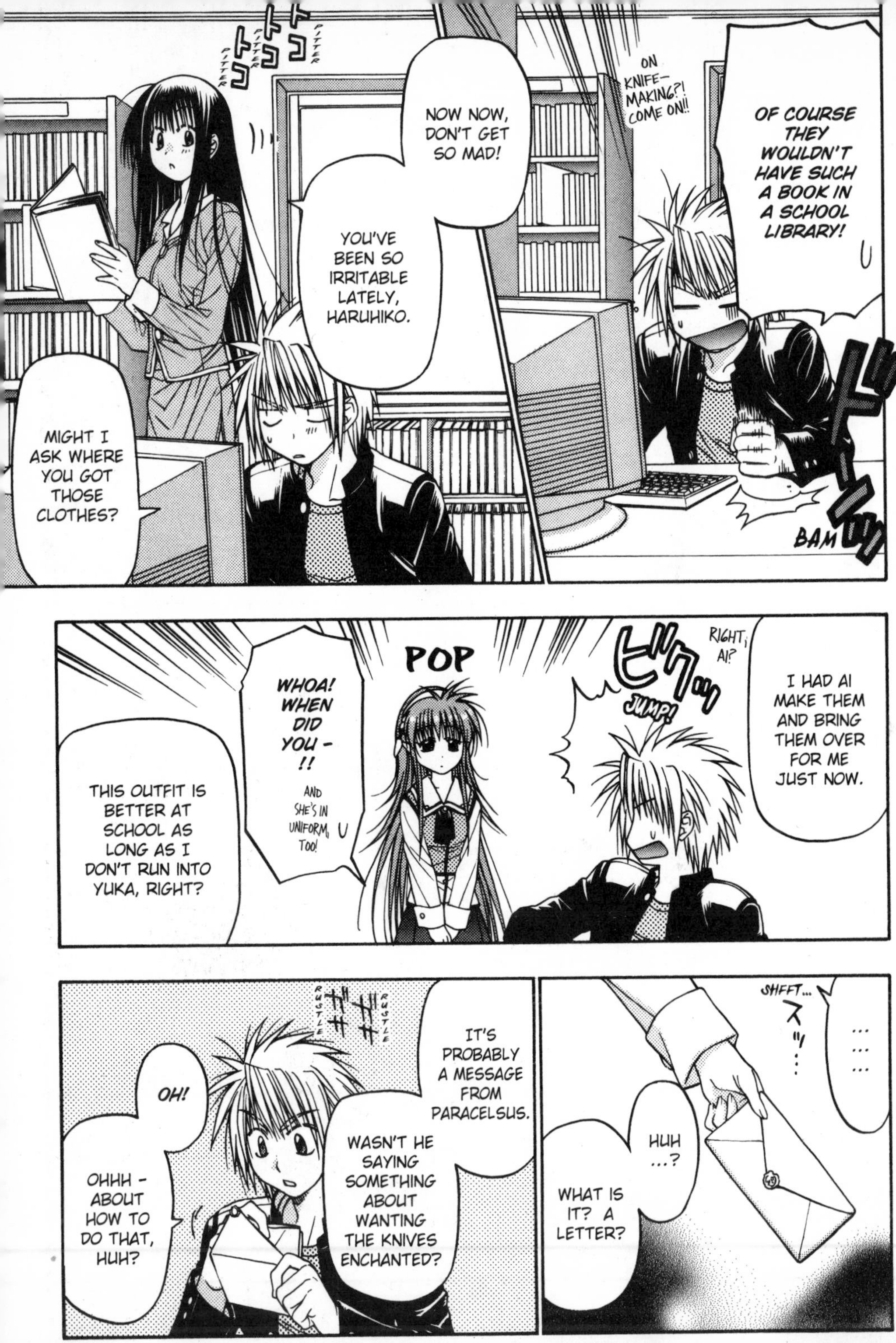
OF COURSE THEY WOULDN'T HAVE SUCH A BOOK IN A SCHOOL LIBRARY!
ON KNIFE-MAKING?! COME ON!!
BAM
NOW NOW, DON'T GET SO MAD!
YOU'VE BEEN SO IRRITABLE LATELY, HARUHIKO.
PITTER PITTER PITTER
MIGHT I ASK WHERE YOU GOT THOSE CLOTHES?
I HAD AI MAKE THEM AND BRING THEM OVER FOR ME JUST NOW.
RIGHT, AI?
JUMP!
POP
WHOA! WHEN DID YOU-!!
AND SHE'S IN UNIFORM, TOO!
THIS OUTFIT IS BETTER AT SCHOOL AS LONG AS I DON'T RUN INTO YUKA, RIGHT?
....
SHFFT...
HUH...?
WHAT IS IT? A LETTER?
IT'S PROBABLY A MESSAGE FROM PARACELSUS.
RUSTLE RUSTLE
WASN'T HE SAYING SOMETHING ABOUT WANTING THE KNIVES ENCHANTED?
OH!
OHHH- ABOUT HOW TO DO THAT, HUH?

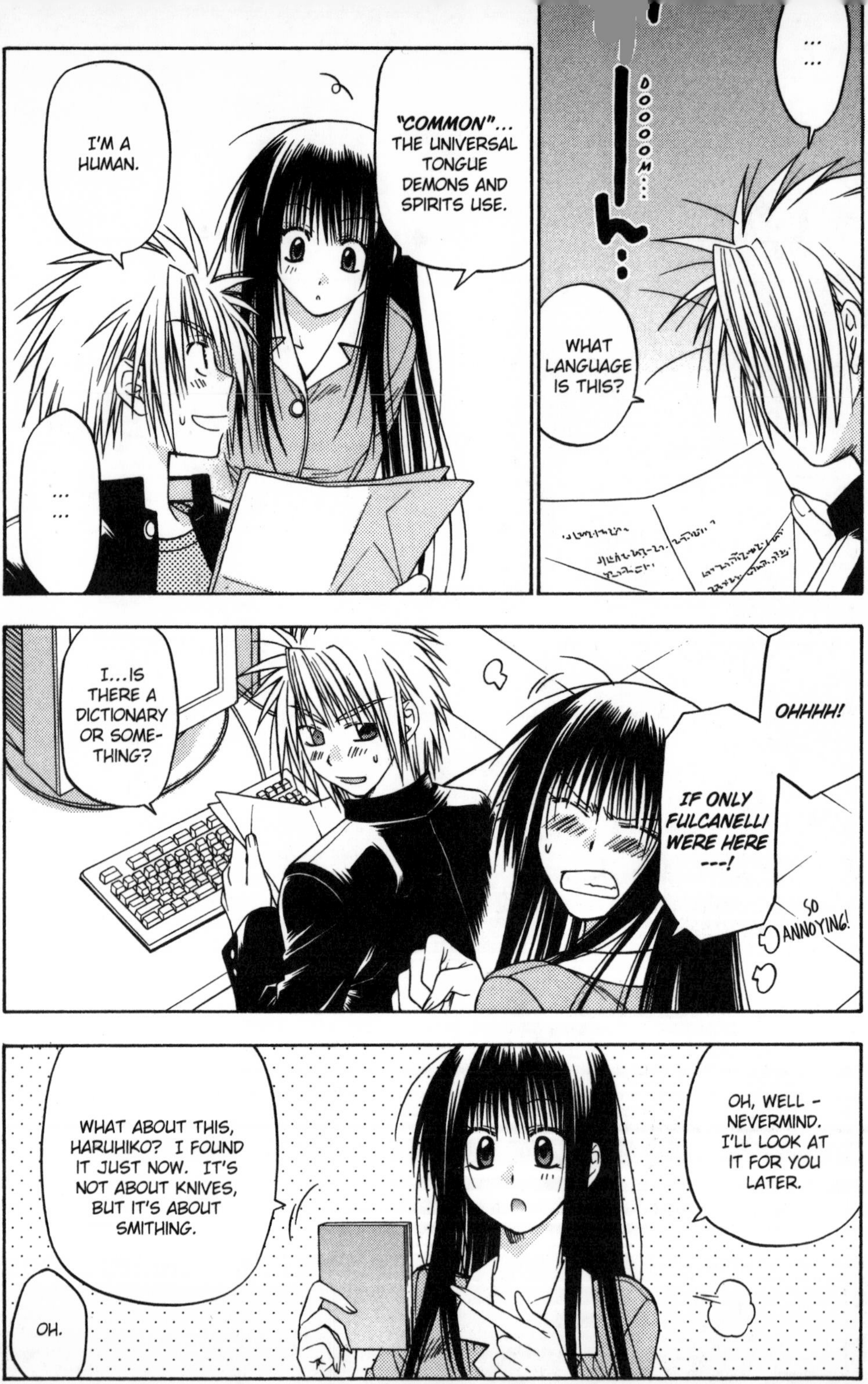
……
DOOOOOM…
WHAT LANGUAGE IS THIS?
"COMMON"… THE UNIVERSAL TONGUE DEMONS AND SPIRITS USE.
I'M A HUMAN.
……
OHHHH!
IF ONLY FULCANELLI WERE HERE---!
SO ANNOYING!
I…IS THERE A DICTIONARY OR SOME-THING?
OH, WELL - NEVERMIND. I'LL LOOK AT IT FOR YOU LATER.
WHAT ABOUT THIS, HARUHIKO? I FOUND IT JUST NOW. IT'S NOT ABOUT KNIVES, BUT IT'S ABOUT SMITHING.
OH.

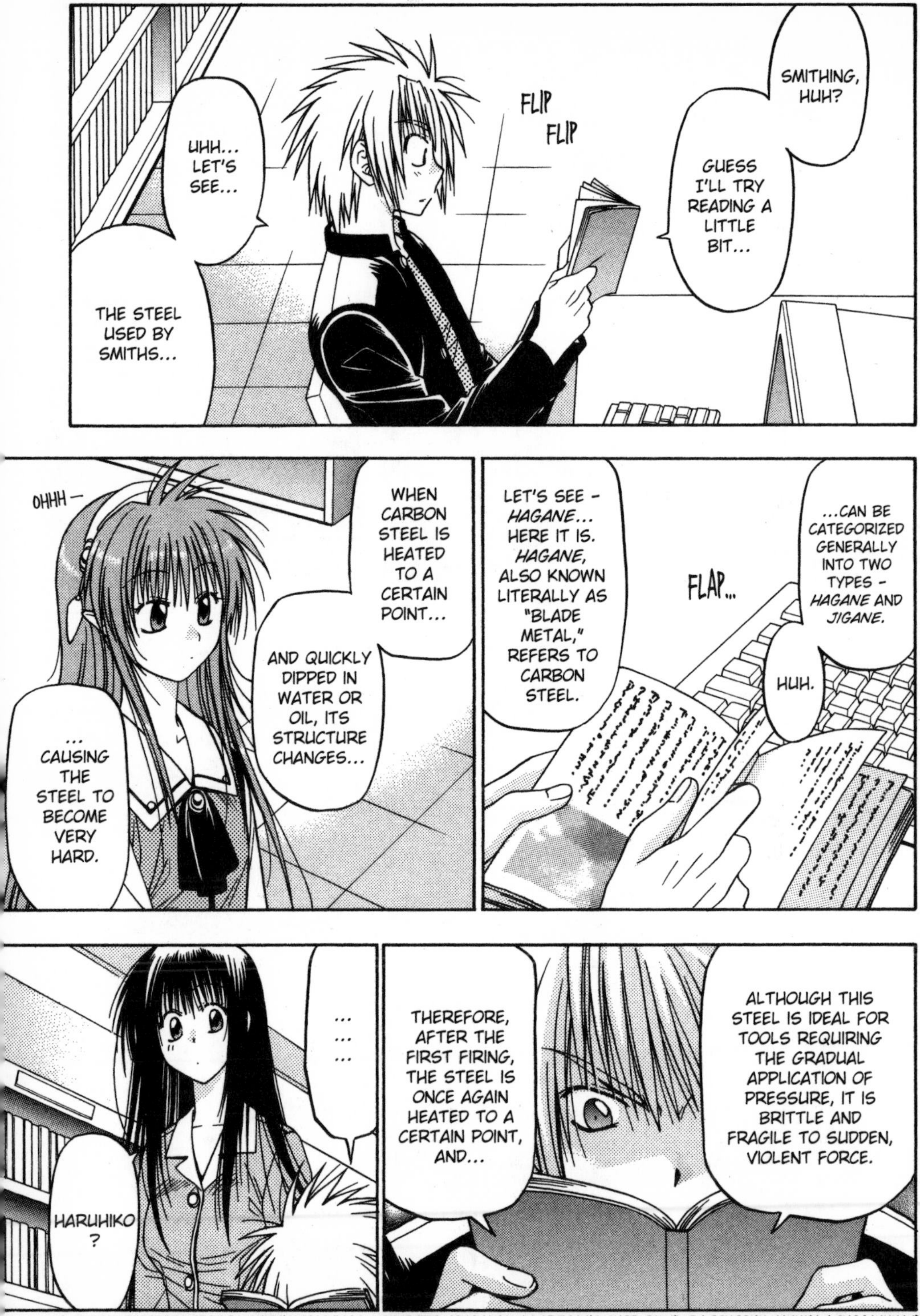
SMITHING, HUH?
GUESS I'LL TRY READING A LITTLE BIT...
FLIP FLIP
UHH... LET'S SEE...
THE STEEL USED BY SMITHS...
...CAN BE CATEGORIZED GENERALLY INTO TWO TYPES - *HAGANE* AND *JIGANE*.
HUH.
FLAP...
LET'S SEE - *HAGANE*... HERE IT IS. *HAGANE*, ALSO KNOWN LITERALLY AS "BLADE METAL," REFERS TO CARBON STEEL.
WHEN CARBON STEEL IS HEATED TO A CERTAIN POINT...
AND QUICKLY DIPPED IN WATER OR OIL, ITS STRUCTURE CHANGES...
OHHH —
... CAUSING THE STEEL TO BECOME VERY HARD.
ALTHOUGH THIS STEEL IS IDEAL FOR TOOLS REQUIRING THE GRADUAL APPLICATION OF PRESSURE, IT IS BRITTLE AND FRAGILE TO SUDDEN, VIOLENT FORCE.
THEREFORE, AFTER THE FIRST FIRING, THE STEEL IS ONCE AGAIN HEATED TO A CERTAIN POINT, AND...
... ...
HARUHIKO?

* QUOTED EXCERPTS FROM "A SMITH'S TEACHINGS - SUKEHIRO YOKOYAMA, AN ARTISAN'S SHOP-TALK" BY TSUTOMU KAKUMA / SHOGAKUKAN)

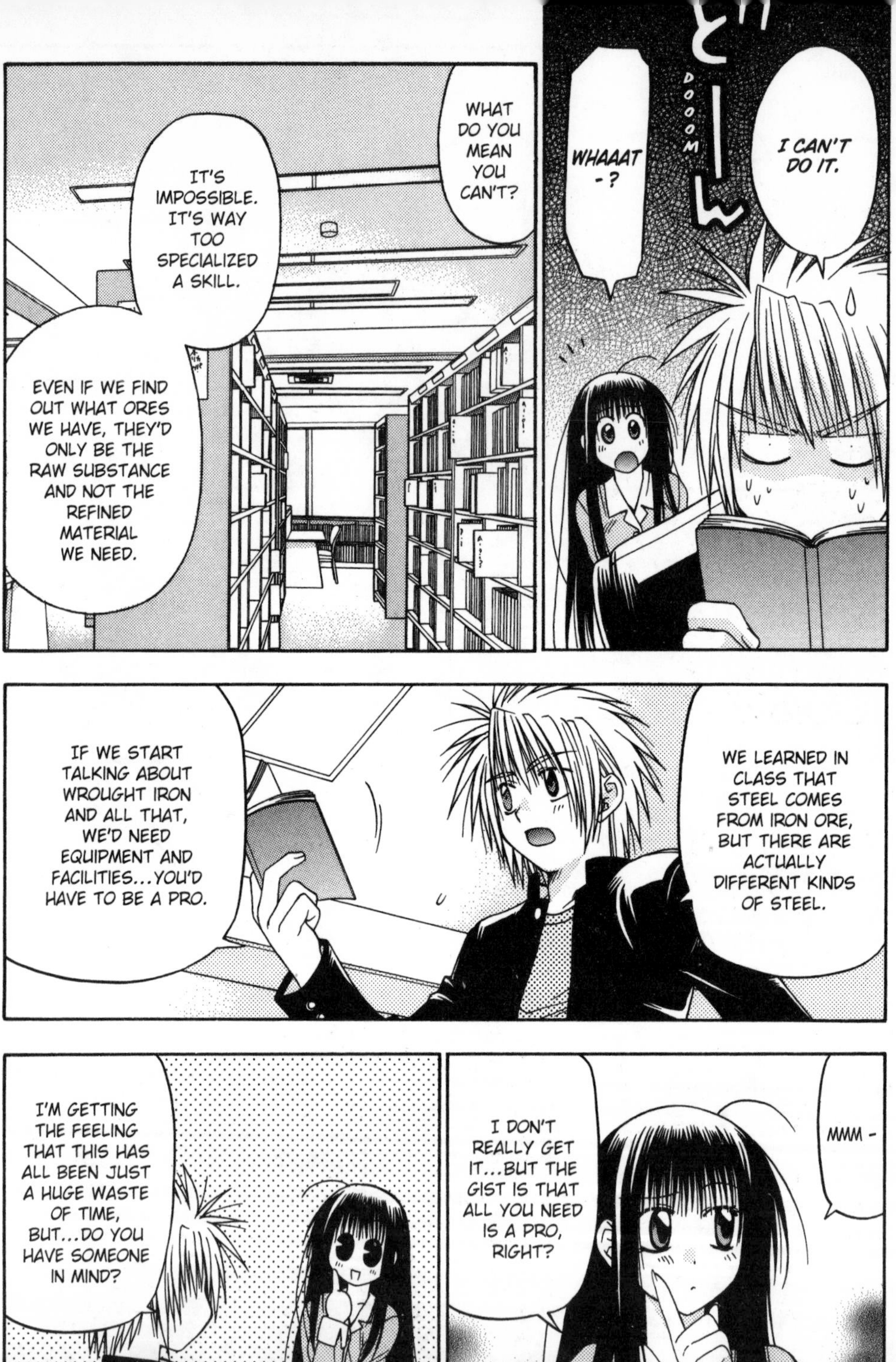
I CAN'T DO IT.
どーん
DOOOOM
WHAAAT-?
WHAT DO YOU MEAN YOU CAN'T?
IT'S IMPOSSIBLE. IT'S WAY TOO SPECIALIZED A SKILL.
EVEN IF WE FIND OUT WHAT ORES WE HAVE, THEY'D ONLY BE THE RAW SUBSTANCE AND NOT THE REFINED MATERIAL WE NEED.
WE LEARNED IN CLASS THAT STEEL COMES FROM IRON ORE, BUT THERE ARE ACTUALLY DIFFERENT KINDS OF STEEL.
IF WE START TALKING ABOUT WROUGHT IRON AND ALL THAT, WE'D NEED EQUIPMENT AND FACILITIES...YOU'D HAVE TO BE A PRO.
MMM-
I DON'T REALLY GET IT...BUT THE GIST IS THAT ALL YOU NEED IS A PRO, RIGHT?
I'M GETTING THE FEELING THAT THIS HAS ALL BEEN JUST A HUGE WASTE OF TIME, BUT...DO YOU HAVE SOMEONE IN MIND?

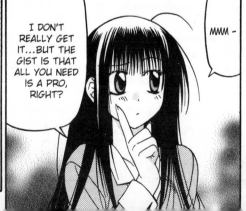

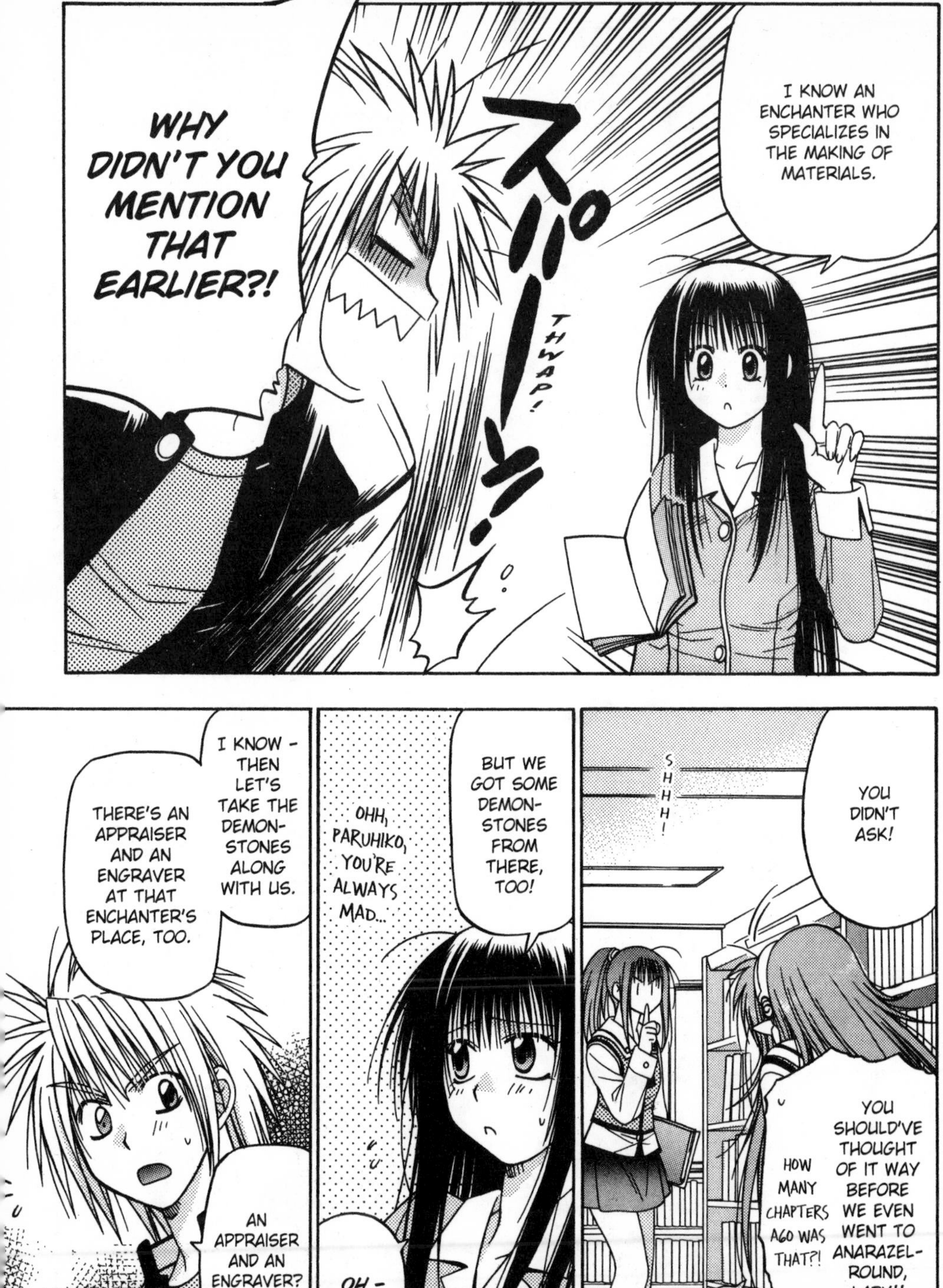
I KNOW AN ENCHANTER WHO SPECIALIZES IN THE MAKING OF MATERIALS.
WHY DIDN'T YOU MENTION THAT EARLIER?!
THWAP!
YOU DIDN'T ASK!
SHHH!
YOU SHOULD'VE THOUGHT OF IT WAY BEFORE WE EVEN WENT TO ANARAZEL-ROUND, LADY!!
HOW MANY CHAPTERS AGO WAS THAT?!
BOW
BUT WE GOT SOME DEMON-STONES FROM THERE, TOO!
OHH, PARUHIKO, YOU'RE ALWAYS MAD...
OH -
I KNOW - THEN LET'S TAKE THE DEMON-STONES ALONG WITH US.
THERE'S AN APPRAISER AND AN ENGRAVER AT THAT ENCHANTER'S PLACE, TOO.
AN APPRAISER AND AN ENGRAVER?

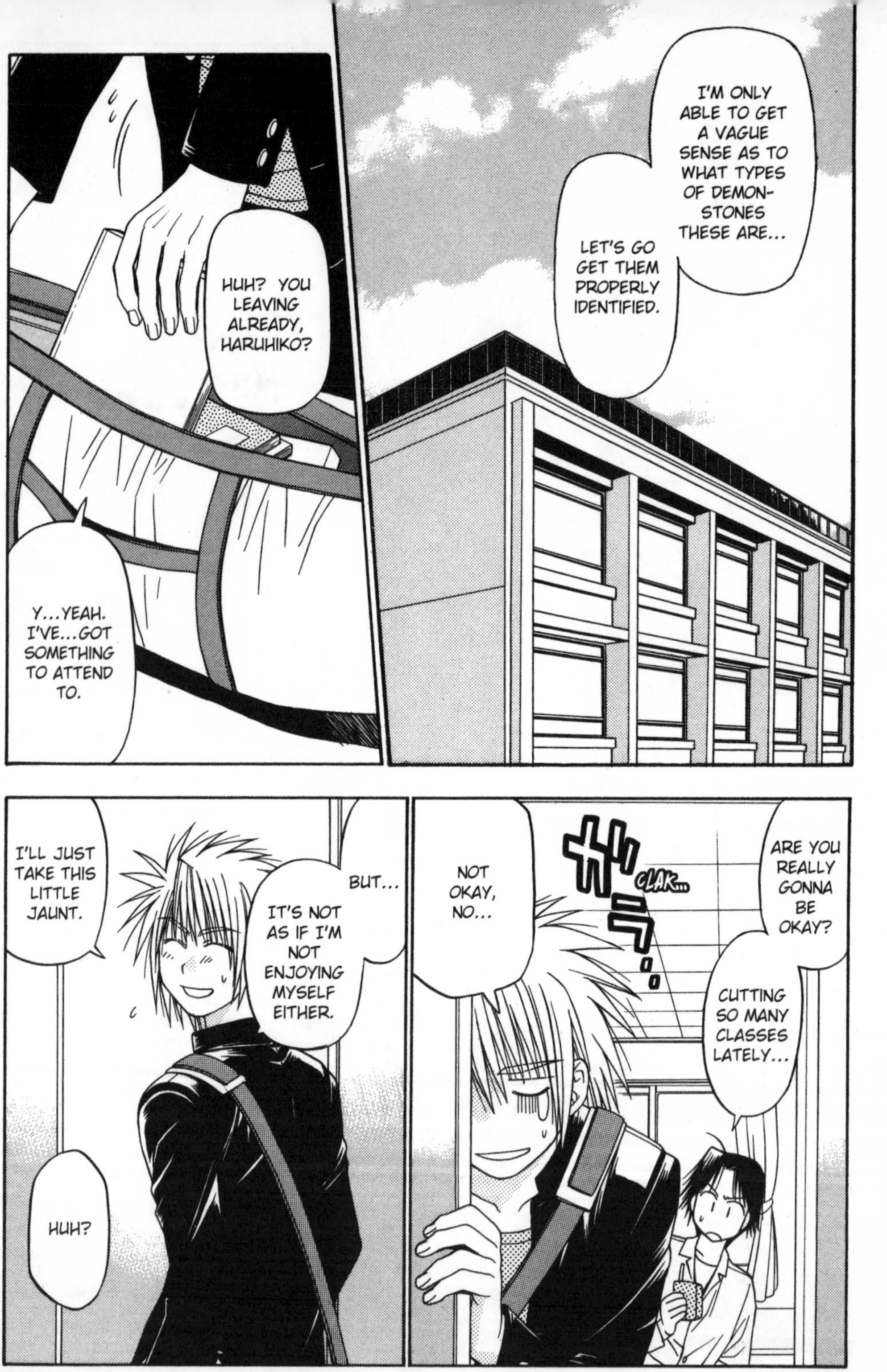
I'M ONLY ABLE TO GET A VAGUE SENSE AS TO WHAT TYPES OF DEMON-STONES THESE ARE...
LET'S GO GET THEM PROPERLY IDENTIFIED.
HUH? YOU LEAVING ALREADY, HARUHIKO?
Y...YEAH. I'VE...GOT SOMETHING TO ATTEND TO.
ARE YOU REALLY GONNA BE OKAY?
CUTTING SO MANY CLASSES LATELY...
ガラ
CLAK...
NOT OKAY, NO...
BUT...
IT'S NOT AS IF I'M NOT ENJOYING MYSELF EITHER.
I'LL JUST TAKE THIS LITTLE JAUNT.
HUH?

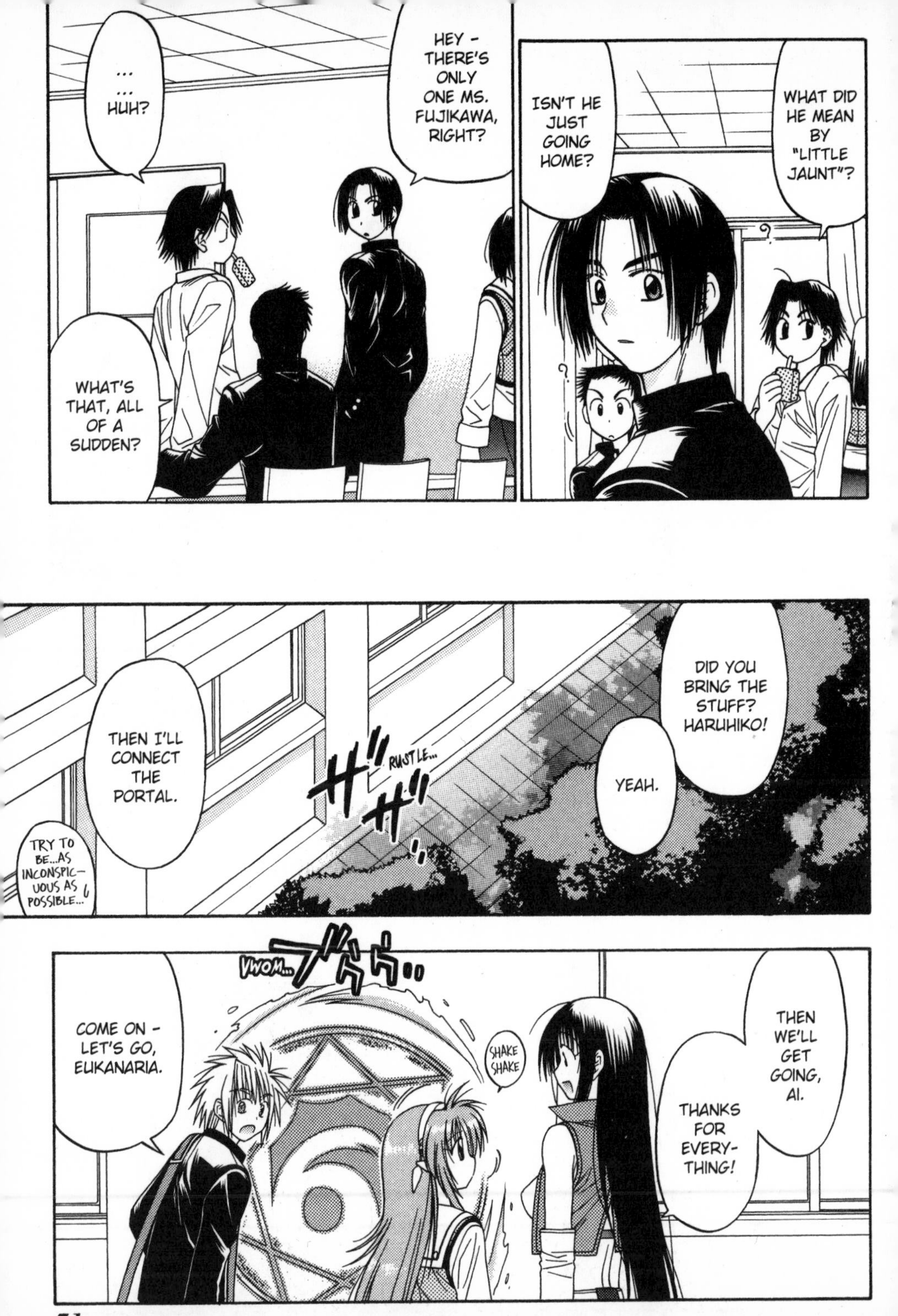
WHAT DID HE MEAN BY "LITTLE JAUNT"?
ISN'T HE JUST GOING HOME?
HEY - THERE'S ONLY ONE MS. FUJIKAWA, RIGHT?
... ... HUH?
WHAT'S THAT, ALL OF A SUDDEN?
DID YOU BRING THE STUFF? HARUHIKO!
YEAH.
RUSTLE...
THEN I'LL CONNECT THE PORTAL.
TRY TO BE...AS INCONSPICUOUS AS POSSIBLE...
THEN WE'LL GET GOING, AI.
THANKS FOR EVERYTHING!
SHAKE SHAKE
VWOM...
COME ON - LET'S GO, EUKANARIA.

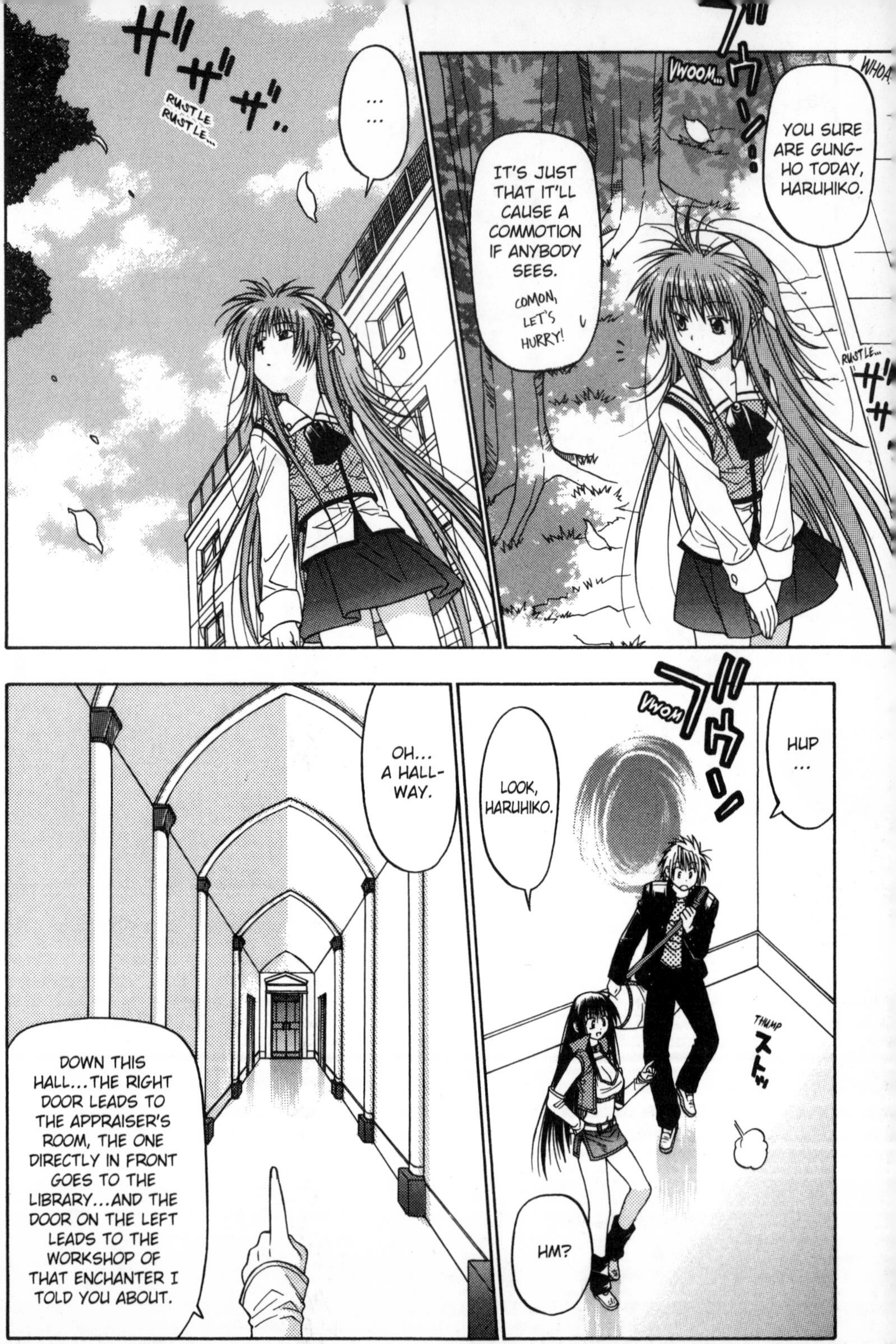
VWOOM...
ブゥーン..
WHOA!
YOU SURE ARE GUNG-HO TODAY, HARUHIKO.
IT'S JUST THAT IT'LL CAUSE A COMMOTION IF ANYBODY SEES.
COMON, LET'S HURRY!
RUSTLE...
……
……
ザザザ..
RUSTLE RUSTLE...
VWOOM
ブゥーン
HUP…
LOOK, HARUHIKO.
THUMP
ストッ
HM?
OH… A HALL-WAY.
DOWN THIS HALL…THE RIGHT DOOR LEADS TO THE APPRAISER'S ROOM, THE ONE DIRECTLY IN FRONT GOES TO THE LIBRARY…AND THE DOOR ON THE LEFT LEADS TO THE WORKSHOP OF THAT ENCHANTER I TOLD YOU ABOUT.

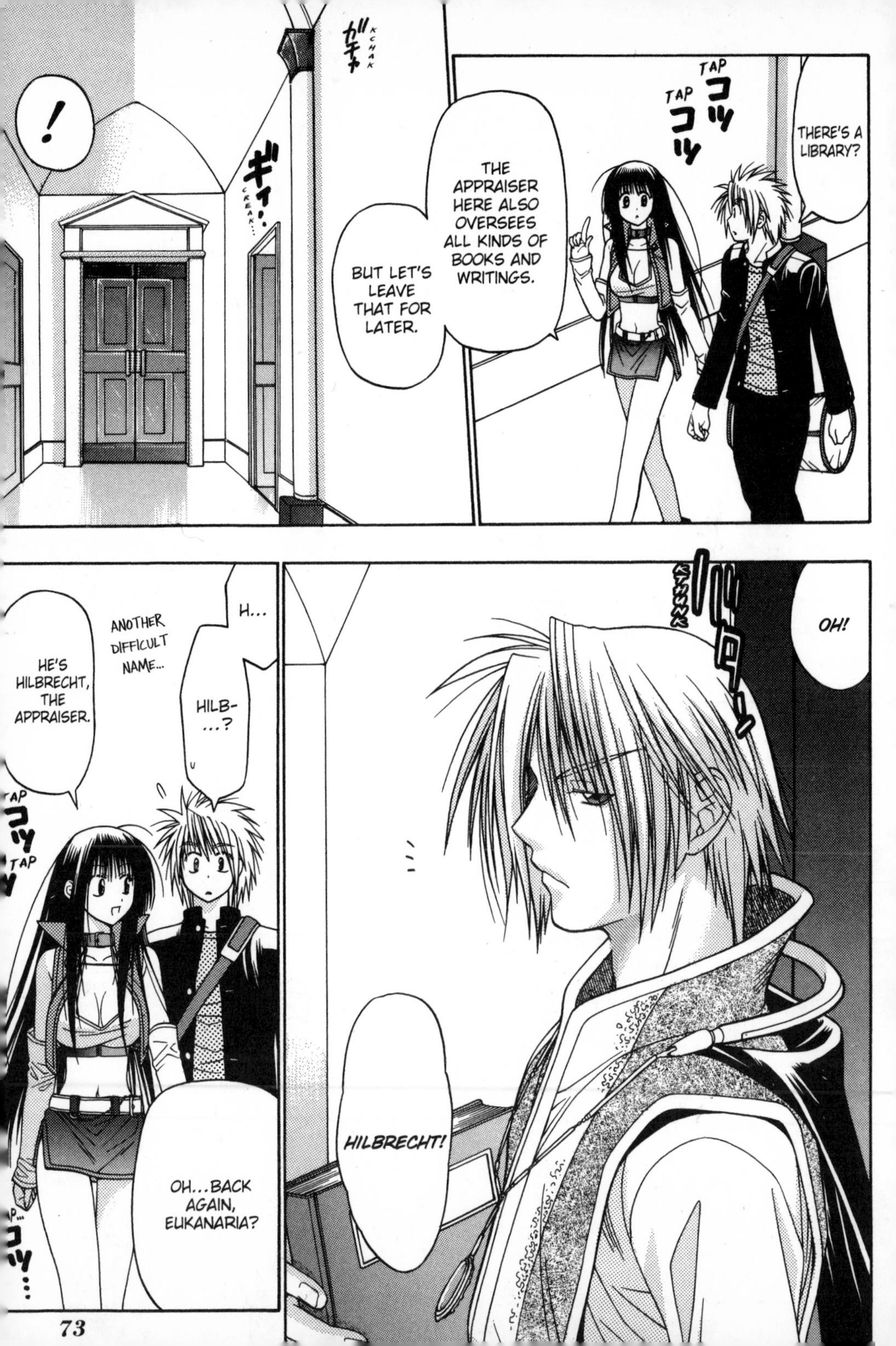

TAP コツ TAP コツ
THERE'S A LIBRARY?
THE APPRAISER HERE ALSO OVERSEES ALL KINDS OF BOOKS AND WRITINGS.
BUT LET'S LEAVE THAT FOR LATER.
ガチャ KCHAK
ギイ… CREAK…
!
KTHUNK
OH!
HILBRECHT!
OH...BACK AGAIN, EUKANARIA?
H...
HILB-...?
ANOTHER DIFFICULT NAME...
HE'S HILBRECHT, THE APPRAISER.
TAP コツ TAP

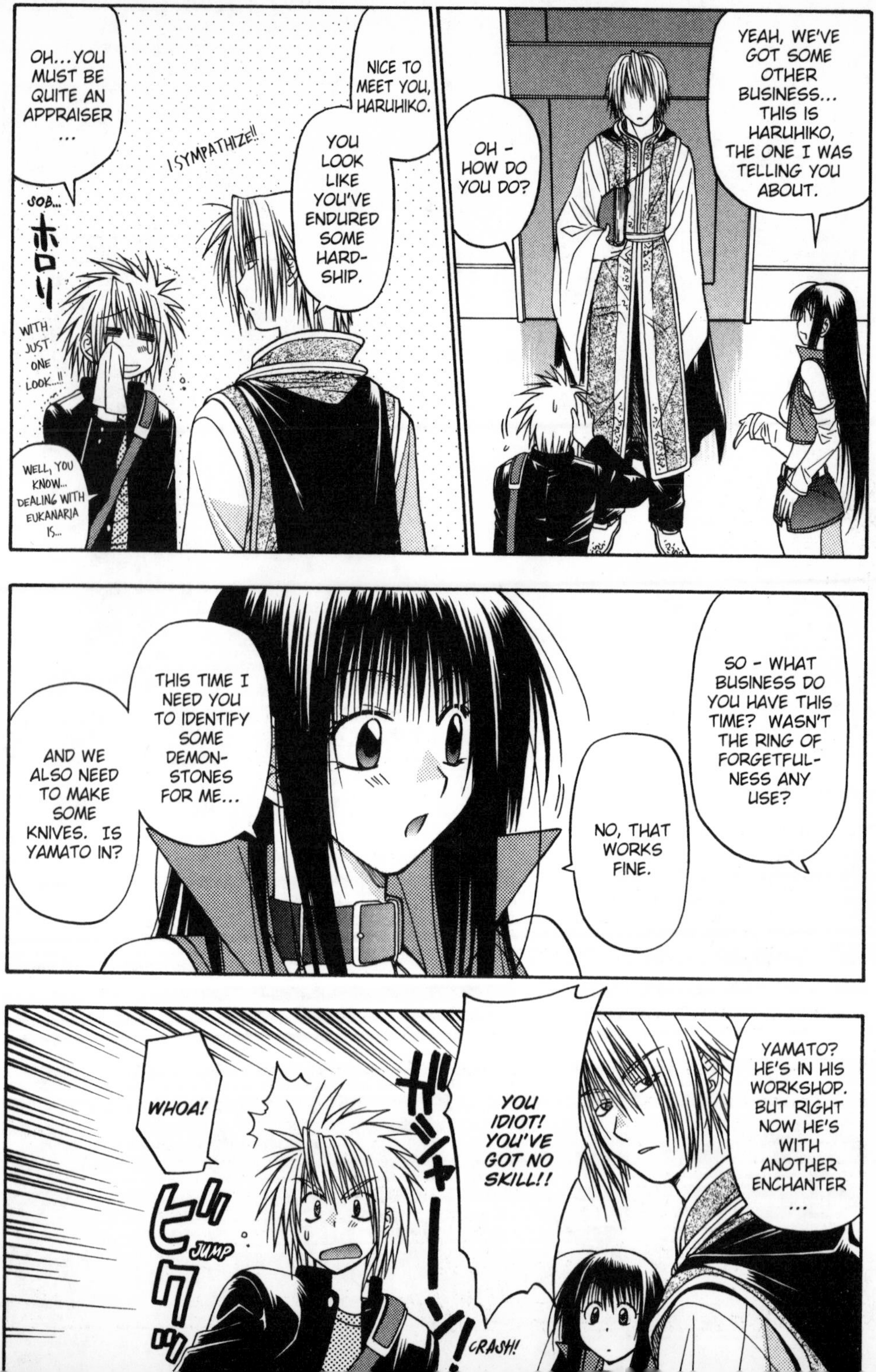
YEAH, WE'VE GOT SOME OTHER BUSINESS... THIS IS HARUHIKO, THE ONE I WAS TELLING YOU ABOUT.
OH - HOW DO YOU DO?
NICE TO MEET YOU, HARUHIKO.
YOU LOOK LIKE YOU'VE ENDURED SOME HARD-SHIP.
I SYMPATHIZE!!
OH...YOU MUST BE QUITE AN APPRAISER ...
SOB...
ホロリ
WITH JUST ONE LOOK...!!
WELL, YOU KNOW... DEALING WITH EUKANARJA IS...
SO - WHAT BUSINESS DO YOU HAVE THIS TIME? WASN'T THE RING OF FORGETFUL-NESS ANY USE?
NO, THAT WORKS FINE.
THIS TIME I NEED YOU TO IDENTIFY SOME DEMON-STONES FOR ME...
AND WE ALSO NEED TO MAKE SOME KNIVES. IS YAMATO IN?
YAMATO? HE'S IN HIS WORKSHOP. BUT RIGHT NOW HE'S WITH ANOTHER ENCHANTER ...
YOU IDIOT! YOU'VE GOT NO SKILL!!
ガシャーン!
CRASH!
WHOA!
ビクッ
JUMP

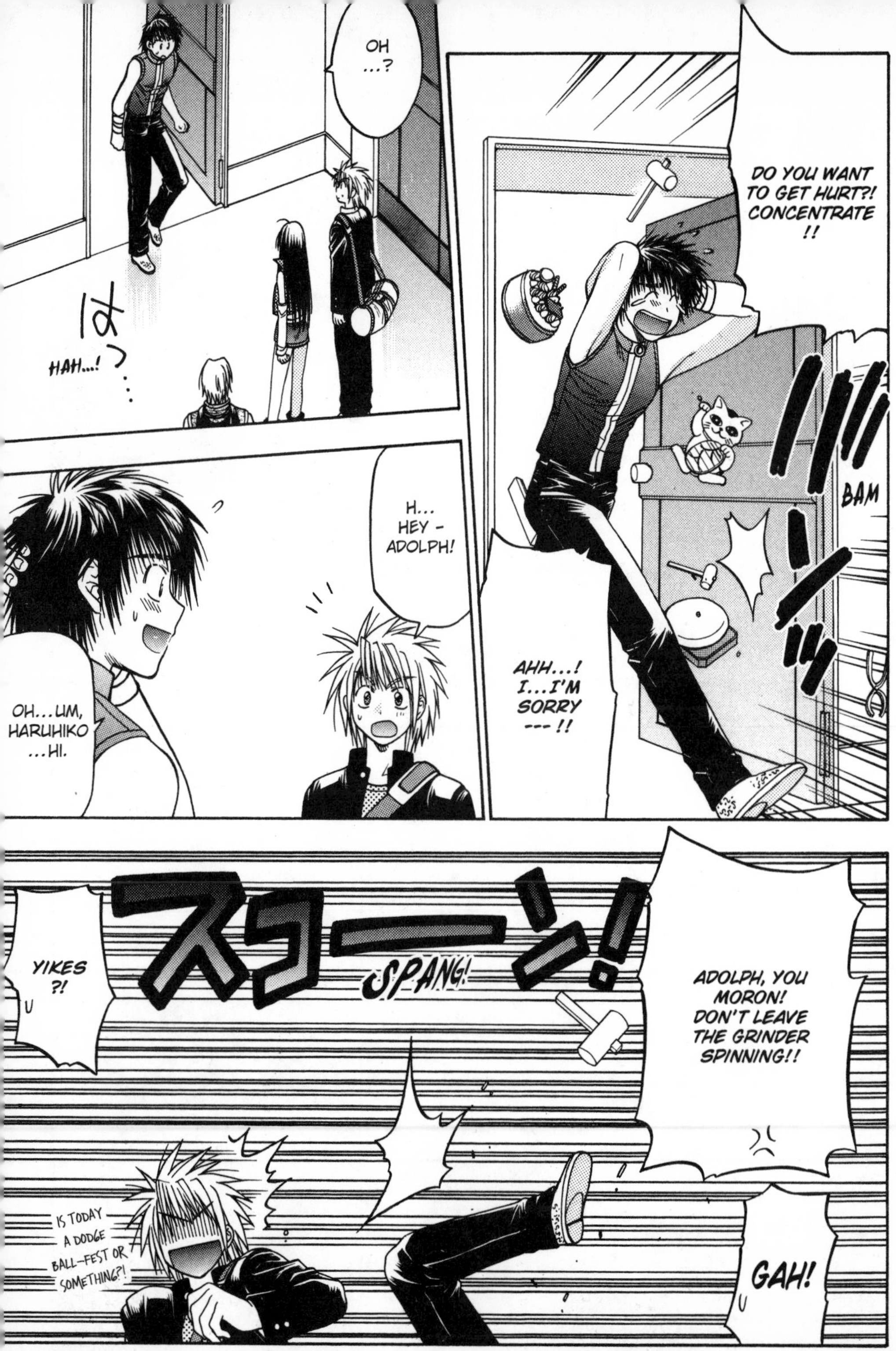
DO YOU WANT TO GET HURT?! CONCENTRATE !!
BAM
AHH...! I...I'M SORRY --- !!
OH ...?
はっ
HAH...!
H... HEY - ADOLPH!
OH...UM, HARUHIKO ...HI.
ADOLPH, YOU MORON! DON'T LEAVE THE GRINDER SPINNING!!
スコーーン!
SPANG!
YIKES ?!
GAH!
IS TODAY A DODGE BALL-FEST OR SOMETHING?!

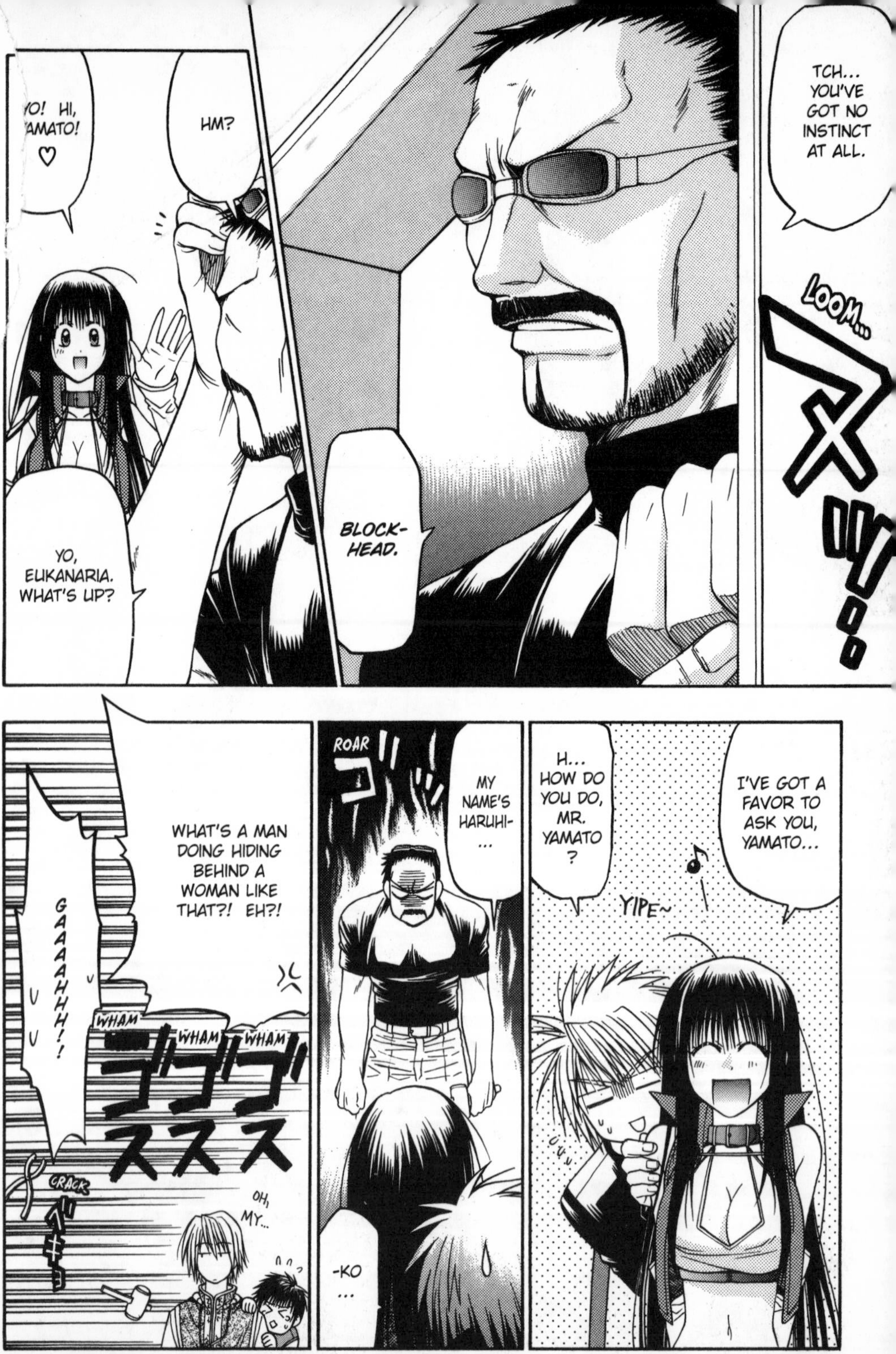

TCH... YOU'VE GOT NO INSTINCT AT ALL.
LOOM...
BLOCK-HEAD.
HM?
YO! HI, YAMATO! ♡
YO, EUKANARIA. WHAT'S UP?
I'VE GOT A FAVOR TO ASK YOU, YAMATO...
H... HOW DO YOU DO, MR. YAMATO?
YIPE~
ROAR
MY NAME'S HARUHI-...
-KO...
WHAT'S A MAN DOING HIDING BEHIND A WOMAN LIKE THAT?! EH?!
GAAAAAHHH!!
WHAM
WHAM
WHAM
CRACK
OH, MY...

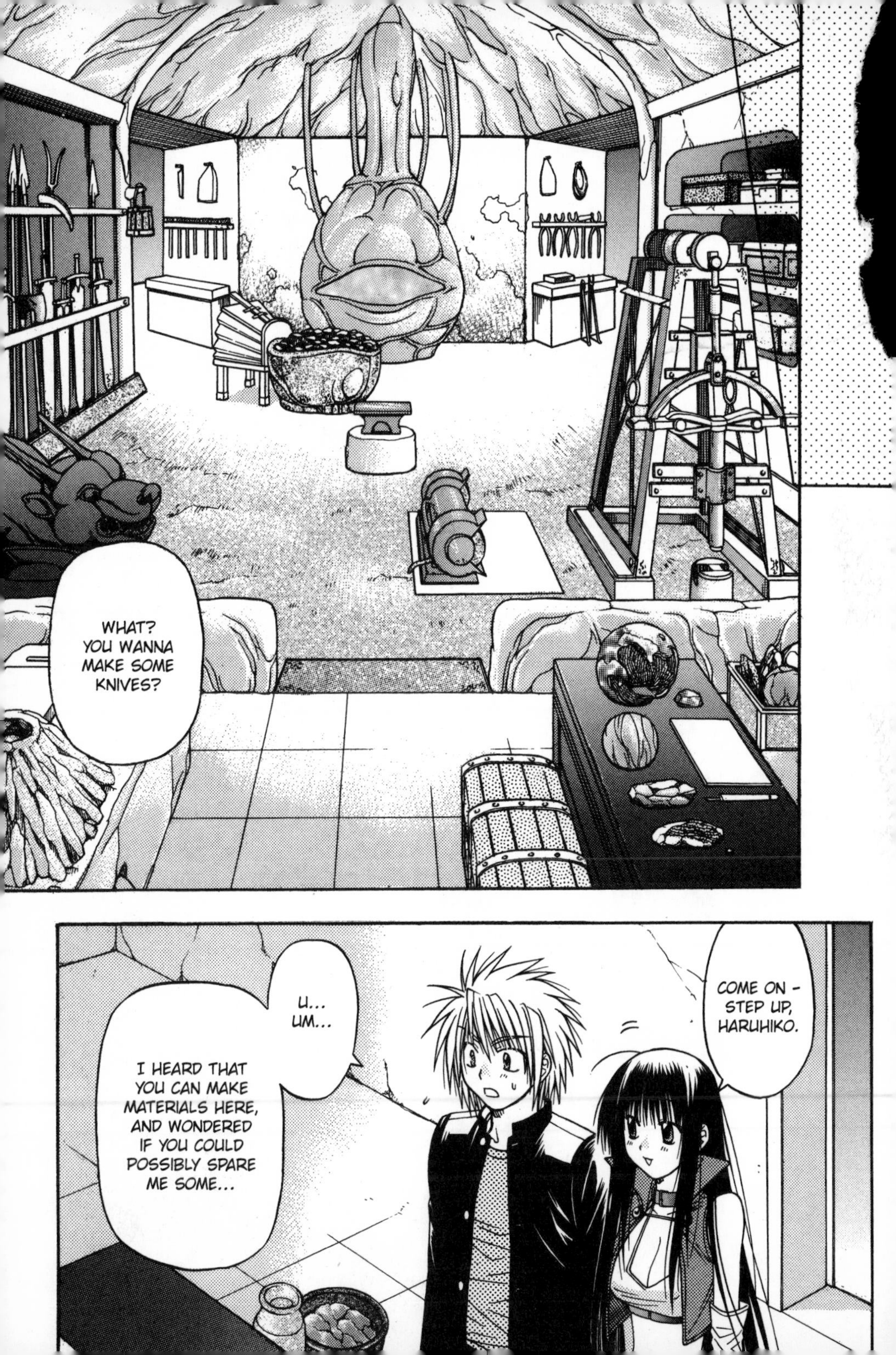
WHAT? YOU WANNA MAKE SOME KNIVES?
COME ON - STEP UP, HARUHIKO.
U... UM...
I HEARD THAT YOU CAN MAKE MATERIALS HERE, AND WONDERED IF YOU COULD POSSIBLY SPARE ME SOME...

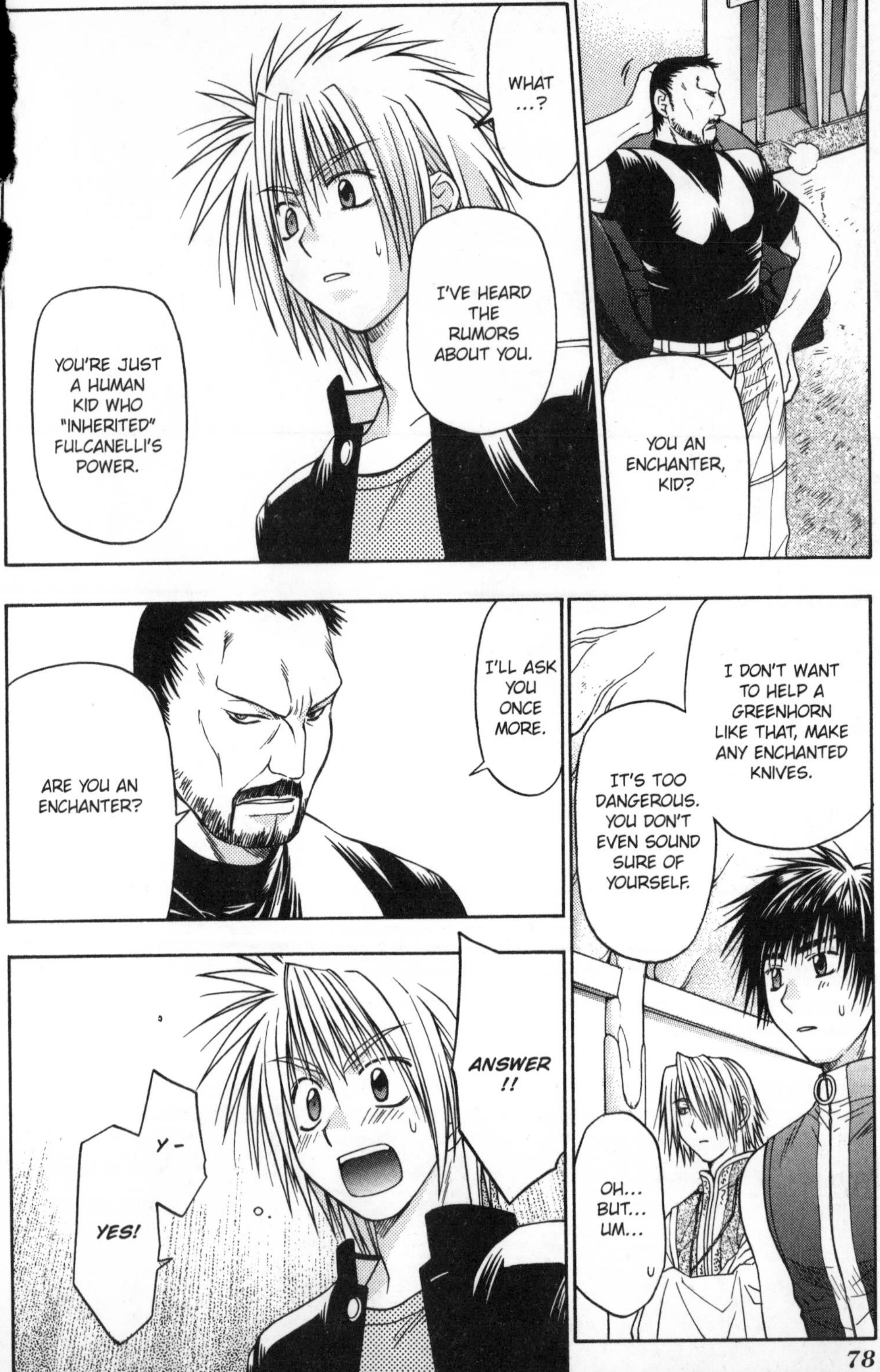
YOU AN ENCHANTER, KID?
WHAT ...?
I'VE HEARD THE RUMORS ABOUT YOU.
YOU'RE JUST A HUMAN KID WHO "INHERITED" FULCANELLI'S POWER.
I DON'T WANT TO HELP A GREENHORN LIKE THAT, MAKE ANY ENCHANTED KNIVES.
IT'S TOO DANGEROUS. YOU DON'T EVEN SOUND SURE OF YOURSELF.
OH... BUT... UM...
I'LL ASK YOU ONCE MORE.
ARE YOU AN ENCHANTER?
ANSWER !!
Y-
YES!

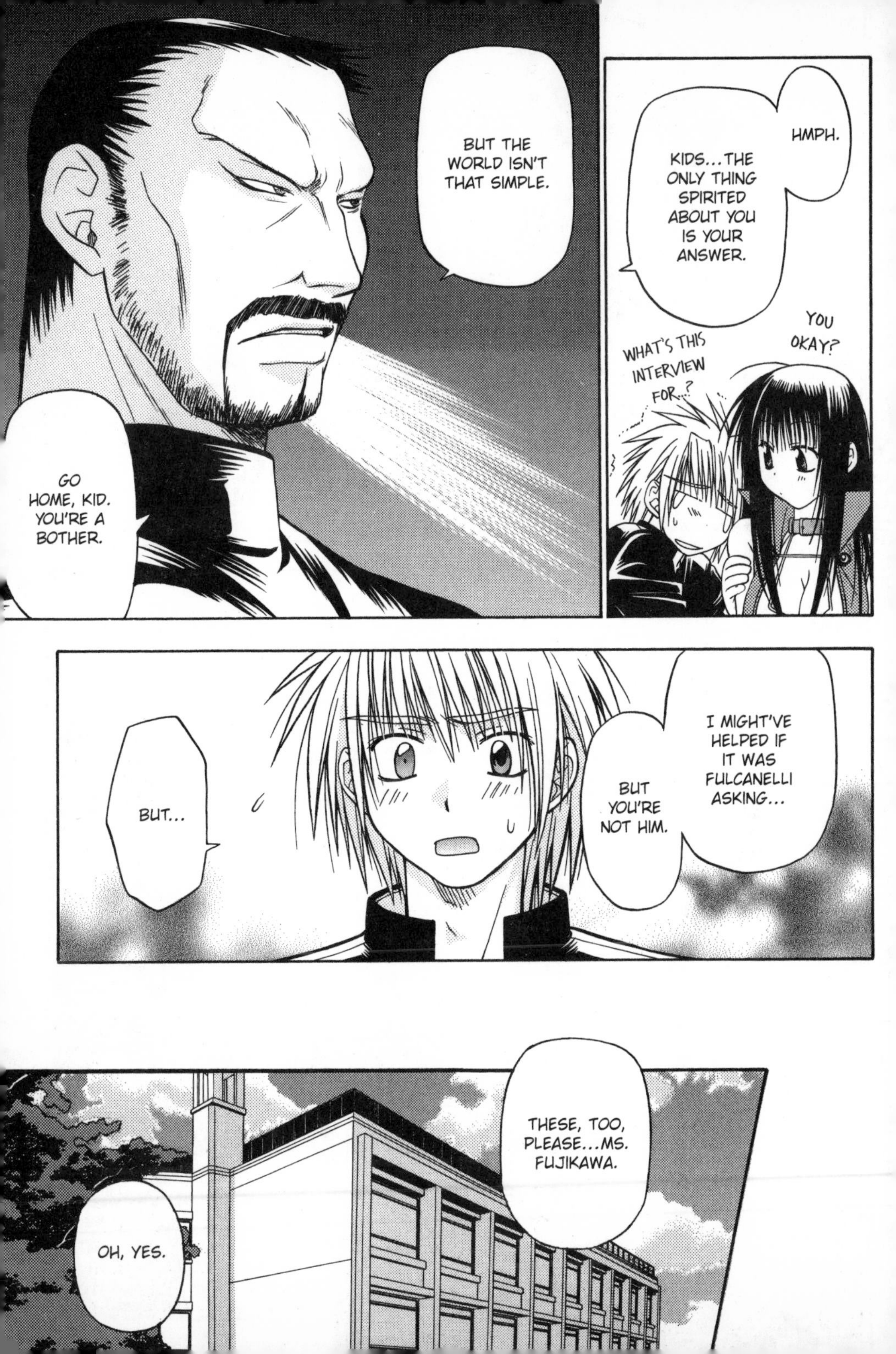
HMPH.
KIDS...THE ONLY THING SPIRITED ABOUT YOU IS YOUR ANSWER.
YOU OKAY?
WHAT'S THIS INTERVIEW FOR..?
BUT THE WORLD ISN'T THAT SIMPLE.
GO HOME, KID. YOU'RE A BOTHER.
I MIGHT'VE HELPED IF IT WAS FULCANELLI ASKING...
BUT YOU'RE NOT HIM.
BUT...
THESE, TOO, PLEASE...MS. FUJIKAWA.
OH, YES.

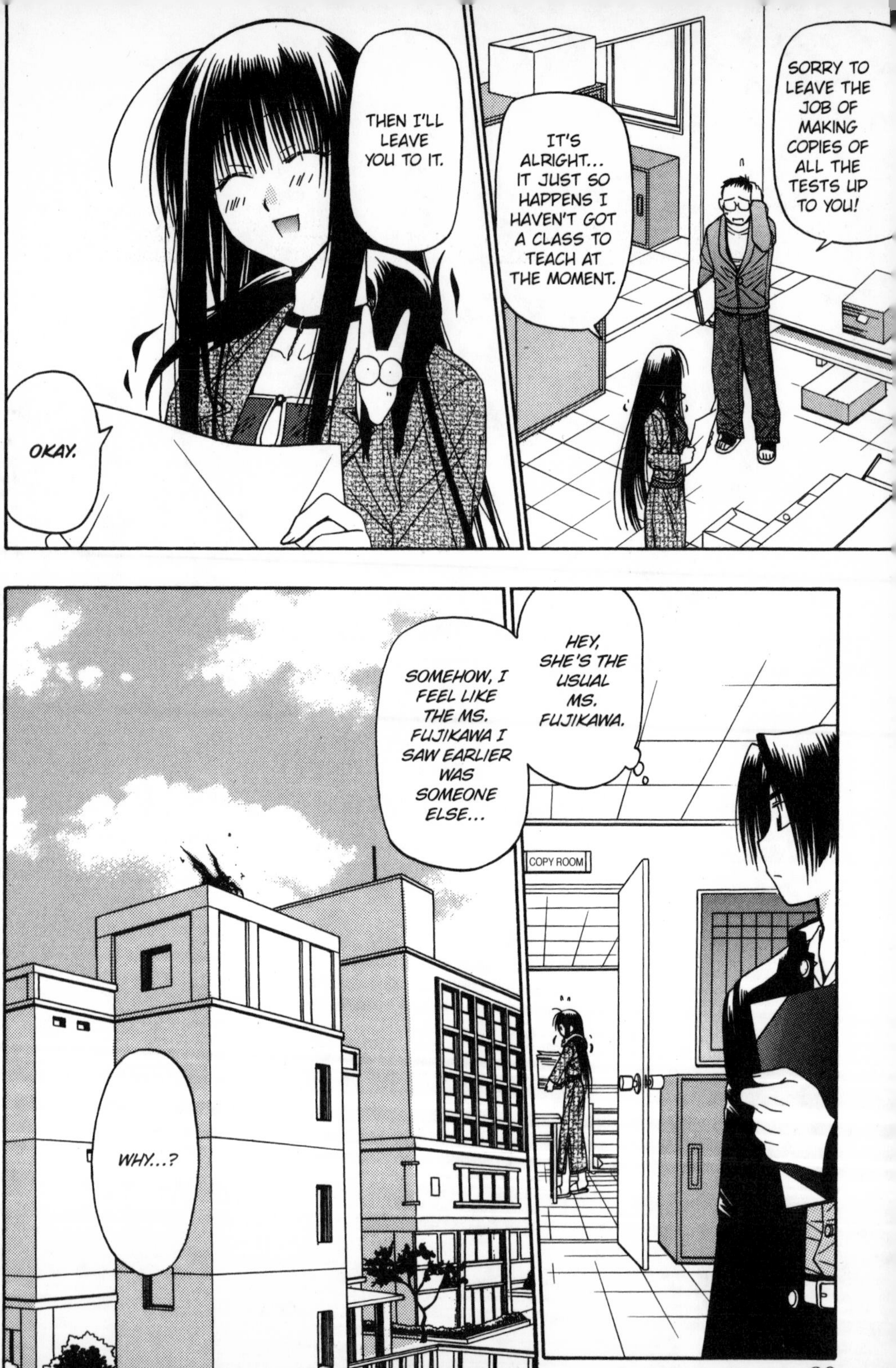
SORRY TO LEAVE THE JOB OF MAKING COPIES OF ALL THE TESTS UP TO YOU!
IT'S ALRIGHT... IT JUST SO HAPPENS I HAVEN'T GOT A CLASS TO TEACH AT THE MOMENT.
THEN I'LL LEAVE YOU TO IT.
OKAY.
HEY, SHE'S THE USUAL MS. FUJIKAWA.
SOMEHOW, I FEEL LIKE THE MS. FUJIKAWA I SAW EARLIER WAS SOMEONE ELSE...
COPY ROOM
WHY...?

エンチャント

enchant. 10

タンジェント

tangent

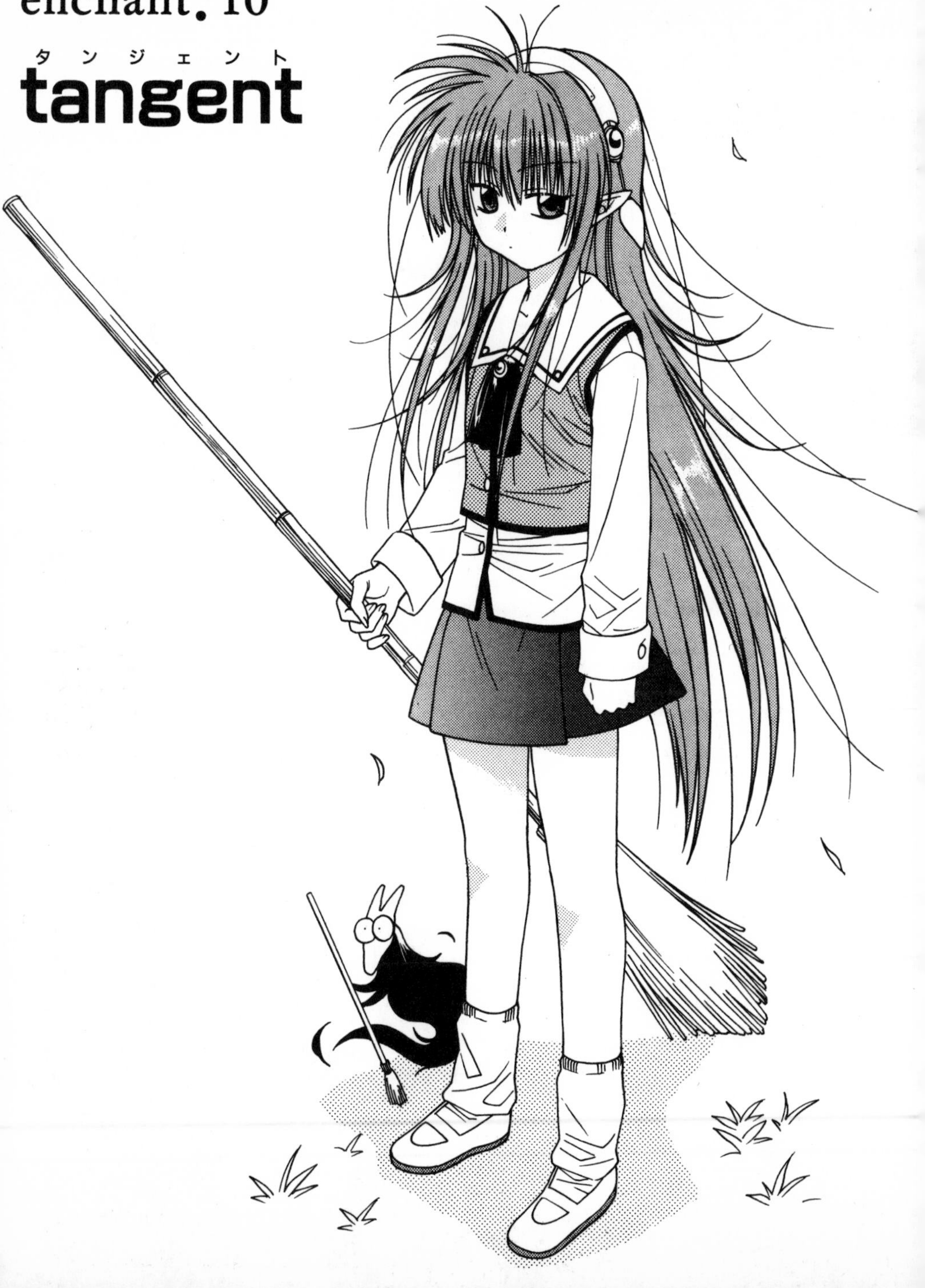

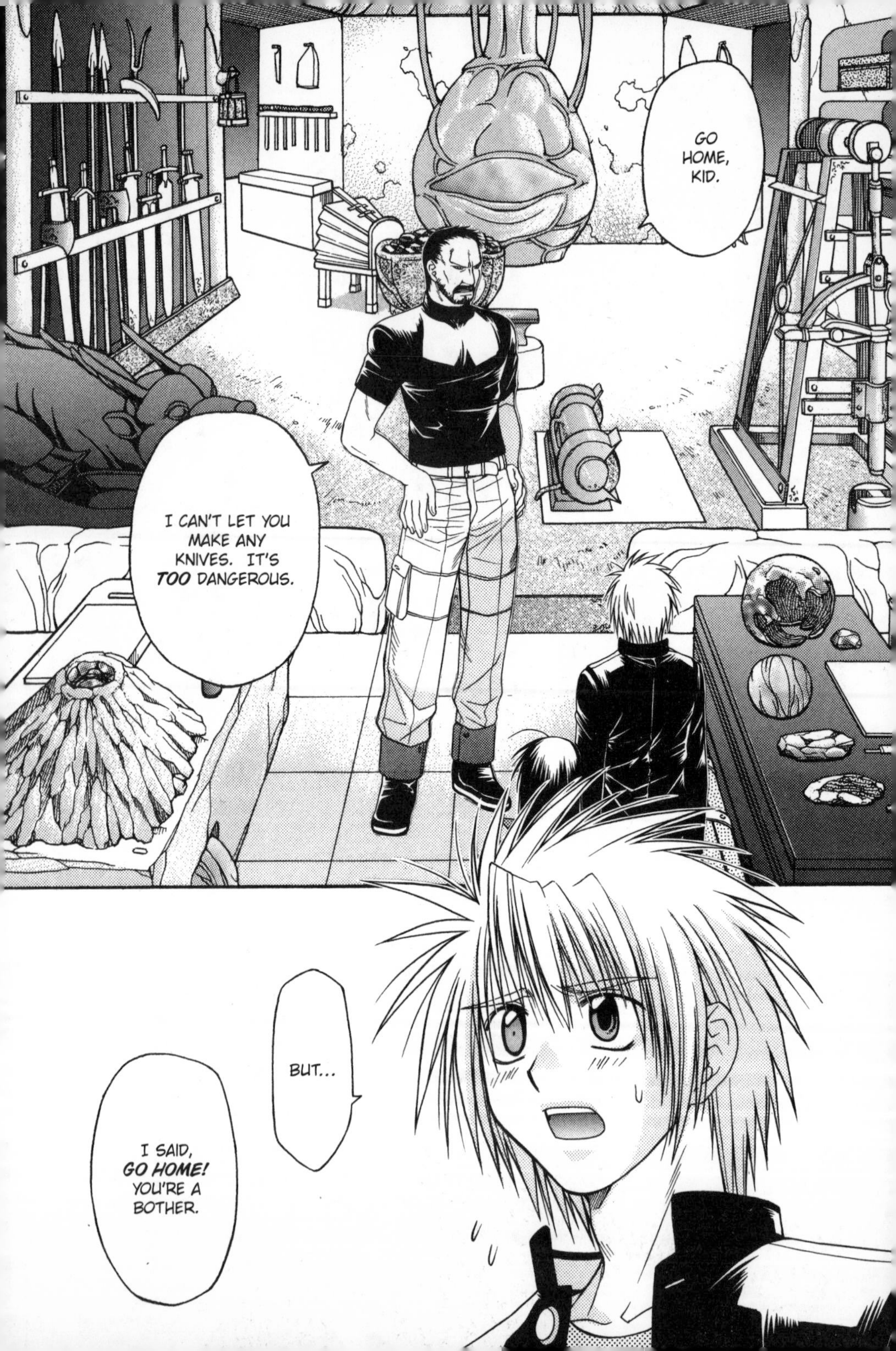
GO HOME, KID.
I CAN'T LET YOU MAKE ANY KNIVES. IT'S *TOO* DANGEROUS.
BUT...
I SAID, ***GO HOME!*** YOU'RE A BOTHER.

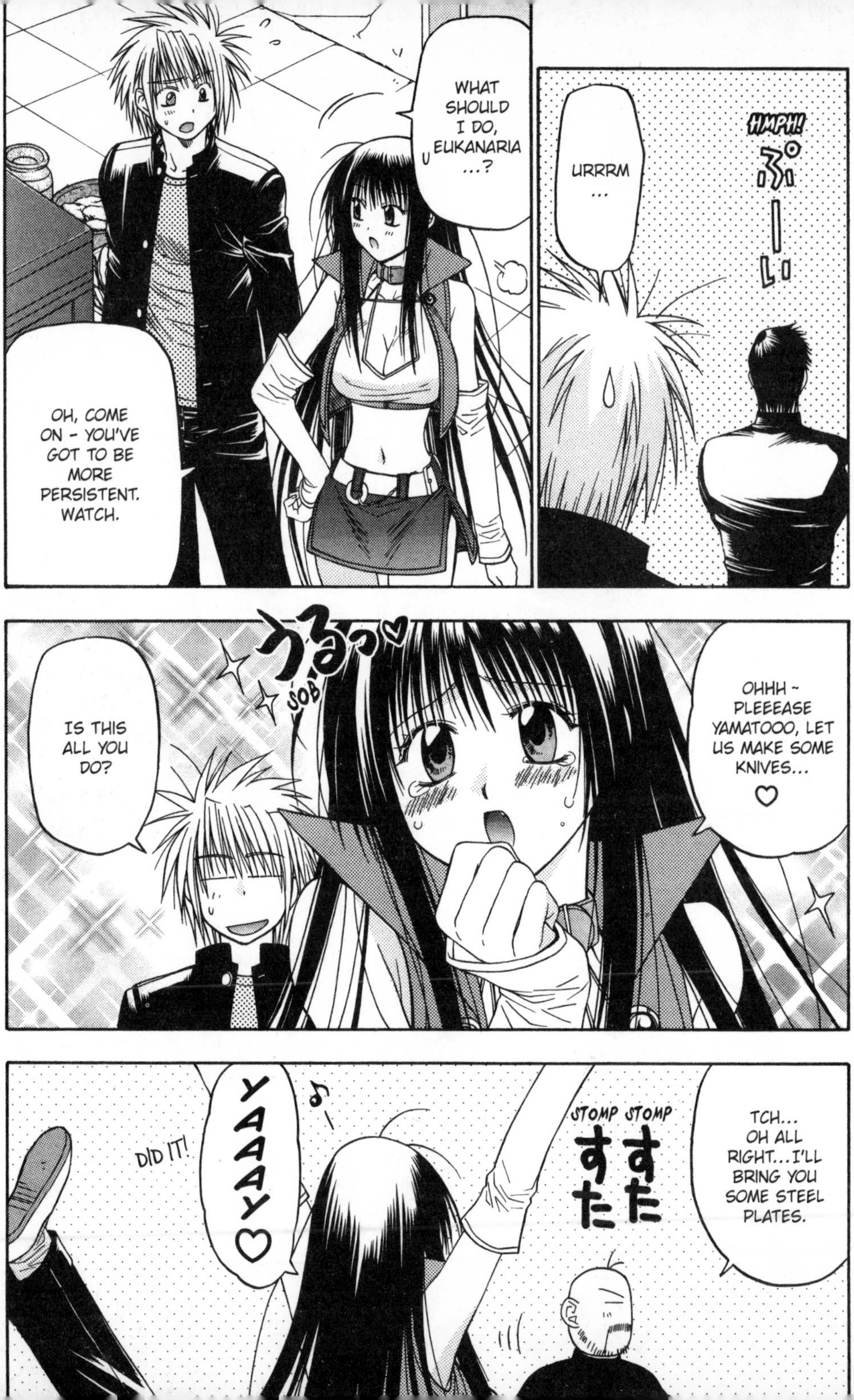
HMPH!
URRRM ...
WHAT SHOULD I DO, EUKANARIA ...?
OH, COME ON - YOU'VE GOT TO BE MORE PERSISTENT. WATCH.
OHHH ~ PLEEEASE YAMATOOO, LET US MAKE SOME KNIVES... ♡
うるっ♡
SOB
IS THIS ALL YOU DO?
TCH... OH ALL RIGHT... I'LL BRING YOU SOME STEEL PLATES.
STOMP STOMP
すたすた
YAAAAY ♡
DID IT!

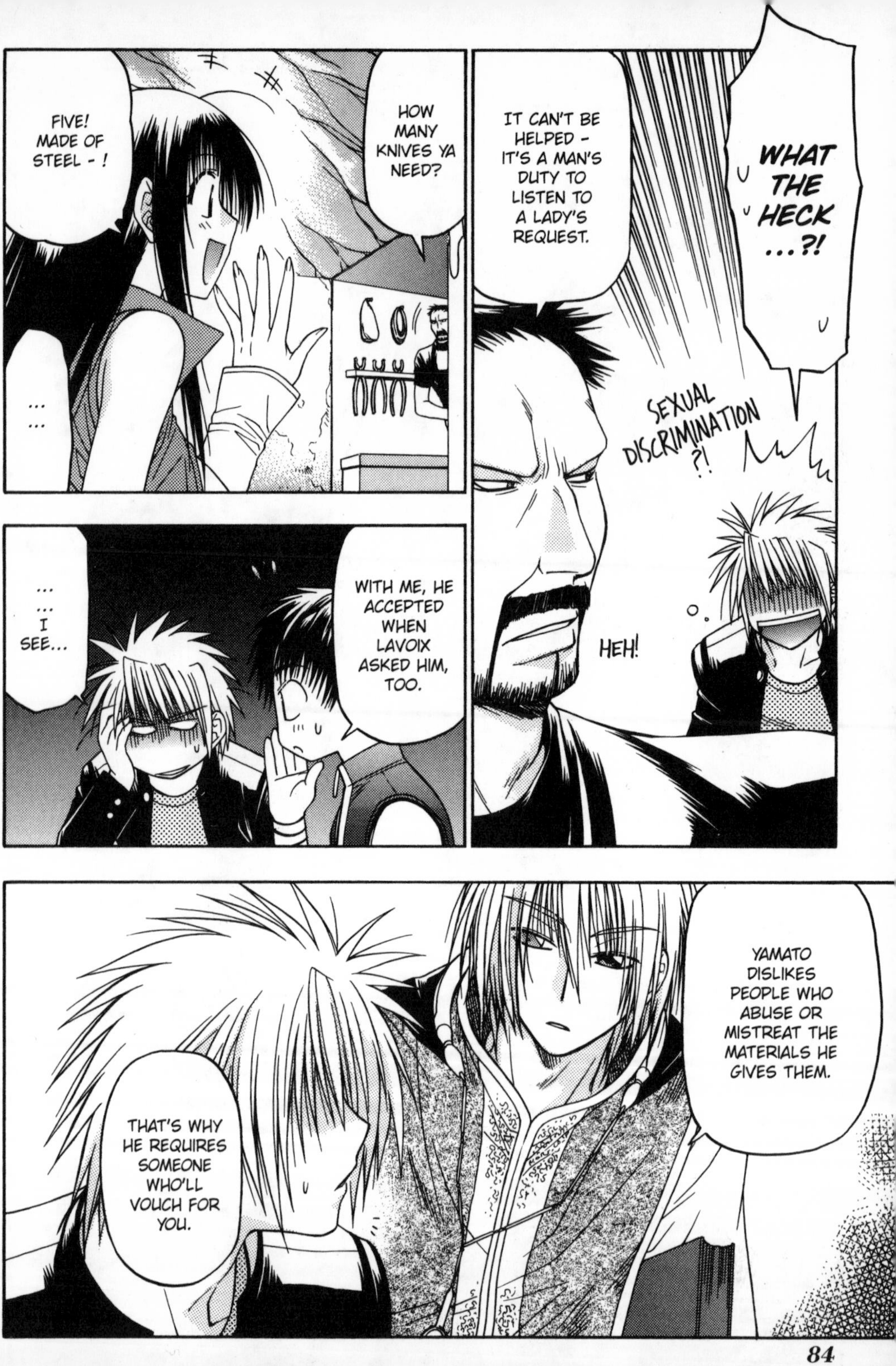
WHAT THE HECK ...?!
IT CAN'T BE HELPED - IT'S A MAN'S DUTY TO LISTEN TO A LADY'S REQUEST.
SEXUAL DISCRIMINATION ?!
HEH!
HOW MANY KNIVES YA NEED?
FIVE! MADE OF STEEL - !
... ...
WITH ME, HE ACCEPTED WHEN LAVOIX ASKED HIM, TOO.
... ... I SEE...
YAMATO DISLIKES PEOPLE WHO ABUSE OR MISTREAT THE MATERIALS HE GIVES THEM.
THAT'S WHY HE REQUIRES SOMEONE WHO'LL VOUCH FOR YOU.

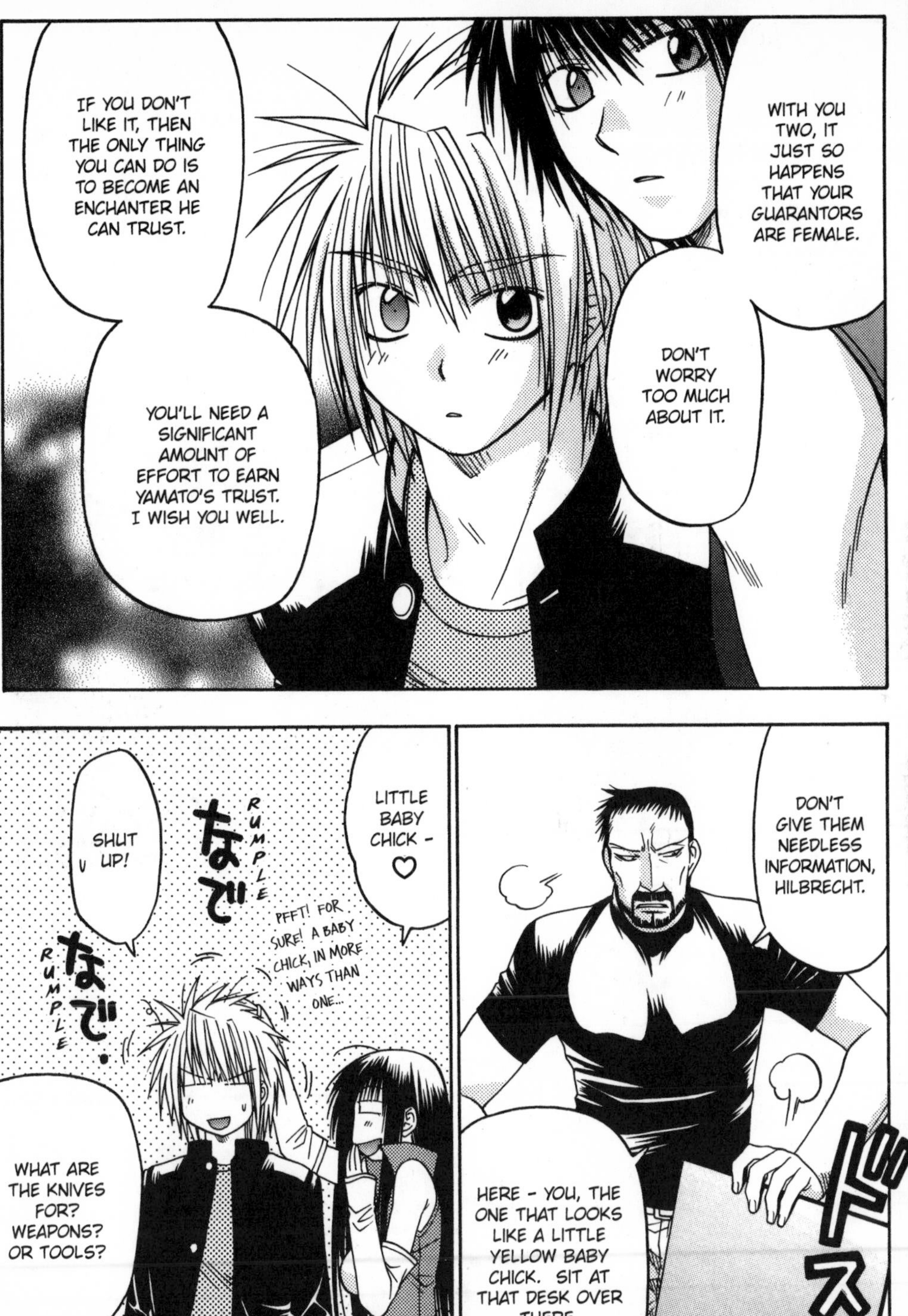
WITH YOU TWO, IT JUST SO HAPPENS THAT YOUR GUARANTORS ARE FEMALE.
DON'T WORRY TOO MUCH ABOUT IT.
IF YOU DON'T LIKE IT, THEN THE ONLY THING YOU CAN DO IS TO BECOME AN ENCHANTER HE CAN TRUST.
YOU'LL NEED A SIGNIFICANT AMOUNT OF EFFORT TO EARN YAMATO'S TRUST. I WISH YOU WELL.
DON'T GIVE THEM NEEDLESS INFORMATION, HILBRECHT.
HERE - YOU, THE ONE THAT LOOKS LIKE A LITTLE YELLOW BABY CHICK. SIT AT THAT DESK OVER THERE.
ドス。
THUD
LITTLE BABY CHICK - ♡
なで
RUMPLE
なで。
RUMPLE
SHUT UP!
PFFT! FOR SURE! A BABY CHICK, IN MORE WAYS THAN ONE...
WHAT ARE THE KNIVES FOR? WEAPONS? OR TOOLS?

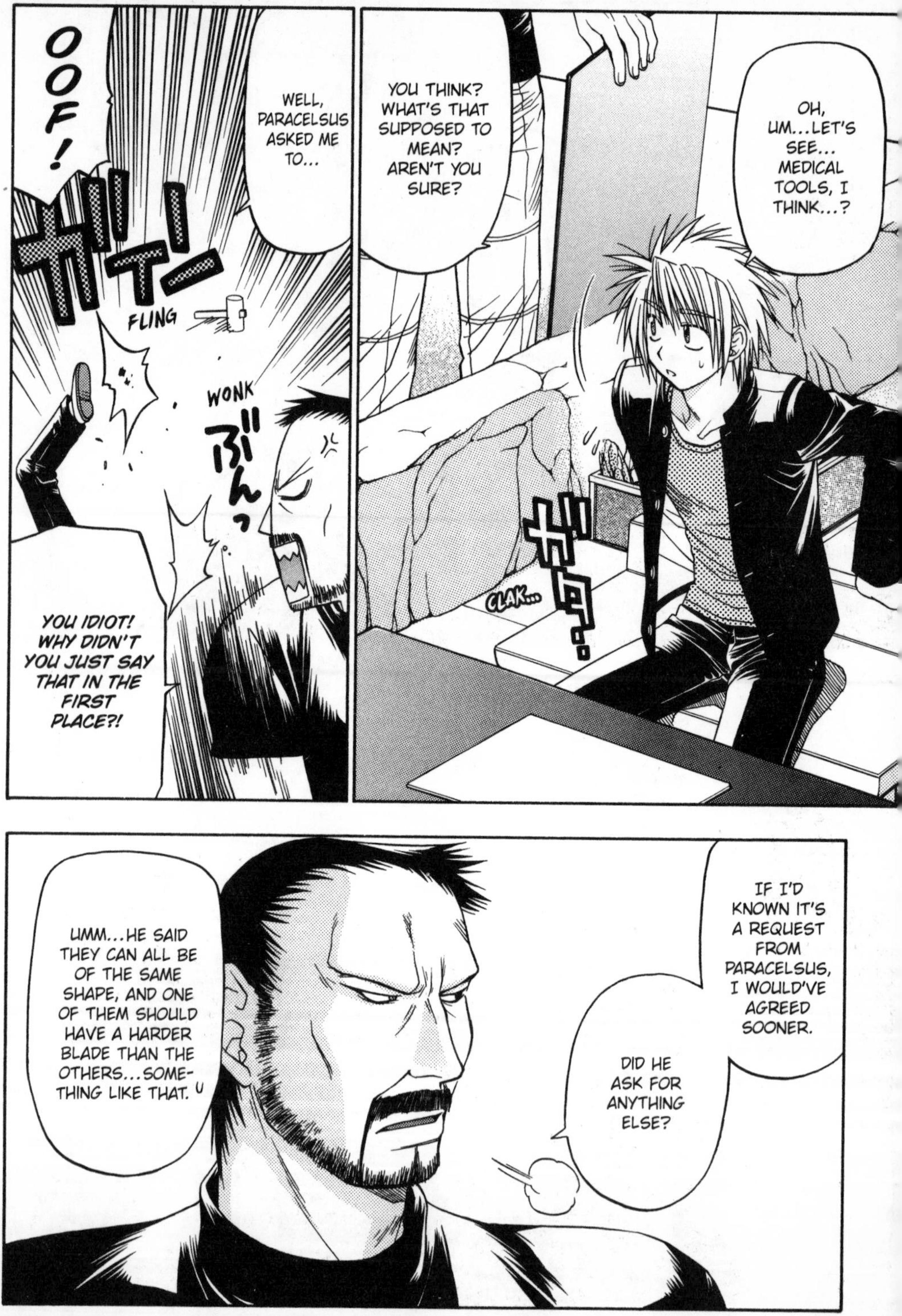
OH, UM...LET'S SEE... MEDICAL TOOLS, I THINK...?
YOU THINK? WHAT'S THAT SUPPOSED TO MEAN? AREN'T YOU SURE?
CLAK...
WELL, PARACELSUS ASKED ME TO...
OOF!
FLING
WONK
ぶんっ
YOU IDIOT! WHY DIDN'T YOU JUST SAY THAT IN THE FIRST PLACE?!
IF I'D KNOWN IT'S A REQUEST FROM PARACELSUS, I WOULD'VE AGREED SOONER.
DID HE ASK FOR ANYTHING ELSE?
UMM...HE SAID THEY CAN ALL BE OF THE SAME SHAPE, AND ONE OF THEM SHOULD HAVE A HARDER BLADE THAN THE OTHERS...SOME-THING LIKE THAT.

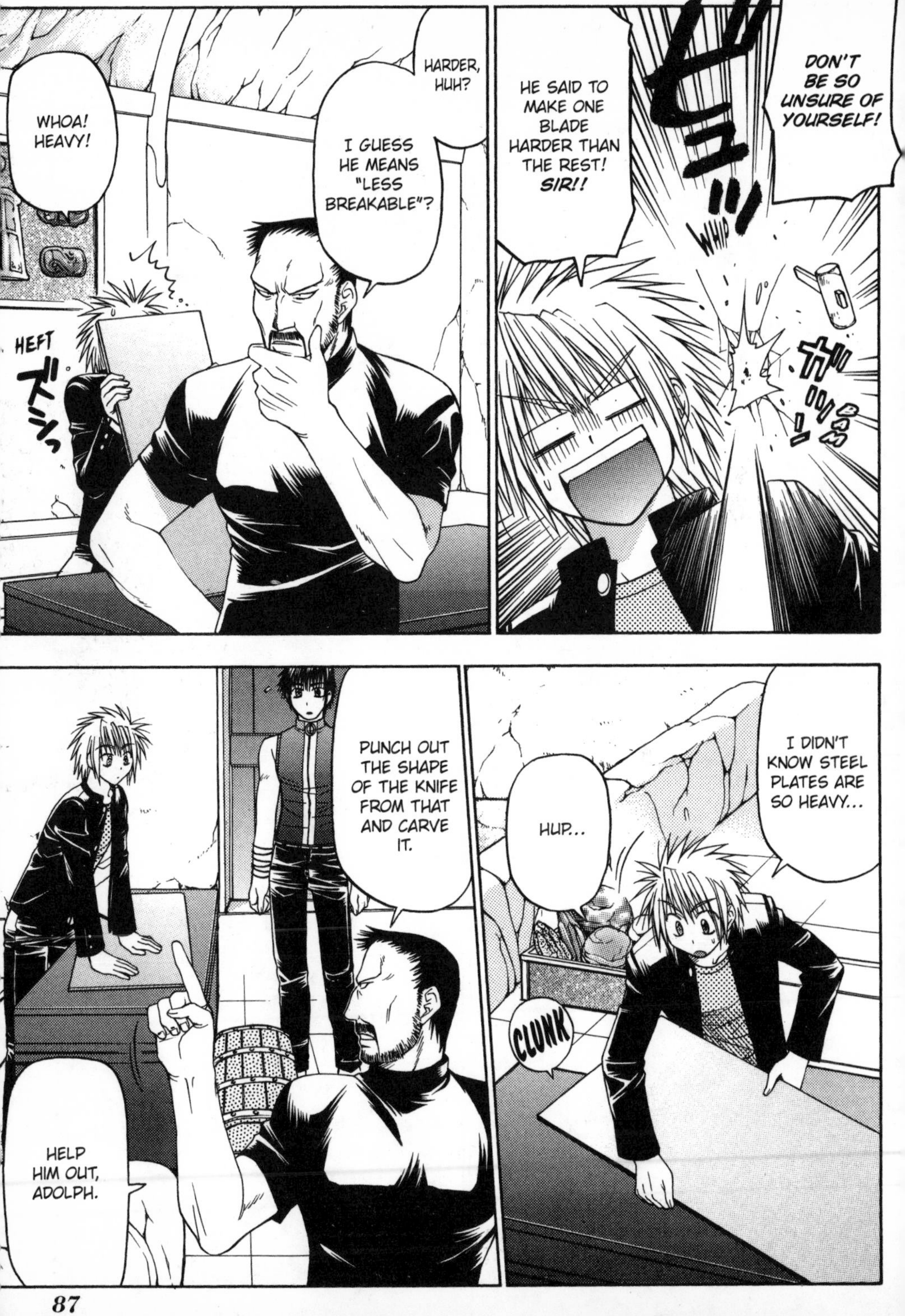
DON'T BE SO UNSURE OF YOURSELF!
HE SAID TO MAKE ONE BLADE HARDER THAN THE REST! SIR!!
WHIP
BAM
HARDER, HUH?
I GUESS HE MEANS "LESS BREAKABLE"?
WHOA! HEAVY!
HEFT
I DIDN'T KNOW STEEL PLATES ARE SO HEAVY...
HUP...
CLUNK
PUNCH OUT THE SHAPE OF THE KNIFE FROM THAT AND CARVE IT.
HELP HIM OUT, ADOLPH.

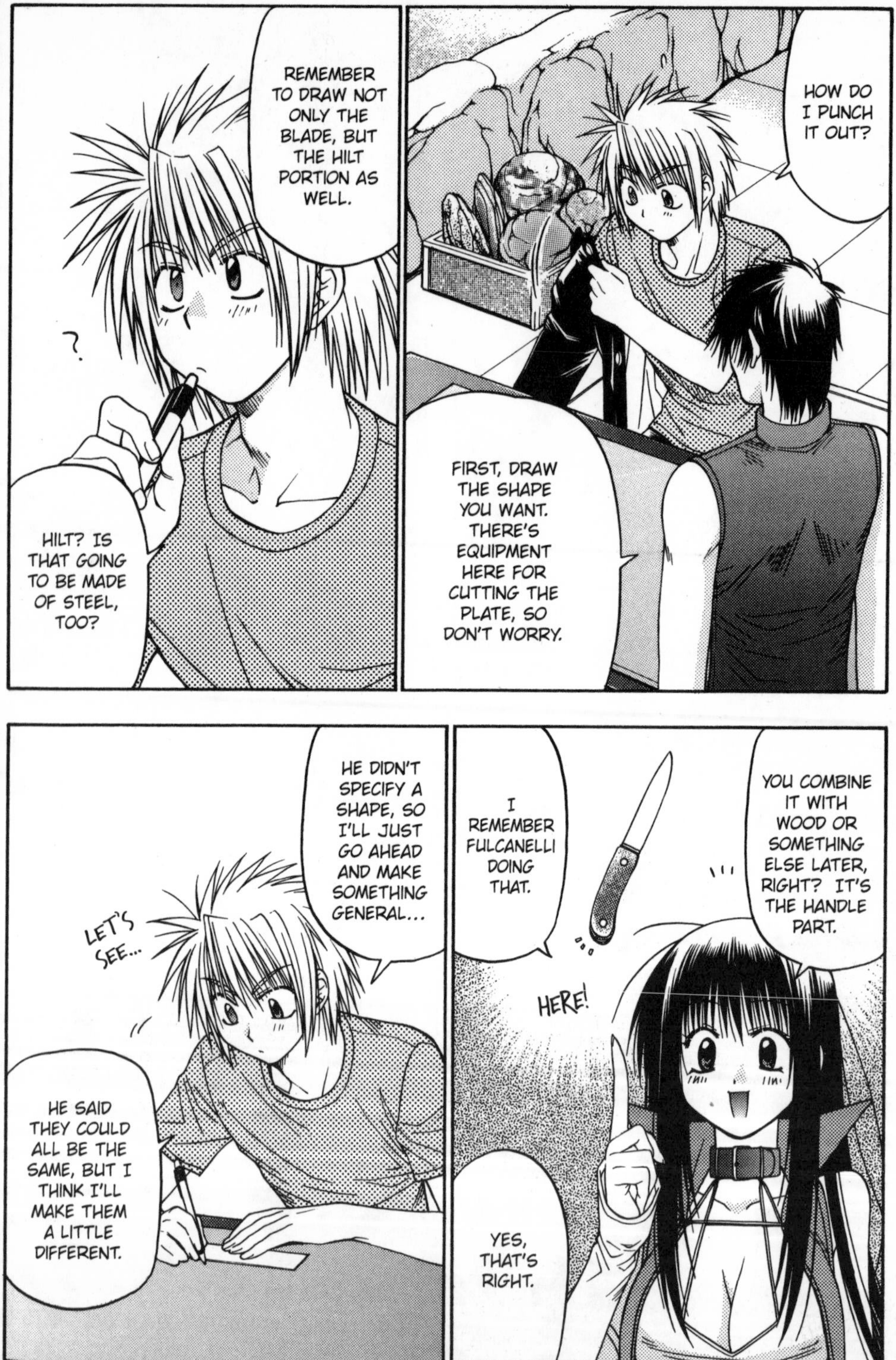
HOW DO I PUNCH IT OUT?
FIRST, DRAW THE SHAPE YOU WANT. THERE'S EQUIPMENT HERE FOR CUTTING THE PLATE, SO DON'T WORRY.
REMEMBER TO DRAW NOT ONLY THE BLADE, BUT THE HILT PORTION AS WELL.
?
HILT? IS THAT GOING TO BE MADE OF STEEL, TOO?
YOU COMBINE IT WITH WOOD OR SOMETHING ELSE LATER, RIGHT? IT'S THE HANDLE PART.
I REMEMBER FULCANELLI DOING THAT.
HERE!
YES, THAT'S RIGHT.
HE DIDN'T SPECIFY A SHAPE, SO I'LL JUST GO AHEAD AND MAKE SOMETHING GENERAL...
LET'S SEE...
HE SAID THEY COULD ALL BE THE SAME, BUT I THINK I'LL MAKE THEM A LITTLE DIFFERENT.

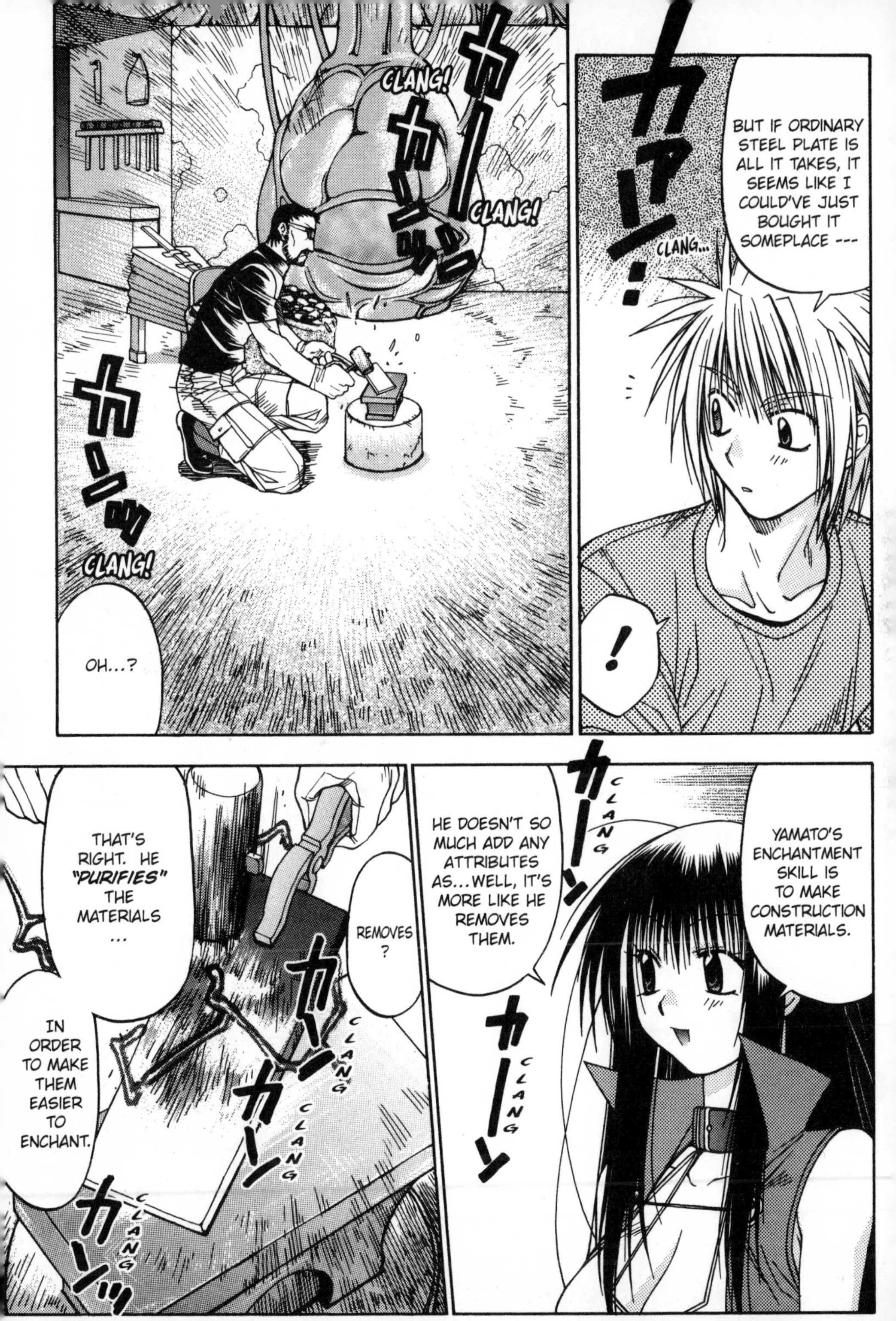
CLANG...
BUT IF ORDINARY STEEL PLATE IS ALL IT TAKES, IT SEEMS LIKE I COULD'VE JUST BOUGHT IT SOMEPLACE ---
!
CLANG!
CLANG!
CLANG!
OH...?
YAMATO'S ENCHANTMENT SKILL IS TO MAKE CONSTRUCTION MATERIALS.
CLANG
HE DOESN'T SO MUCH ADD ANY ATTRIBUTES AS...WELL, IT'S MORE LIKE HE REMOVES THEM.
CLANG
REMOVES?
THAT'S RIGHT. HE *"PURIFIES"* THE MATERIALS ...
CLANG
CLANG
IN ORDER TO MAKE THEM EASIER TO ENCHANT.
CLANG

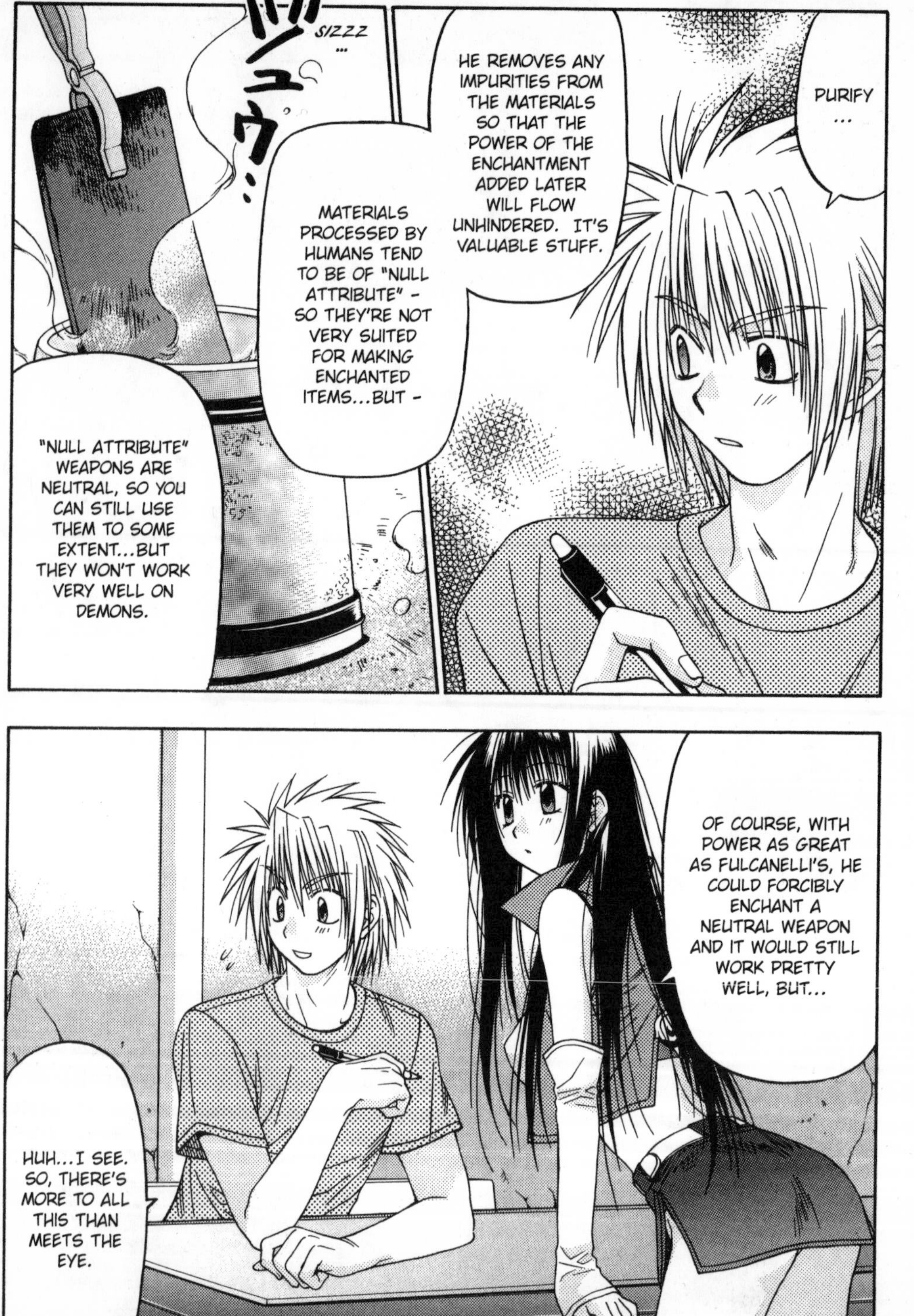
PURIFY...
HE REMOVES ANY IMPURITIES FROM THE MATERIALS SO THAT THE POWER OF THE ENCHANTMENT ADDED LATER WILL FLOW UNHINDERED. IT'S VALUABLE STUFF.
ジュウ…
SIZZZ...
MATERIALS PROCESSED BY HUMANS TEND TO BE OF "NULL ATTRIBUTE" - SO THEY'RE NOT VERY SUITED FOR MAKING ENCHANTED ITEMS...BUT -
"NULL ATTRIBUTE" WEAPONS ARE NEUTRAL, SO YOU CAN STILL USE THEM TO SOME EXTENT...BUT THEY WON'T WORK VERY WELL ON DEMONS.
OF COURSE, WITH POWER AS GREAT AS FULCANELLI'S, HE COULD FORCIBLY ENCHANT A NEUTRAL WEAPON AND IT WOULD STILL WORK PRETTY WELL, BUT...
HUH...I SEE. SO, THERE'S MORE TO ALL THIS THAN MEETS THE EYE.

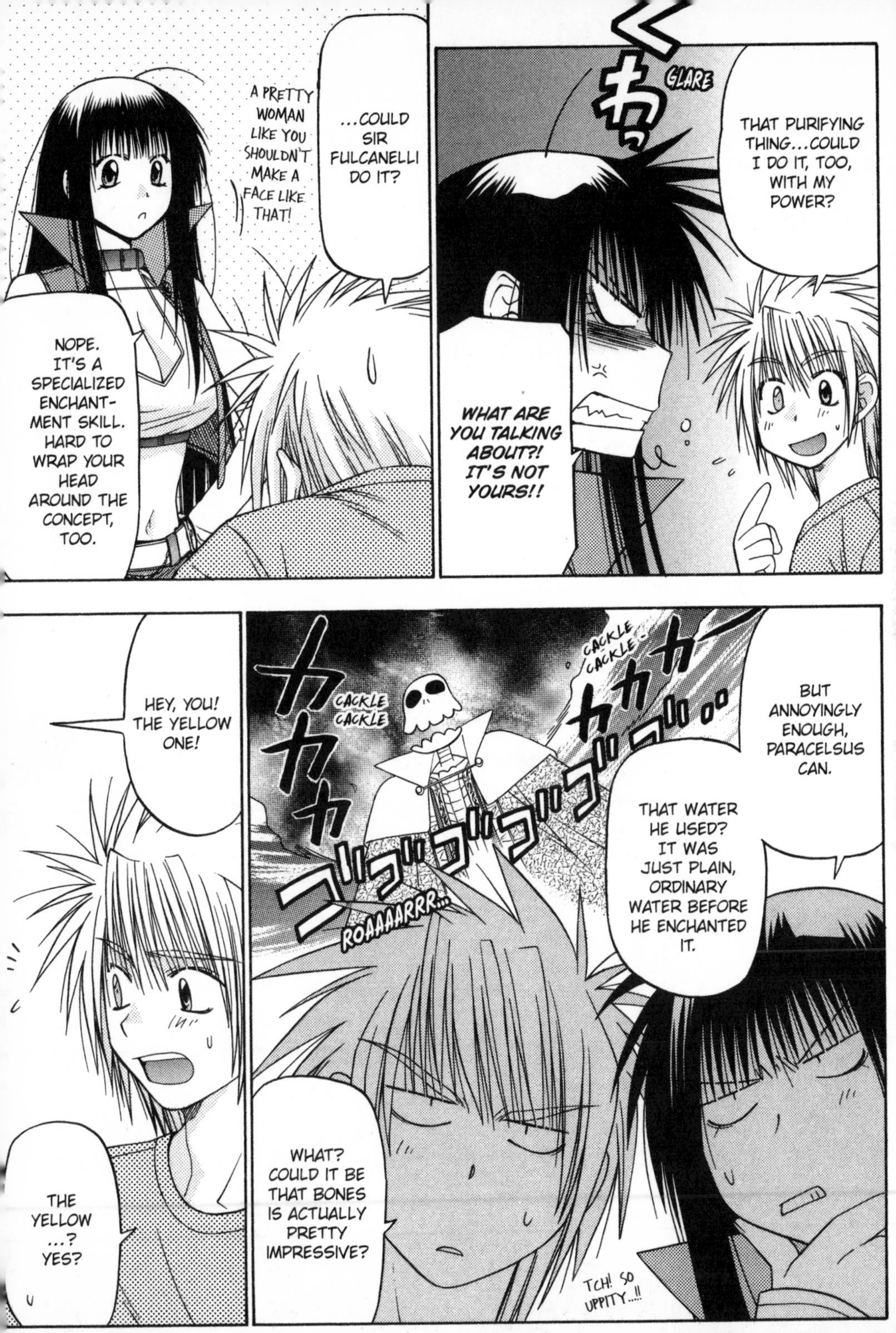
THAT PURIFYING THING...COULD I DO IT, TOO, WITH MY POWER?
GLARE
WHAT ARE YOU TALKING ABOUT?! IT'S NOT YOURS!!
...COULD SIR FULCANELLI DO IT?
A PRETTY WOMAN LIKE YOU SHOULDN'T MAKE A FACE LIKE THAT!
NOPE. IT'S A SPECIALIZED ENCHANT-MENT SKILL. HARD TO WRAP YOUR HEAD AROUND THE CONCEPT, TOO.
CACKLE CACKLE
CACKLE CACKLE
BUT ANNOYINGLY ENOUGH, PARACELSUS CAN.
THAT WATER HE USED? IT WAS JUST PLAIN, ORDINARY WATER BEFORE HE ENCHANTED IT.
ROAAAARRR...
WHAT? COULD IT BE THAT BONES IS ACTUALLY PRETTY IMPRESSIVE?
TCH! SO UPPITY...!!
HEY, YOU! THE YELLOW ONE!
THE YELLOW ...? YES?

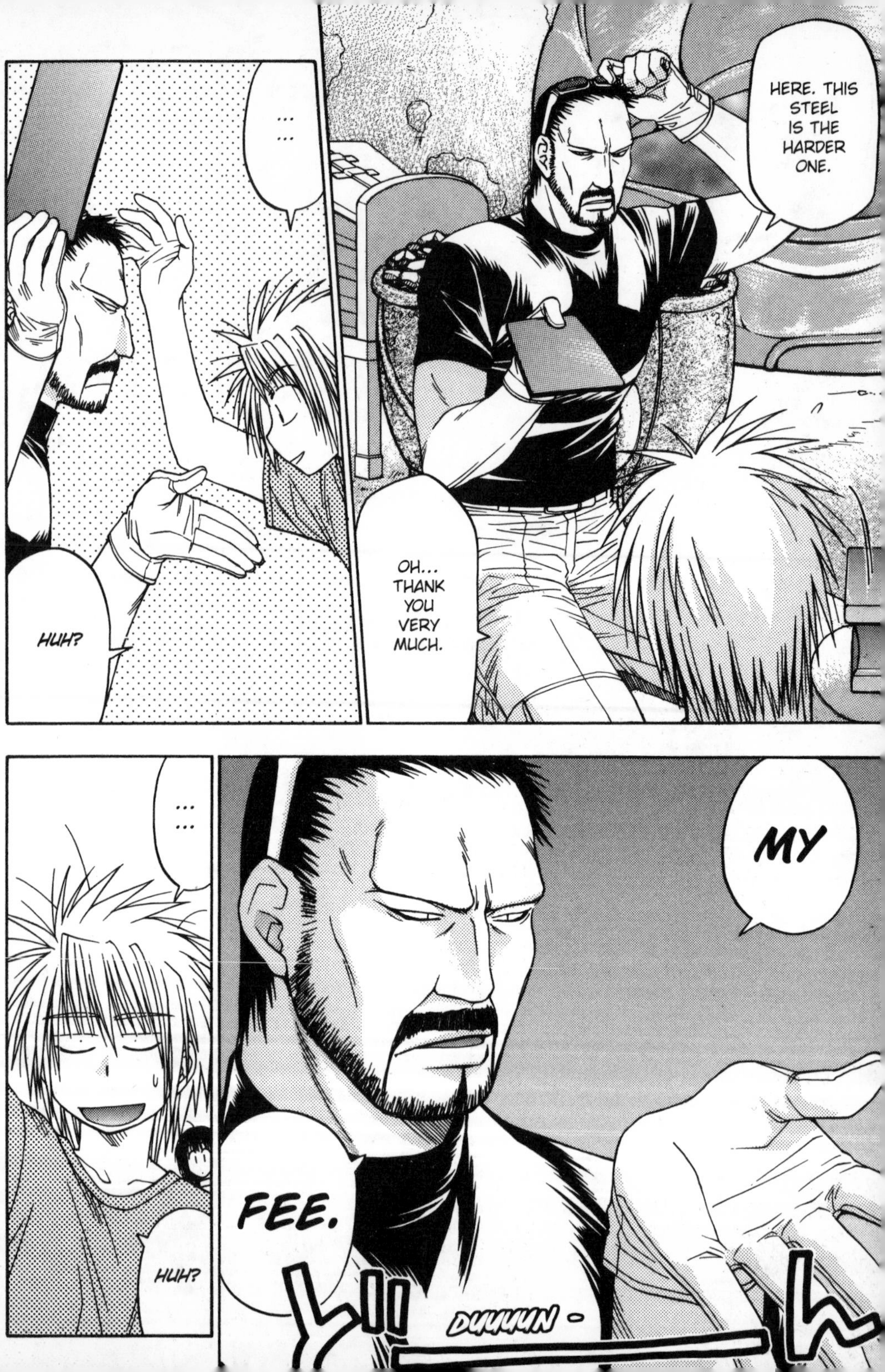
HERE. THIS STEEL IS THE HARDER ONE.
OH... THANK YOU VERY MUCH.
...
...
HUH?
MY
FEE.
DUUUUN -
...
...
HUH?

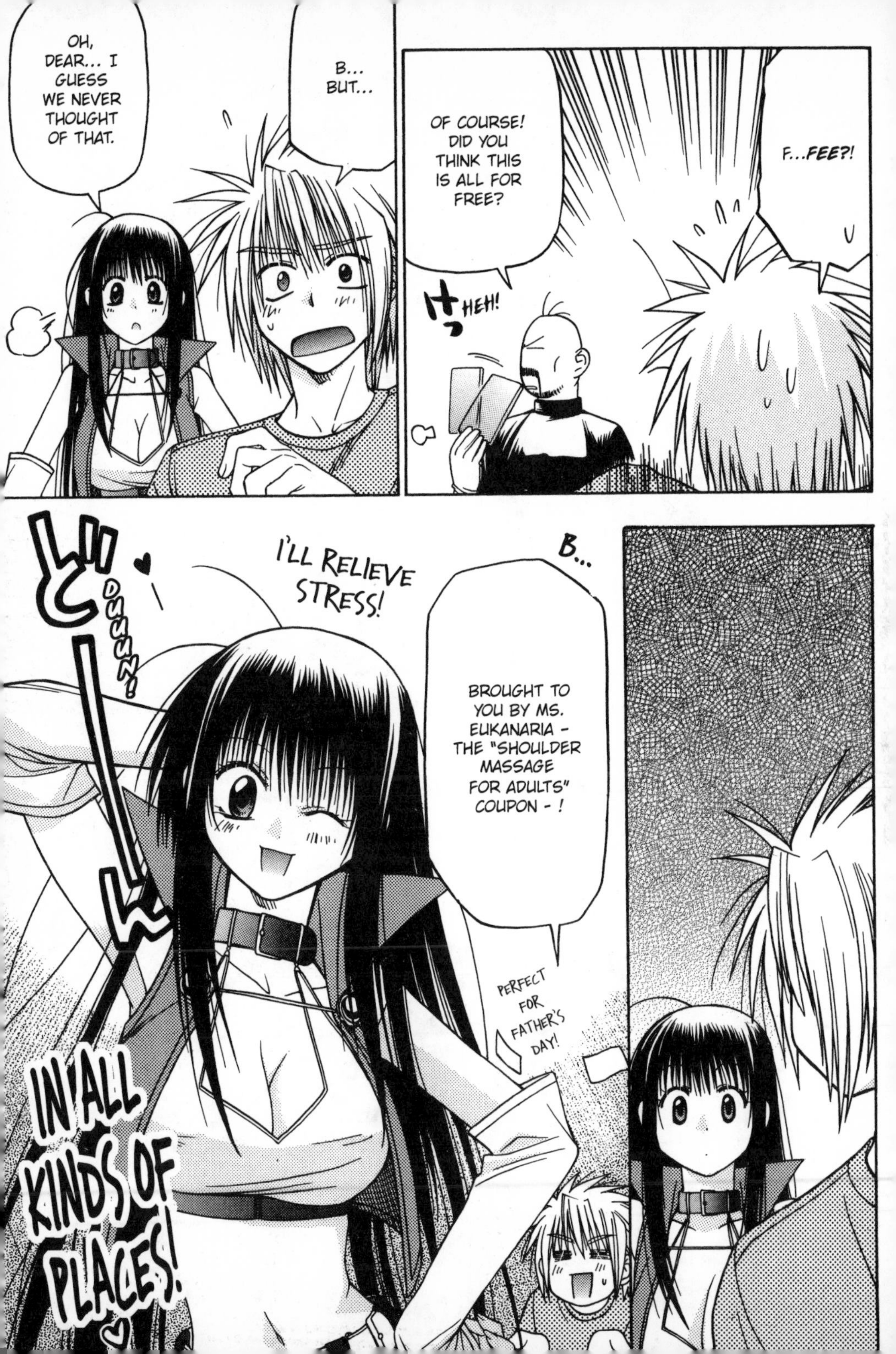
F...FEE?!
OF COURSE! DID YOU THINK THIS IS ALL FOR FREE?
けっ HEH!
B... BUT...
OH, DEAR... I GUESS WE NEVER THOUGHT OF THAT.
B...
BROUGHT TO YOU BY MS. EUKANARIA - THE "SHOULDER MASSAGE FOR ADULTS" COUPON - !
PERFECT FOR FATHER'S DAY!
I'LL RELIEVE STRESS!
DUUUN!
IN ALL KINDS OF PLACES!

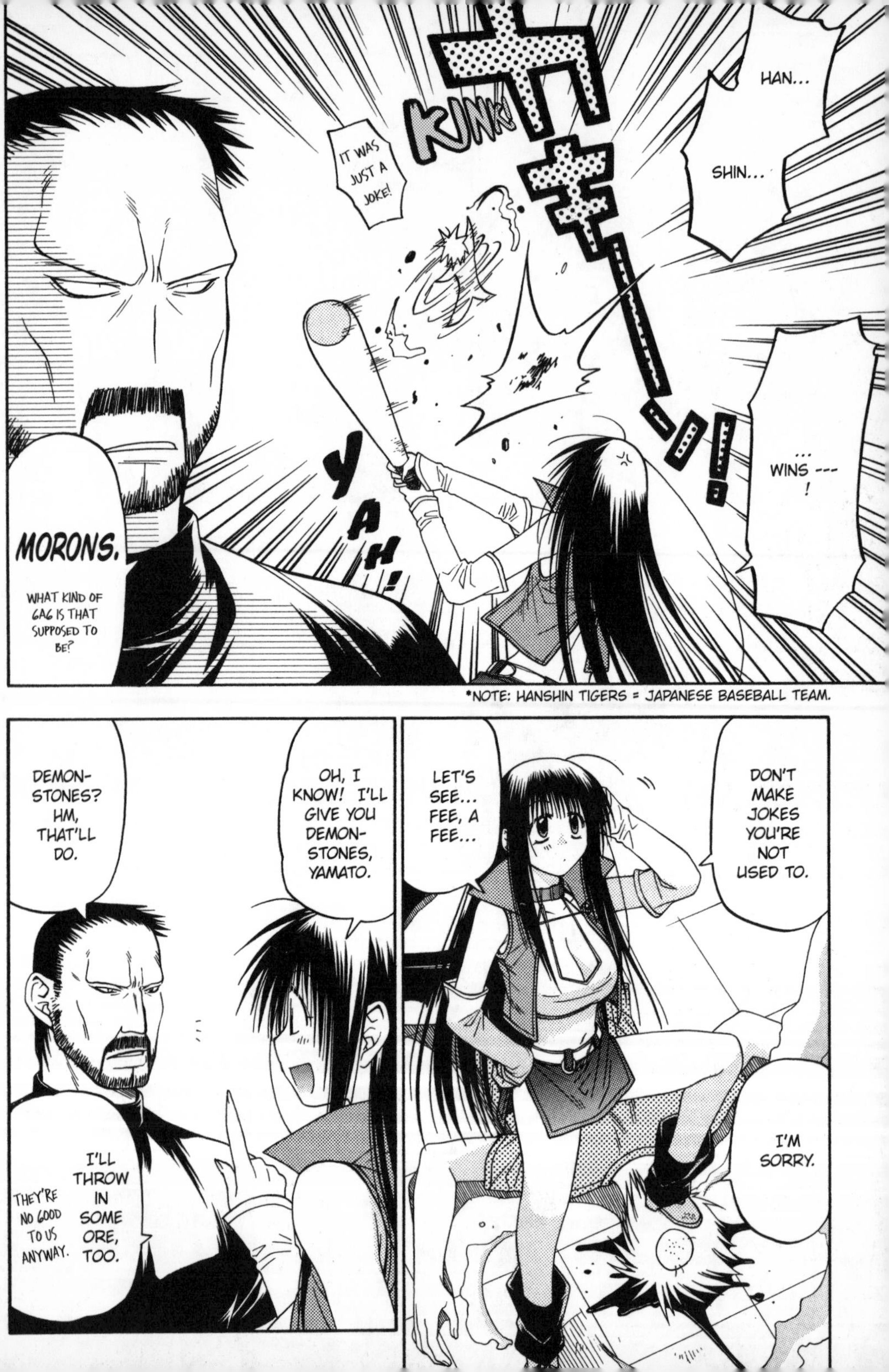
HAN...
SHIN...
... WINS ---!
KINK!
IT WAS JUST A JOKE!
YAH!
MORONS.
WHAT KIND OF GAG IS THAT SUPPOSED TO BE?
DON'T MAKE JOKES YOU'RE NOT USED TO.
LET'S SEE... FEE, A FEE...
I'M SORRY.
OH, I KNOW! I'LL GIVE YOU DEMON-STONES, YAMATO.
DEMON-STONES? HM, THAT'LL DO.
I'LL THROW IN SOME ORE, TOO.
THEY'RE NO GOOD TO US ANYWAY.

*NOTE: HANSHIN TIGERS = JAPANESE BASEBALL TEAM.

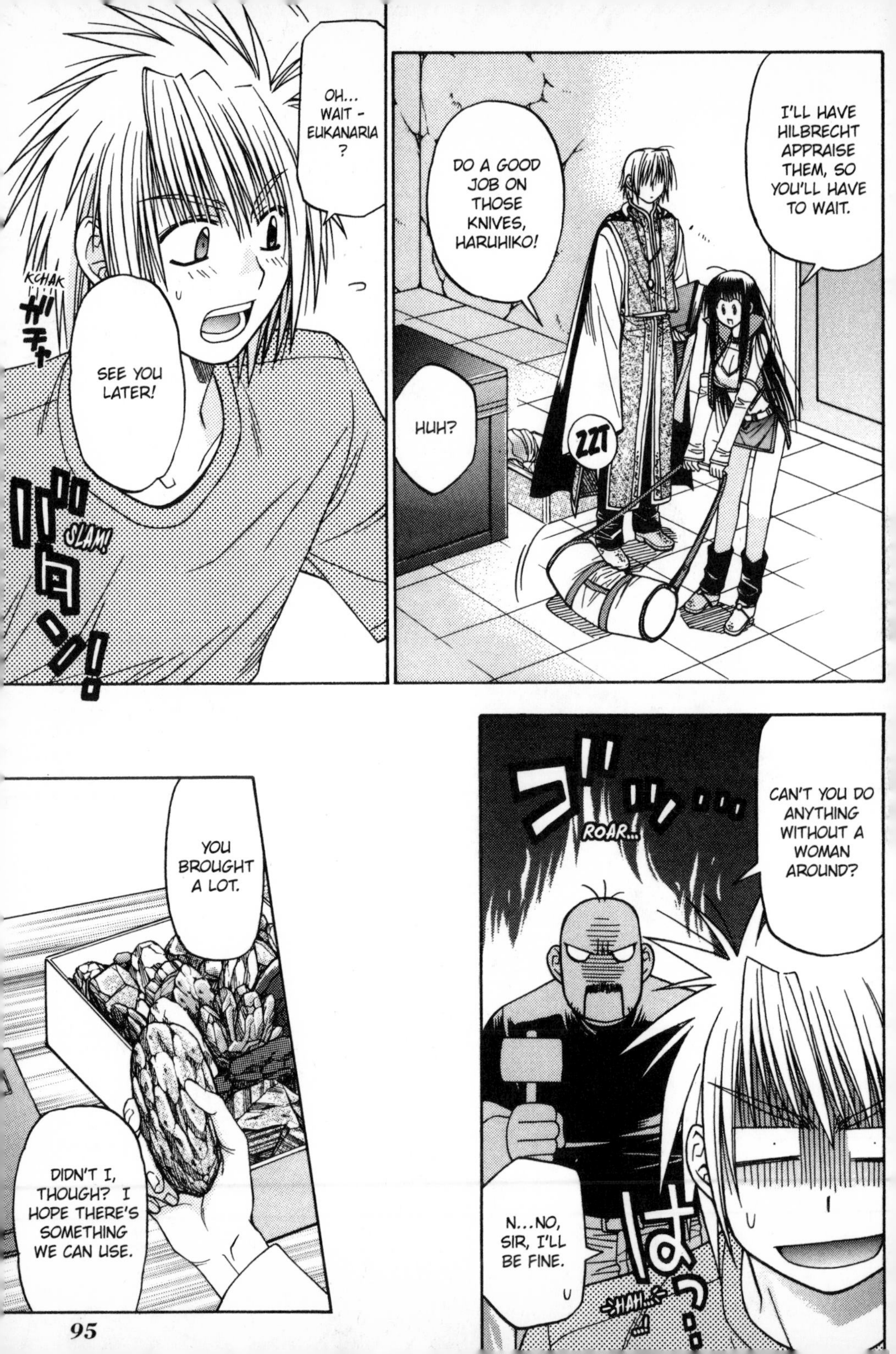
I'LL HAVE HILBRECHT APPRAISE THEM, SO YOU'LL HAVE TO WAIT.
DO A GOOD JOB ON THOSE KNIVES, HARUHIKO!
ZZT
HUH?
OH... WAIT - EUKANARIA ?
KCHAK
SEE YOU LATER!
SLAM!
CAN'T YOU DO ANYTHING WITHOUT A WOMAN AROUND?
ROAR...
N...NO, SIR, I'LL BE FINE.
HAH...
YOU BROUGHT A LOT.
DIDN'T I, THOUGH? I HOPE THERE'S SOMETHING WE CAN USE.

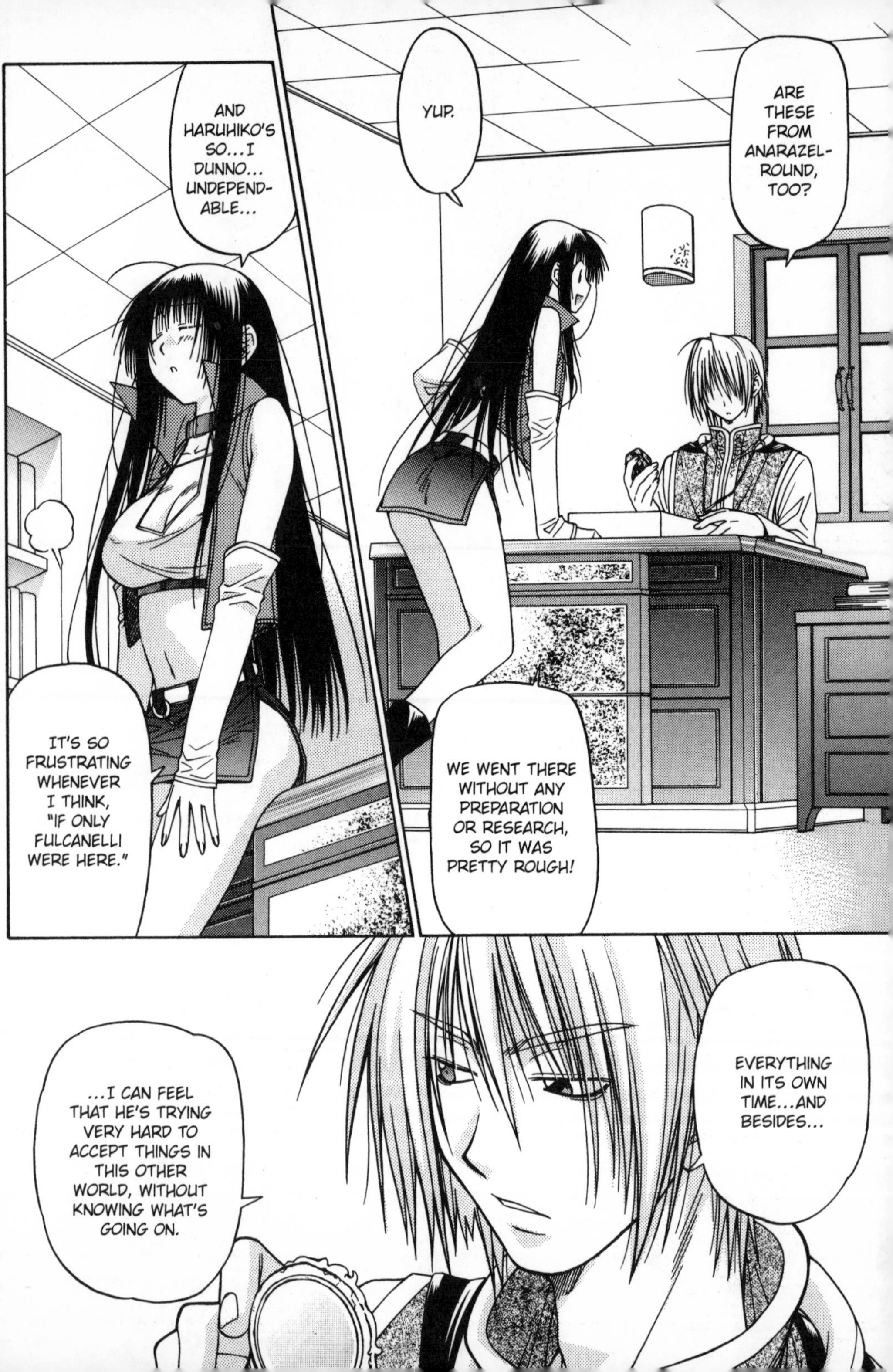
ARE THESE FROM ANARAZEL-ROUND, TOO?
YUP.
WE WENT THERE WITHOUT ANY PREPARATION OR RESEARCH, SO IT WAS PRETTY ROUGH!
AND HARUHIKO'S SO...I DUNNO... UNDEPENDABLE...
IT'S SO FRUSTRATING WHENEVER I THINK, "IF ONLY FULCANELLI WERE HERE."
EVERYTHING IN ITS OWN TIME...AND BESIDES...
...I CAN FEEL THAT HE'S TRYING VERY HARD TO ACCEPT THINGS IN THIS OTHER WORLD, WITHOUT KNOWING WHAT'S GOING ON.

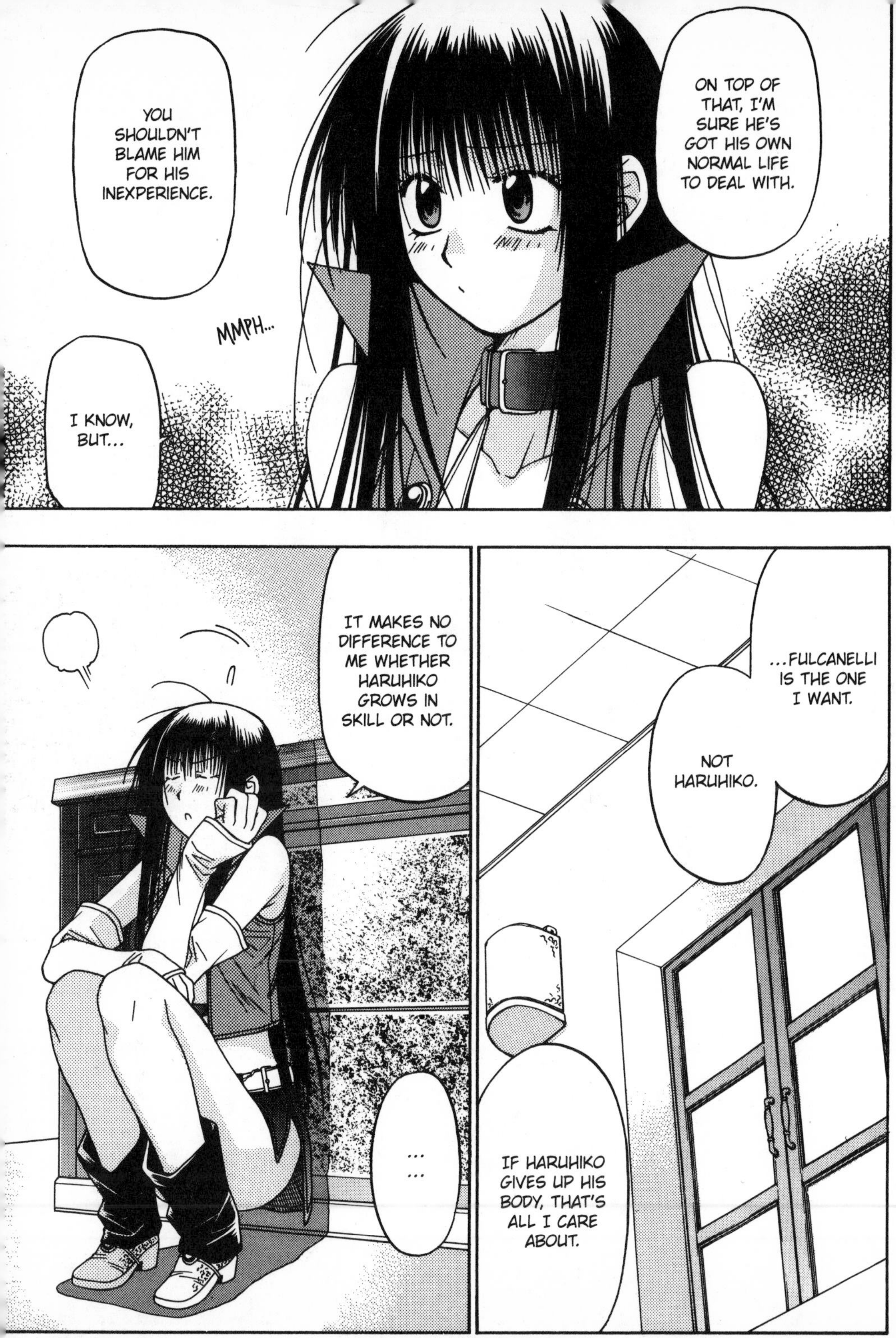
ON TOP OF THAT, I'M SURE HE'S GOT HIS OWN NORMAL LIFE TO DEAL WITH.
YOU SHOULDN'T BLAME HIM FOR HIS INEXPERIENCE.
MMPH...
I KNOW, BUT...
...FULCANELLI IS THE ONE I WANT.
NOT HARUHIKO.
IF HARUHIKO GIVES UP HIS BODY, THAT'S ALL I CARE ABOUT.
IT MAKES NO DIFFERENCE TO ME WHETHER HARUHIKO GROWS IN SKILL OR NOT.
......

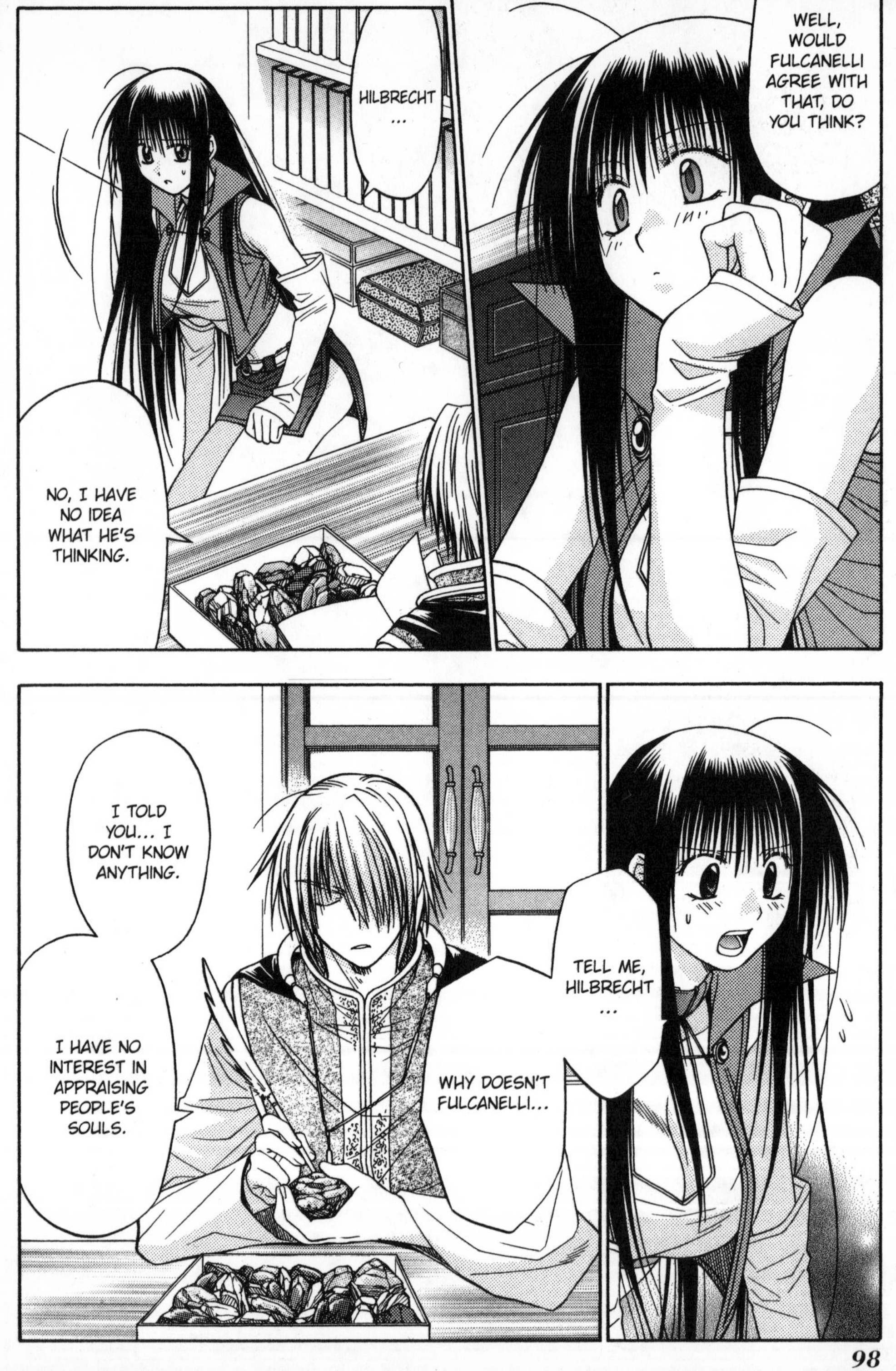
WELL, WOULD FULCANELLI AGREE WITH THAT, DO YOU THINK?
HILBRECHT ...
NO, I HAVE NO IDEA WHAT HE'S THINKING.
TELL ME, HILBRECHT ...
WHY DOESN'T FULCANELLI...
I TOLD YOU... I DON'T KNOW ANYTHING.
I HAVE NO INTEREST IN APPRAISING PEOPLE'S SOULS.

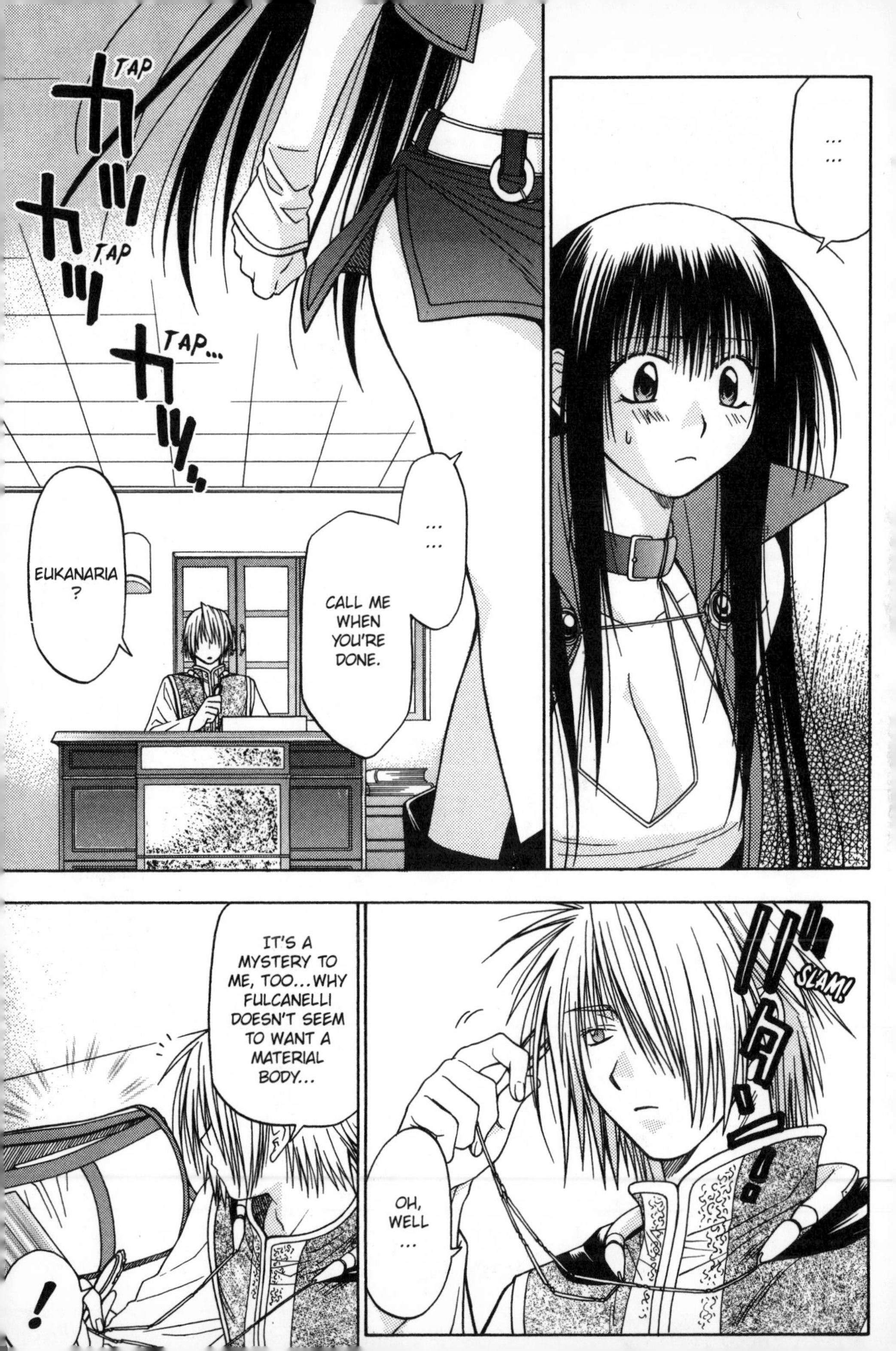
……
TAP
TAP
TAP…
…… CALL ME WHEN YOU'RE DONE.
EUKANARIA ?
SLAM!
OH, WELL …
IT'S A MYSTERY TO ME, TOO…WHY FULCANELLI DOESN'T SEEM TO WANT A MATERIAL BODY…
!

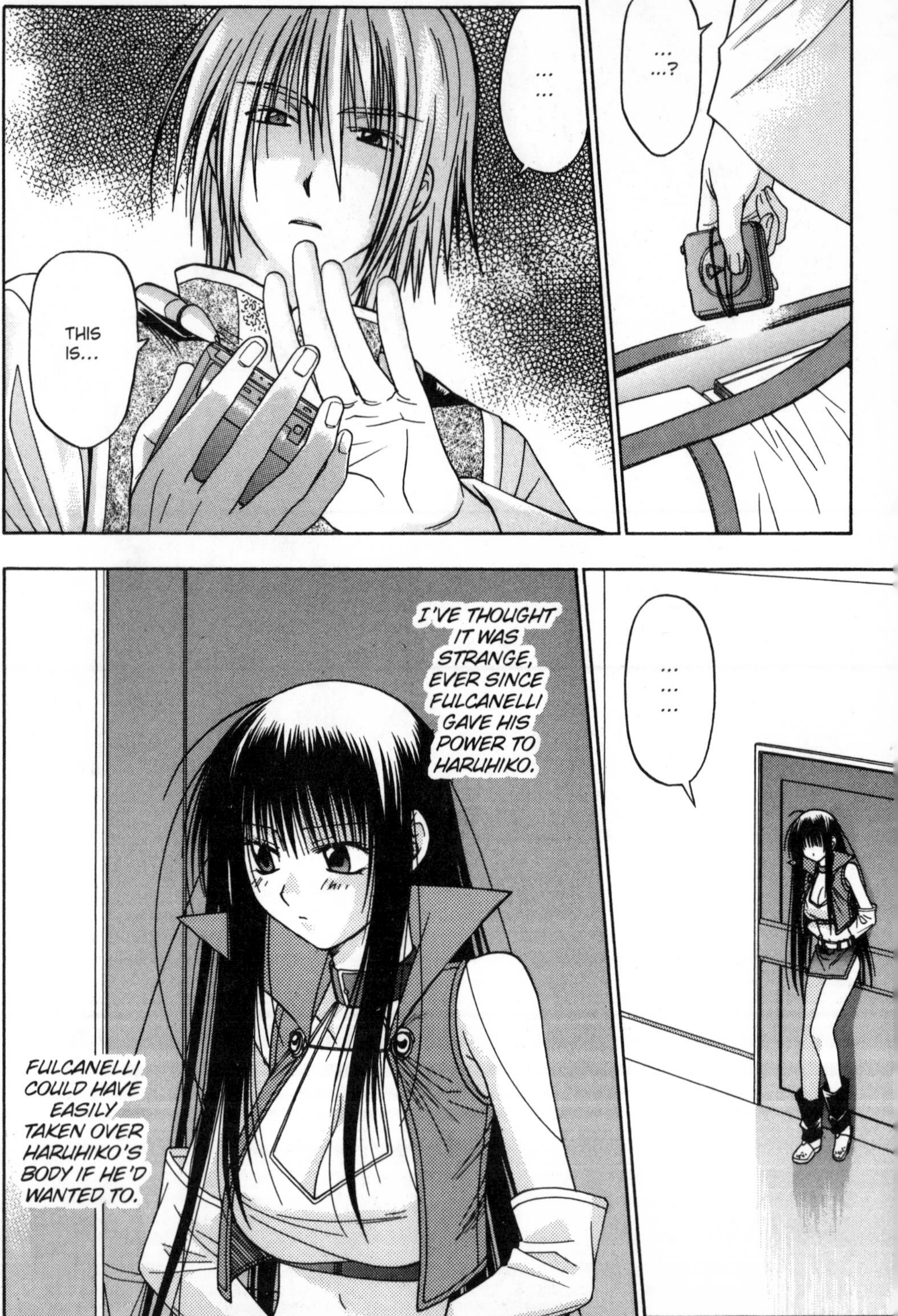
... ...?
... ...
THIS IS...
... ...
I'VE THOUGHT IT WAS STRANGE, EVER SINCE FULCANELLI GAVE HIS POWER TO HARUHIKO.
FULCANELLI COULD HAVE EASILY TAKEN OVER HARUHIKO'S BODY IF HE'D WANTED TO.

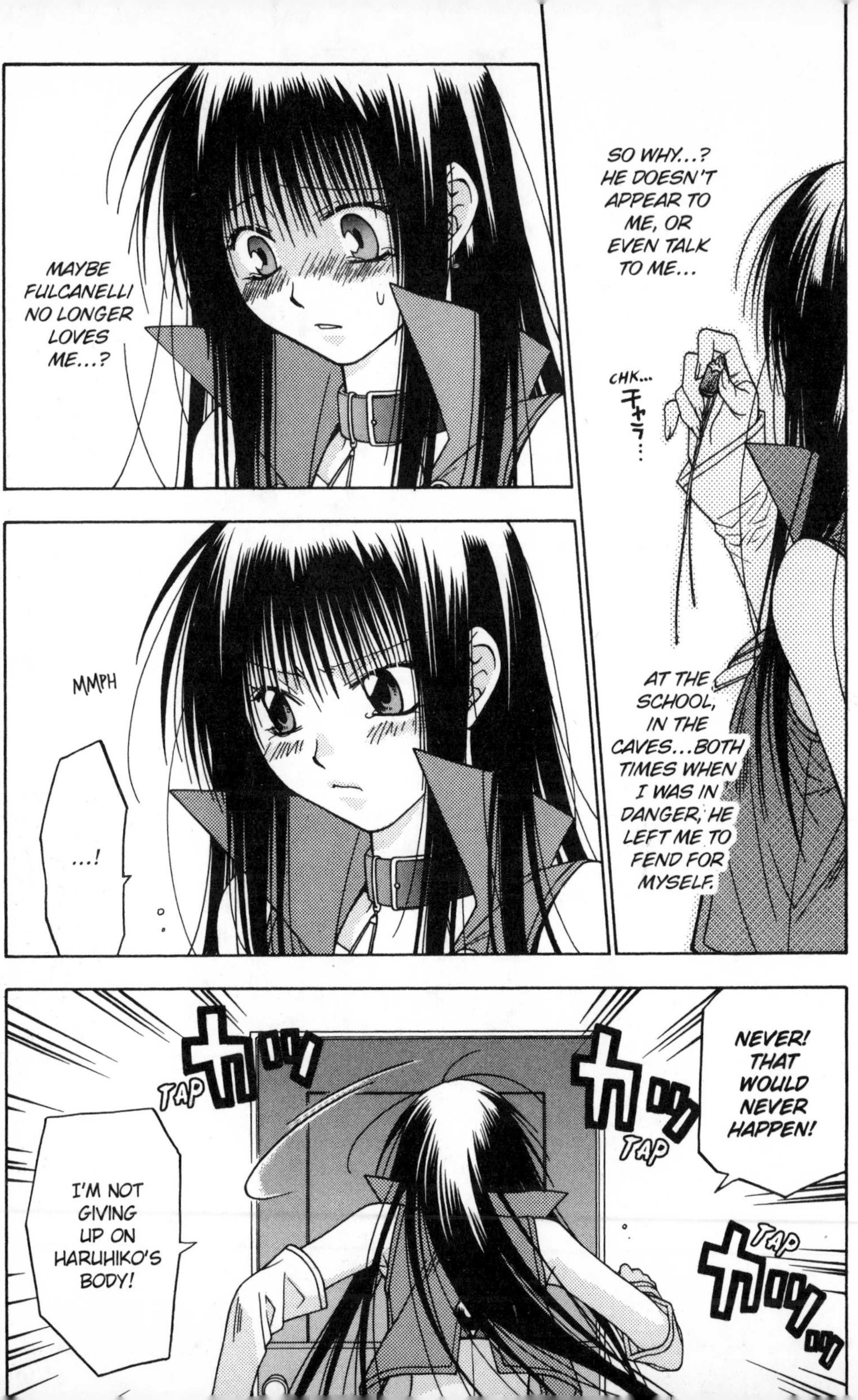
SO WHY...? HE DOESN'T APPEAR TO ME, OR EVEN TALK TO ME...
CHK...
チャラ...
AT THE SCHOOL, IN THE CAVES...BOTH TIMES WHEN I WAS IN DANGER, HE LEFT ME TO FEND FOR MYSELF.
MAYBE FULCANELLI NO LONGER LOVES ME...?
MMPH
...!
NEVER! THAT WOULD NEVER HAPPEN!
TAP
TAP
TAP
I'M NOT GIVING UP ON HARUHIKO'S BODY!

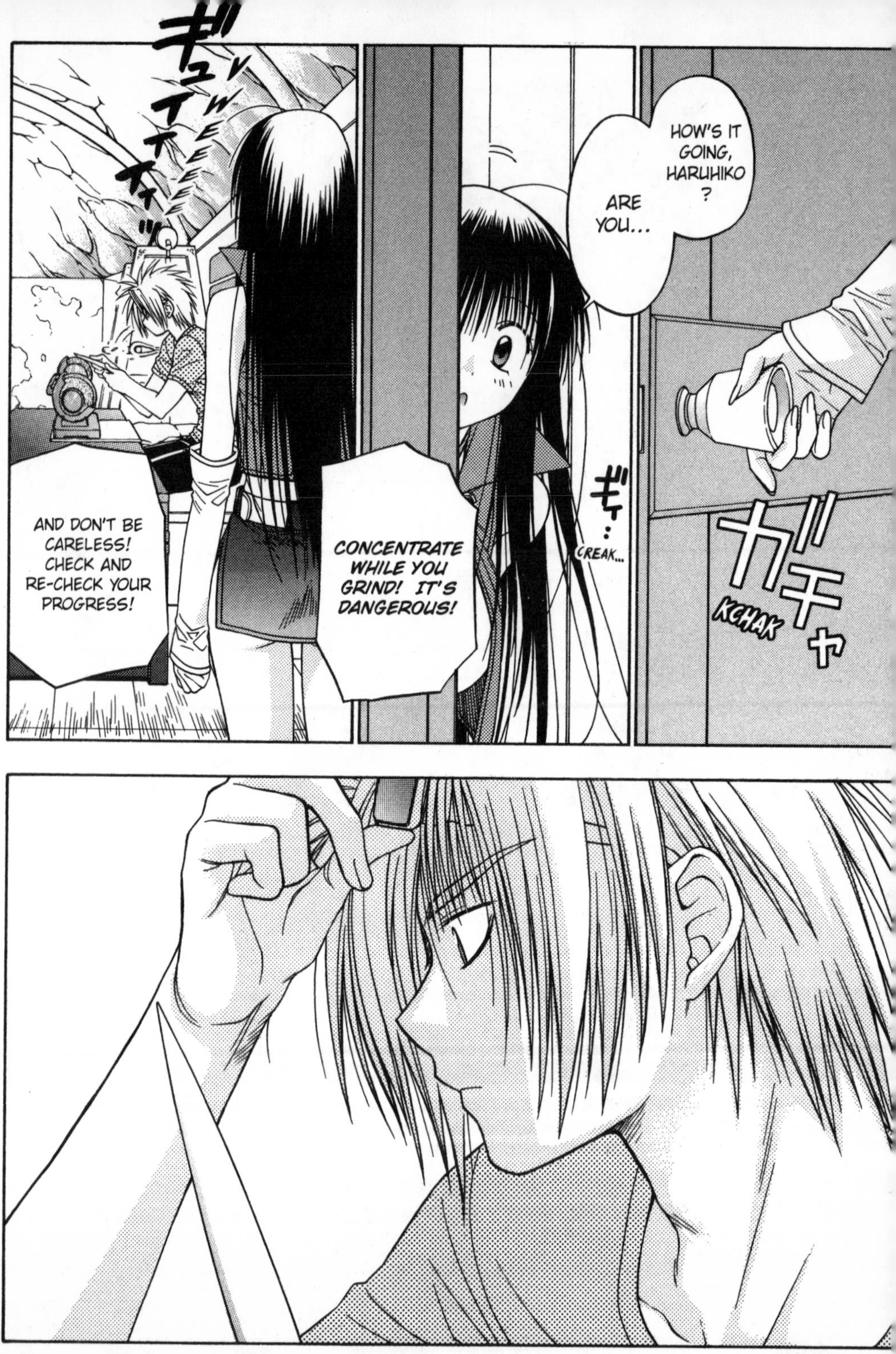
ガチャ
KCHAK
HOW'S IT GOING, HARUHIKO?
ARE YOU...
ギィ…
CREAK...
ギュイイイイイィッ
VWEEEEE
CONCENTRATE WHILE YOU GRIND! IT'S DANGEROUS!
AND DON'T BE CARELESS! CHECK AND RE-CHECK YOUR PROGRESS!

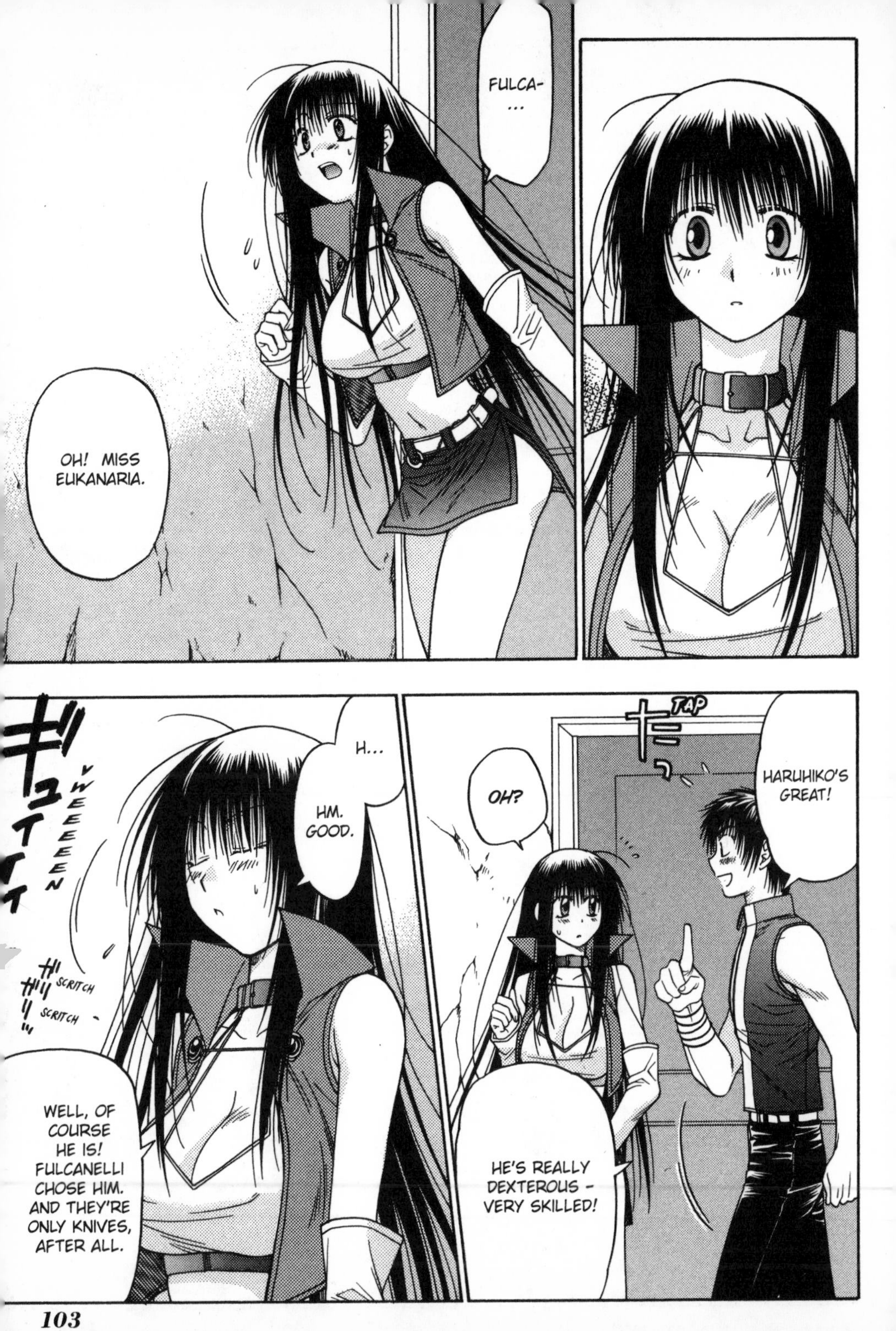
FULCA-
...
OH! MISS EUKANARIA.
TAP
HARUHIKO'S GREAT!
OH?
HE'S REALLY DEXTEROUS - VERY SKILLED!
H...
HM. GOOD.
VWEEEEEEN
SCRITCH
SCRITCH
WELL, OF COURSE HE IS! FULCANELLI CHOSE HIM. AND THEY'RE ONLY KNIVES, AFTER ALL.

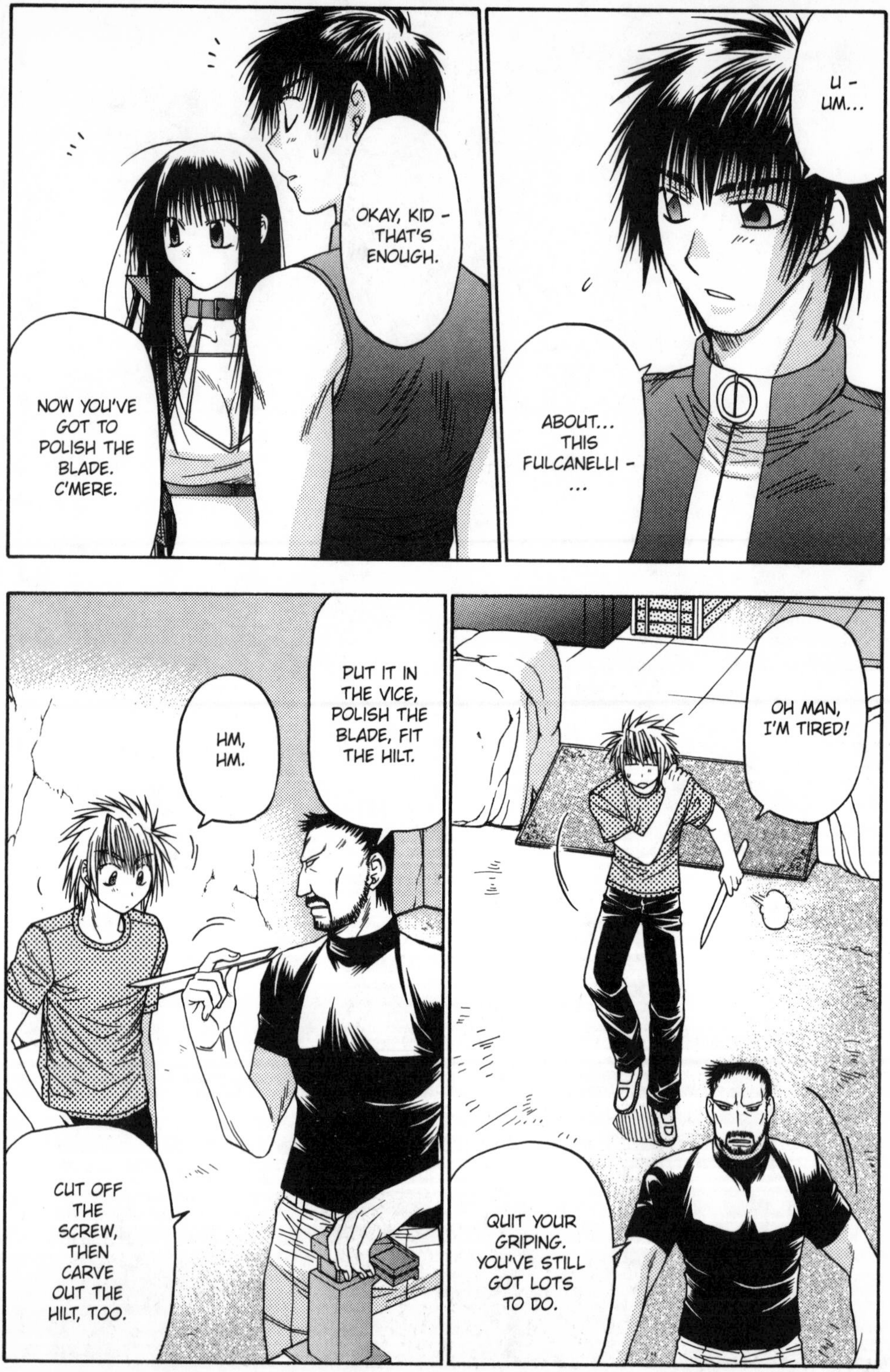
U - UM...
ABOUT... THIS FULCANELLI - ...
OKAY, KID - THAT'S ENOUGH.
NOW YOU'VE GOT TO POLISH THE BLADE. C'MERE.
OH MAN, I'M TIRED!
QUIT YOUR GRIPING. YOU'VE STILL GOT LOTS TO DO.
PUT IT IN THE VICE, POLISH THE BLADE, FIT THE HILT.
HM, HM.
CUT OFF THE SCREW, THEN CARVE OUT THE HILT, TOO.

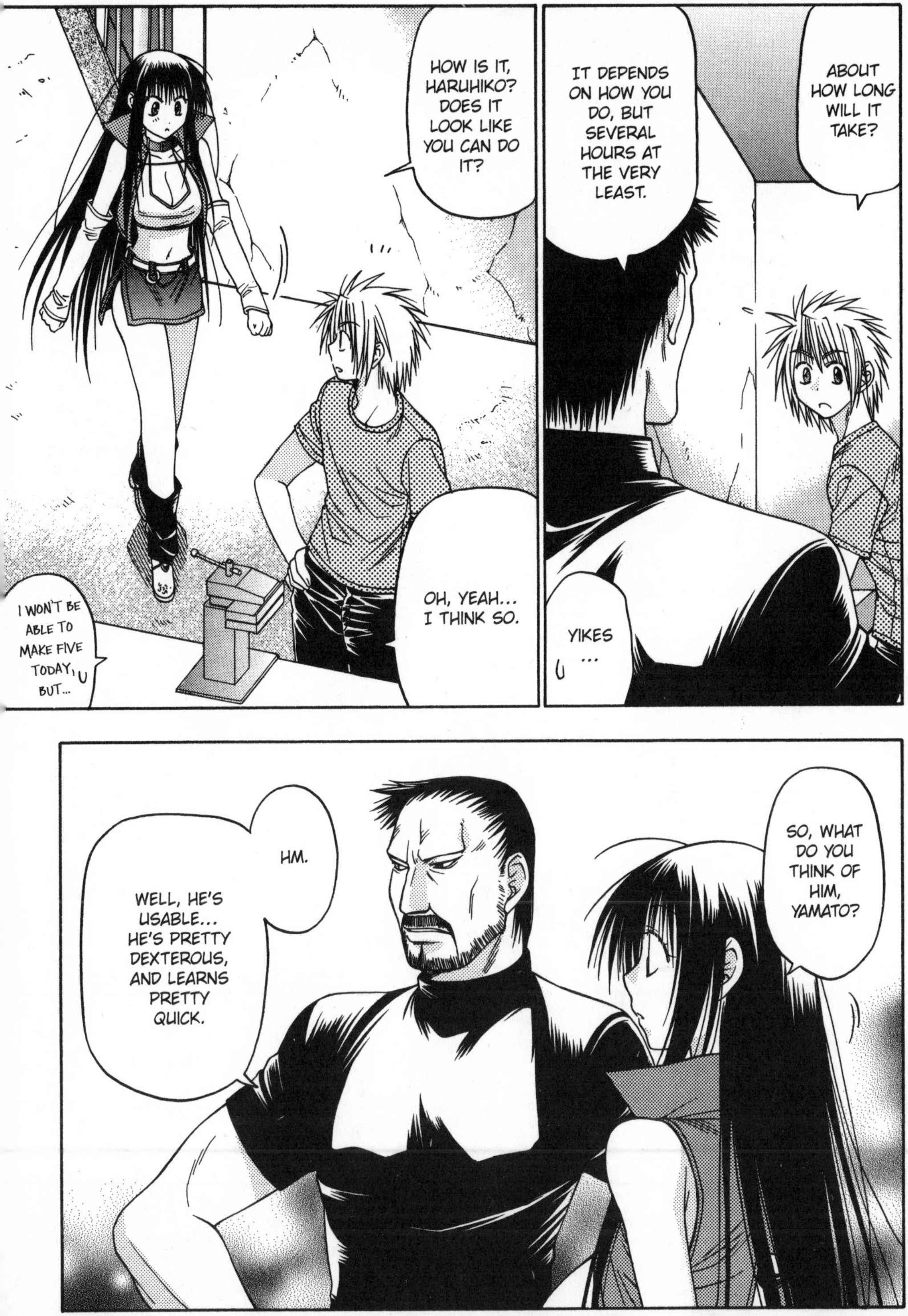
HOW IS IT, HARUHIKO? DOES IT LOOK LIKE YOU CAN DO IT?
OH, YEAH... I THINK SO.
I WON'T BE ABLE TO MAKE FIVE TODAY, BUT...
ABOUT HOW LONG WILL IT TAKE?
IT DEPENDS ON HOW YOU DO, BUT SEVERAL HOURS AT THE VERY LEAST.
YIKES ...
SO, WHAT DO YOU THINK OF HIM, YAMATO?
HM.
WELL, HE'S USABLE... HE'S PRETTY DEXTEROUS, AND LEARNS PRETTY QUICK.

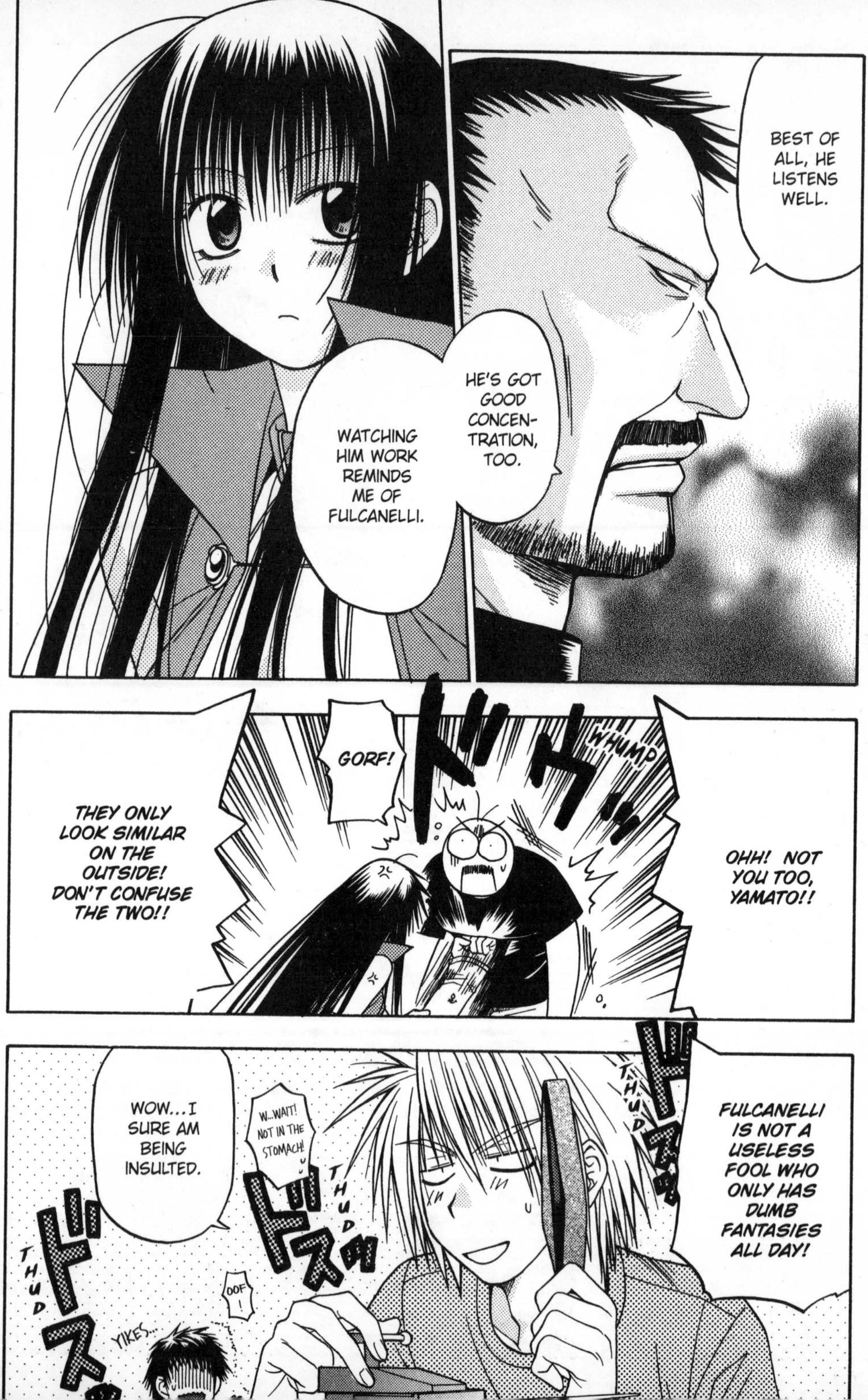
BEST OF ALL, HE LISTENS WELL.
HE'S GOT GOOD CONCENTRATION, TOO.
WATCHING HIM WORK REMINDS ME OF FULCANELLI.
OHH! NOT YOU TOO, YAMATO!!
WHUMP
GORF!
THEY ONLY LOOK SIMILAR ON THE OUTSIDE! DON'T CONFUSE THE TWO!!
FULCANELLI IS NOT A USELESS FOOL WHO ONLY HAS DUMB FANTASIES ALL DAY!
THUD
THUD
W...WAIT! NOT IN THE STOMACH!
WOW...I SURE AM BEING INSULTED.
OOF!
THUD
YIKES...

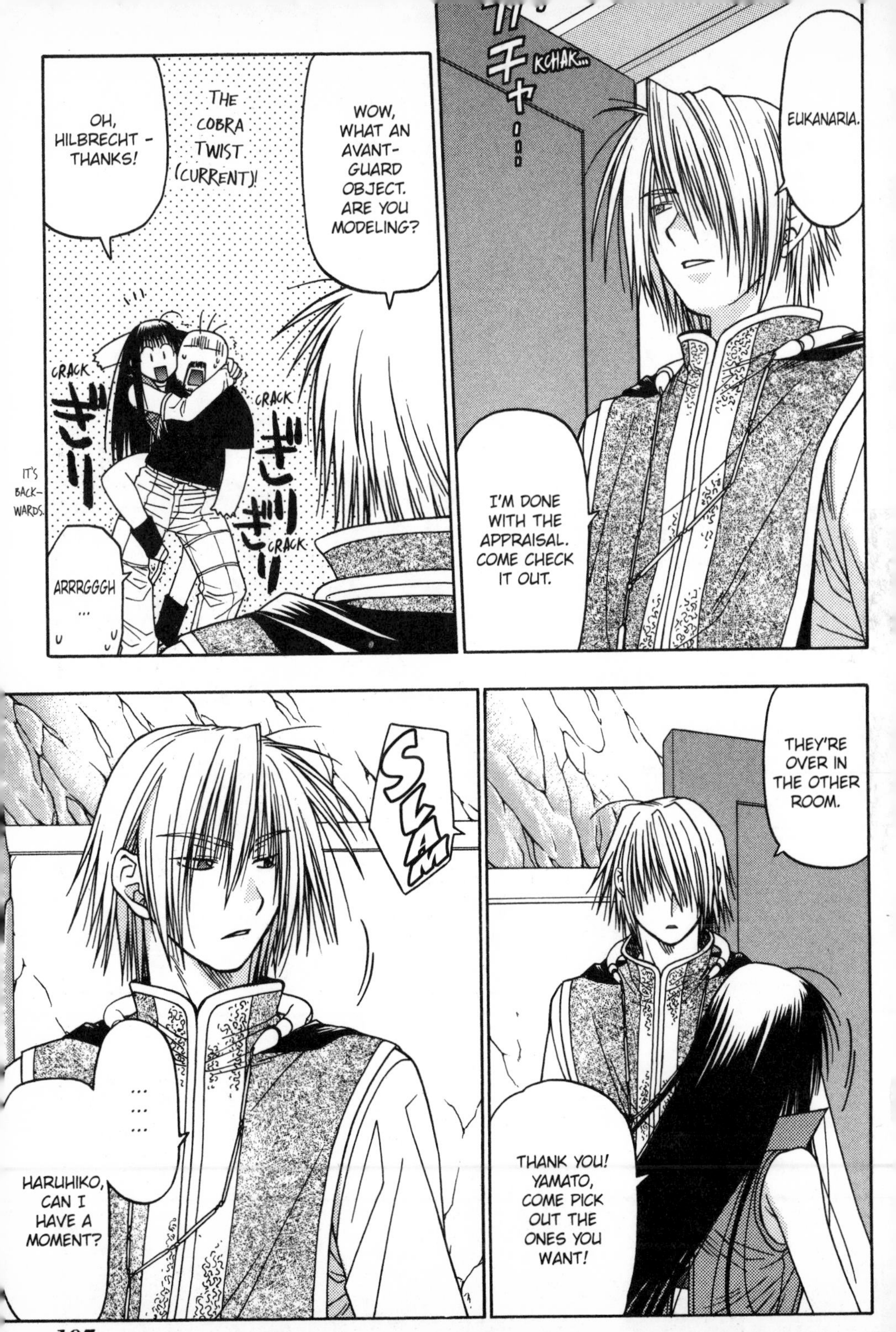
KCHAK...
EUKANARIA.
I'M DONE WITH THE APPRAISAL. COME CHECK IT OUT.
WOW, WHAT AN AVANT-GUARD OBJECT. ARE YOU MODELING?
THE COBRA TWIST (CURRENT)!
OH, HILBRECHT - THANKS!
CRACK
CRACK
CRACK
ARRRGGGH ...
IT'S BACKWARDS.
THEY'RE OVER IN THE OTHER ROOM.
THANK YOU! YAMATO, COME PICK OUT THE ONES YOU WANT!
SLAM
... ...
HARUHIKO, CAN I HAVE A MOMENT?

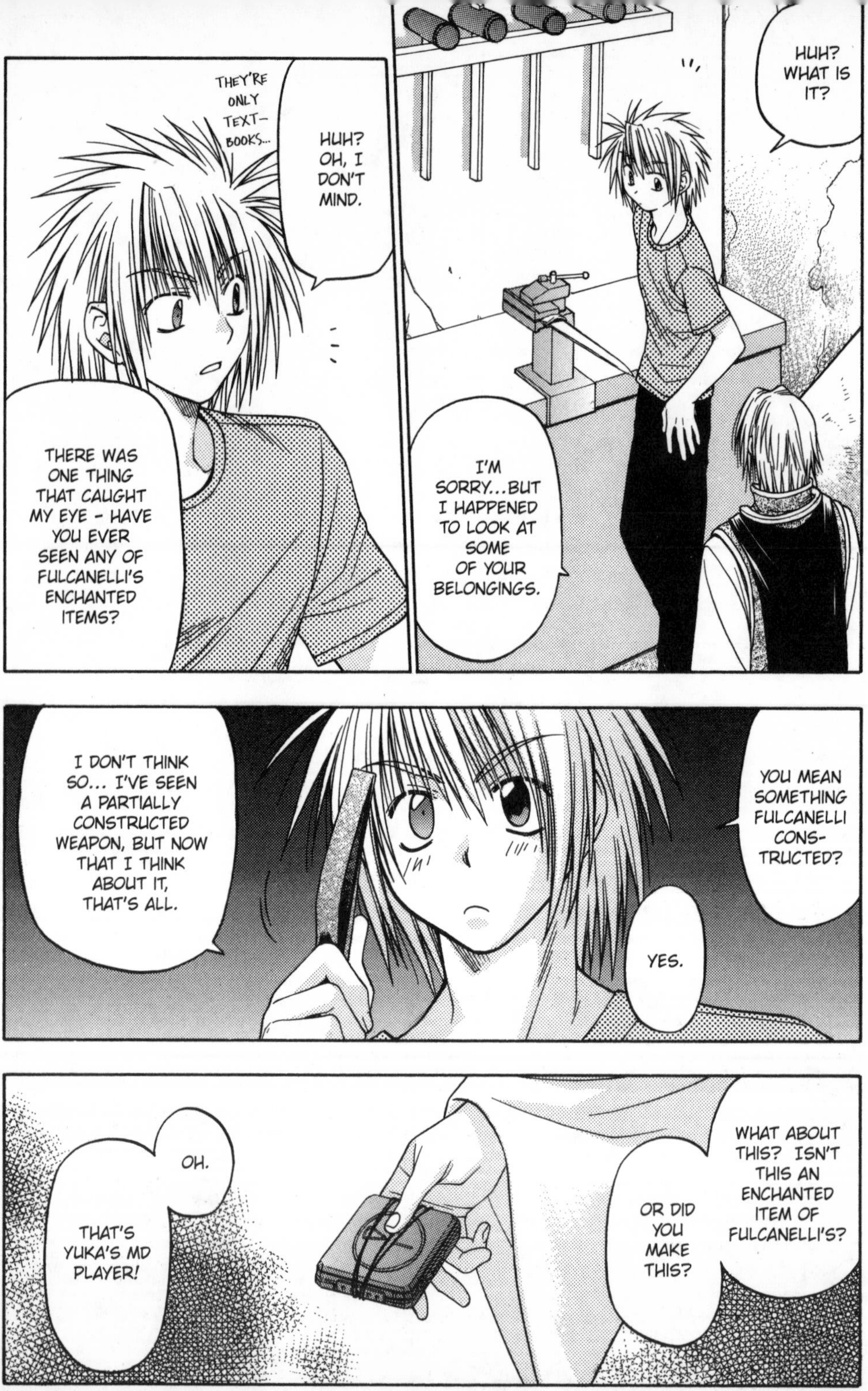
HUH? WHAT IS IT?
I'M SORRY...BUT I HAPPENED TO LOOK AT SOME OF YOUR BELONGINGS.
THEY'RE ONLY TEXT-BOOKS...
HUH? OH, I DON'T MIND.
THERE WAS ONE THING THAT CAUGHT MY EYE - HAVE YOU EVER SEEN ANY OF FULCANELLI'S ENCHANTED ITEMS?
YOU MEAN SOMETHING FULCANELLI CONS-TRUCTED?
YES.
I DON'T THINK SO... I'VE SEEN A PARTIALLY CONSTRUCTED WEAPON, BUT NOW THAT I THINK ABOUT IT, THAT'S ALL.
WHAT ABOUT THIS? ISN'T THIS AN ENCHANTED ITEM OF FULCANELLI'S?
OR DID YOU MAKE THIS?
OH.
THAT'S YUKA'S MD PLAYER!

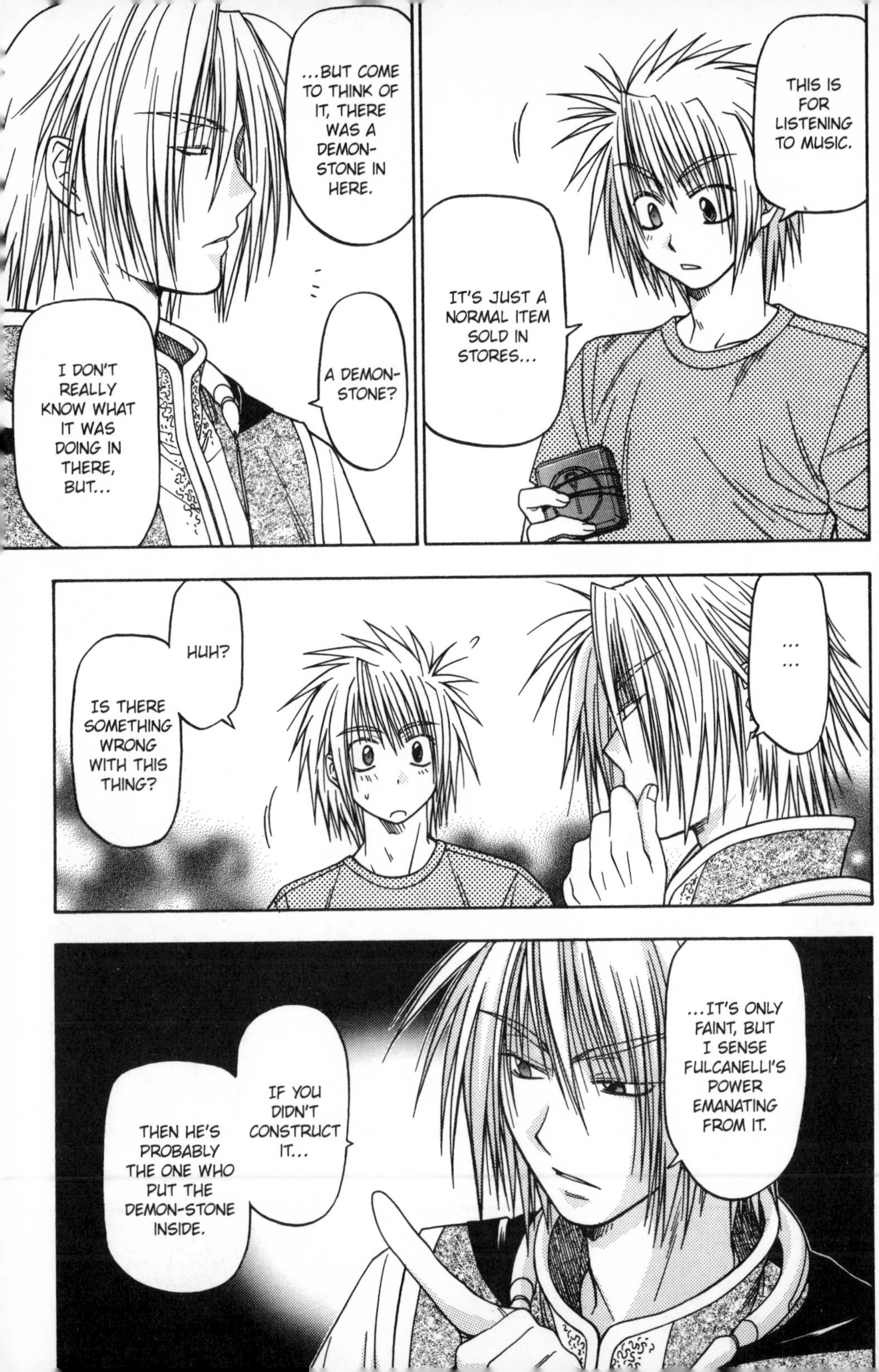
THIS IS FOR LISTENING TO MUSIC.
IT'S JUST A NORMAL ITEM SOLD IN STORES...
...BUT COME TO THINK OF IT, THERE WAS A DEMON-STONE IN HERE.
A DEMON-STONE?
I DON'T REALLY KNOW WHAT IT WAS DOING IN THERE, BUT...
......
HUH? IS THERE SOMETHING WRONG WITH THIS THING?
...IT'S ONLY FAINT, BUT I SENSE FULCANELLI'S POWER EMANATING FROM IT.
IF YOU DIDN'T CONSTRUCT IT...
THEN HE'S PROBABLY THE ONE WHO PUT THE DEMON-STONE INSIDE.

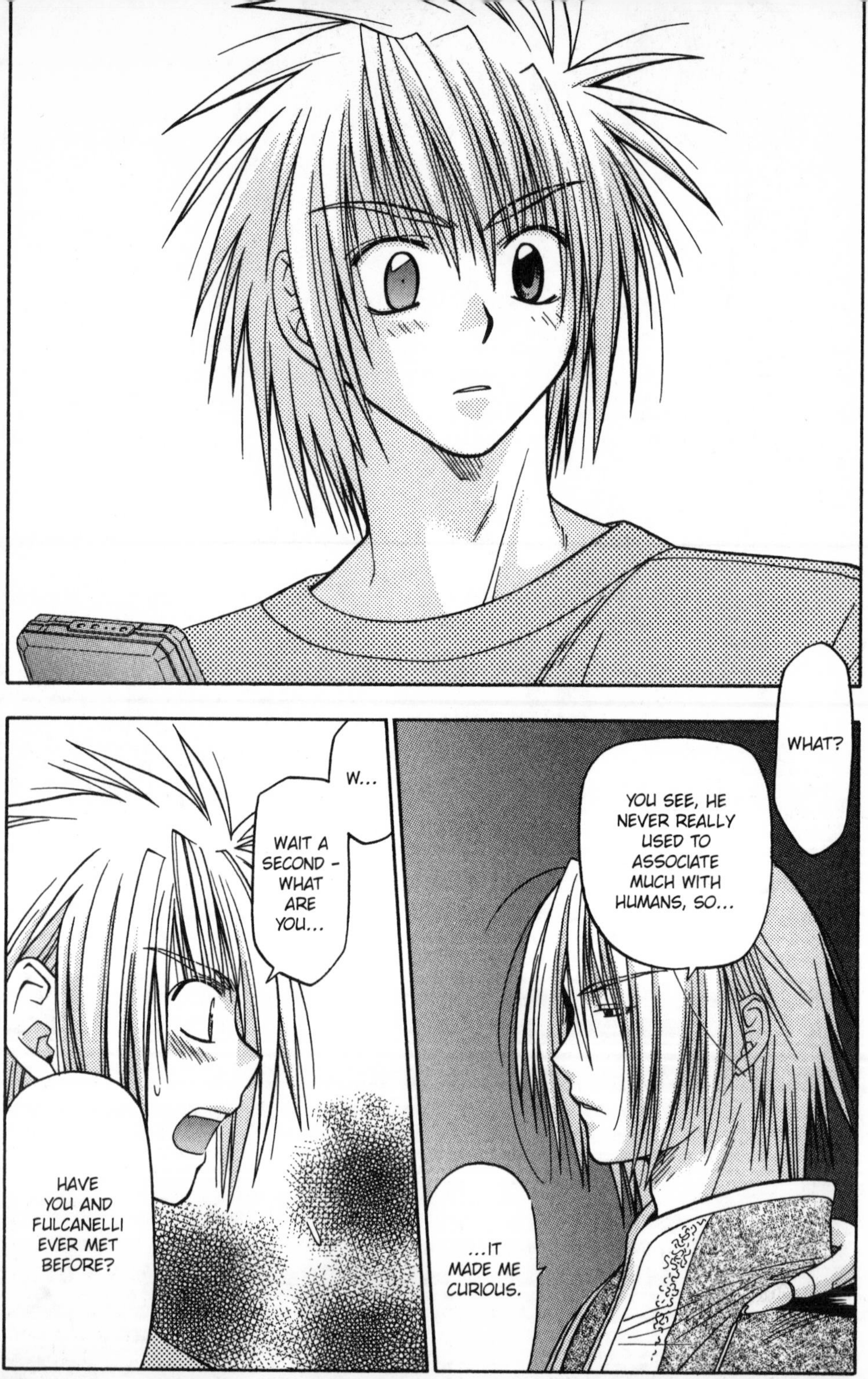
WHAT?
YOU SEE, HE NEVER REALLY USED TO ASSOCIATE MUCH WITH HUMANS, SO...
...IT MADE ME CURIOUS.
W...
WAIT A SECOND - WHAT ARE YOU...
HAVE YOU AND FULCANELLI EVER MET BEFORE?

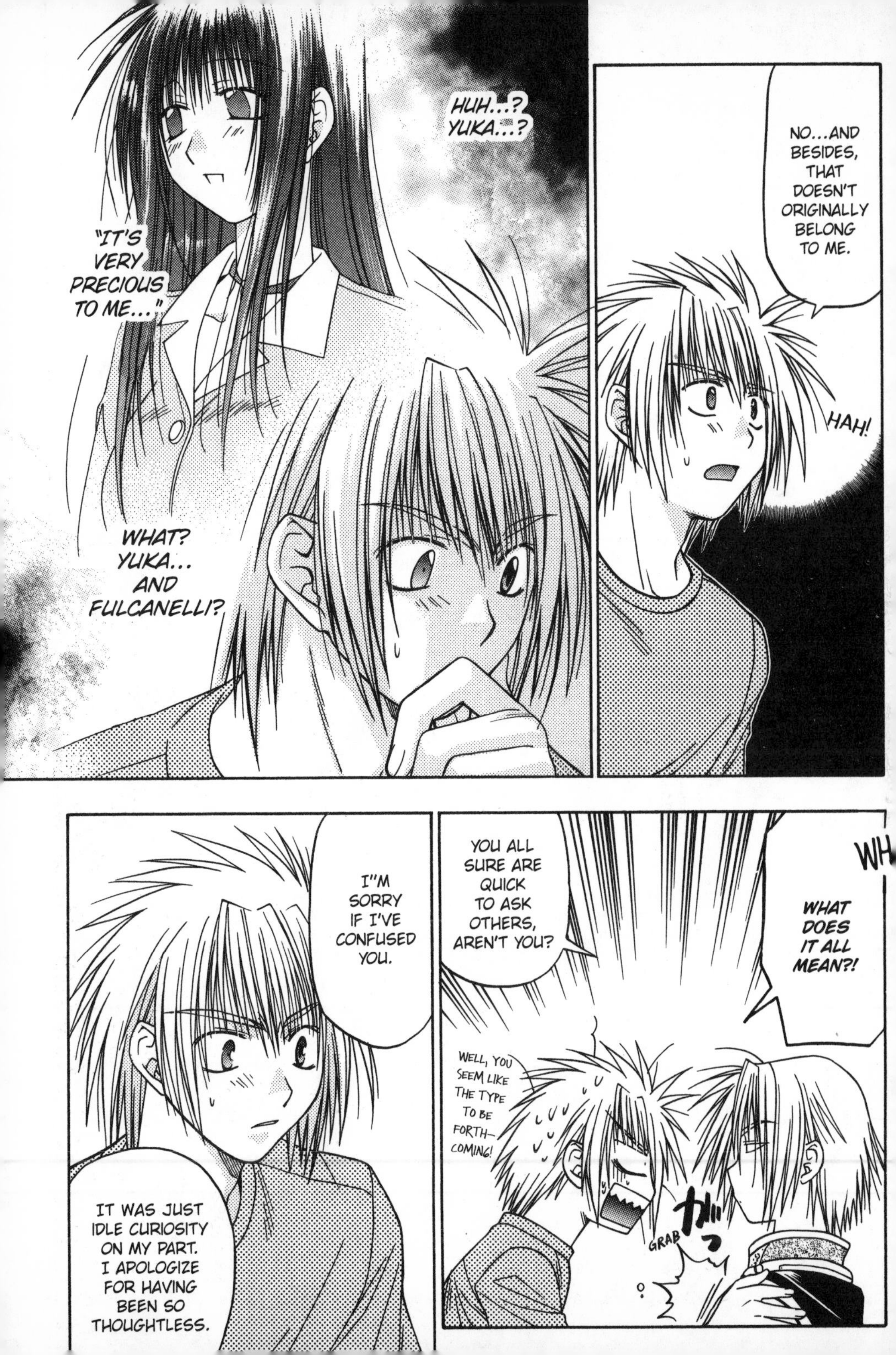
NO...AND BESIDES, THAT DOESN'T ORIGINALLY BELONG TO ME.
HAH!
HUH...? YUKA...?
"IT'S VERY PRECIOUS TO ME..."
WHAT? YUKA... AND FULCANELLI?
WH
WHAT DOES IT ALL MEAN?!
YOU ALL SURE ARE QUICK TO ASK OTHERS, AREN'T YOU?
WELL, YOU SEEM LIKE THE TYPE TO BE FORTH-COMING!
GRAB
I'M SORRY IF I'VE CONFUSED YOU.
IT WAS JUST IDLE CURIOSITY ON MY PART. I APOLOGIZE FOR HAVING BEEN SO THOUGHTLESS.

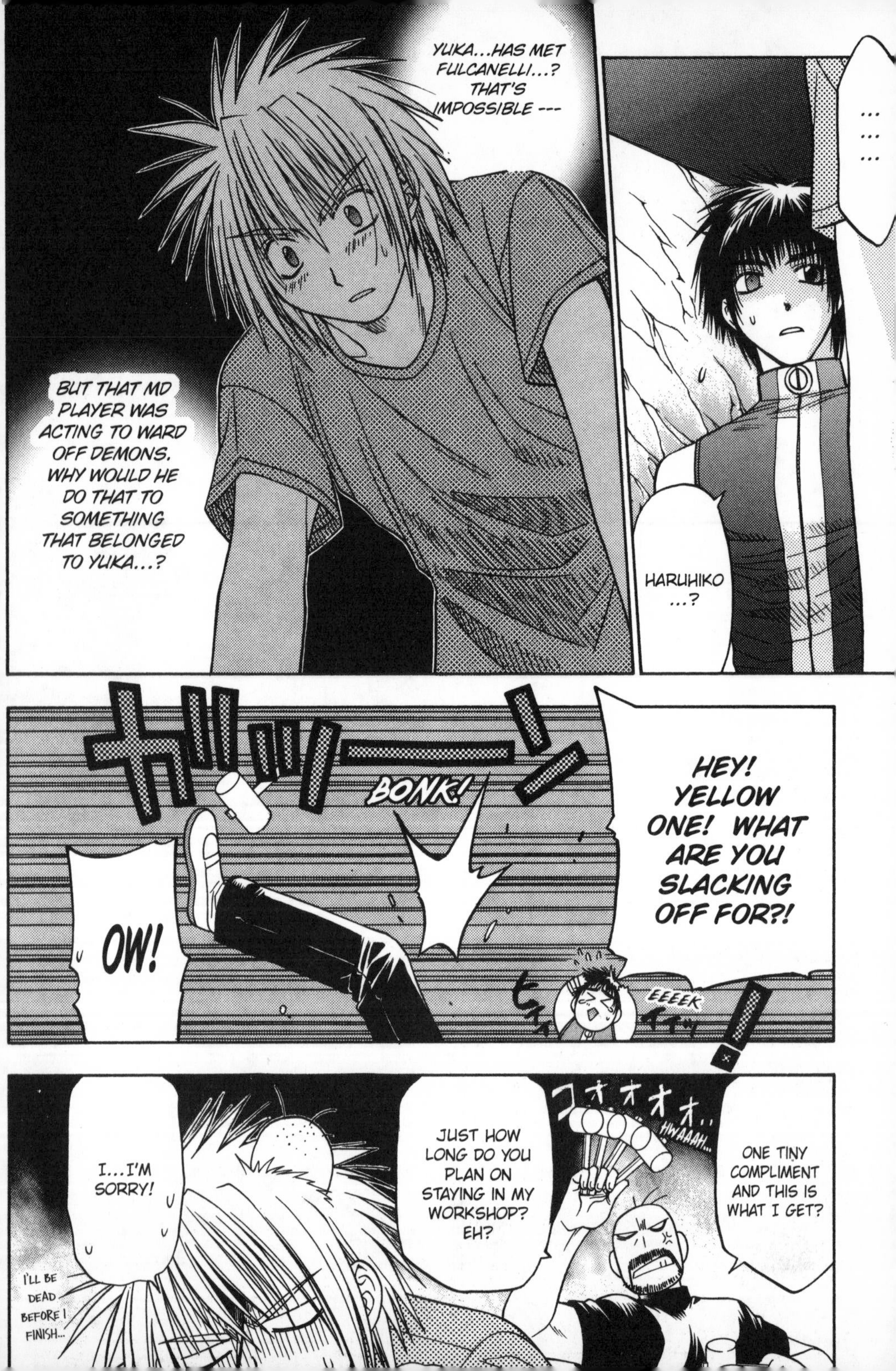

... ...
HARUHIKO ...?
YUKA...HAS MET FULCANELLI...? THAT'S IMPOSSIBLE ---
BUT THAT MD PLAYER WAS ACTING TO WARD OFF DEMONS. WHY WOULD HE DO THAT TO SOMETHING THAT BELONGED TO YUKA...?
HEY! YELLOW ONE! WHAT ARE YOU SLACKING OFF FOR?!
BONK!
OW!
EEEEK
ONE TINY COMPLIMENT AND THIS IS WHAT I GET?
HWAAAH...
JUST HOW LONG DO YOU PLAN ON STAYING IN MY WORKSHOP? EH?
I...I'M SORRY!
I'LL BE DEAD BEFORE I FINISH...

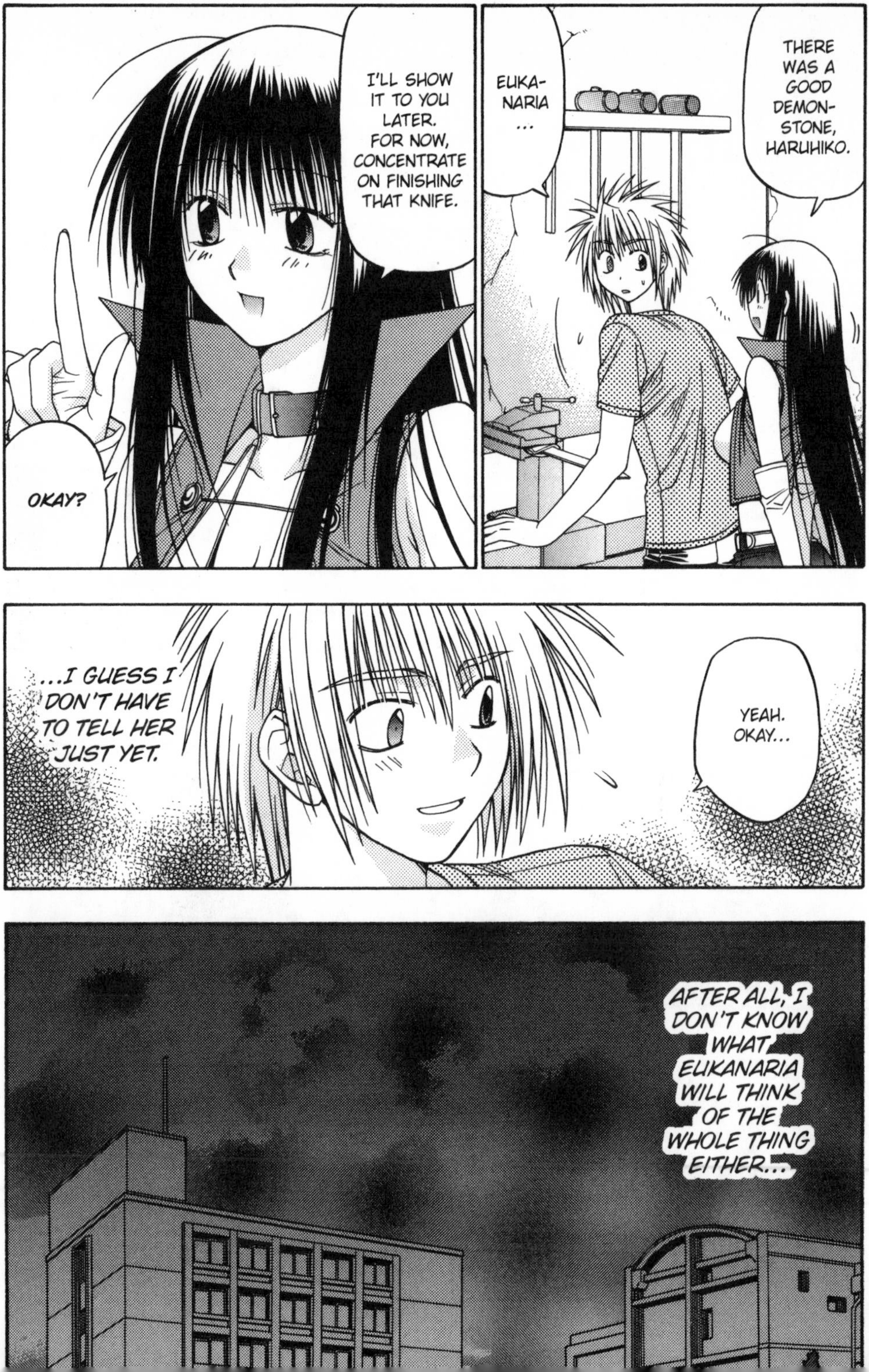
THERE WAS A GOOD DEMON-STONE, HARUHIKO.
EUKA-NARIA ...
I'LL SHOW IT TO YOU LATER. FOR NOW, CONCENTRATE ON FINISHING THAT KNIFE.
OKAY?
YEAH. OKAY...
...I GUESS I DON'T HAVE TO TELL HER JUST YET.
AFTER ALL, I DON'T KNOW WHAT EUKANARIA WILL THINK OF THE WHOLE THING EITHER...

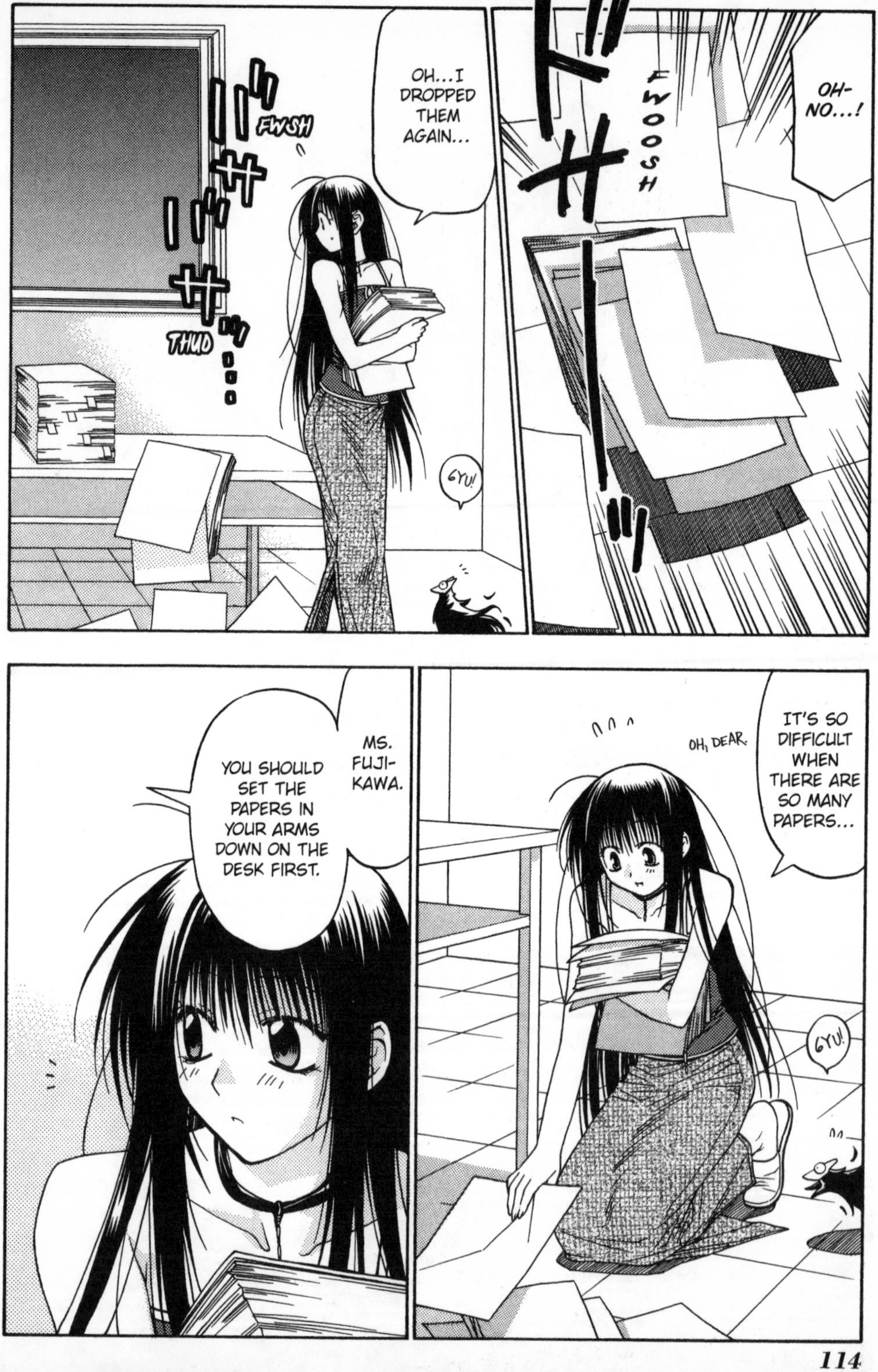
OH-NO...!
FWOOSH
OH...I DROPPED THEM AGAIN...
FWSH
THUD
GYU!
IT'S SO DIFFICULT WHEN THERE ARE SO MANY PAPERS...
OH, DEAR.
GYU!
MS. FUJIKAWA.
YOU SHOULD SET THE PAPERS IN YOUR ARMS DOWN ON THE DESK FIRST.

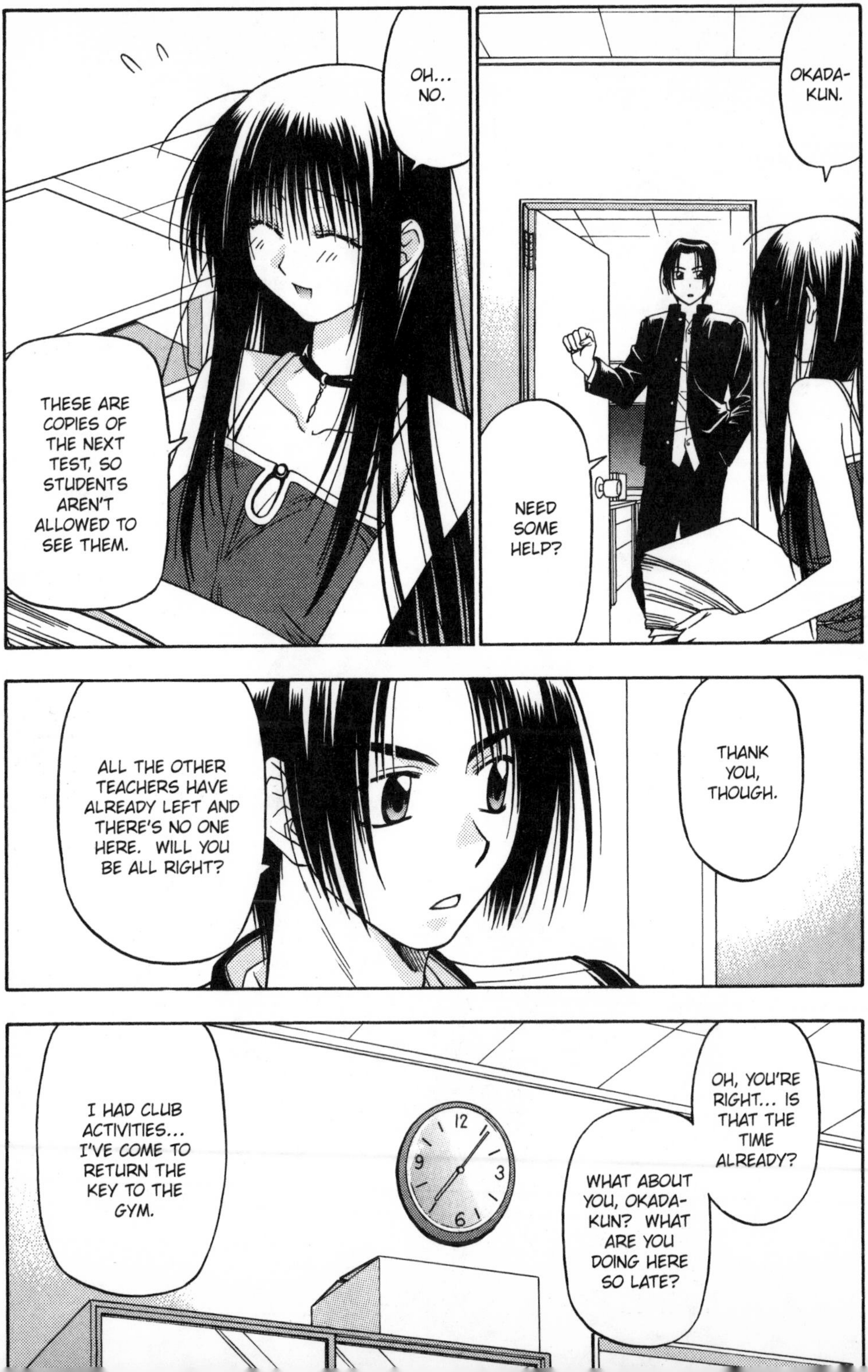
OKADA-KUN.
NEED SOME HELP?
OH... NO.
THESE ARE COPIES OF THE NEXT TEST, SO STUDENTS AREN'T ALLOWED TO SEE THEM.
THANK YOU, THOUGH.
ALL THE OTHER TEACHERS HAVE ALREADY LEFT AND THERE'S NO ONE HERE. WILL YOU BE ALL RIGHT?
OH, YOU'RE RIGHT... IS THAT THE TIME ALREADY?
WHAT ABOUT YOU, OKADA-KUN? WHAT ARE YOU DOING HERE SO LATE?
I HAD CLUB ACTIVITIES... I'VE COME TO RETURN THE KEY TO THE GYM.

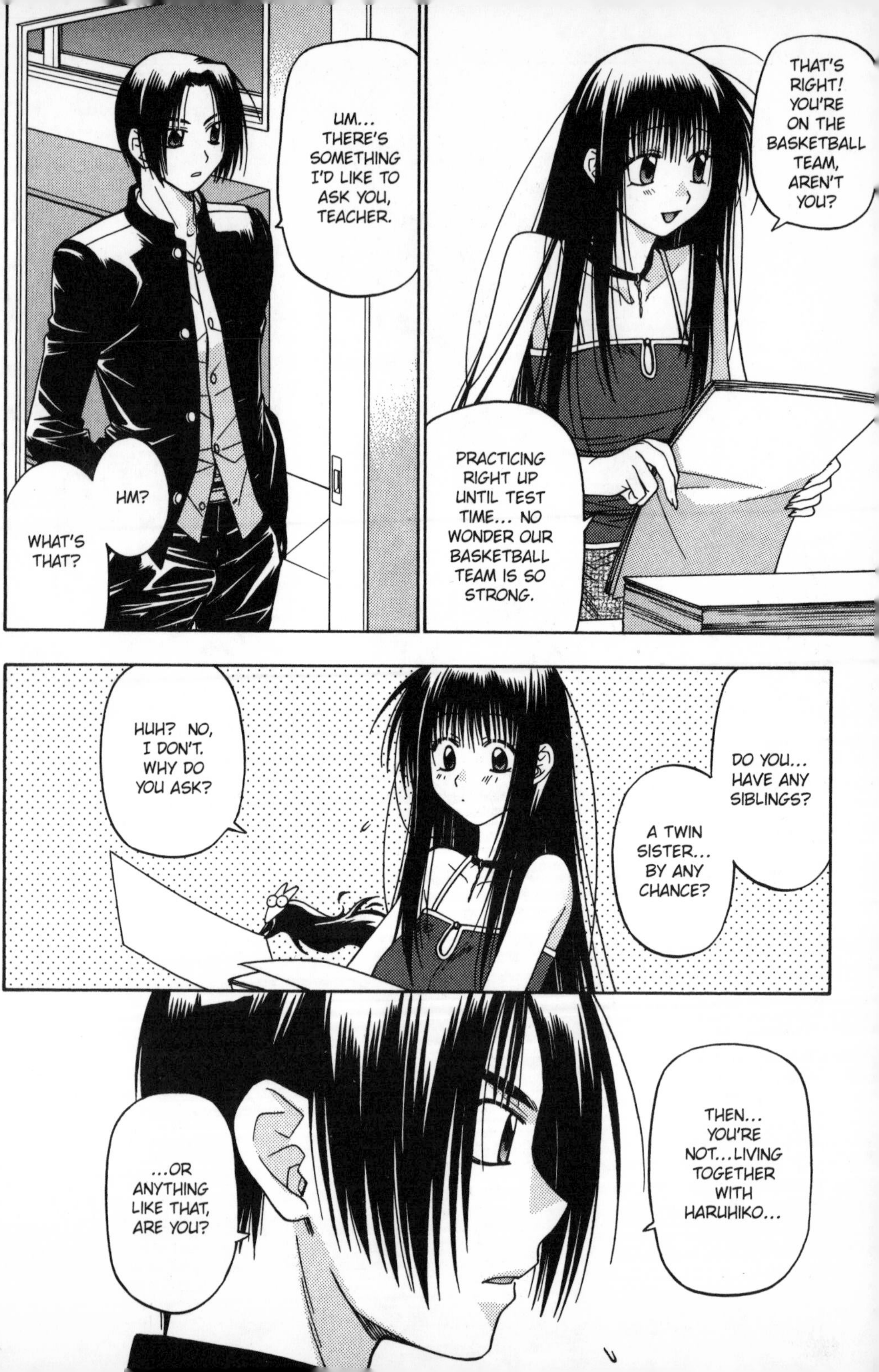
THAT'S RIGHT! YOU'RE ON THE BASKETBALL TEAM, AREN'T YOU?
PRACTICING RIGHT UP UNTIL TEST TIME... NO WONDER OUR BASKETBALL TEAM IS SO STRONG.
UM... THERE'S SOMETHING I'D LIKE TO ASK YOU, TEACHER.
HM?
WHAT'S THAT?
DO YOU... HAVE ANY SIBLINGS?
A TWIN SISTER... BY ANY CHANCE?
HUH? NO, I DON'T. WHY DO YOU ASK?
THEN... YOU'RE NOT...LIVING TOGETHER WITH HARUHIKO...
...OR ANYTHING LIKE THAT, ARE YOU?

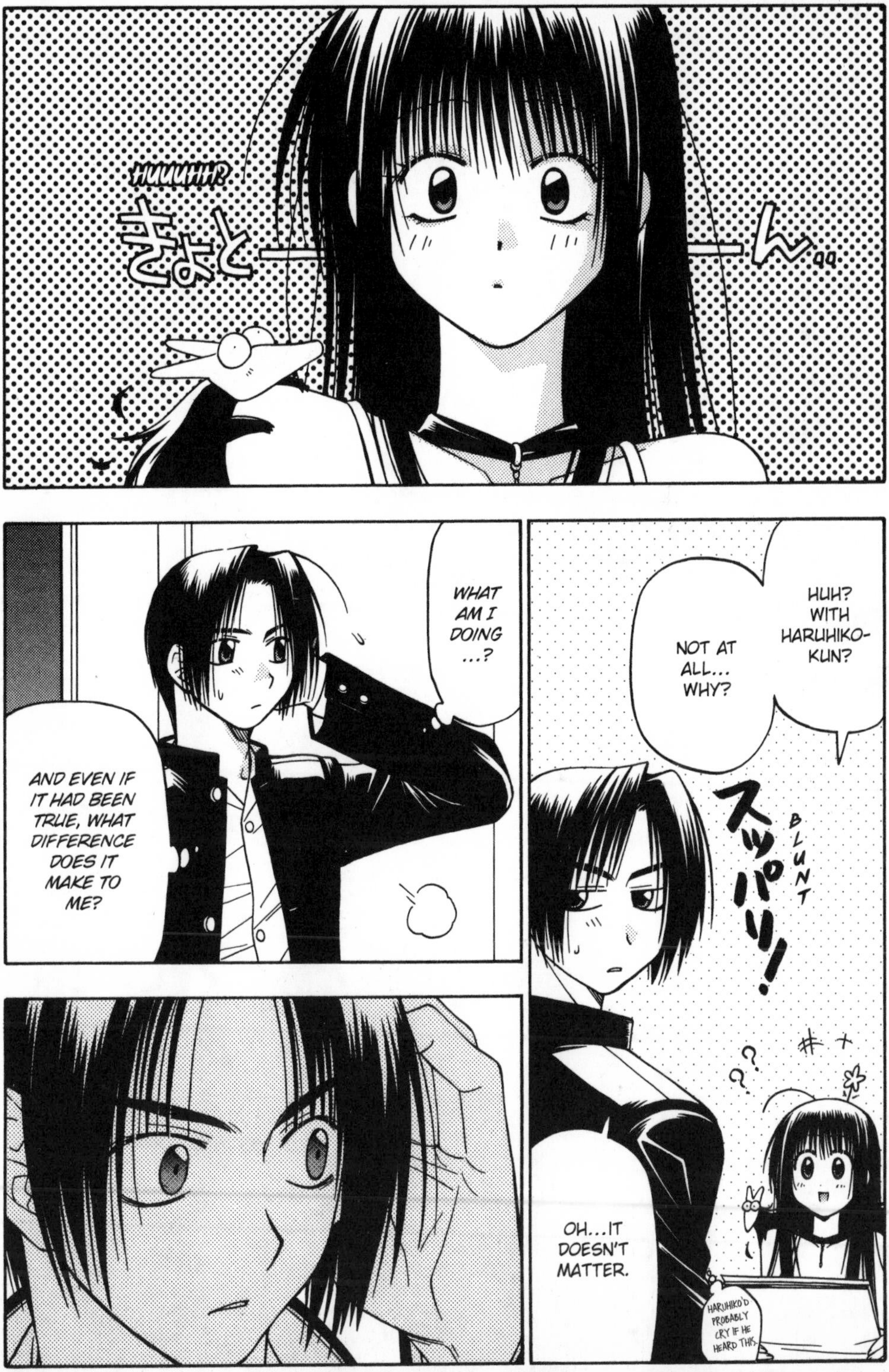
HUUUHH?
きょとーーーん。。
HUH? WITH HARUHIKO-KUN?
NOT AT ALL... WHY?
スッパリ!
BLUNT
OH...IT DOESN'T MATTER.
HARUHIKO'D PROBABLY CRY IF HE HEARD THIS.
WHAT AM I DOING ...?
AND EVEN IF IT HAD BEEN TRUE, WHAT DIFFERENCE DOES IT MAKE TO ME?

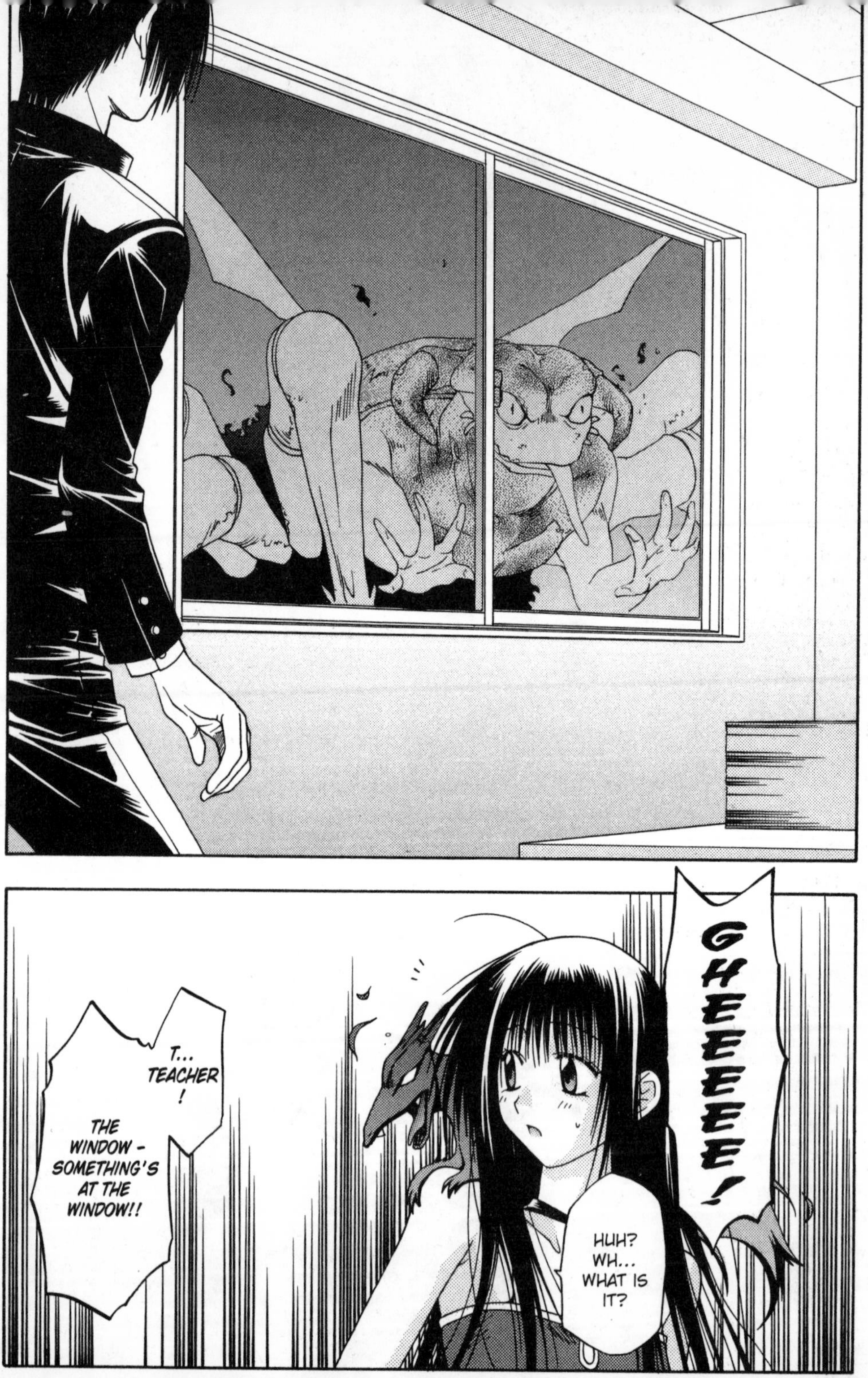
GHEEEEEE!
HUH? WH... WHAT IS IT?
T... TEACHER!
THE WINDOW - SOMETHING'S AT THE WINDOW!!

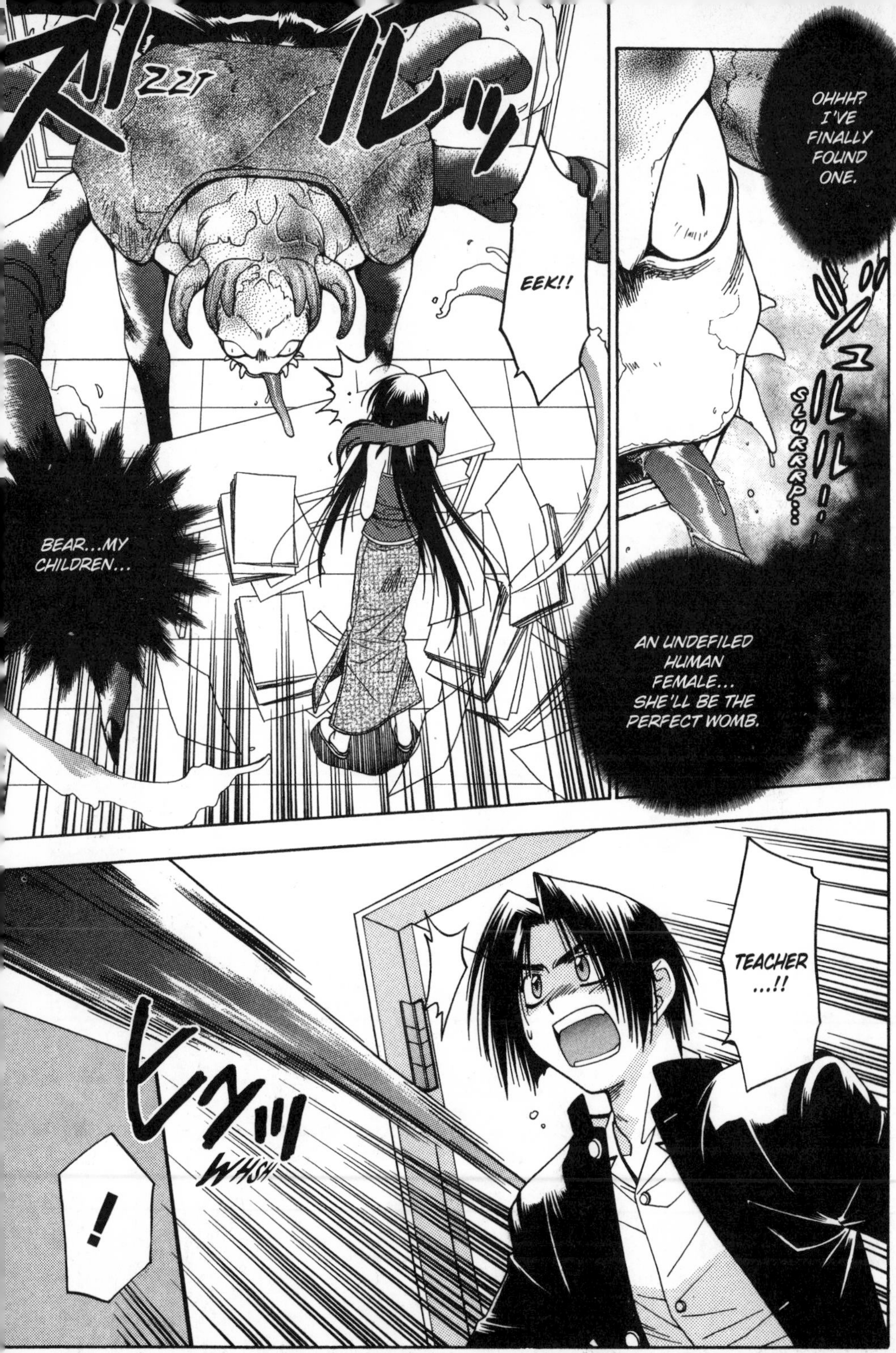
OHHH? I'VE FINALLY FOUND ONE.
SLURRRP...
AN UNDEFILED HUMAN FEMALE... SHE'LL BE THE PERFECT WOMB.
ZZZT
EEK!!
BEAR...MY CHILDREN...
TEACHER ...!!
WHSH
!

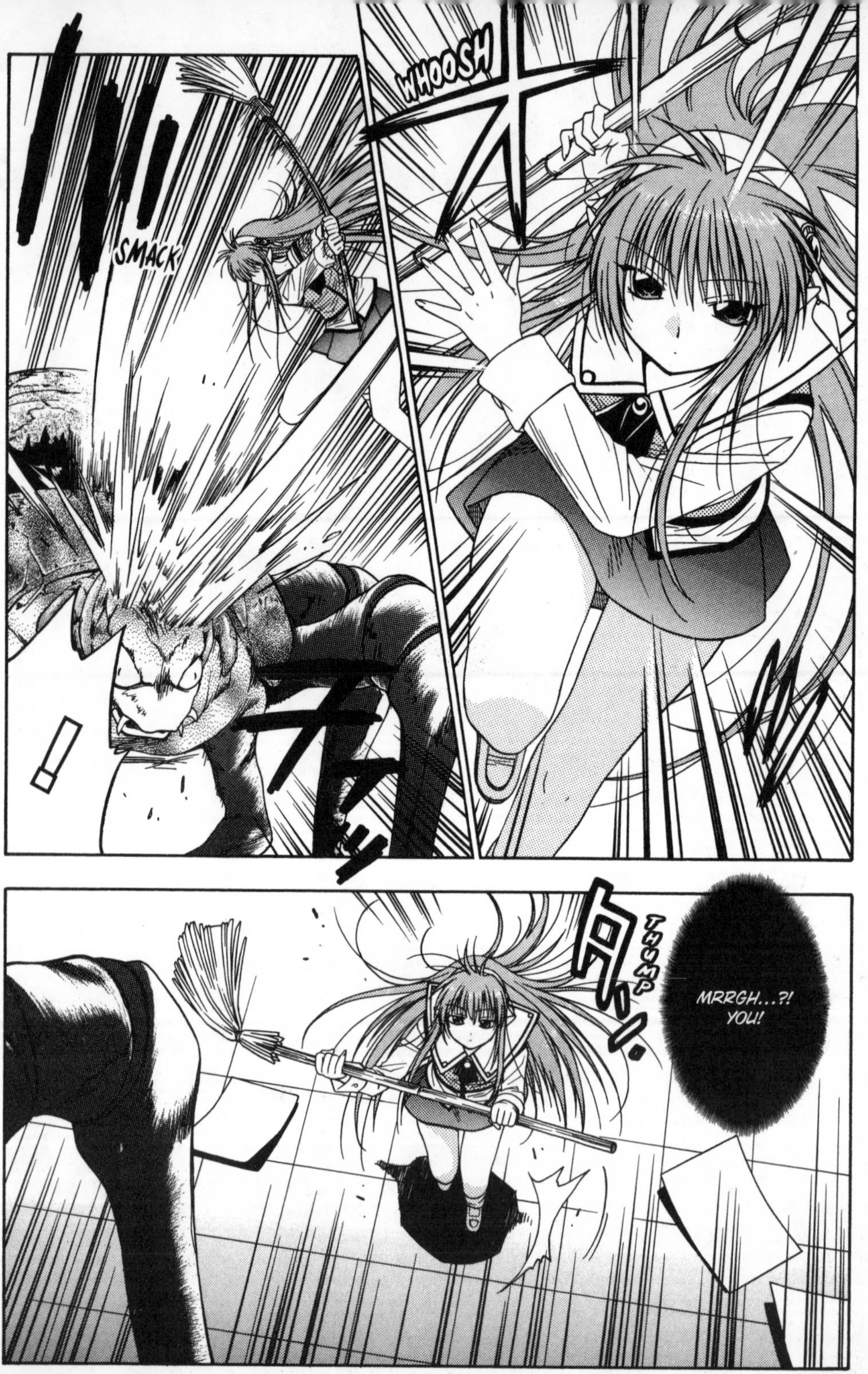
WHOOSH
SMACK
!
THUMP
MRRGH...?! YOU!

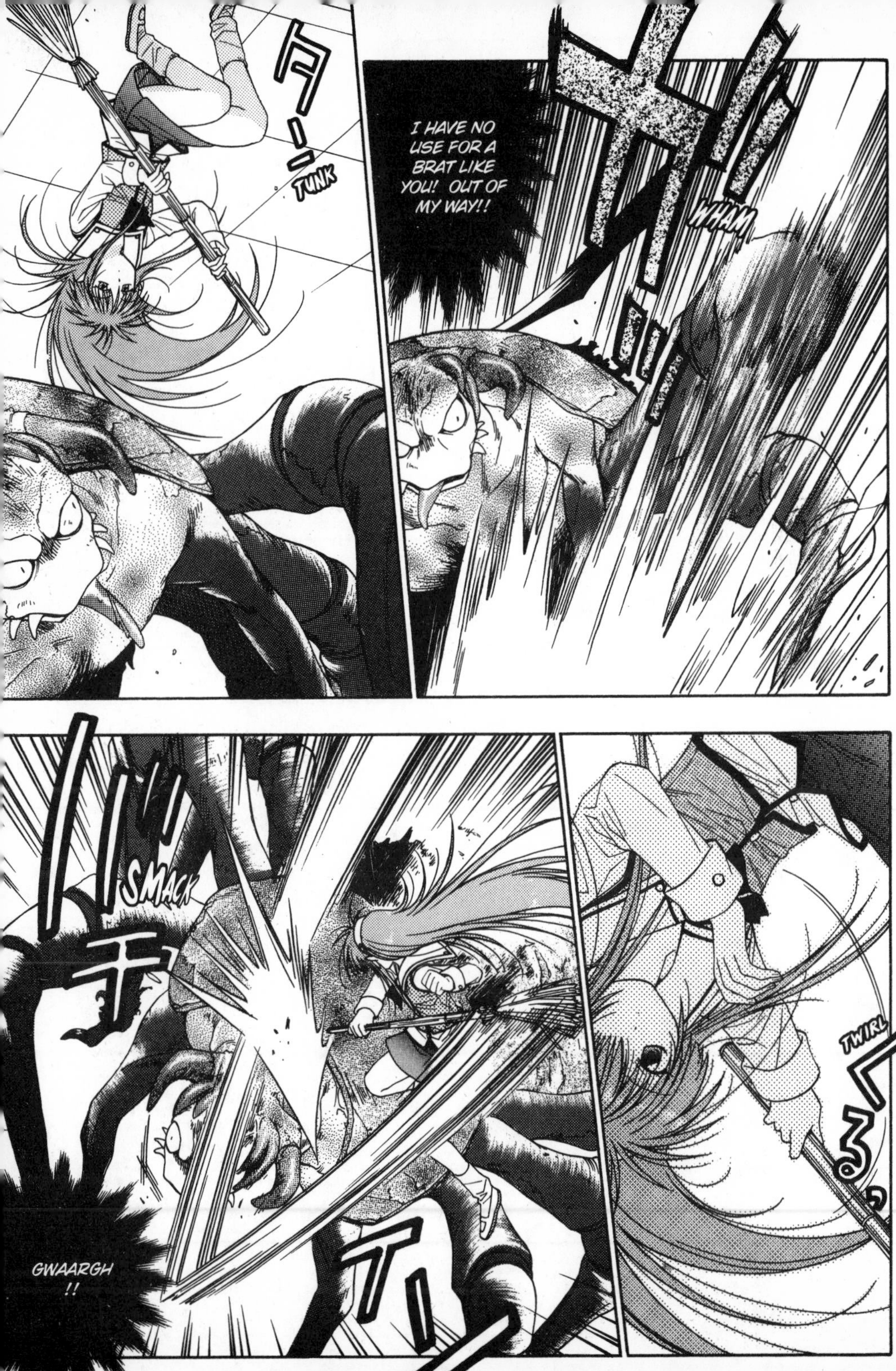
I HAVE NO USE FOR A BRAT LIKE YOU!! OUT OF MY WAY!!
WHAM
TUNK
TWIRL
SMACK
GWAARGH !!

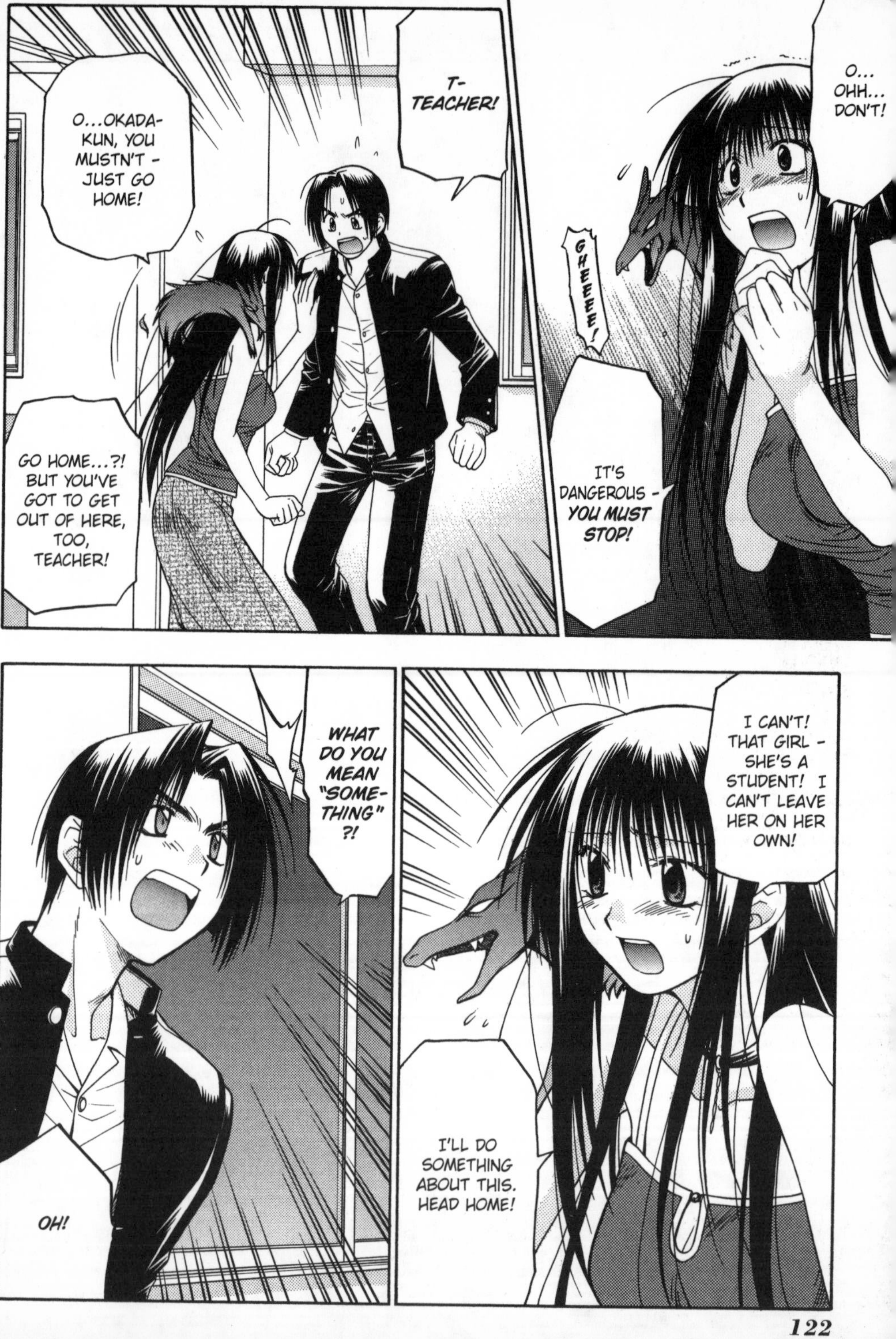
O... OHH... DON'T!
GHEEEEE!
IT'S DANGEROUS - YOU MUST STOP!
T- TEACHER!
O...OKADA-KUN, YOU MUSTN'T - JUST GO HOME!
GO HOME...?! BUT YOU'VE GOT TO GET OUT OF HERE, TOO, TEACHER!
I CAN'T! THAT GIRL - SHE'S A STUDENT! I CAN'T LEAVE HER ON HER OWN!
I'LL DO SOMETHING ABOUT THIS. HEAD HOME!
WHAT DO YOU MEAN "SOMETHING"?!
OH!

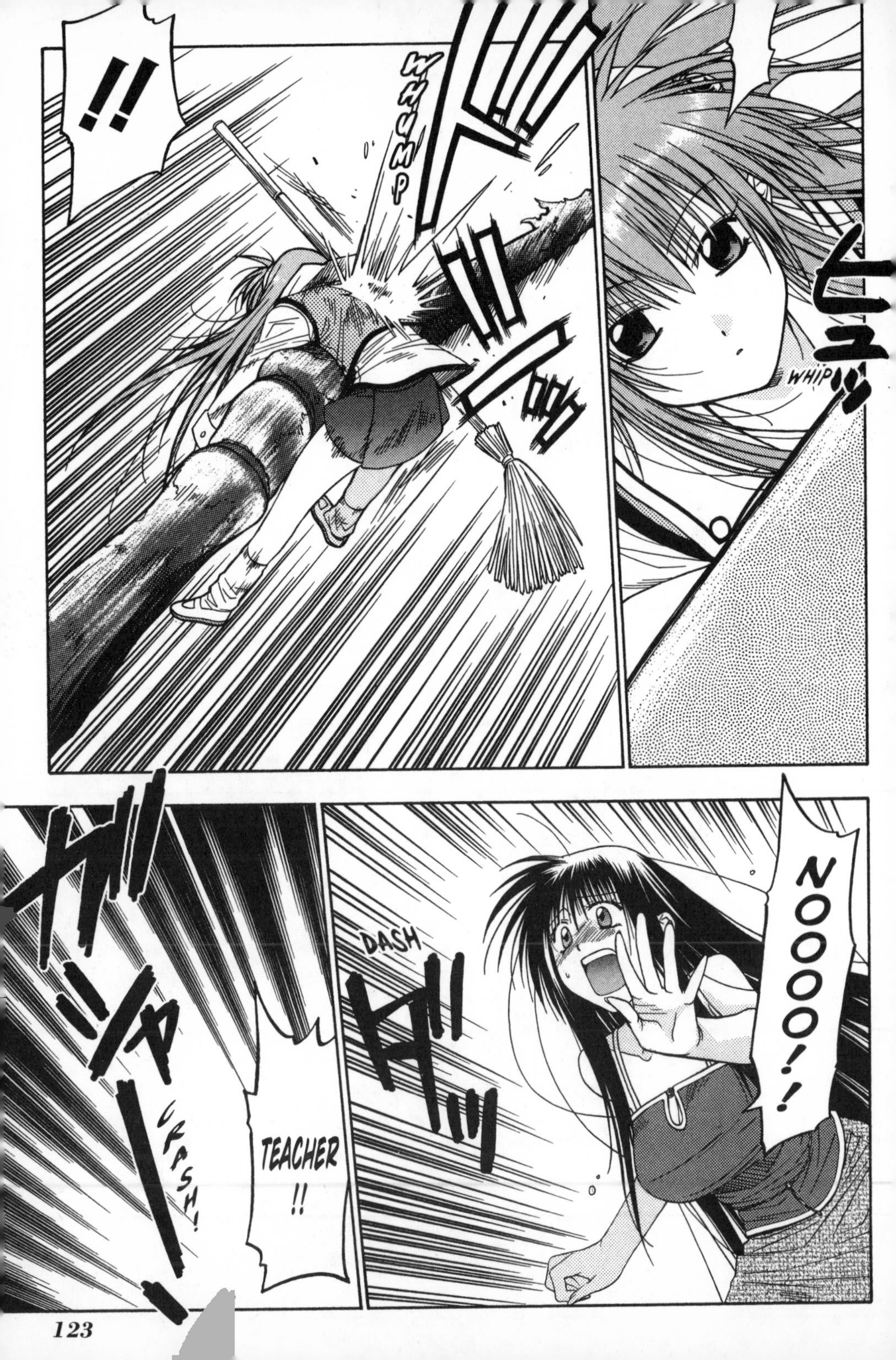
WHIP
!!
WHUMP
NOOOOO!!
DASH
TEACHER !!
CRASH!

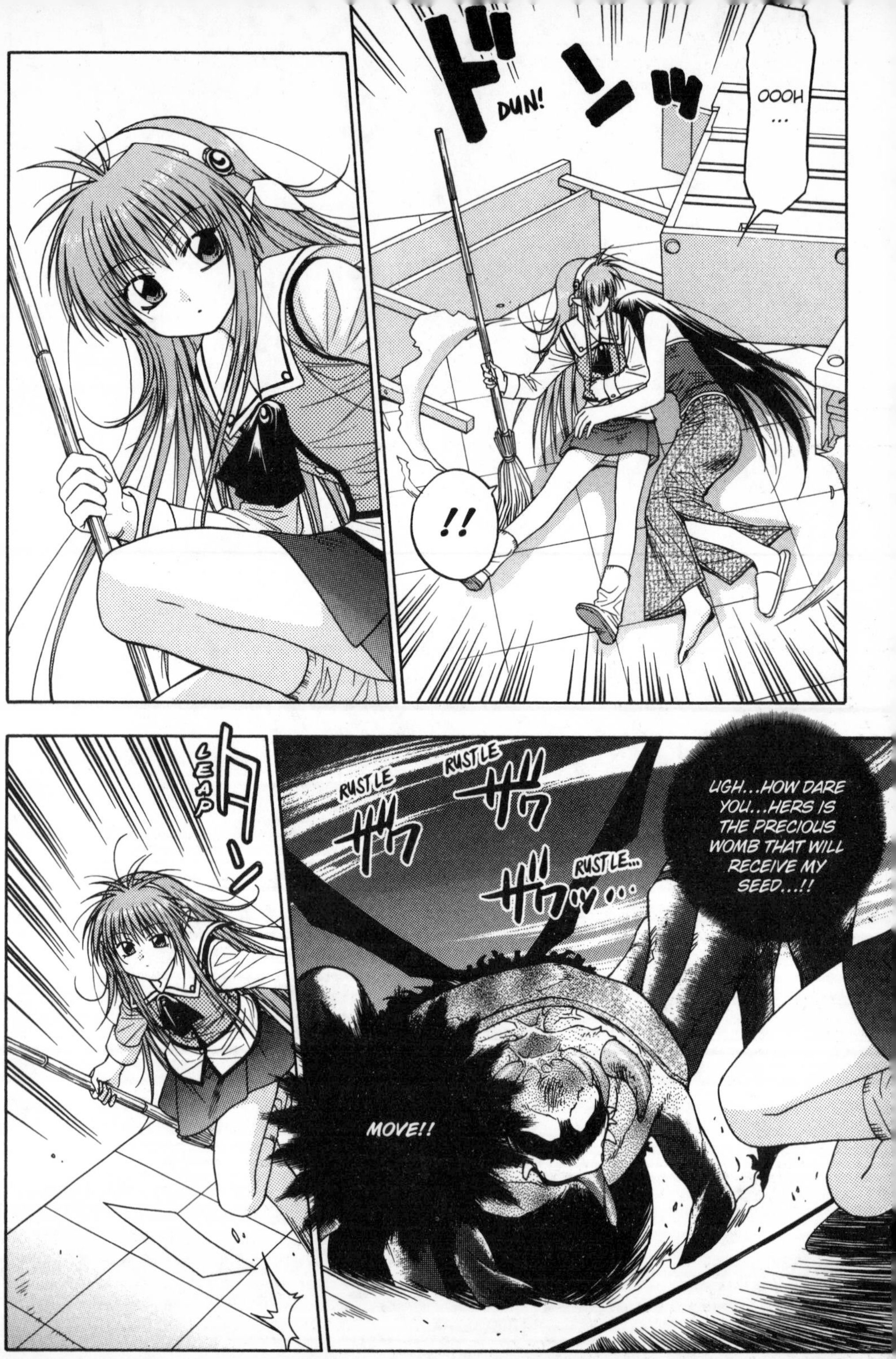

OOOH ...
ドンッ
DUN!
!!
UGH...HOW DARE YOU...HERS IS THE PRECIOUS WOMB THAT WILL RECEIVE MY SEED...!!
RUSTLE
ザワ
RUSTLE
ザワ
RUSTLE...
ザワッ...
MOVE!!
タンッ
LEAP

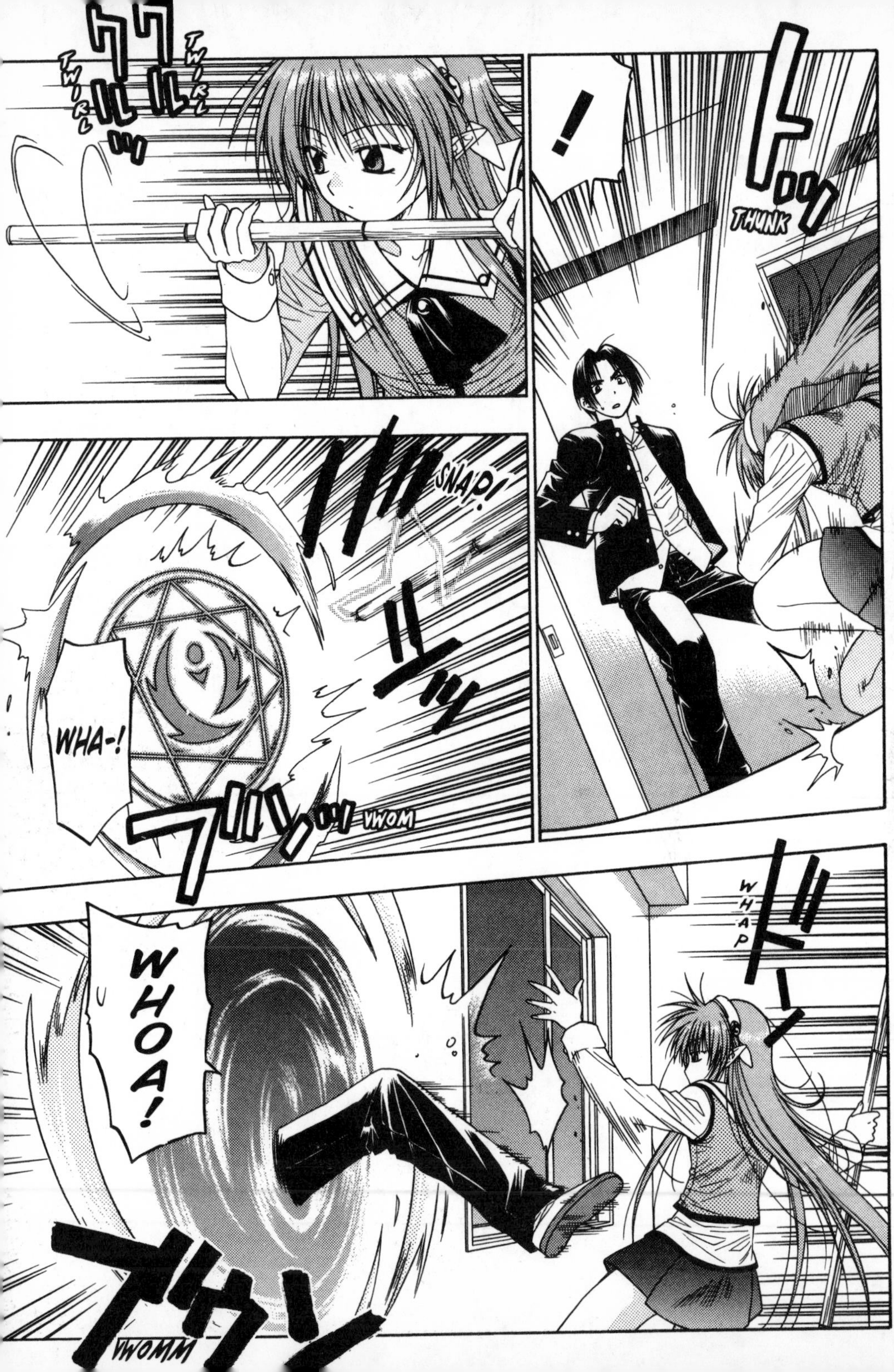
!
THUNK
TWIRL TWIRL
SNAP!
WHA-!
VWOM
WHAP
WHOA!
VWOMM

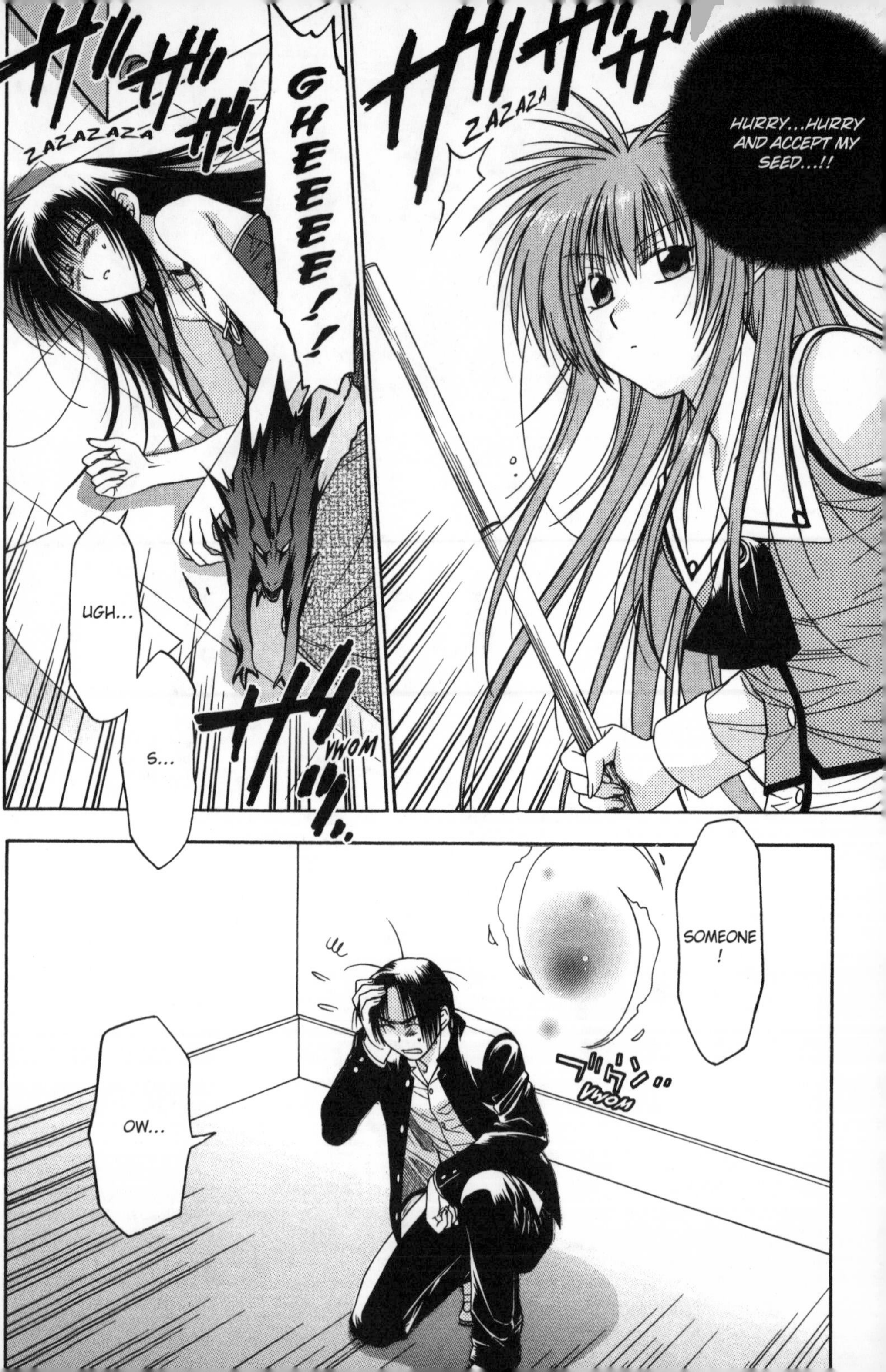
ZAZAZA
HURRY...HURRY AND ACCEPT MY SEED...!!
ZAZAZAZA
GHEEEEEE!!
UGH...
S...
VWOM
SOMEONE!
VWOM
OW...

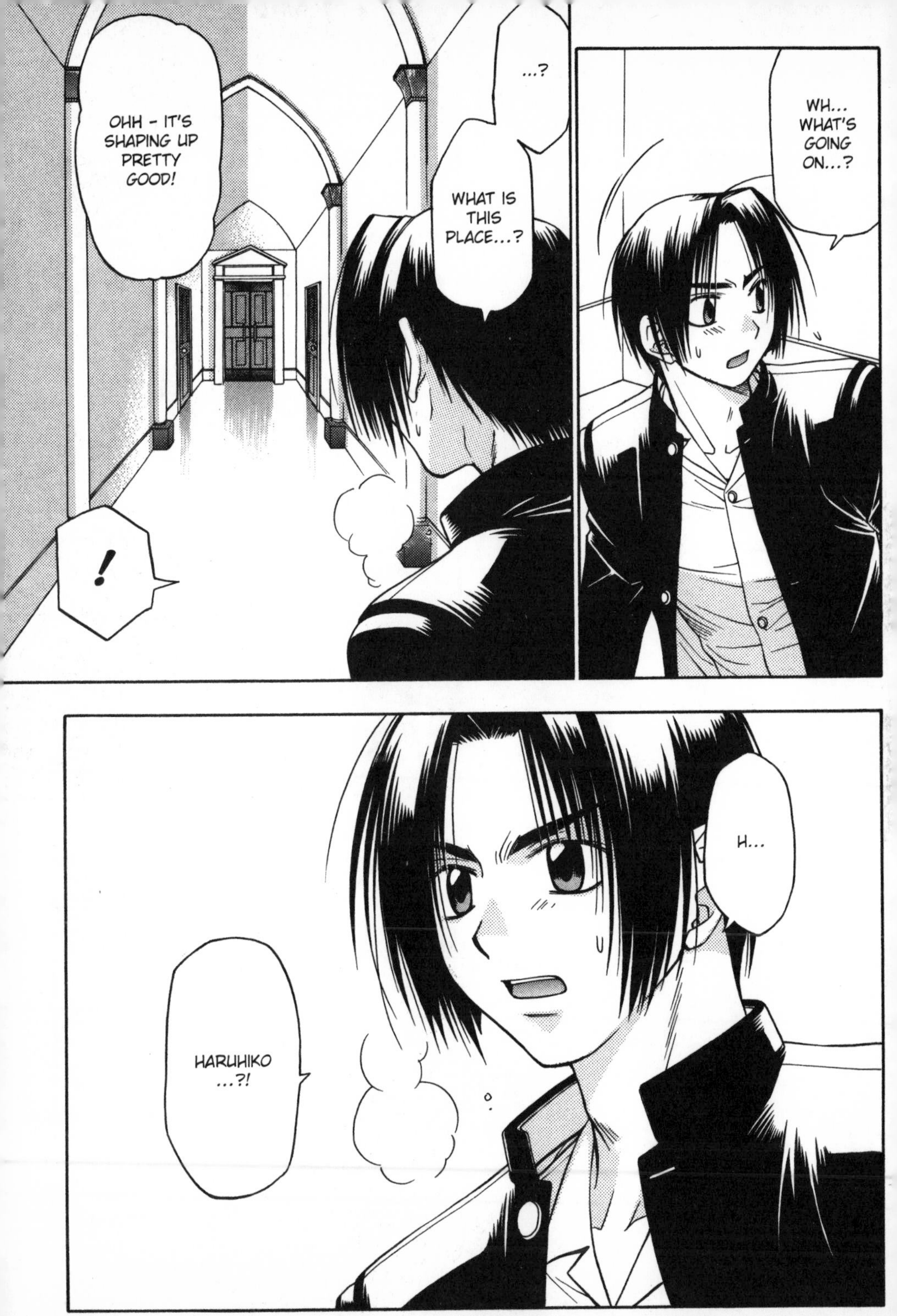
WH... WHAT'S GOING ON...?
...?
WHAT IS THIS PLACE...?
OHH - IT'S SHAPING UP PRETTY GOOD!
!
H...
HARUHIKO ...?!

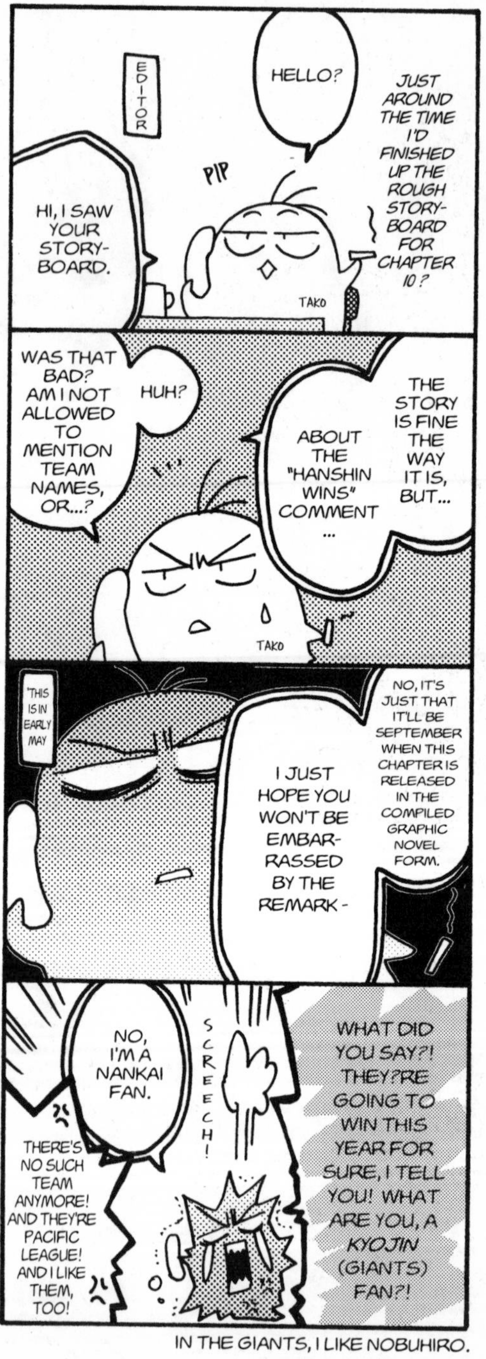
JUST AROUND THE TIME I'D FINISHED UP THE ROUGH STORY-BOARD FOR CHAPTER 10?
HELLO?
PIP
EDITOR
HI, I SAW YOUR STORY-BOARD.
TAKO
THE STORY IS FINE THE WAY IT IS, BUT...
ABOUT THE "HANSHIN WINS" COMMENT ...
HUH?
WAS THAT BAD? AM I NOT ALLOWED TO MENTION TEAM NAMES, OR...?
TAKO
NO, IT'S JUST THAT IT'LL BE SEPTEMBER WHEN THIS CHAPTER IS RELEASED IN THE COMPILED GRAPHIC NOVEL FORM.
I JUST HOPE YOU WON'T BE EMBAR-RASSED BY THE REMARK -
*THIS IS IN EARLY MAY
WHAT DID YOU SAY?! THEY?RE GOING TO WIN THIS YEAR FOR SURE, I TELL YOU! WHAT ARE YOU, A *KYOJIN* (GIANTS) FAN?!
SCREECH!
NO, I'M A NANKAI FAN.
THERE'S NO SUCH TEAM ANYMORE! AND THEY'RE PACIFIC LEAGUE! AND I LIKE THEM, TOO!
IN THE GIANTS, I LIKE NOBUHIRO.

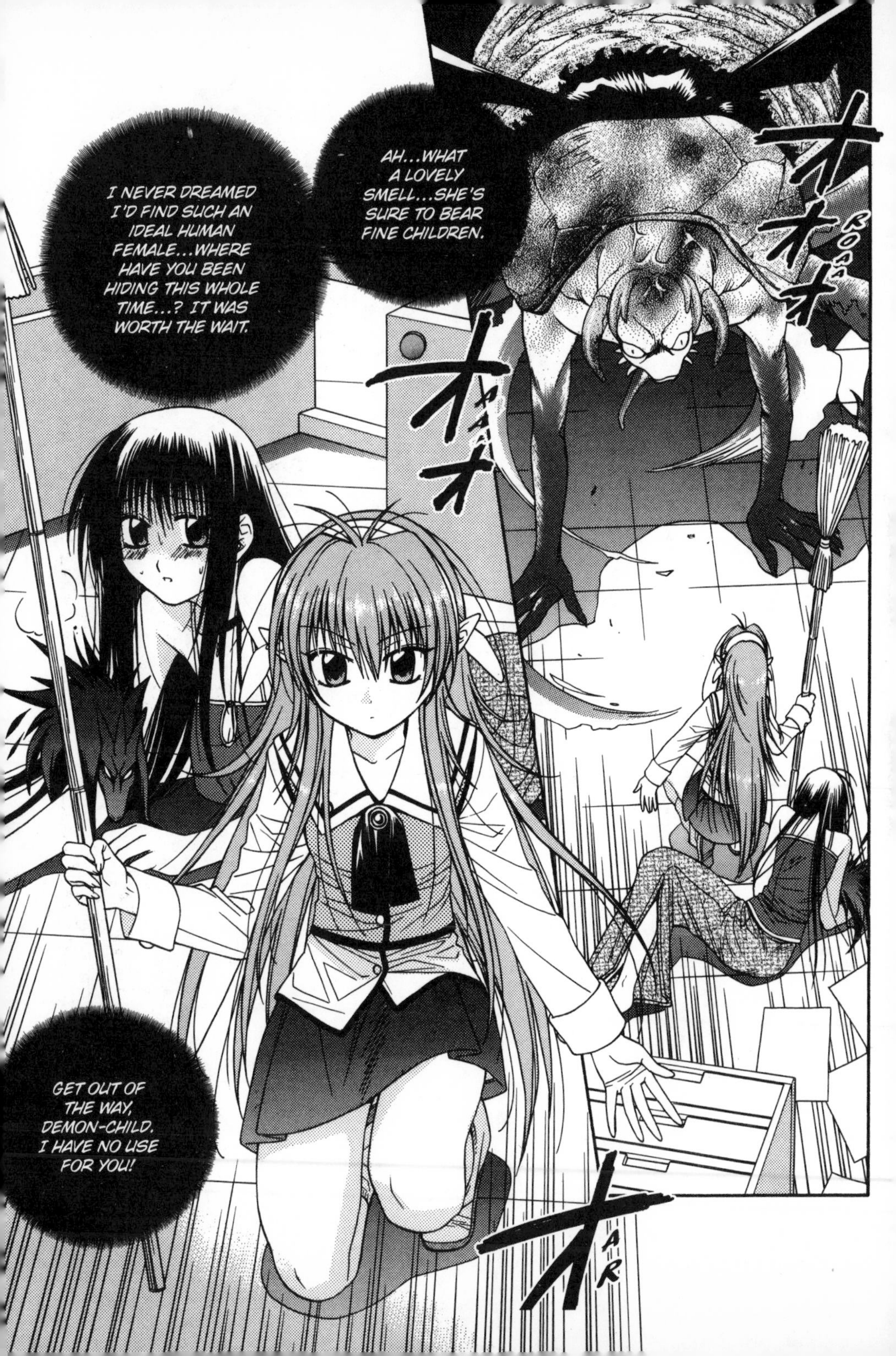
ROAA
AH...WHAT A LOVELY SMELL...SHE'S SURE TO BEAR FINE CHILDREN.
I NEVER DREAMED I'D FIND SUCH AN IDEAL HUMAN FEMALE...WHERE HAVE YOU BEEN HIDING THIS WHOLE TIME...? IT WAS WORTH THE WAIT.
GET OUT OF THE WAY, DEMON-CHILD. I HAVE NO USE FOR YOU!
AR

エンチャント
enchant. 11

騎士(きし)の憂鬱(ゆううつ)

A KNIGHT'S MELANCHOLY

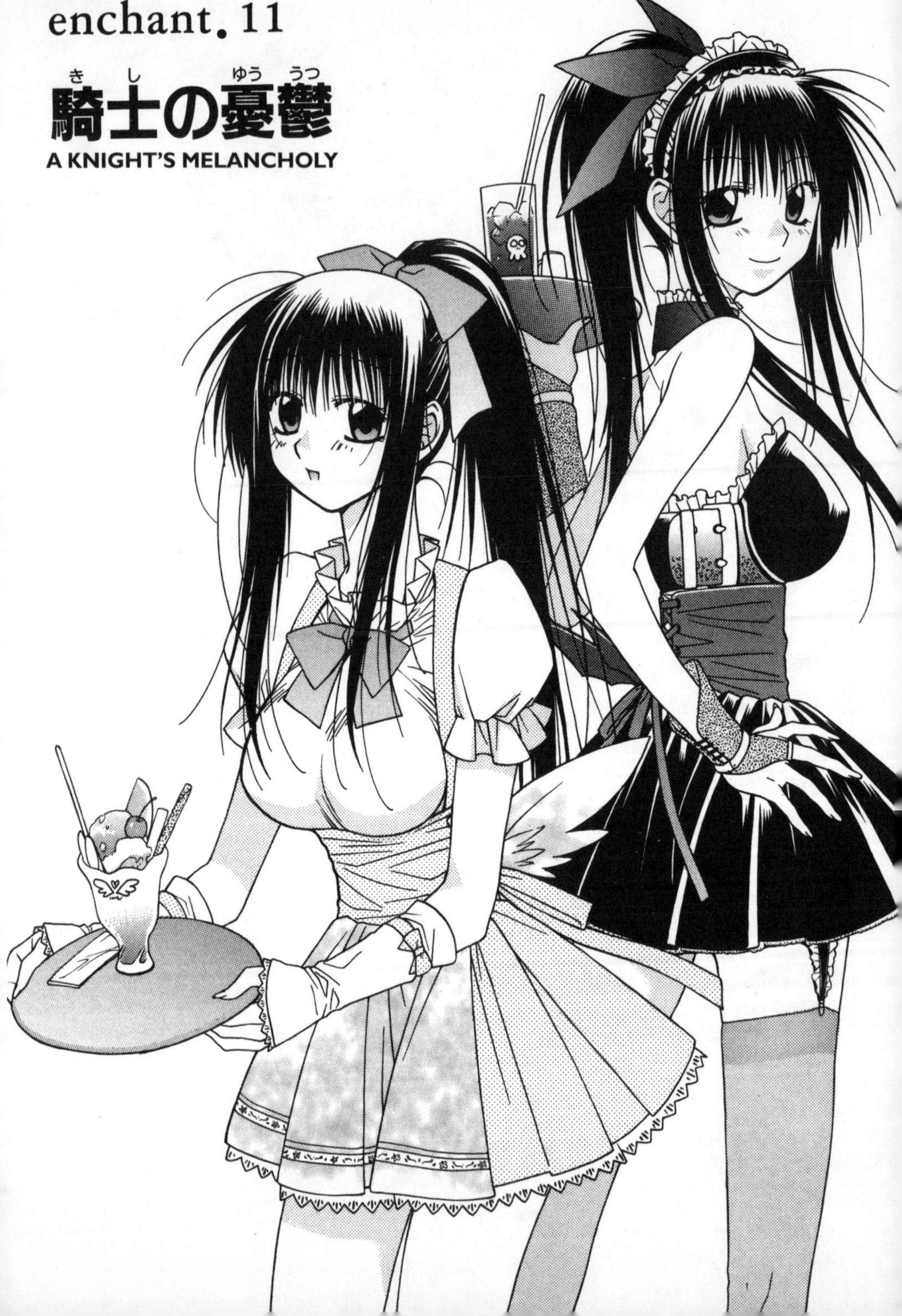

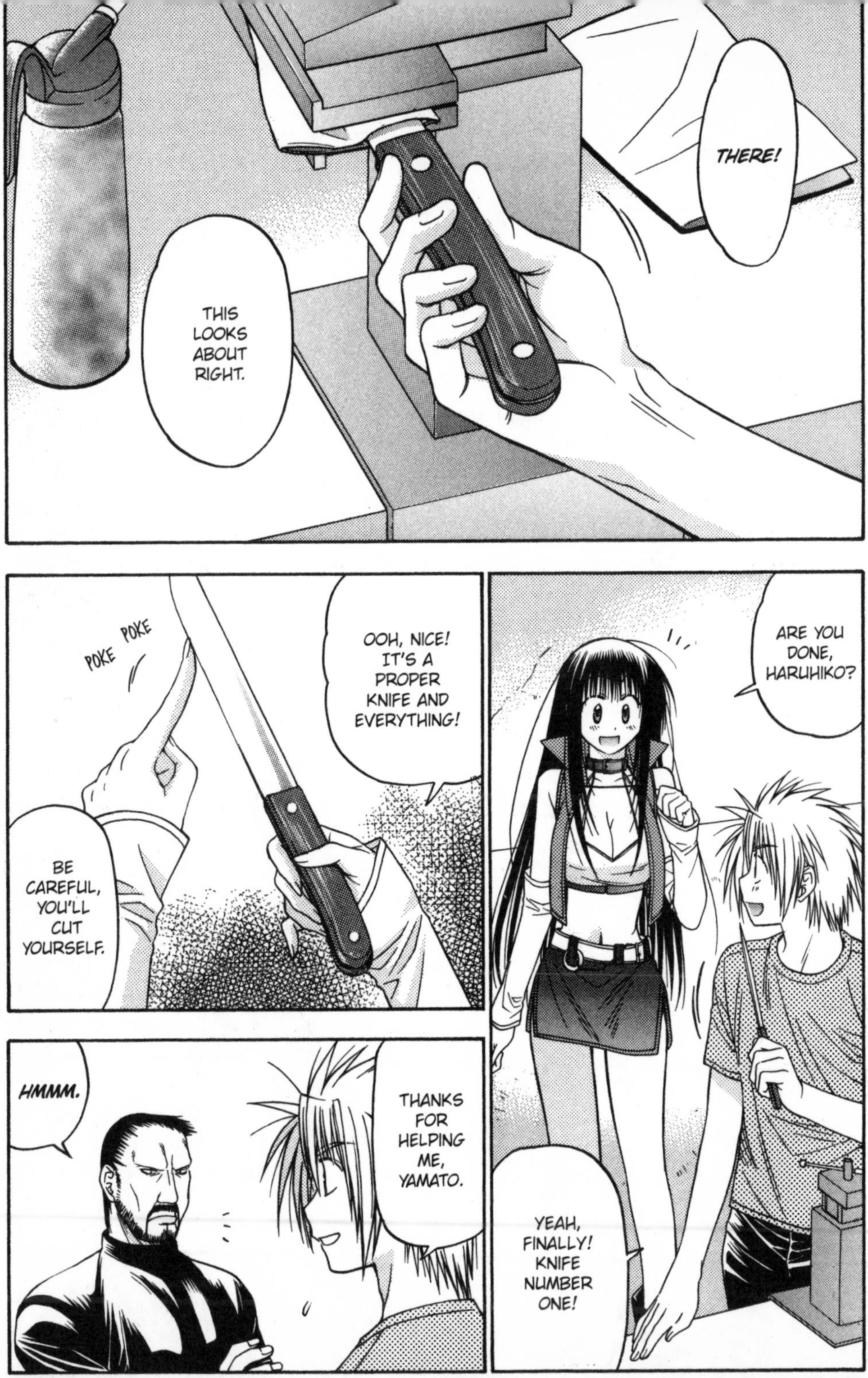
THERE!
THIS LOOKS ABOUT RIGHT.
ARE YOU DONE, HARUHIKO?
YEAH, FINALLY! KNIFE NUMBER ONE!
OOH, NICE! IT'S A PROPER KNIFE AND EVERYTHING!
POKE POKE
BE CAREFUL, YOU'LL CUT YOURSELF.
THANKS FOR HELPING ME, YAMATO.
HMMM.

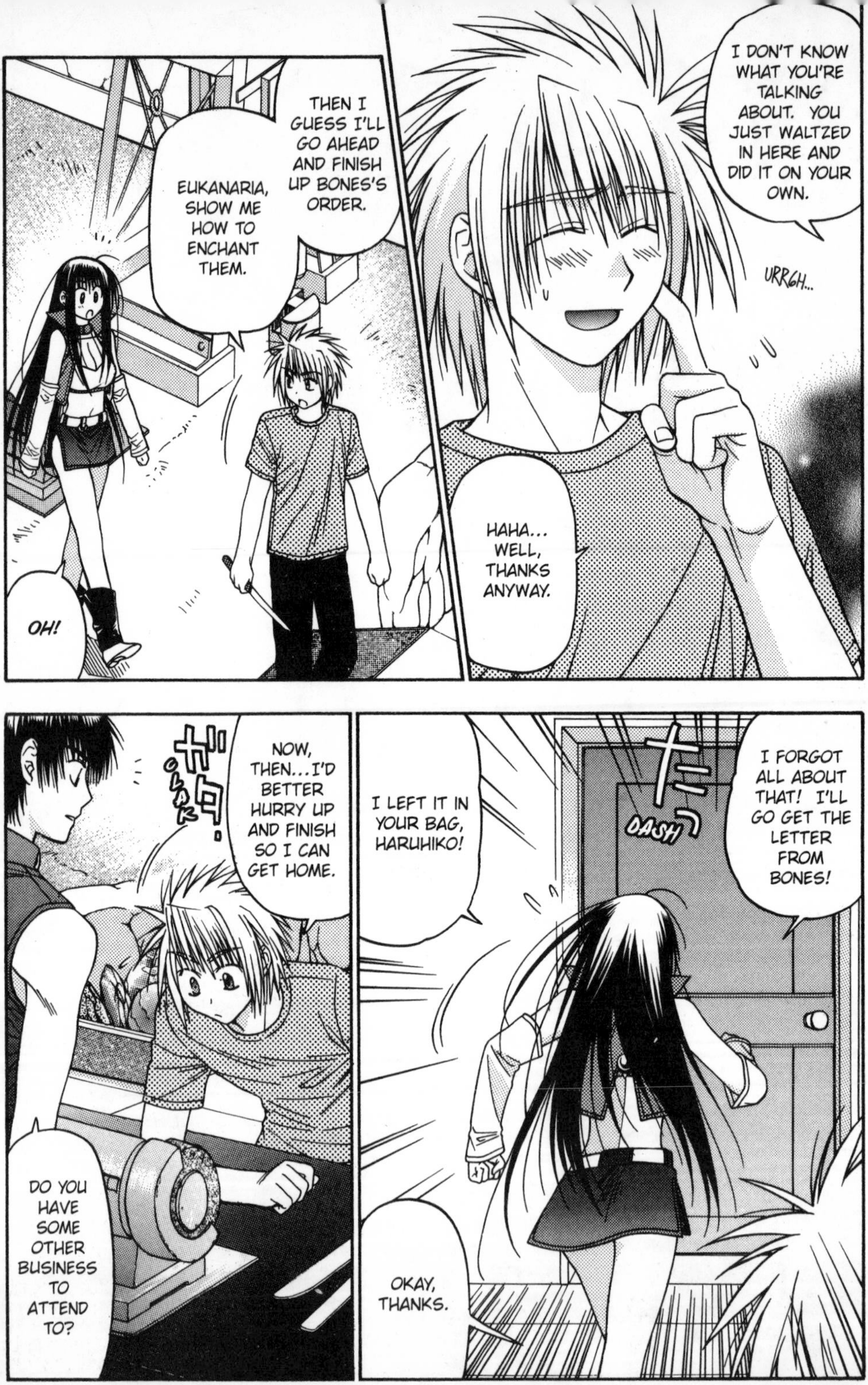
I DON'T KNOW WHAT YOU'RE TALKING ABOUT. YOU JUST WALTZED IN HERE AND DID IT ON YOUR OWN.
URRGH...
HAHA... WELL, THANKS ANYWAY.
THEN I GUESS I'LL GO AHEAD AND FINISH UP BONES'S ORDER.
EUKANARIA, SHOW ME HOW TO ENCHANT THEM.
OH!
I FORGOT ALL ABOUT THAT! I'LL GO GET THE LETTER FROM BONES!
DASH
I LEFT IT IN YOUR BAG, HARUHIKO!
OKAY, THANKS.
NOW, THEN...I'D BETTER HURRY UP AND FINISH SO I CAN GET HOME.
CLAK
DO YOU HAVE SOME OTHER BUSINESS TO ATTEND TO?

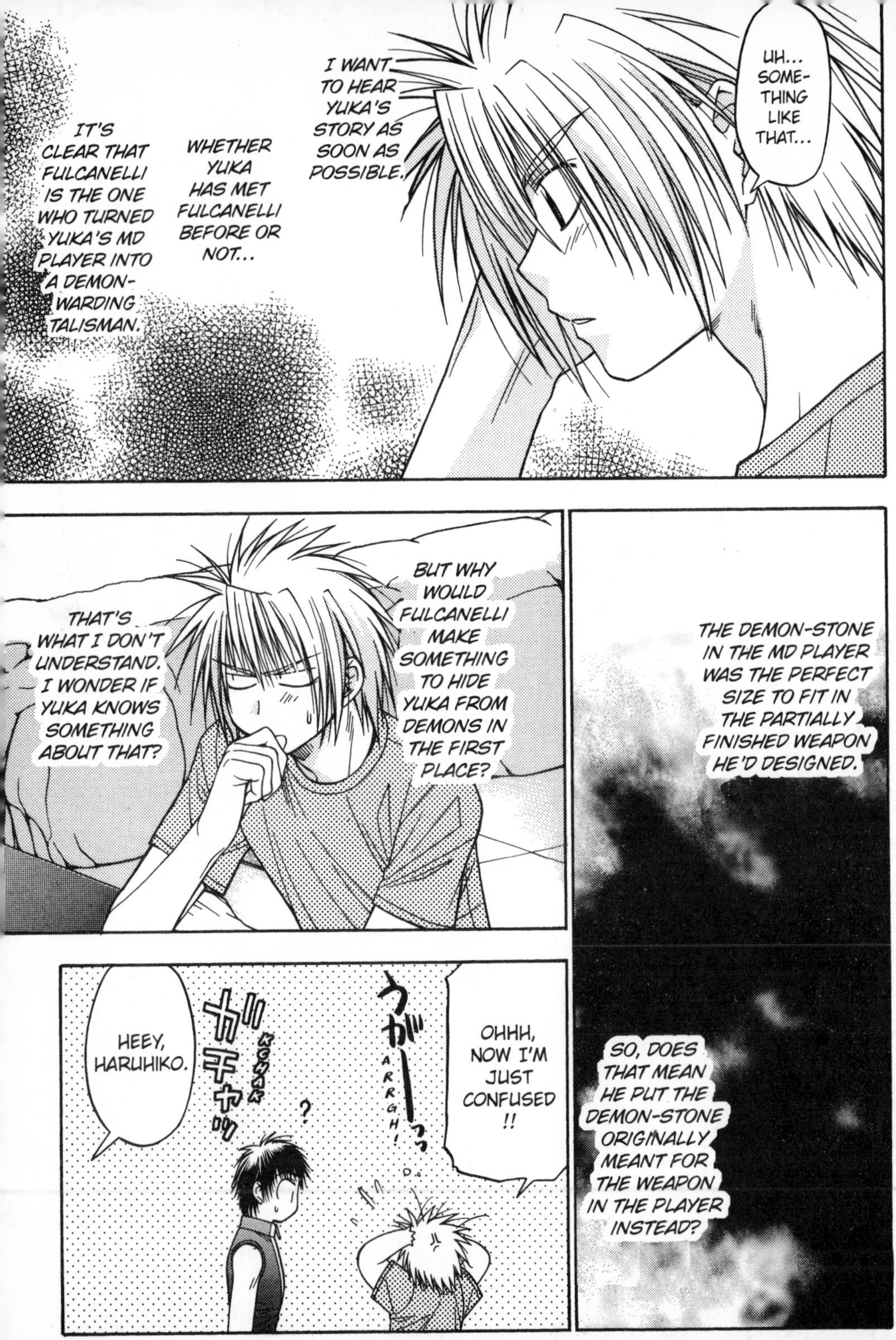
UH... SOME-THING LIKE THAT...
I WANT TO HEAR YUKA'S STORY AS SOON AS POSSIBLE.
WHETHER YUKA HAS MET FULCANELLI BEFORE OR NOT...
IT'S CLEAR THAT FULCANELLI IS THE ONE WHO TURNED YUKA'S MD PLAYER INTO A DEMON-WARDING TALISMAN.
THE DEMON-STONE IN THE MD PLAYER WAS THE PERFECT SIZE TO FIT IN THE PARTIALLY FINISHED WEAPON HE'D DESIGNED.
SO, DOES THAT MEAN HE PUT THE DEMON-STONE ORIGINALLY MEANT FOR THE WEAPON IN THE PLAYER INSTEAD?
BUT WHY WOULD FULCANELLI MAKE SOMETHING TO HIDE YUKA FROM DEMONS IN THE FIRST PLACE?
THAT'S WHAT I DON'T UNDERSTAND. I WONDER IF YUKA KNOWS SOMETHING ABOUT THAT?
OHHH, NOW I'M JUST CONFUSED !!
うがーっ
ARRGH!
ガチャッ
KCHAK
HEEY, HARUHIKO.
?

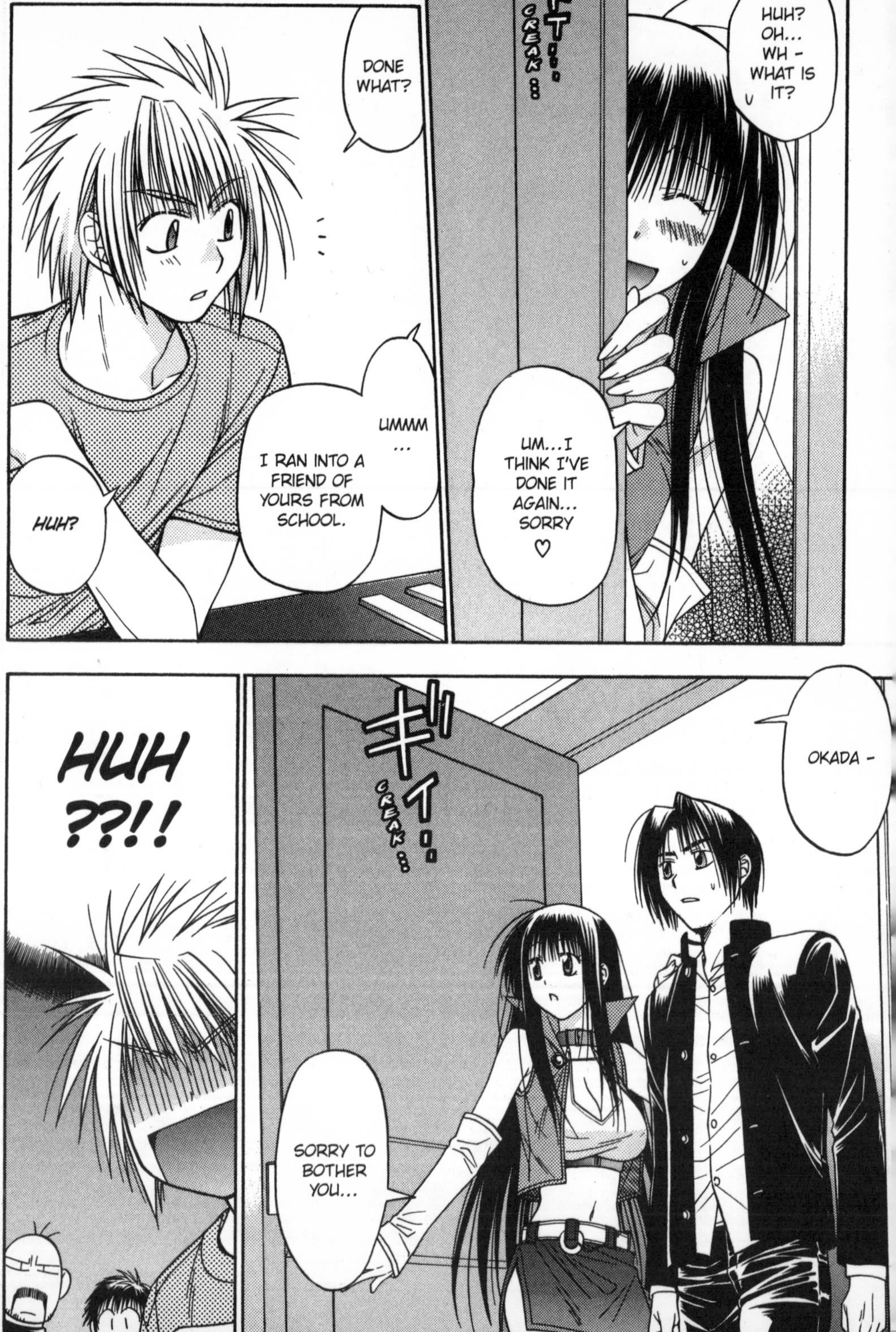
HUH? OH... WH - WHAT IS IT?
CREAK...
UM...I THINK I'VE DONE IT AGAIN... SORRY ♡
DONE WHAT?
UMMM...
I RAN INTO A FRIEND OF YOURS FROM SCHOOL.
HUH?
OKADA -
CREAK...
SORRY TO BOTHER YOU...
HUH ??!!

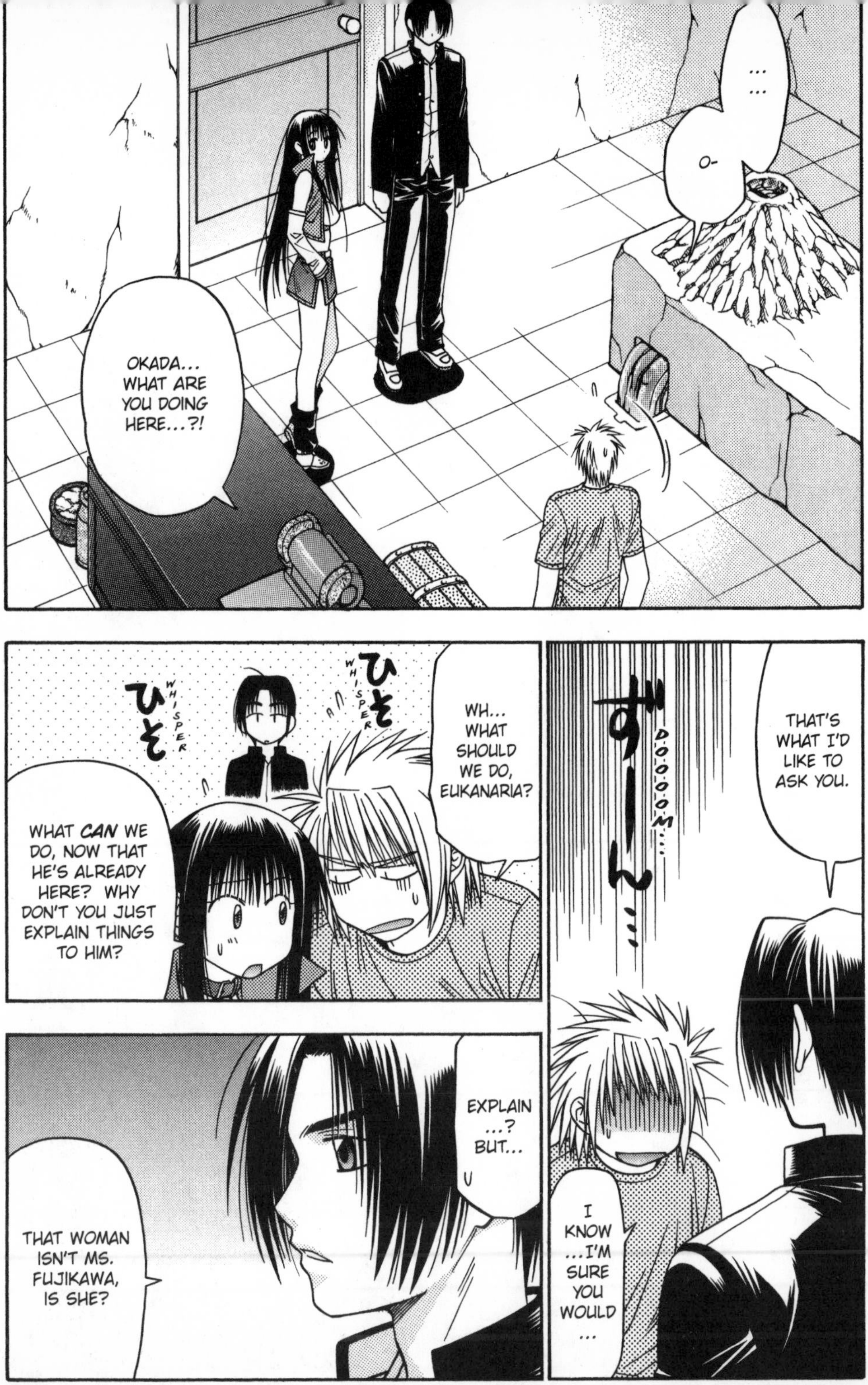
...
...
O-
OKADA... WHAT ARE YOU DOING HERE...?!
THAT'S WHAT I'D LIKE TO ASK YOU.
ずーん...
D-O-O-O-O-O-M...
I KNOW ...I'M SURE YOU WOULD ...
ひそ
WHISPER
WH... WHAT SHOULD WE DO, EUKANARIA?
ひそ
WHISPER
WHAT *CAN* WE DO, NOW THAT HE'S ALREADY HERE? WHY DON'T YOU JUST EXPLAIN THINGS TO HIM?
EXPLAIN ...? BUT...
THAT WOMAN ISN'T MS. FUJIKAWA, IS SHE?

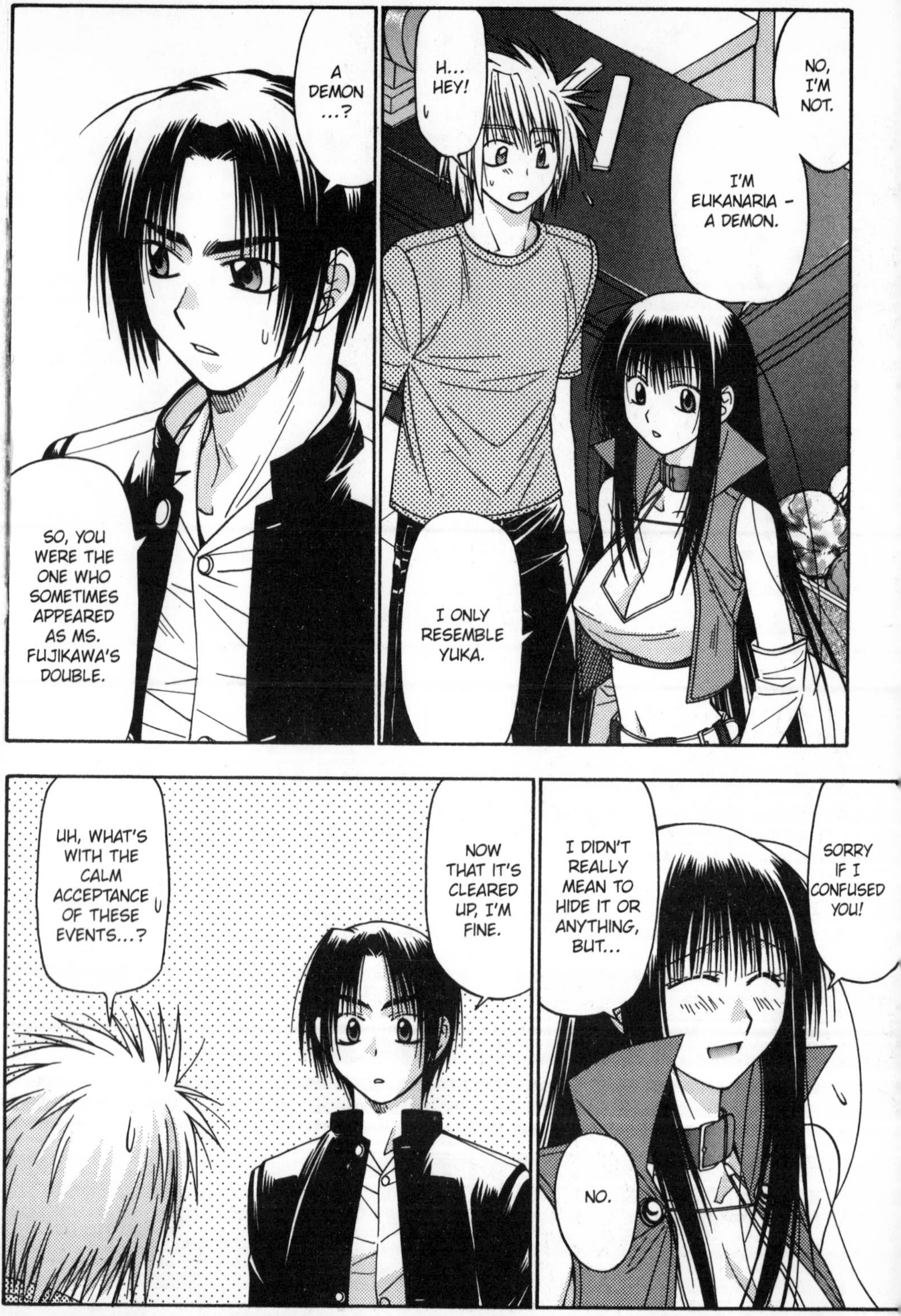
NO, I'M NOT.
I'M EUKANARIA - A DEMON.
H... HEY!
I ONLY RESEMBLE YUKA.
A DEMON ...?
SO, YOU WERE THE ONE WHO SOMETIMES APPEARED AS MS. FUJIKAWA'S DOUBLE.
SORRY IF I CONFUSED YOU!
I DIDN'T REALLY MEAN TO HIDE IT OR ANYTHING, BUT...
NO.
NOW THAT IT'S CLEARED UP, I'M FINE.
UH, WHAT'S WITH THE CALM ACCEPTANCE OF THESE EVENTS...?

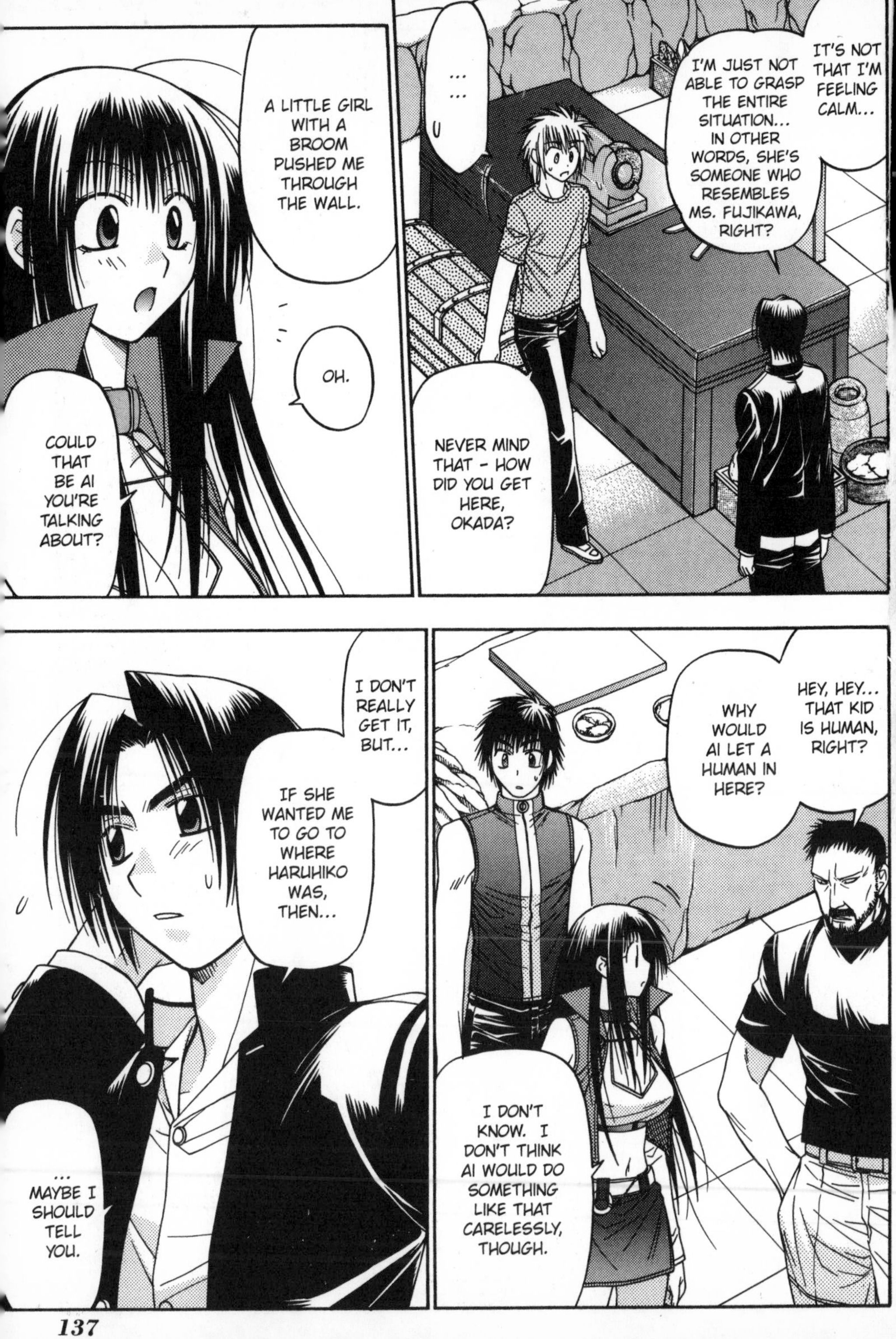
IT'S NOT THAT I'M FEELING CALM...
I'M JUST NOT ABLE TO GRASP THE ENTIRE SITUATION... IN OTHER WORDS, SHE'S SOMEONE WHO RESEMBLES MS. FUJIKAWA, RIGHT?
......
NEVER MIND THAT - HOW DID YOU GET HERE, OKADA?
A LITTLE GIRL WITH A BROOM PUSHED ME THROUGH THE WALL.
OH.
COULD THAT BE AI YOU'RE TALKING ABOUT?
HEY, HEY... THAT KID IS HUMAN, RIGHT?
WHY WOULD AI LET A HUMAN IN HERE?
I DON'T KNOW. I DON'T THINK AI WOULD DO SOMETHING LIKE THAT CARELESSLY, THOUGH.
I DON'T REALLY GET IT, BUT...
IF SHE WANTED ME TO GO TO WHERE HARUHIKO WAS, THEN...
... MAYBE I SHOULD TELL YOU.

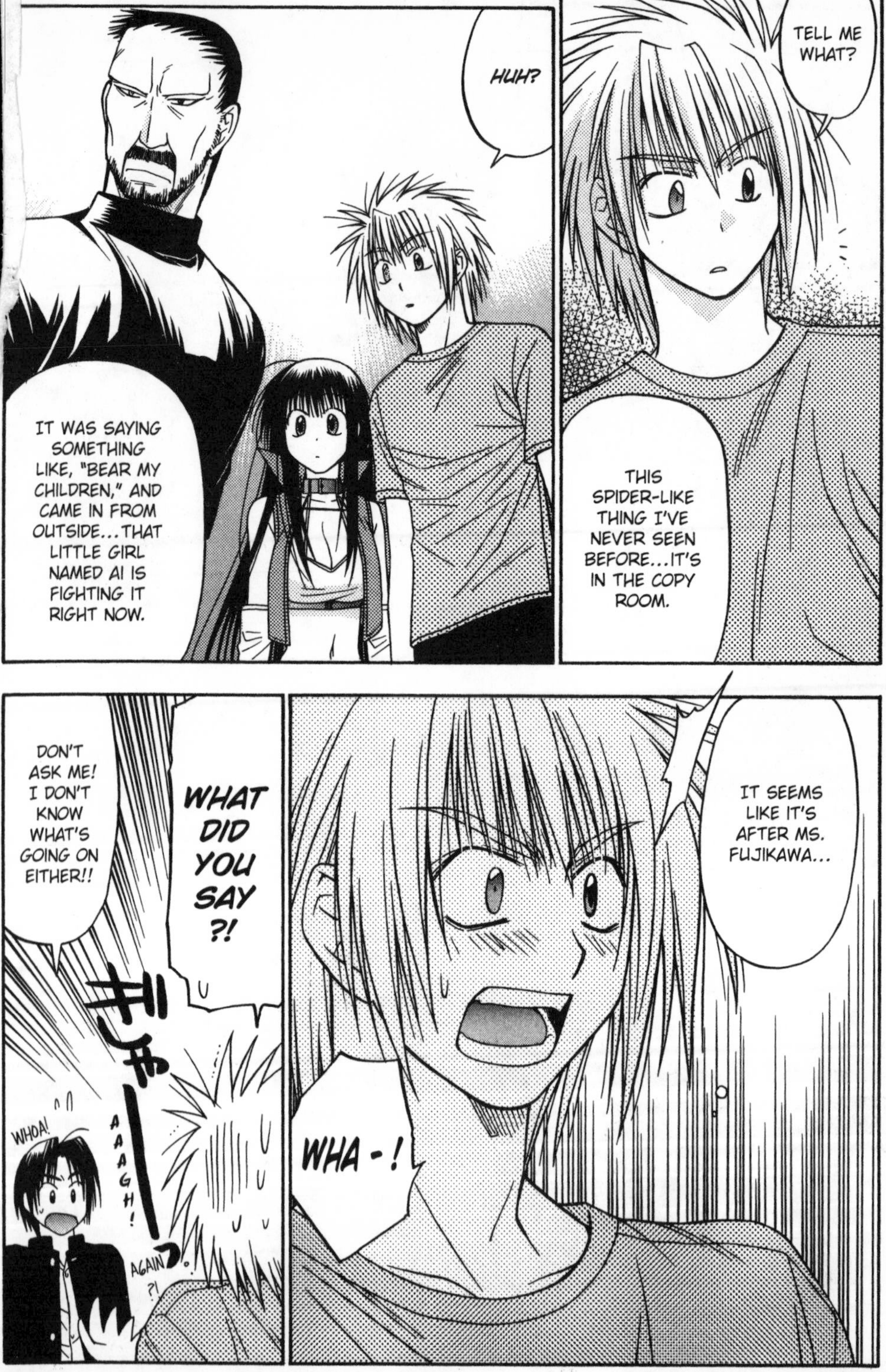
TELL ME WHAT?
THIS SPIDER-LIKE THING I'VE NEVER SEEN BEFORE...IT'S IN THE COPY ROOM.
HUH?
IT WAS SAYING SOMETHING LIKE, "BEAR MY CHILDREN," AND CAME IN FROM OUTSIDE...THAT LITTLE GIRL NAMED AI IS FIGHTING IT RIGHT NOW.
IT SEEMS LIKE IT'S AFTER MS. FUJIKAWA...
WHA-!
WHAT DID YOU SAY?!
DON'T ASK ME! I DON'T KNOW WHAT'S GOING ON EITHER!!
WHOA!
AAAGH!
AGAIN?!

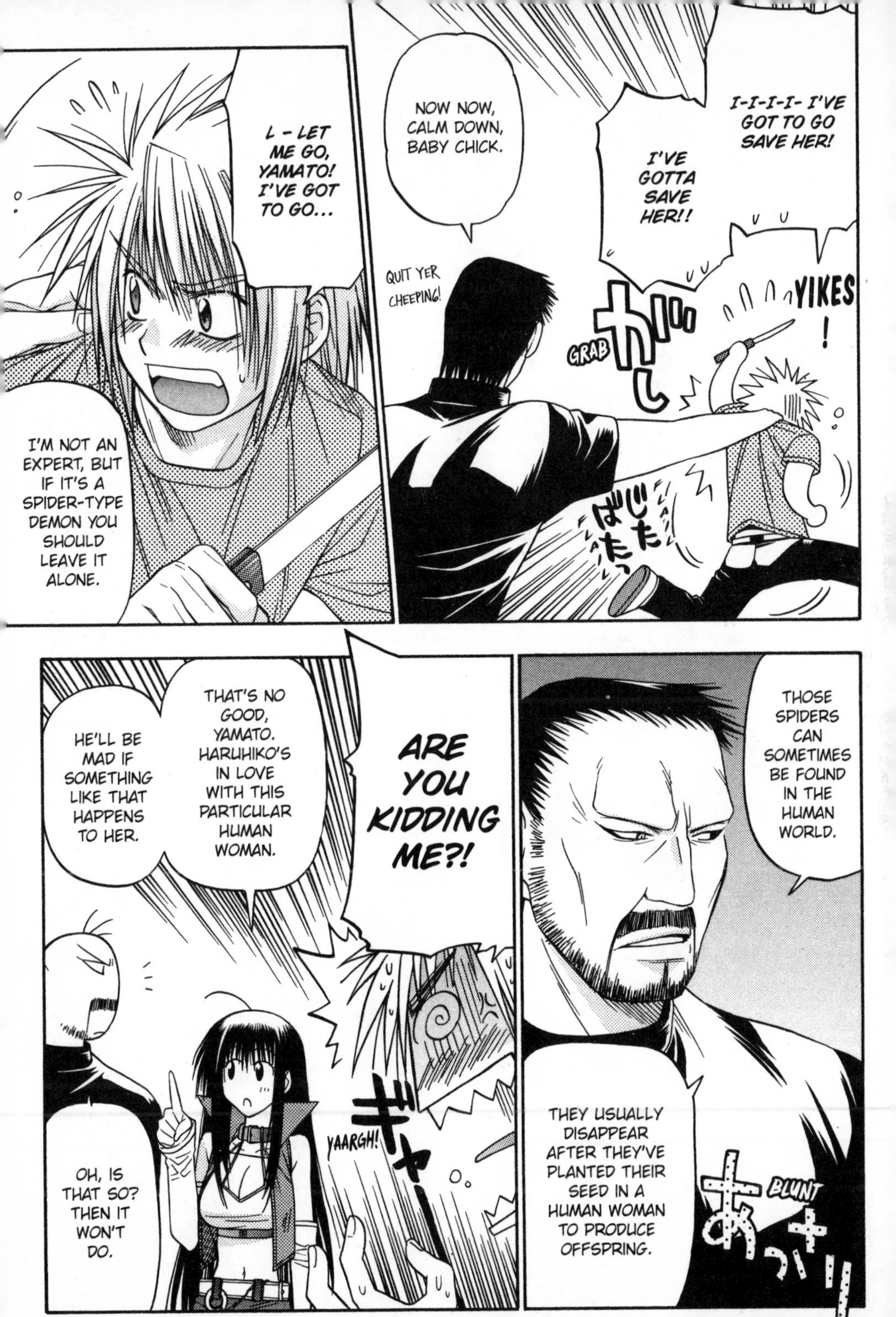
I-I-I-I- I'VE GOT TO GO SAVE HER!
I'VE GOTTA SAVE HER!!
NOW NOW, CALM DOWN, BABY CHICK.
YIKES!
GRAB
QUIT YER CHEEPING!
L - LET ME GO, YAMATO! I'VE GOT TO GO...
I'M NOT AN EXPERT, BUT IF IT'S A SPIDER-TYPE DEMON YOU SHOULD LEAVE IT ALONE.
THOSE SPIDERS CAN SOMETIMES BE FOUND IN THE HUMAN WORLD.
THEY USUALLY DISAPPEAR AFTER THEY'VE PLANTED THEIR SEED IN A HUMAN WOMAN TO PRODUCE OFFSPRING.
BLUNT
ARE YOU KIDDING ME?!
THAT'S NO GOOD, YAMATO. HARUHIKO'S IN LOVE WITH THIS PARTICULAR HUMAN WOMAN.
HE'LL BE MAD IF SOMETHING LIKE THAT HAPPENS TO HER.
YAARGH!
OH, IS THAT SO? THEN IT WON'T DO.

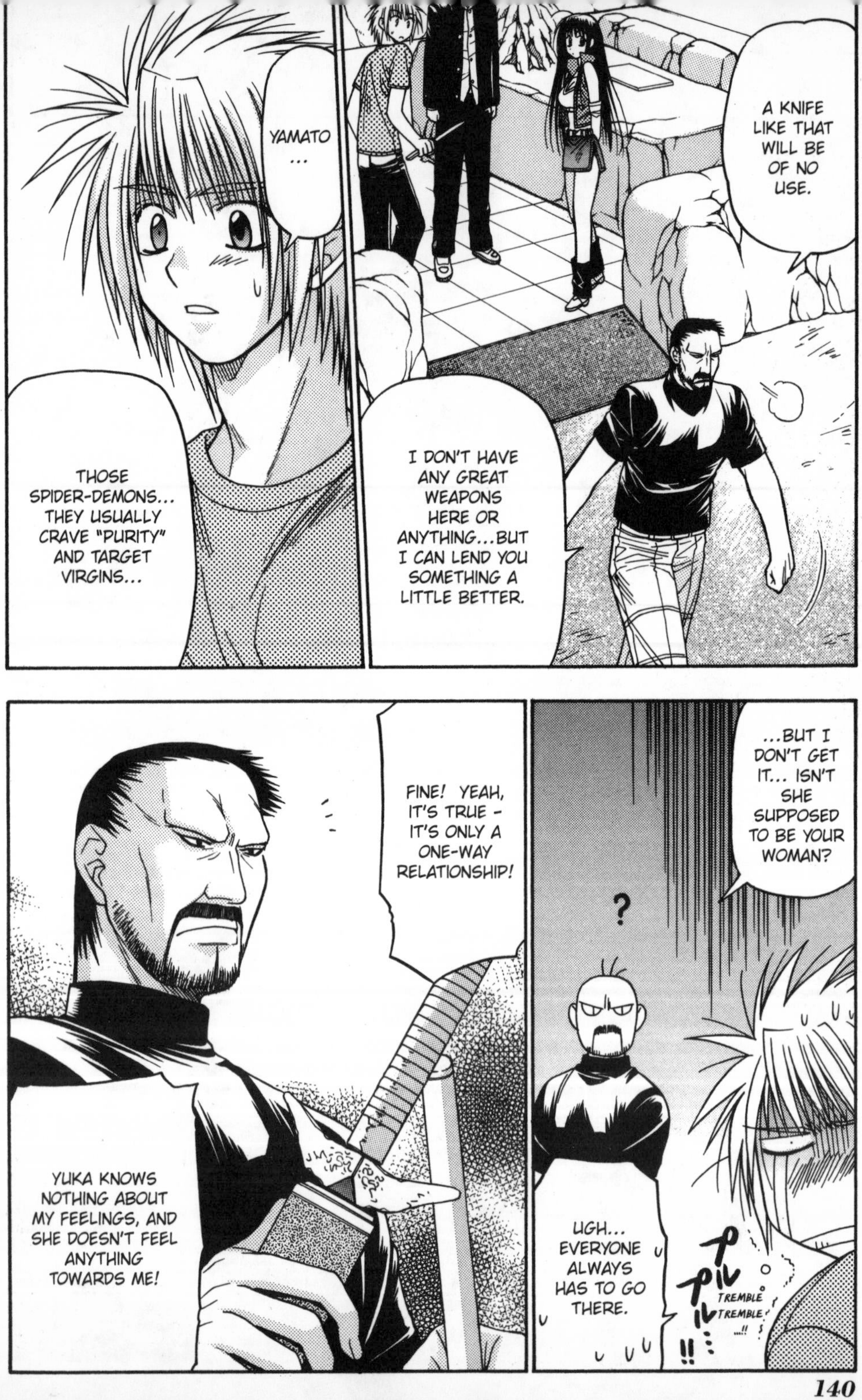
A KNIFE LIKE THAT WILL BE OF NO USE.
I DON'T HAVE ANY GREAT WEAPONS HERE OR ANYTHING...BUT I CAN LEND YOU SOMETHING A LITTLE BETTER.
YAMATO ...
THOSE SPIDER-DEMONS... THEY USUALLY CRAVE "PURITY" AND TARGET VIRGINS...
...BUT I DON'T GET IT... ISN'T SHE SUPPOSED TO BE YOUR WOMAN?
?
UGH... EVERYONE ALWAYS HAS TO GO THERE.
プルプル
TREMBLE TREMBLE ...!!
FINE! YEAH, IT'S TRUE - IT'S ONLY A ONE-WAY RELATIONSHIP!
YUKA KNOWS NOTHING ABOUT MY FEELINGS, AND SHE DOESN'T FEEL ANYTHING TOWARDS ME!

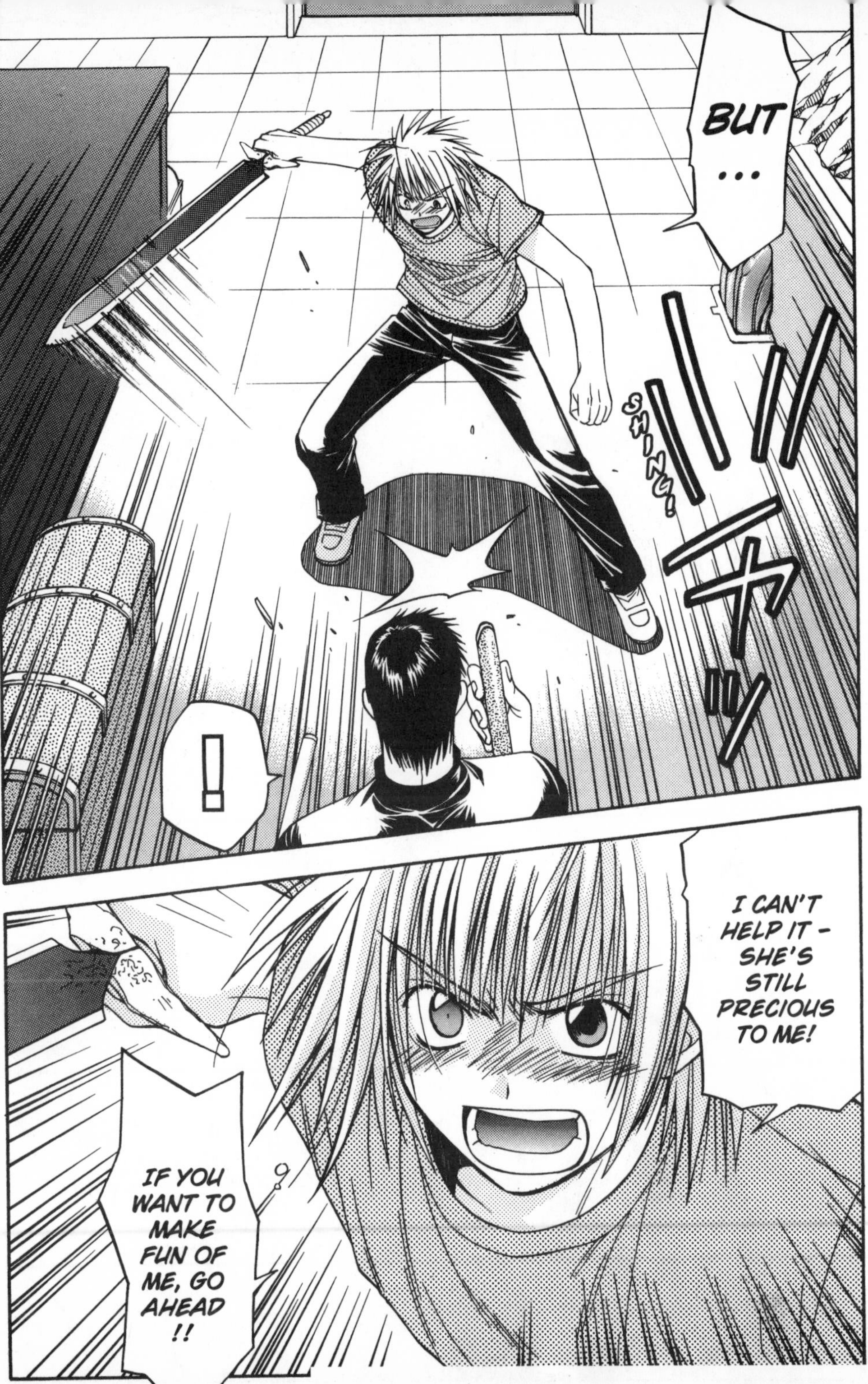
BUT ...
SHING!
!
I CAN'T HELP IT - SHE'S STILL PRECIOUS TO ME!
IF YOU WANT TO MAKE FUN OF ME, GO AHEAD !!

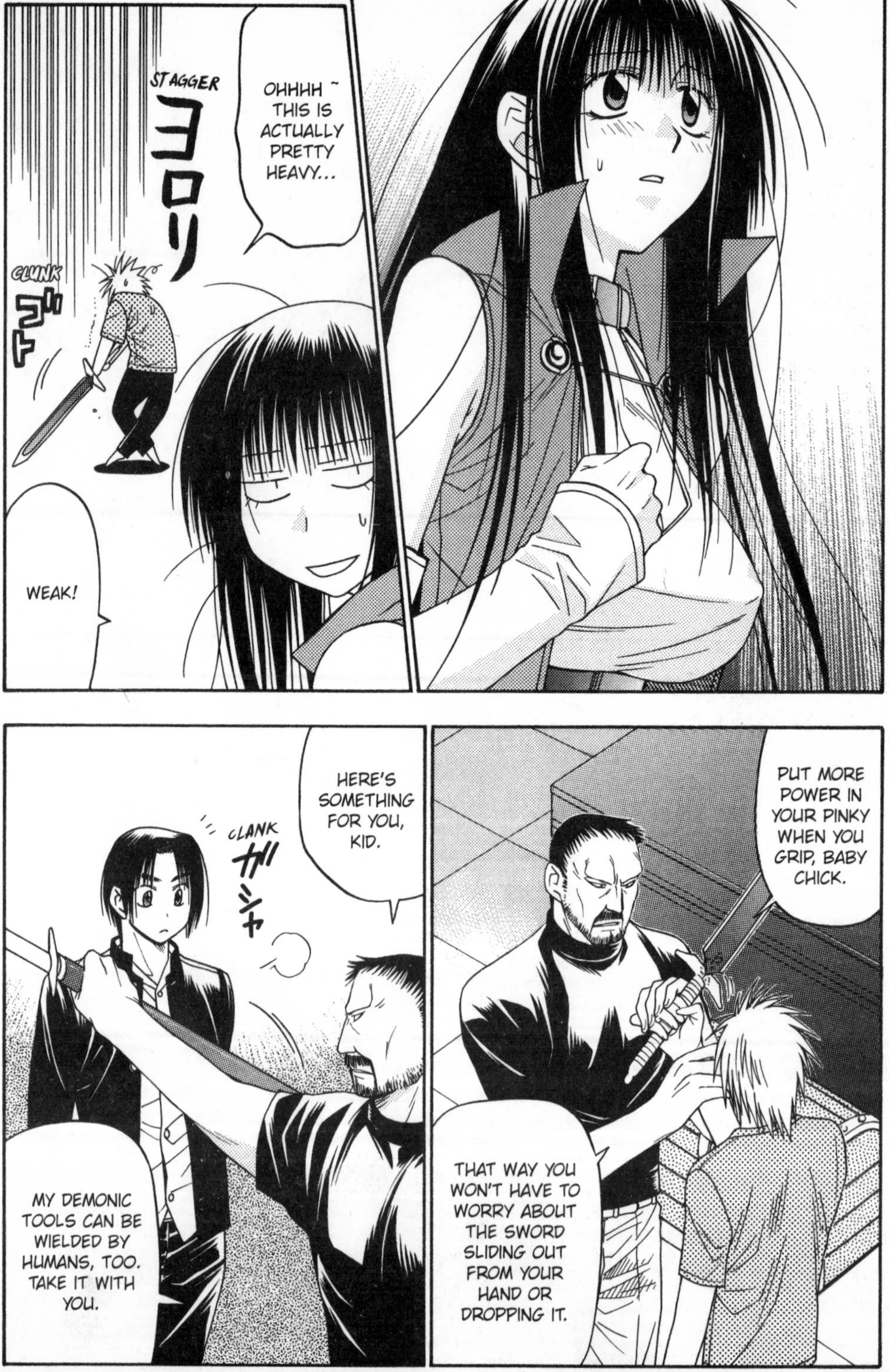
OHHHH ~ THIS IS ACTUALLY PRETTY HEAVY...
STAGGER
ヨロリ
CLUNK
ゴト
WEAK!
PUT MORE POWER IN YOUR PINKY WHEN YOU GRIP, BABY CHICK.
THAT WAY YOU WON'T HAVE TO WORRY ABOUT THE SWORD SLIDING OUT FROM YOUR HAND OR DROPPING IT.
HERE'S SOMETHING FOR YOU, KID.
CLANK
ガシャ
MY DEMONIC TOOLS CAN BE WIELDED BY HUMANS, TOO. TAKE IT WITH YOU.

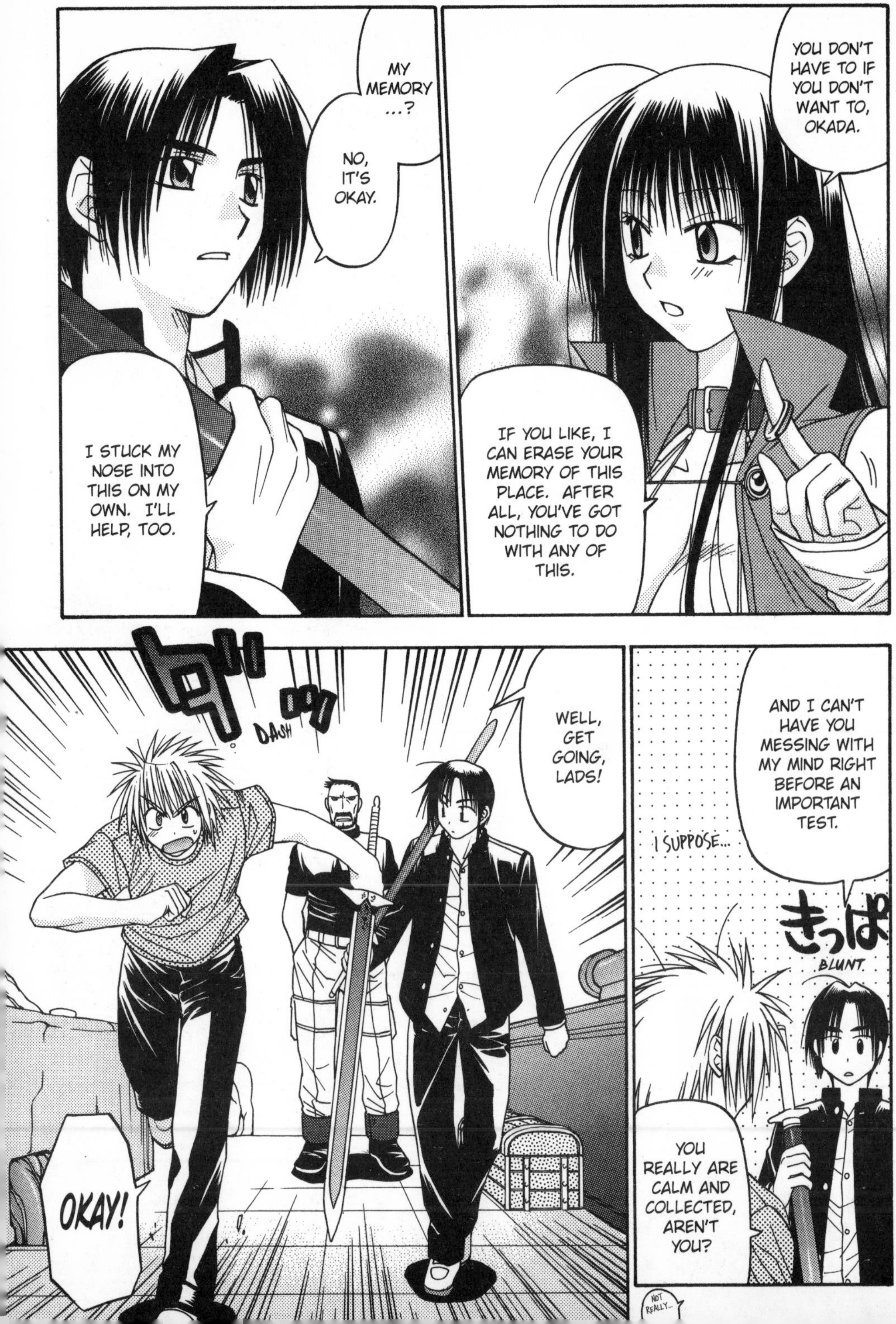
YOU DON'T HAVE TO IF YOU DON'T WANT TO, OKADA.
IF YOU LIKE, I CAN ERASE YOUR MEMORY OF THIS PLACE. AFTER ALL, YOU'VE GOT NOTHING TO DO WITH ANY OF THIS.
MY MEMORY ...?
NO, IT'S OKAY.
I STUCK MY NOSE INTO THIS ON MY OWN. I'LL HELP, TOO.
AND I CAN'T HAVE YOU MESSING WITH MY MIND RIGHT BEFORE AN IMPORTANT TEST.
I SUPPOSE...
きっぱ
BLUNT.
YOU REALLY ARE CALM AND COLLECTED, AREN'T YOU?
NOT REALLY...
WELL, GET GOING, LADS!
DASH
OKAY!

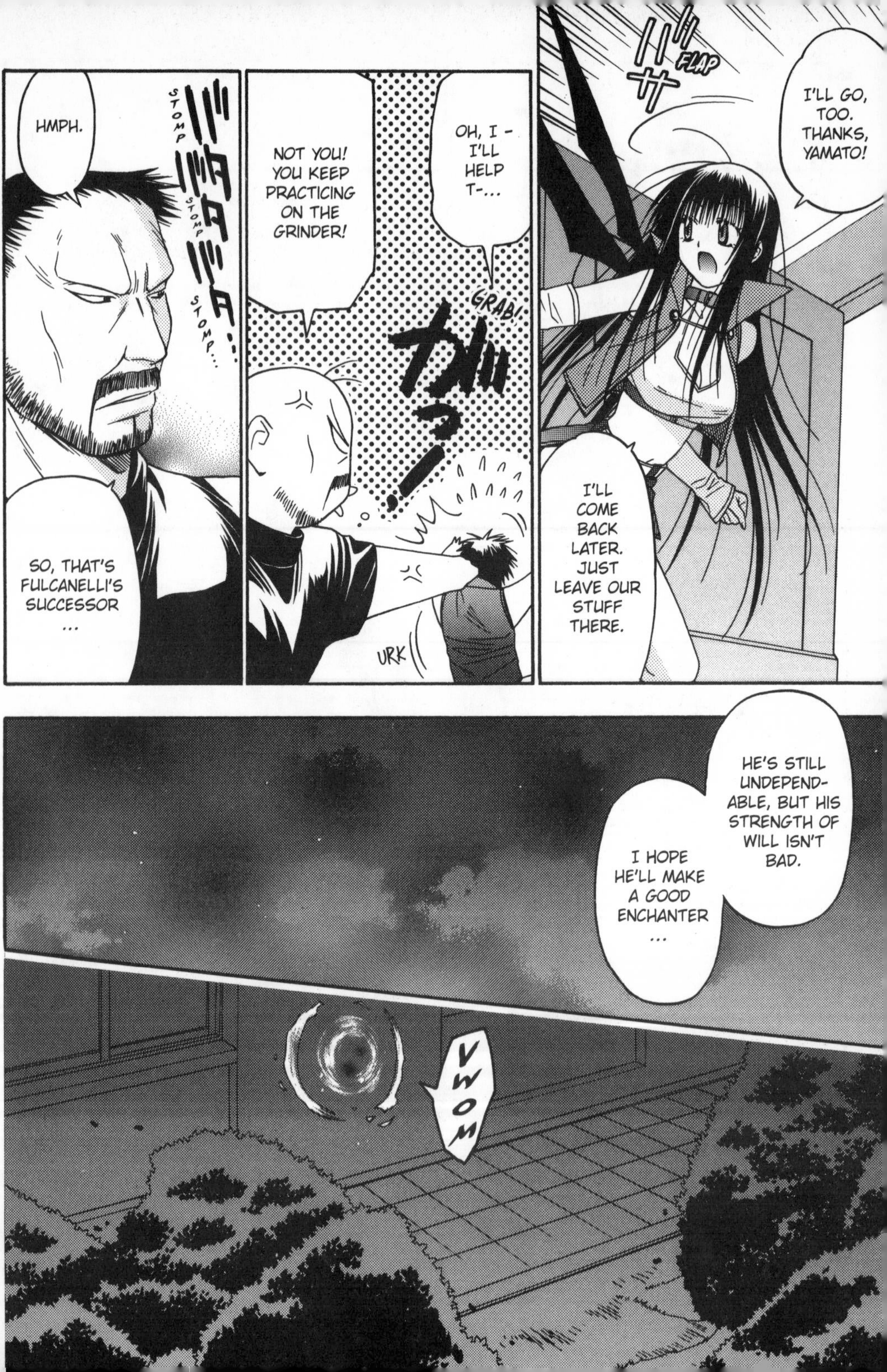
FLAP
I'LL GO, TOO. THANKS, YAMATO!
I'LL COME BACK LATER. JUST LEAVE OUR STUFF THERE.
OH, I - I'LL HELP T-...
NOT YOU! YOU KEEP PRACTICING ON THE GRINDER!
GRAB!
URK
HMPH.
STOMP STOMP STOMP...
SO, THAT'S FULCANELLI'S SUCCESSOR ...
HE'S STILL UNDEPENDABLE, BUT HIS STRENGTH OF WILL ISN'T BAD.
I HOPE HE'LL MAKE A GOOD ENCHANTER ...
VWOM

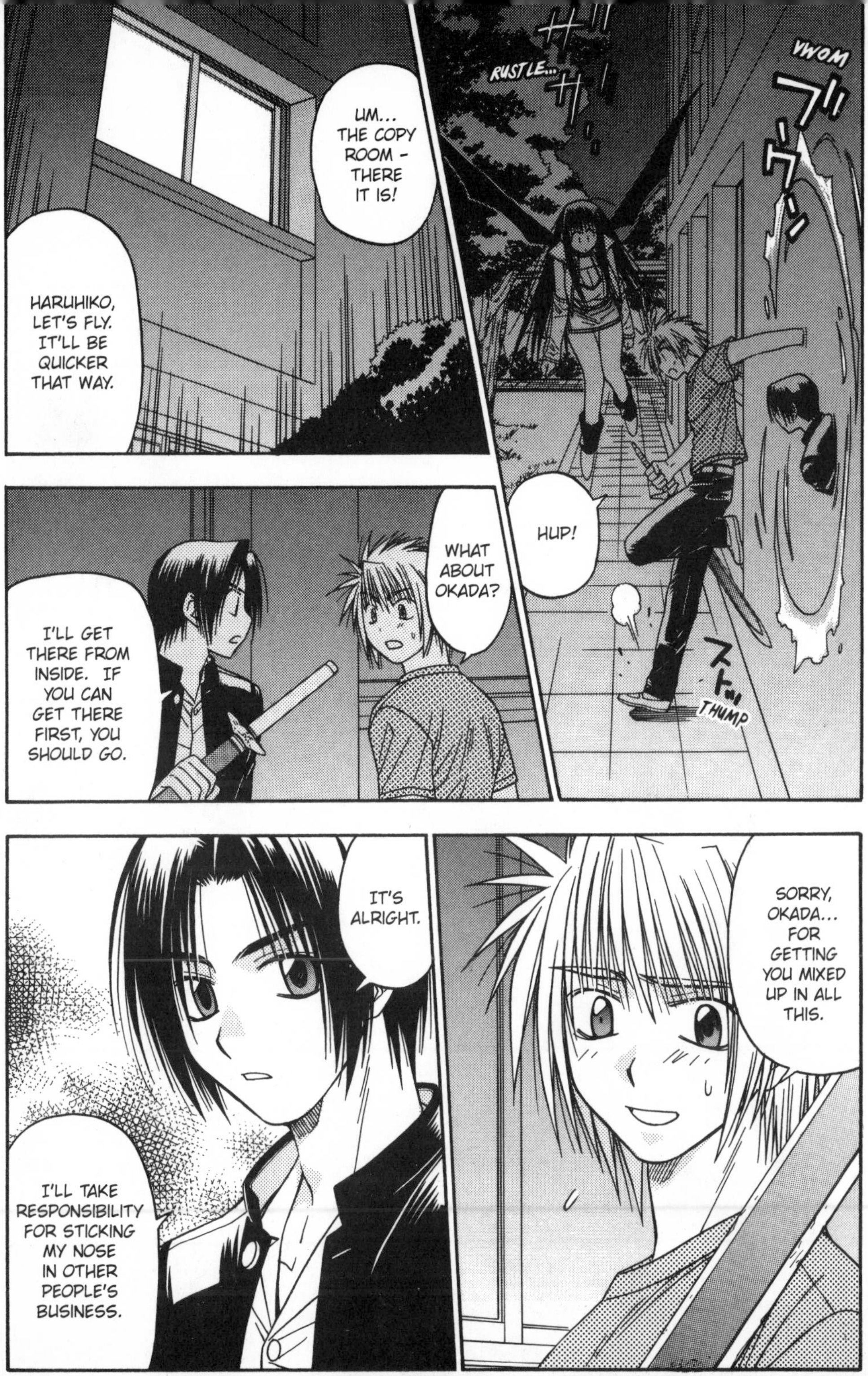
VWOM
RUSTLE...
HUP!
THUMP
UM... THE COPY ROOM - THERE IT IS!
HARUHIKO, LET'S FLY. IT'LL BE QUICKER THAT WAY.
WHAT ABOUT OKADA?
I'LL GET THERE FROM INSIDE. IF YOU CAN GET THERE FIRST, YOU SHOULD GO.
SORRY, OKADA... FOR GETTING YOU MIXED UP IN ALL THIS.
IT'S ALRIGHT.
I'LL TAKE RESPONSIBILITY FOR STICKING MY NOSE IN OTHER PEOPLE'S BUSINESS.

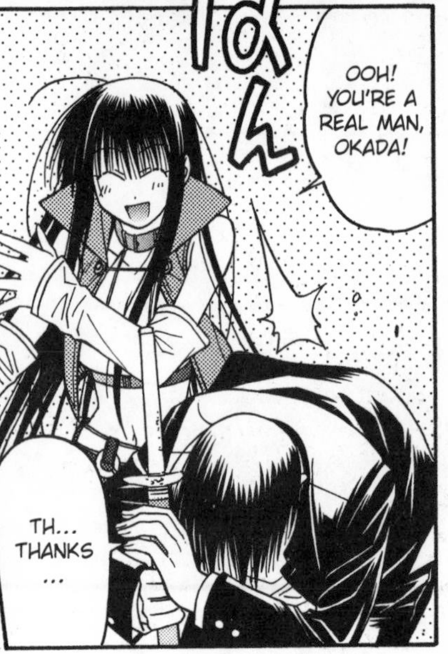
THWACK
ばん
OOH! YOU'RE A REAL MAN, OKADA!
TH... THANKS ...
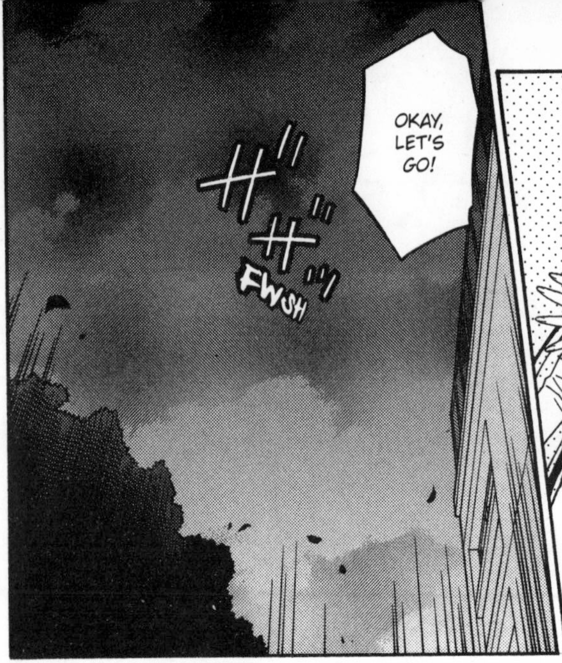
OKAY, LET'S GO!
FWSH
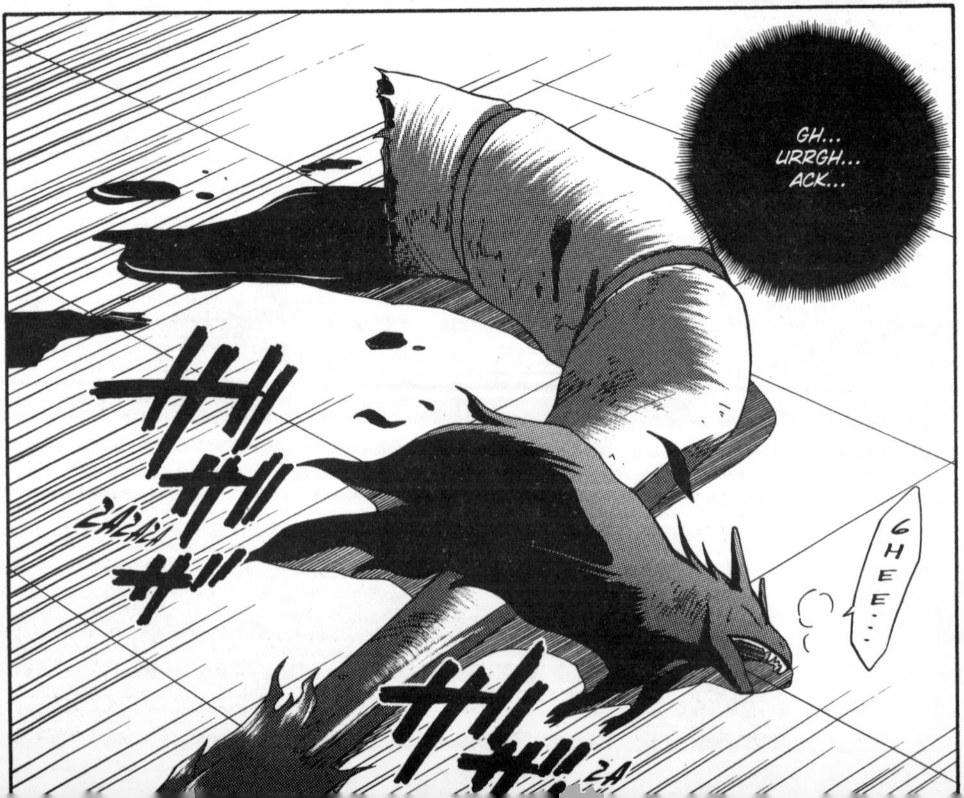
GH... URRGH... ACK...
GHEE...
ZAZAZA
ZA

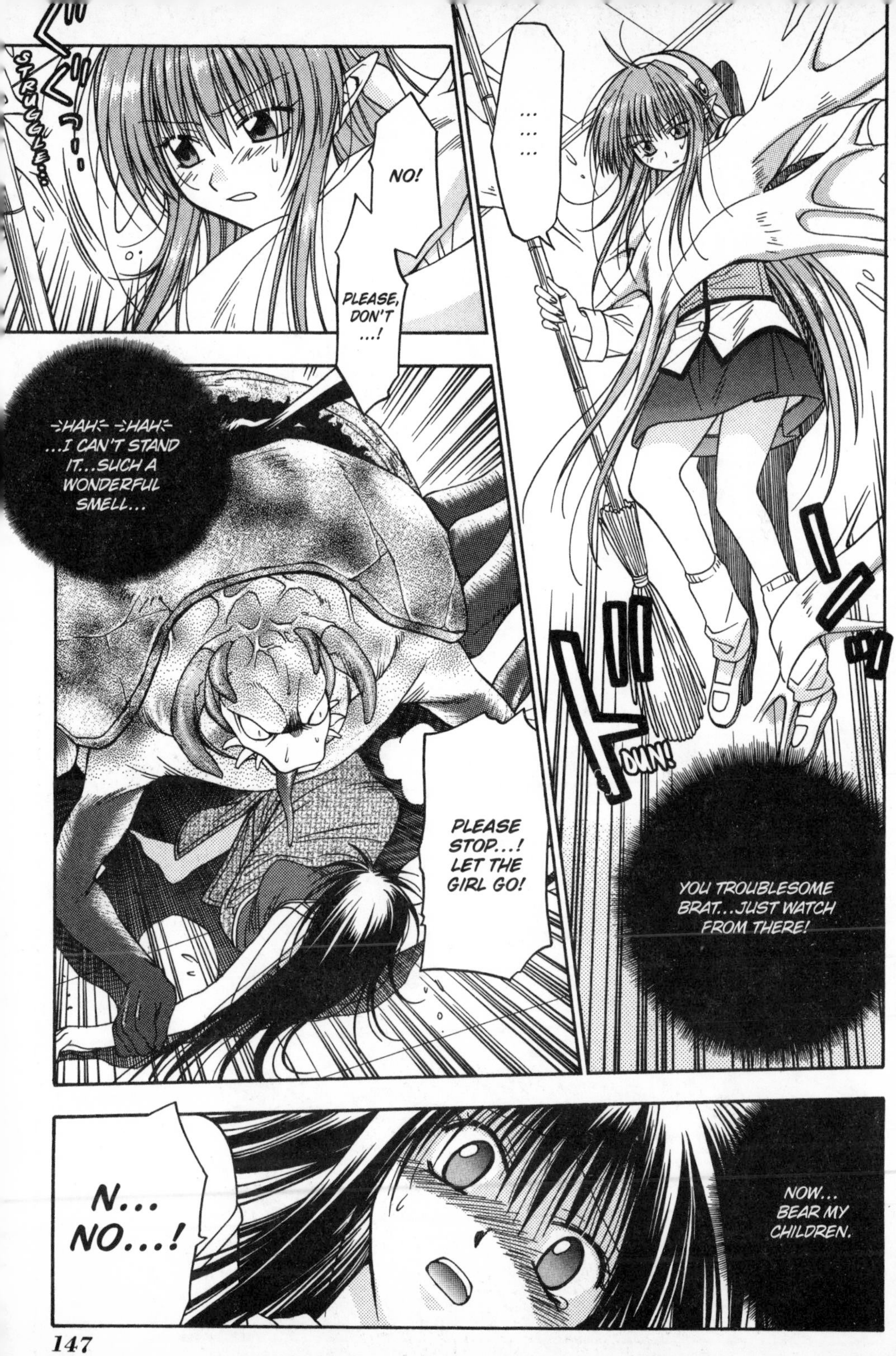

......
DOUN!
YOU TROUBLESOME BRAT...JUST WATCH FROM THERE!
STRUGGLE...
NO!
PLEASE, DON'T ...!
HAH HAH ...I CAN'T STAND IT...SUCH A WONDERFUL SMELL...
PLEASE STOP...! LET THE GIRL GO!
NOW... BEAR MY CHILDREN.
N... NO...!

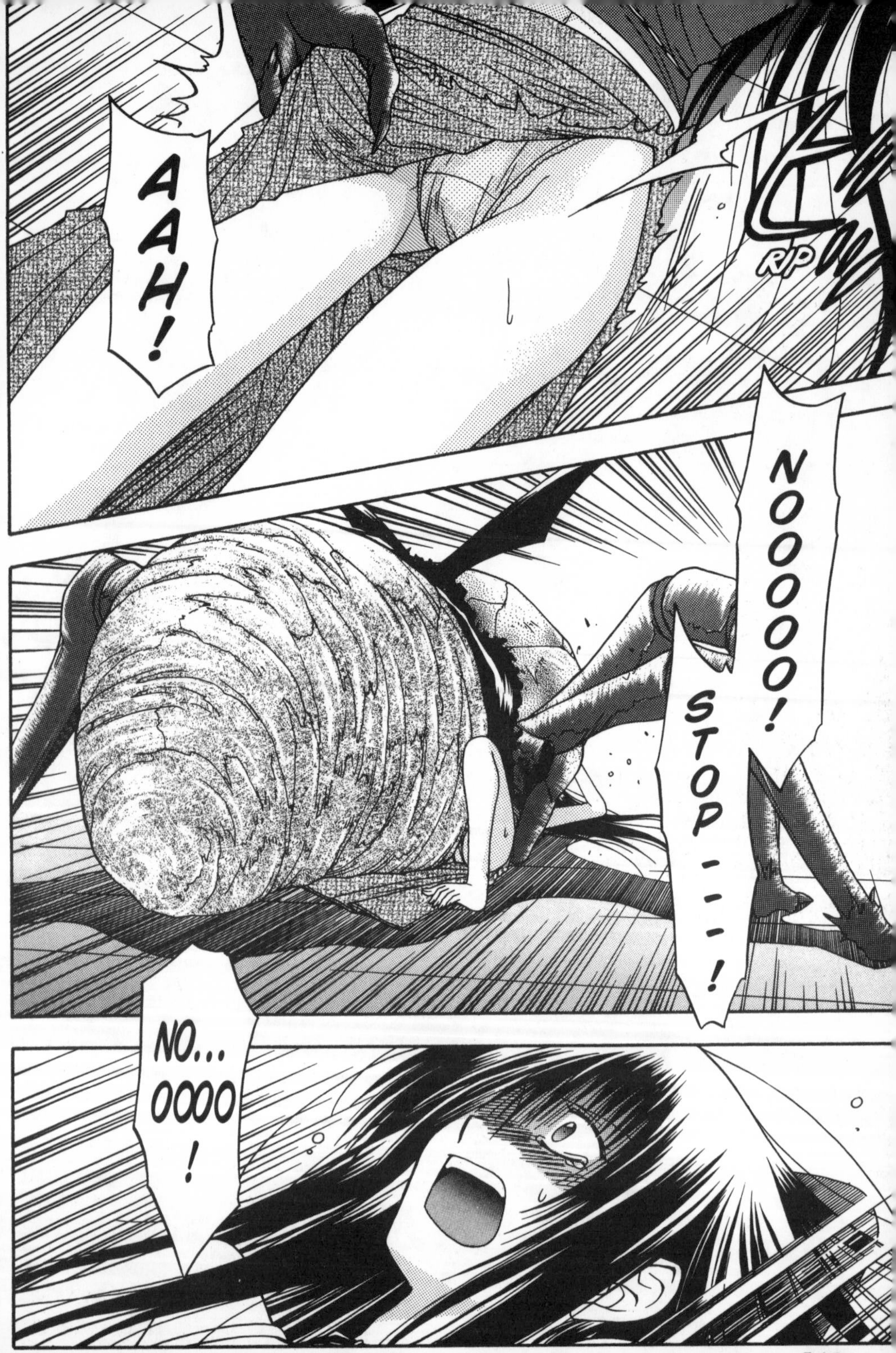
RIP
AAH!
NOOOOOOO! STOP---!
NO... OOOO!

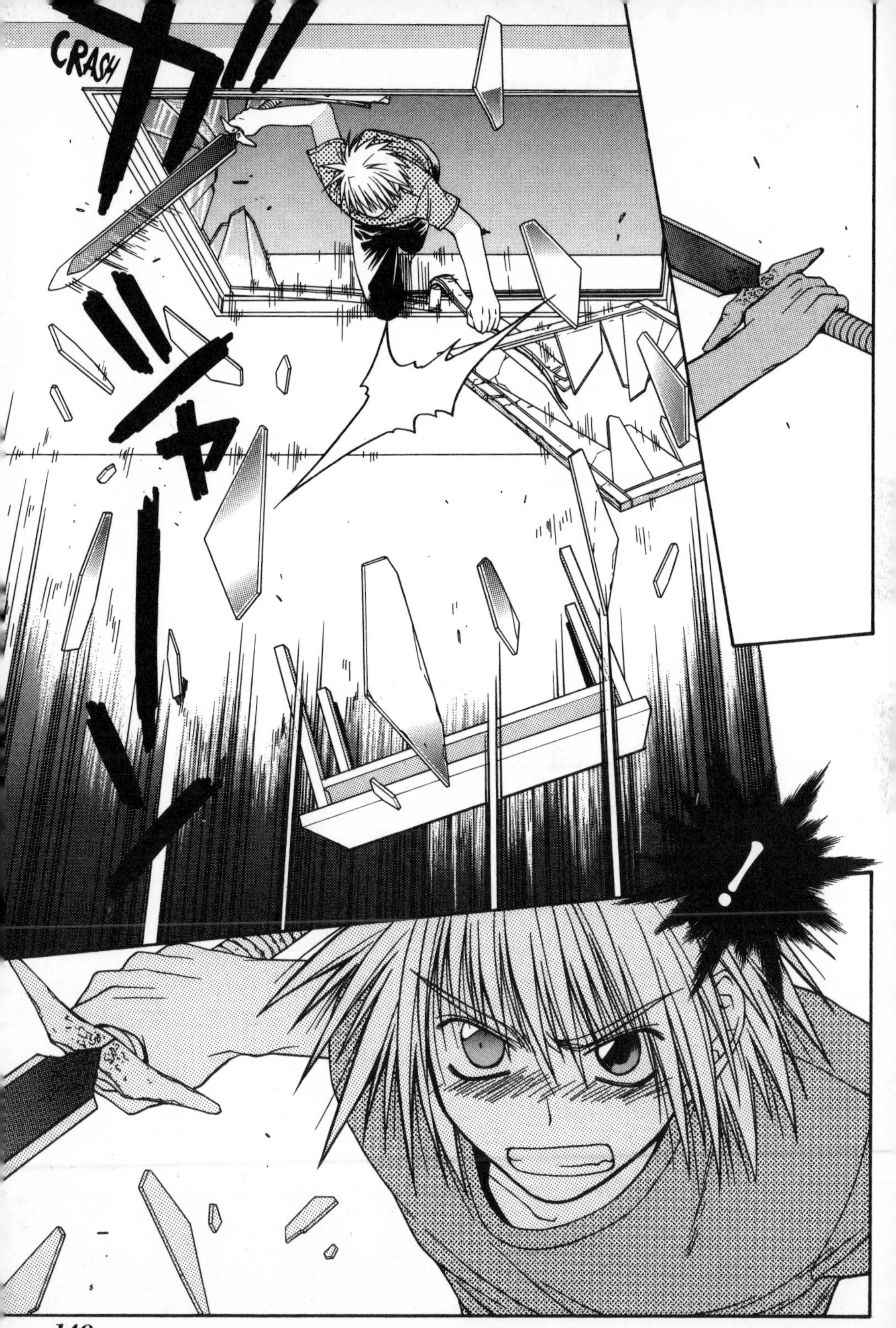
CRASH
ガシャーン
!

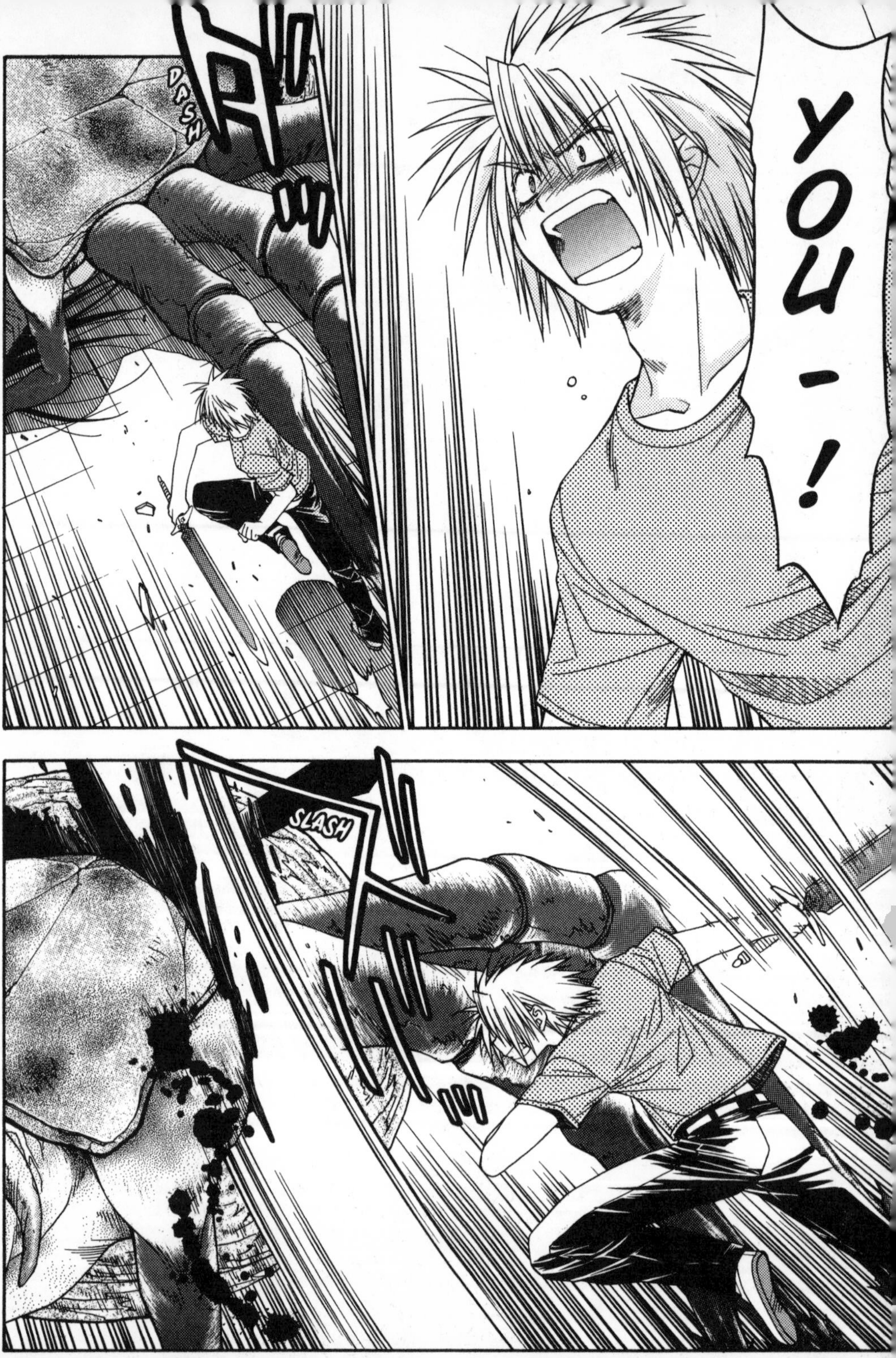
YOU--!
DASH
SLASH

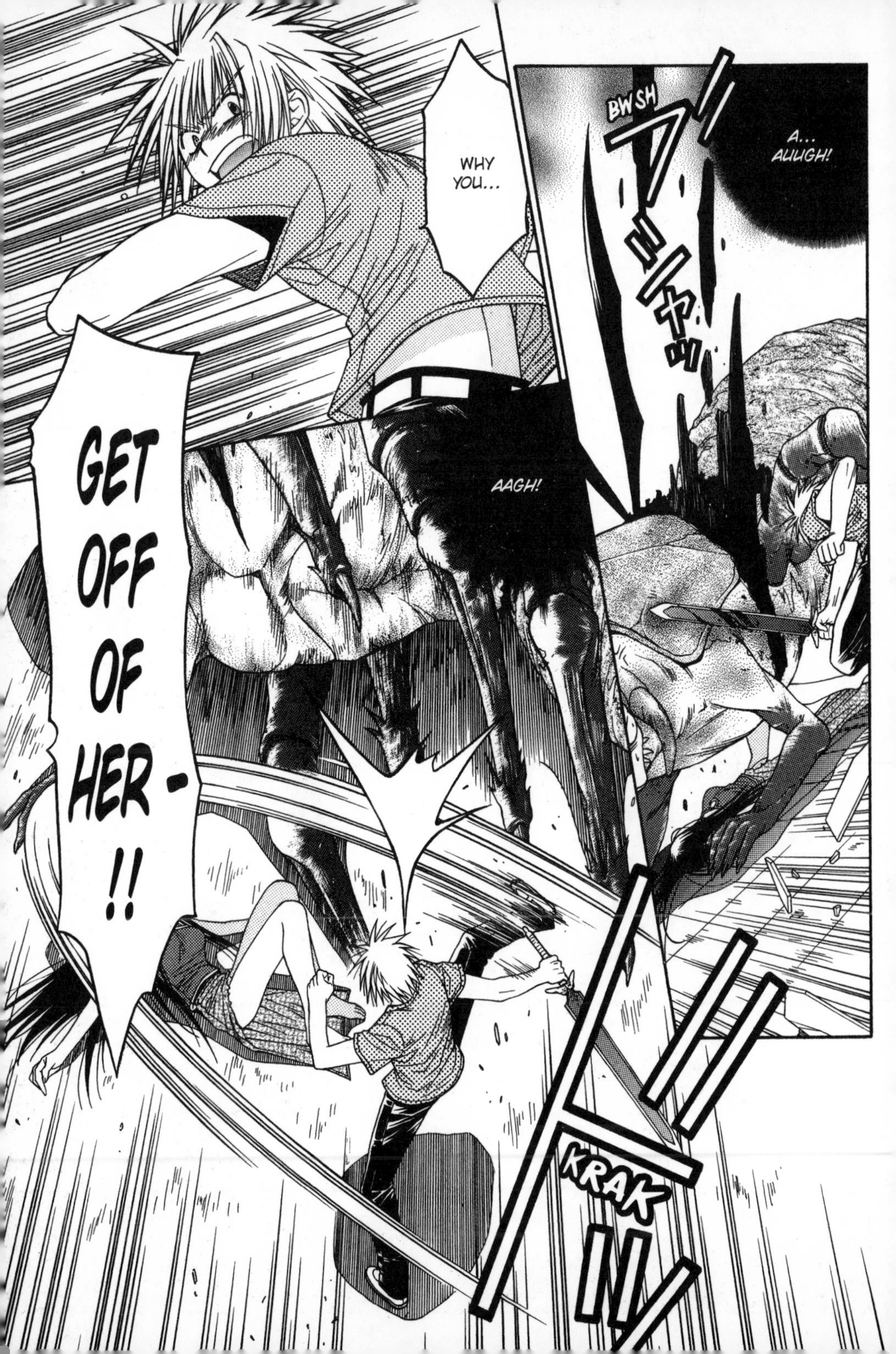
BWSH
A... AUUGH!
WHY YOU...
AAGH!
GET OFF OF HER -!!
KRAK

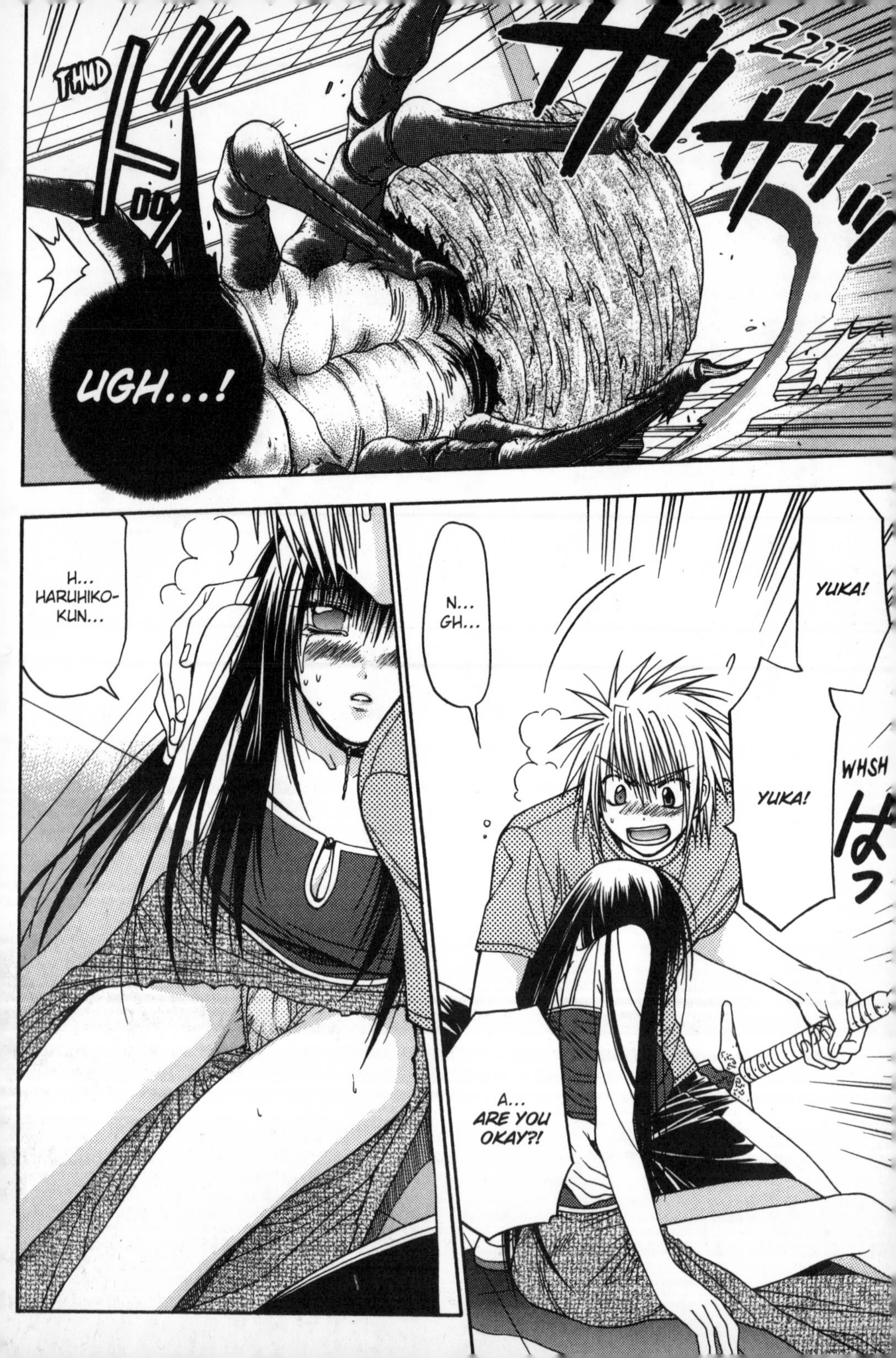

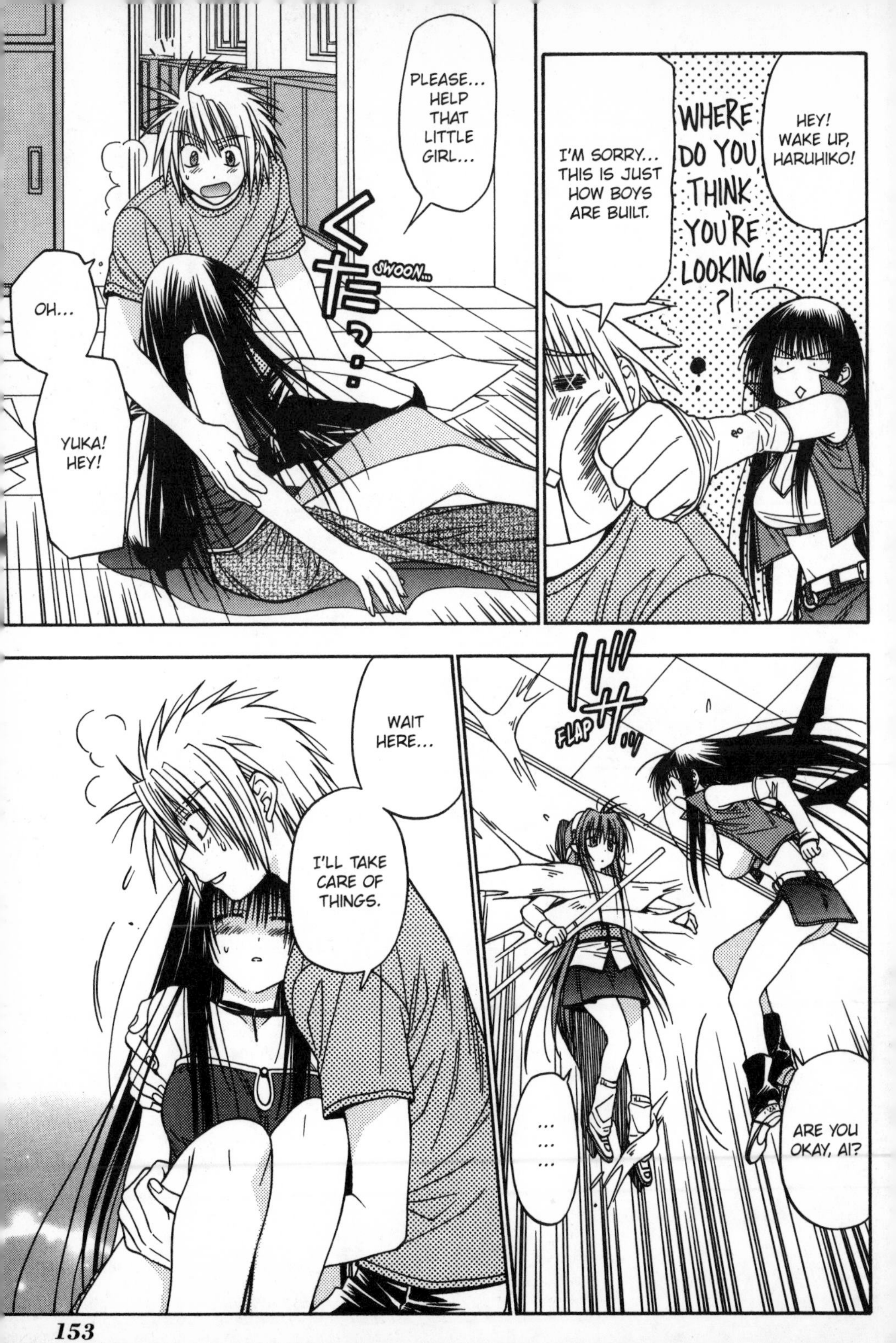
HEY! WAKE UP, HARUHIKO!
WHERE DO YOU THINK YOU'RE LOOKING ?!
I'M SORRY... THIS IS JUST HOW BOYS ARE BUILT.
PLEASE... HELP THAT LITTLE GIRL...
くたっ
SWOON...
OH...
YUKA! HEY!
FLAP
ARE YOU OKAY, AI?
....
WAIT HERE...
I'LL TAKE CARE OF THINGS.

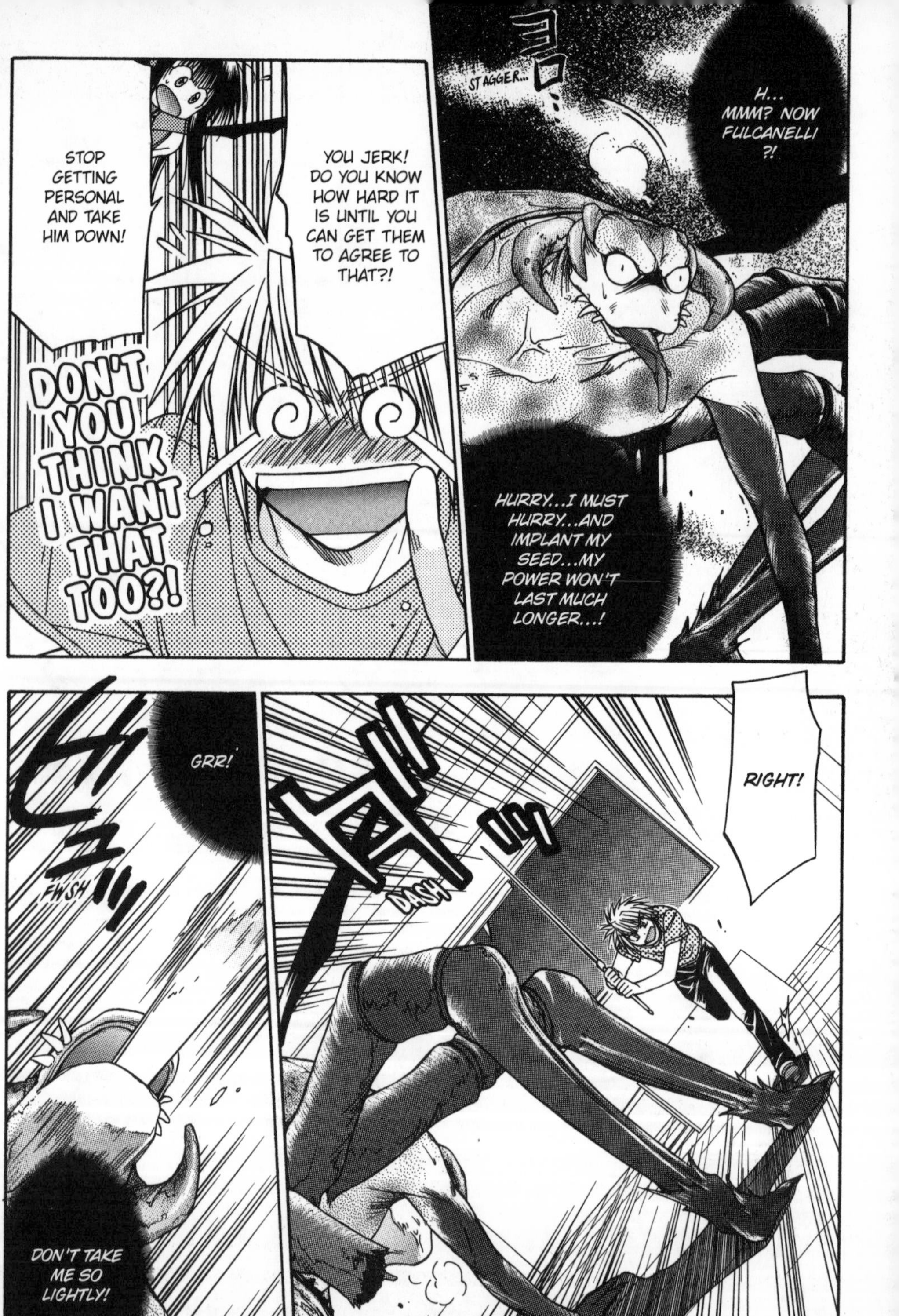
STAGGER...
H... MMM? NOW FULCANELLI ?!
HURRY...I MUST HURRY...AND IMPLANT MY SEED...MY POWER WON'T LAST MUCH LONGER...!
YOU JERK! DO YOU KNOW HOW HARD IT IS UNTIL YOU CAN GET THEM TO AGREE TO THAT?!
STOP GETTING PERSONAL AND TAKE HIM DOWN!
DON'T YOU THINK I WANT THAT TOO?!
RIGHT!
DASH
GRR!
FWSH
DON'T TAKE ME SO LIGHTLY!

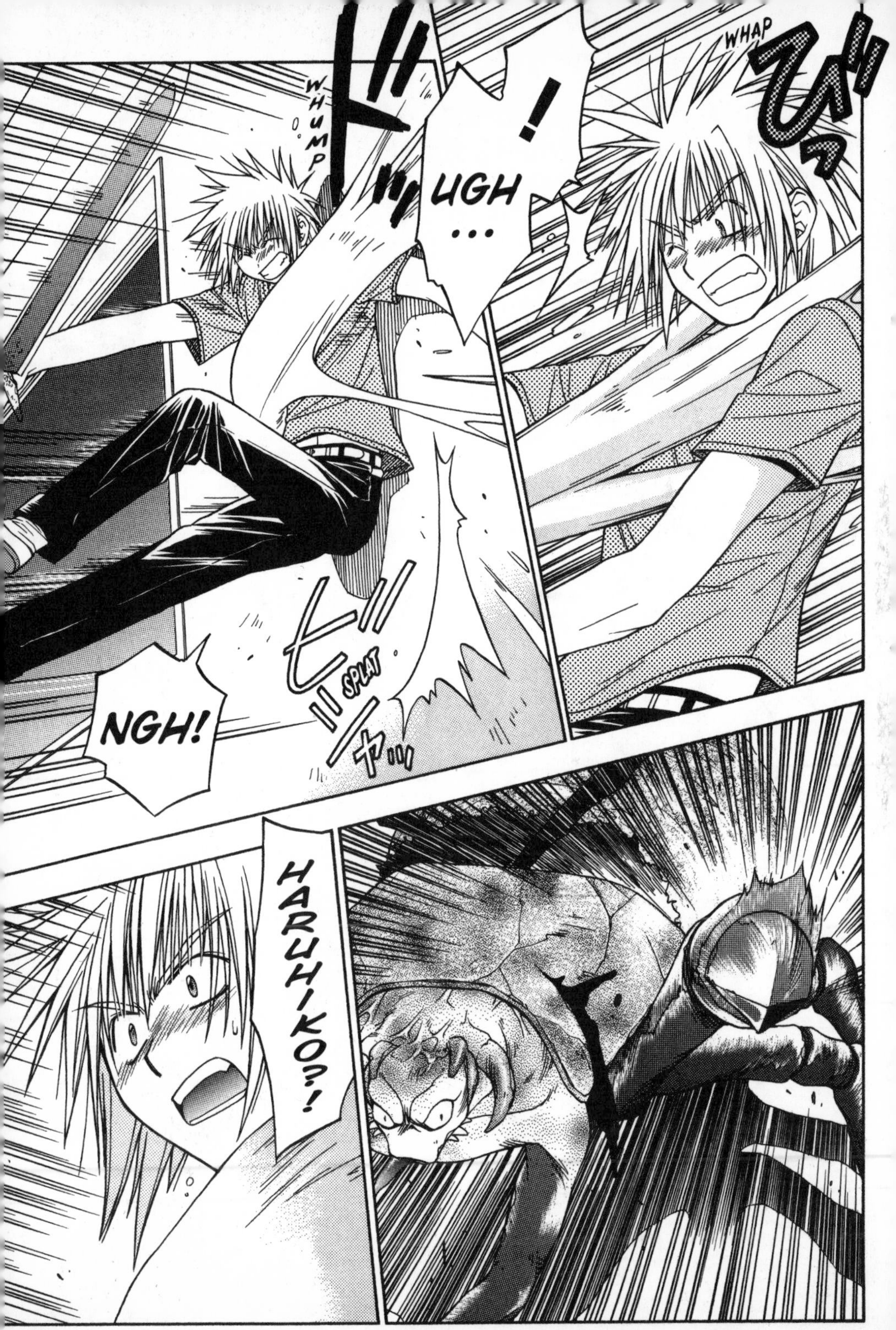
WHAP
!
UGH ...
WHUMP
SPLAT
NGH!
HARUHIKO?!

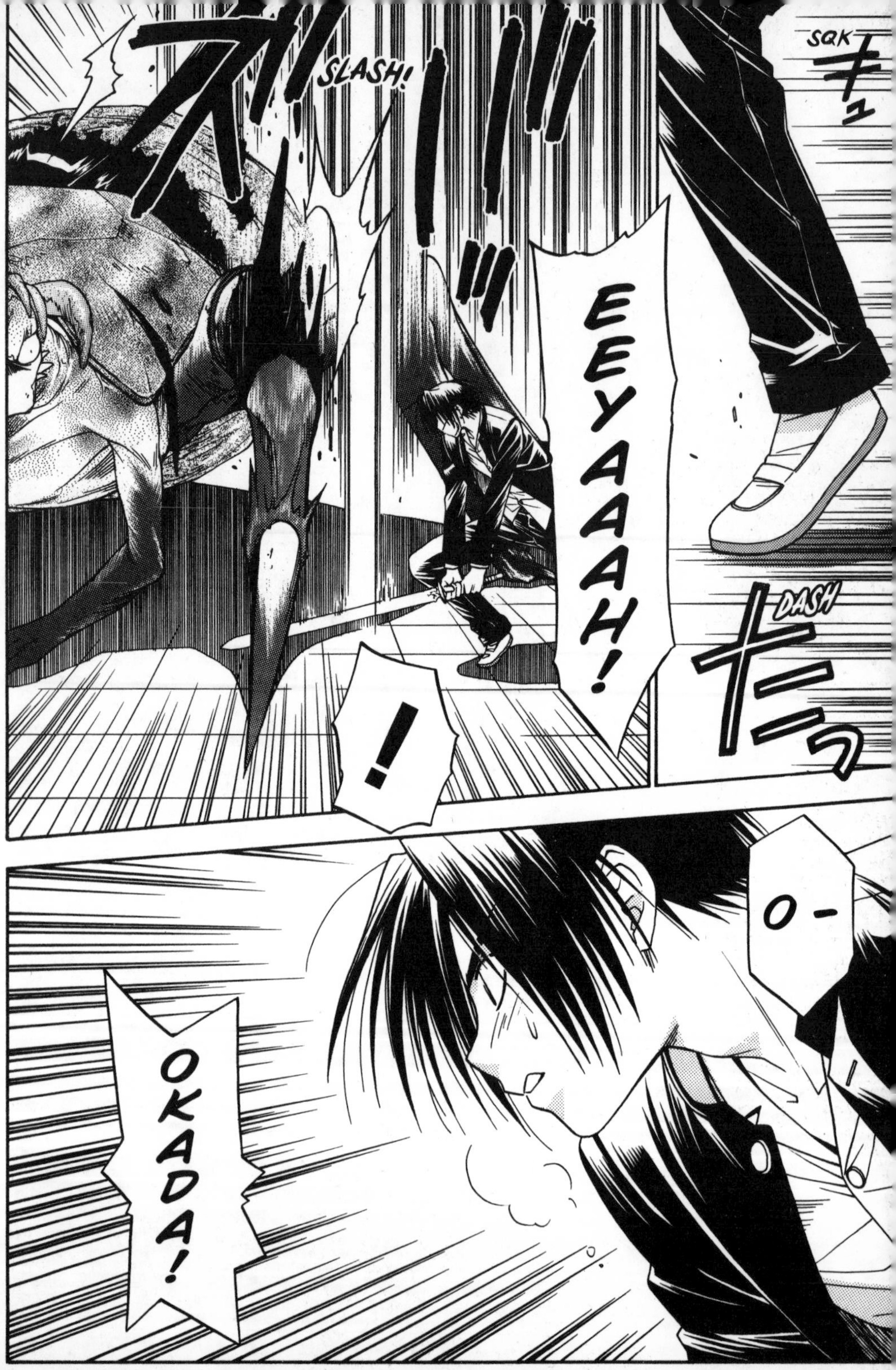
SQK
DASH
SLASH!
EEYAAAAH!
!
O-
OKADA!

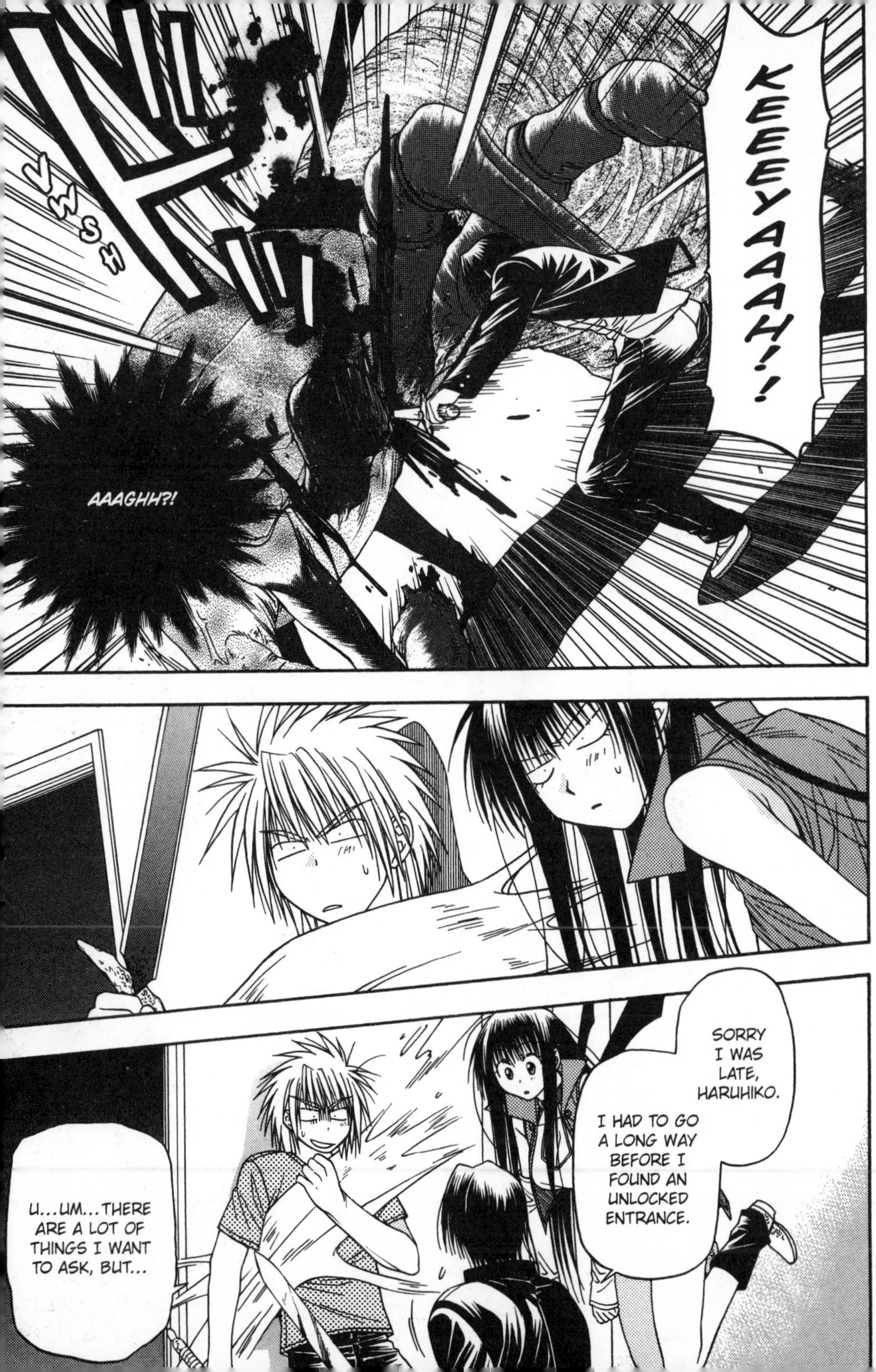
KEEEYAAAAH!!
VWSH
AAAGHH?!
SORRY I WAS LATE, HARUHIKO.
I HAD TO GO A LONG WAY BEFORE I FOUND AN UNLOCKED ENTRANCE.
U...UM...THERE ARE A LOT OF THINGS I WANT TO ASK, BUT...

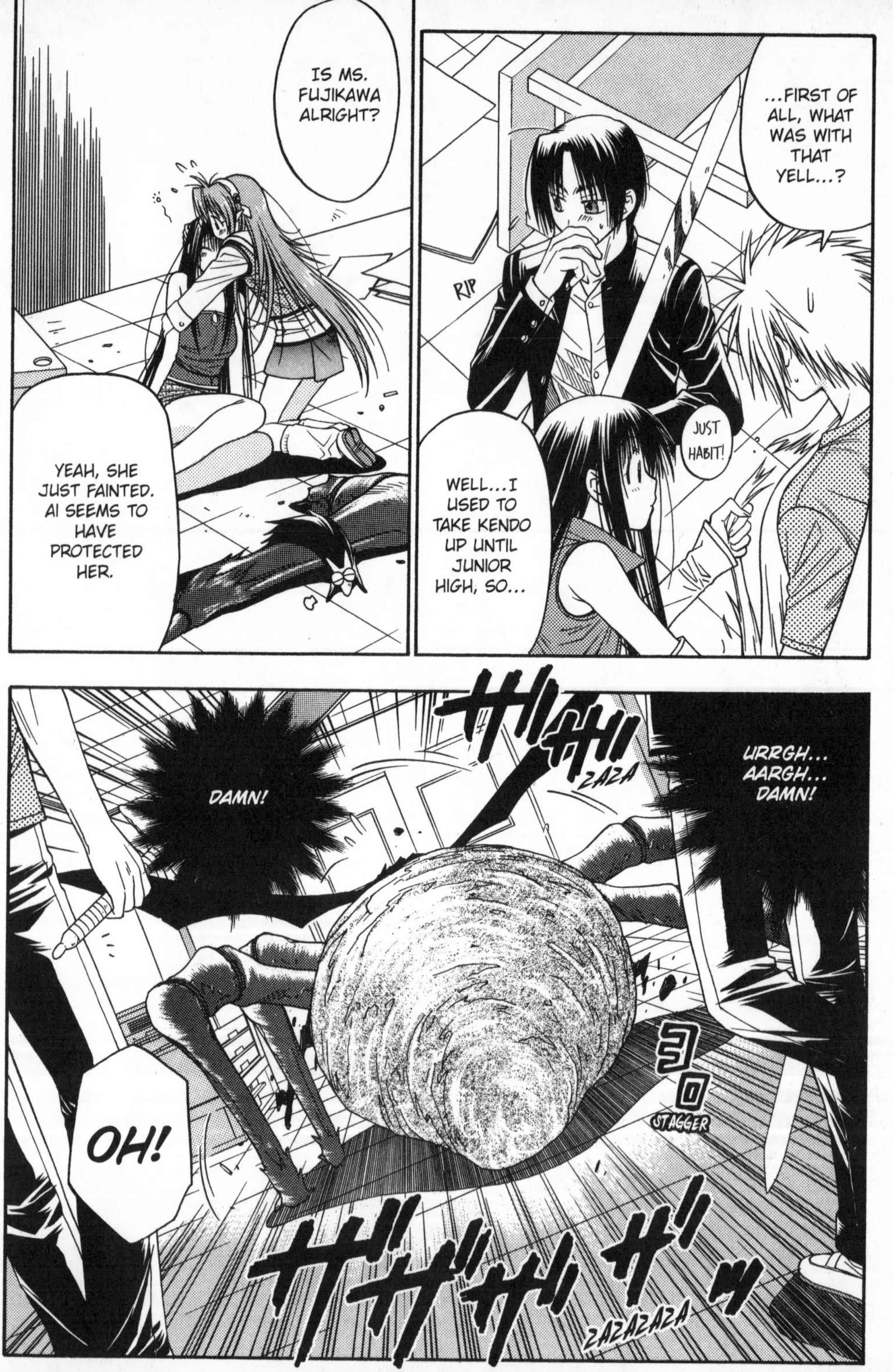
...FIRST OF ALL, WHAT WAS WITH THAT YELL...?
JUST HABIT!
RIP
WELL...I USED TO TAKE KENDO UP UNTIL JUNIOR HIGH, SO...
IS MS. FUJIKAWA ALRIGHT?
YEAH, SHE JUST FAINTED. AI SEEMS TO HAVE PROTECTED HER.
ZAZA
URRGH... AARGH... DAMN!
DAMN!
STAGGER
OH!
ZAZAZAZA

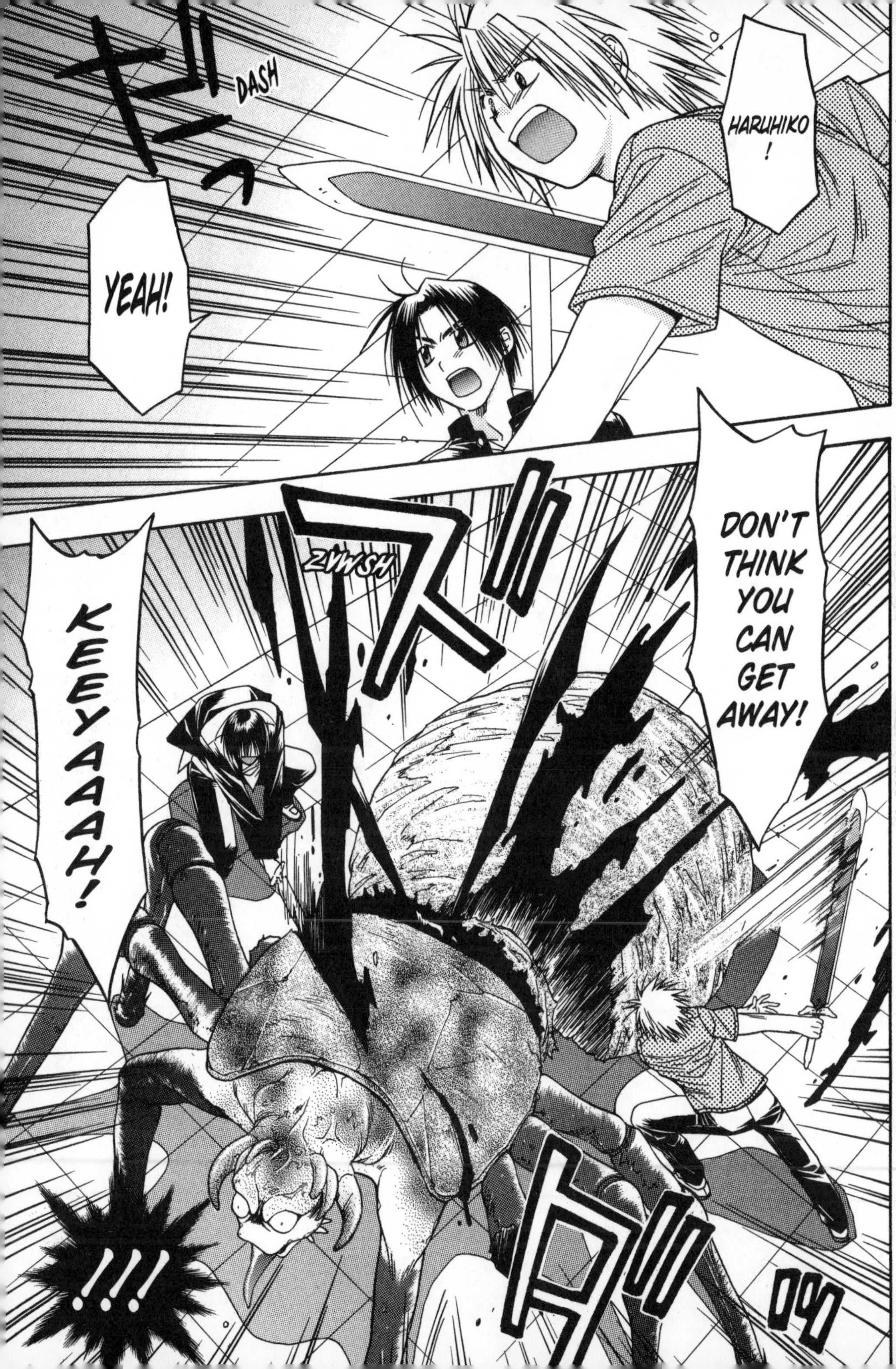
HARUHIKO
!
DASH
YEAH!
DON'T THINK YOU CAN GET AWAY!
ZWSH
KEEYAAAAH!
!!!
DOO

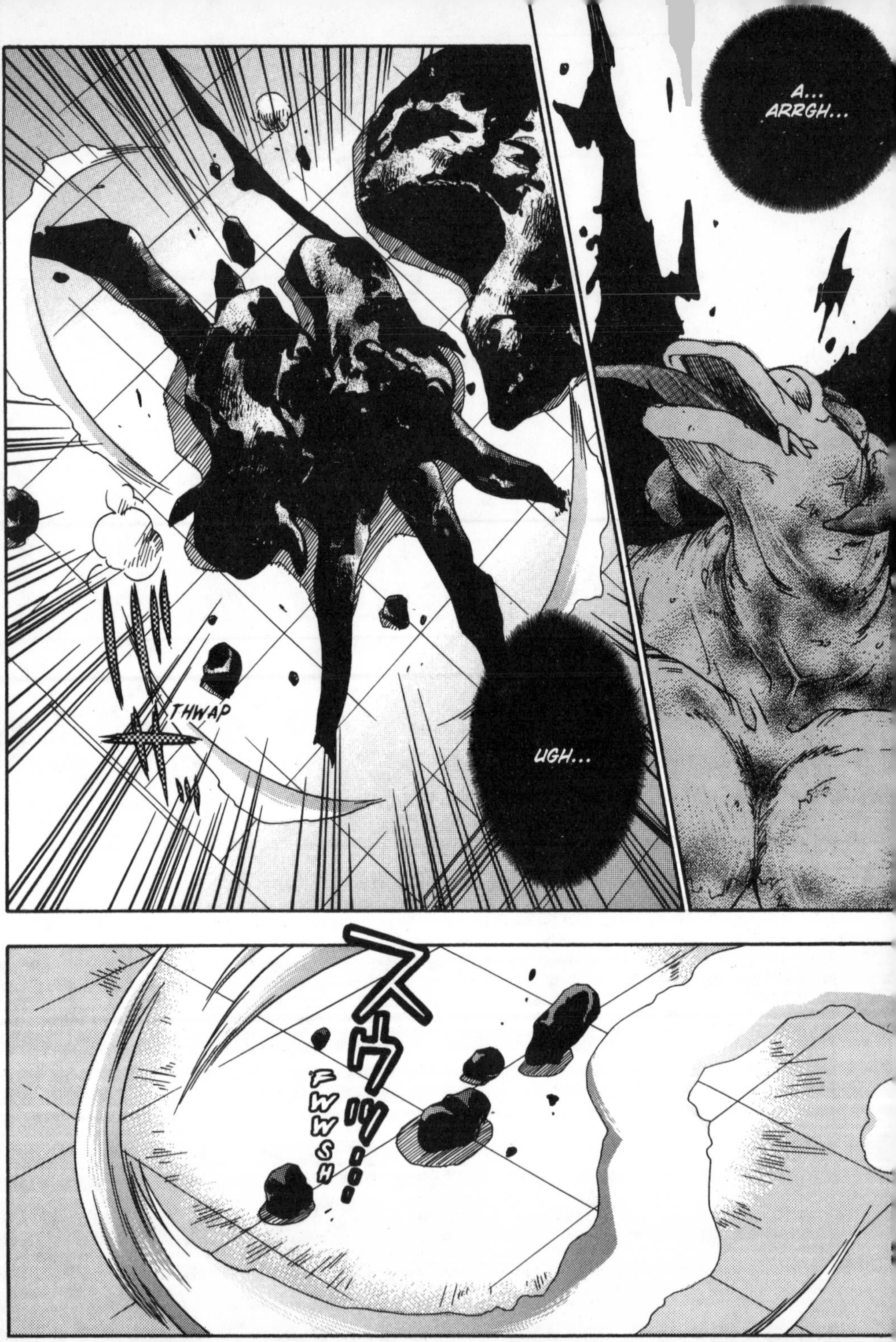
A... ARRGH...
THWAP
UGH...
FWWSH

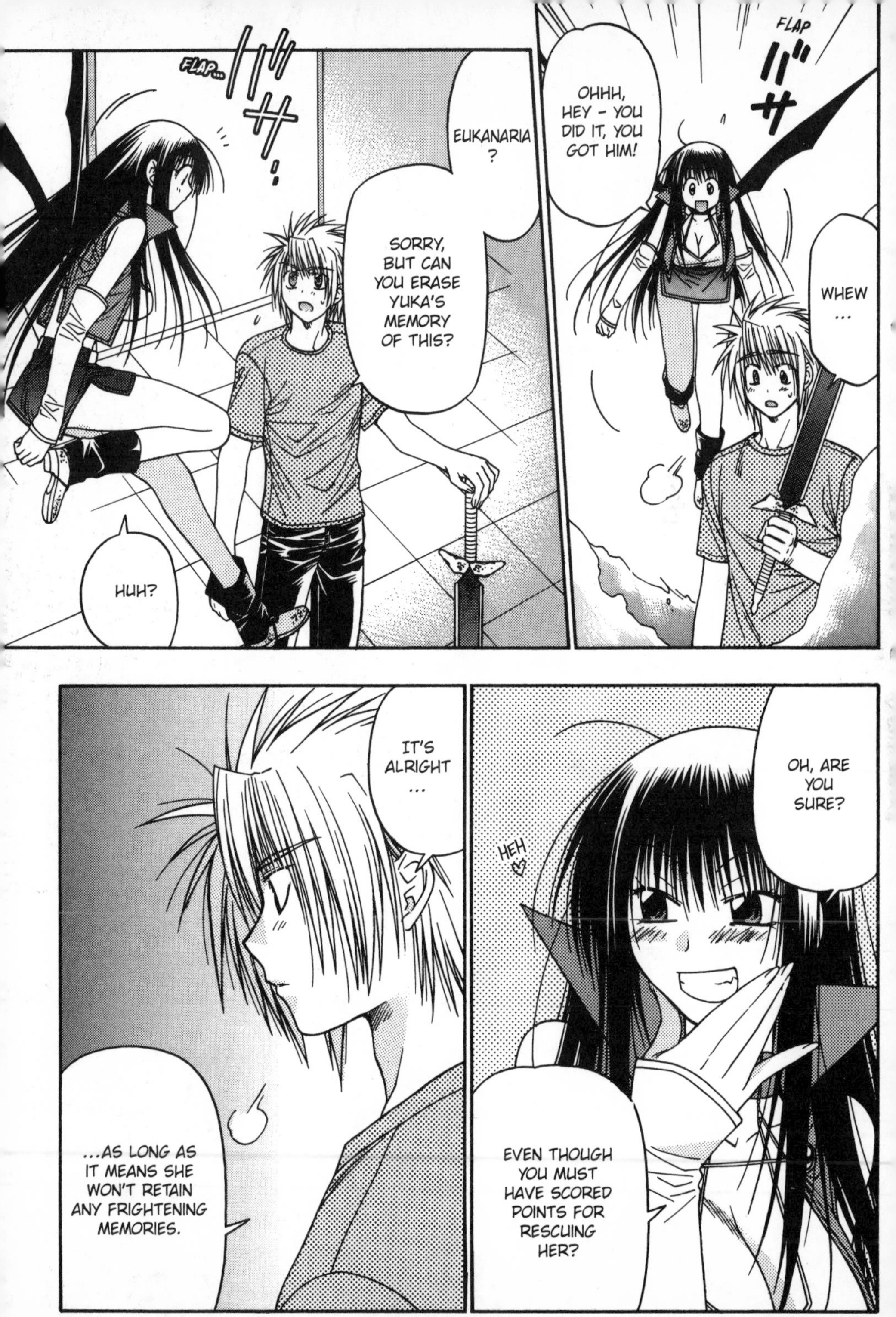
FLAP
OHHH, HEY - YOU DID IT, YOU GOT HIM!
WHEW ...
FLAP...
EUKANARIA ?
SORRY, BUT CAN YOU ERASE YUKA'S MEMORY OF THIS?
HUH?
OH, ARE YOU SURE?
HEH
EVEN THOUGH YOU MUST HAVE SCORED POINTS FOR RESCUING HER?
IT'S ALRIGHT ...
...AS LONG AS IT MEANS SHE WON'T RETAIN ANY FRIGHTENING MEMORIES.

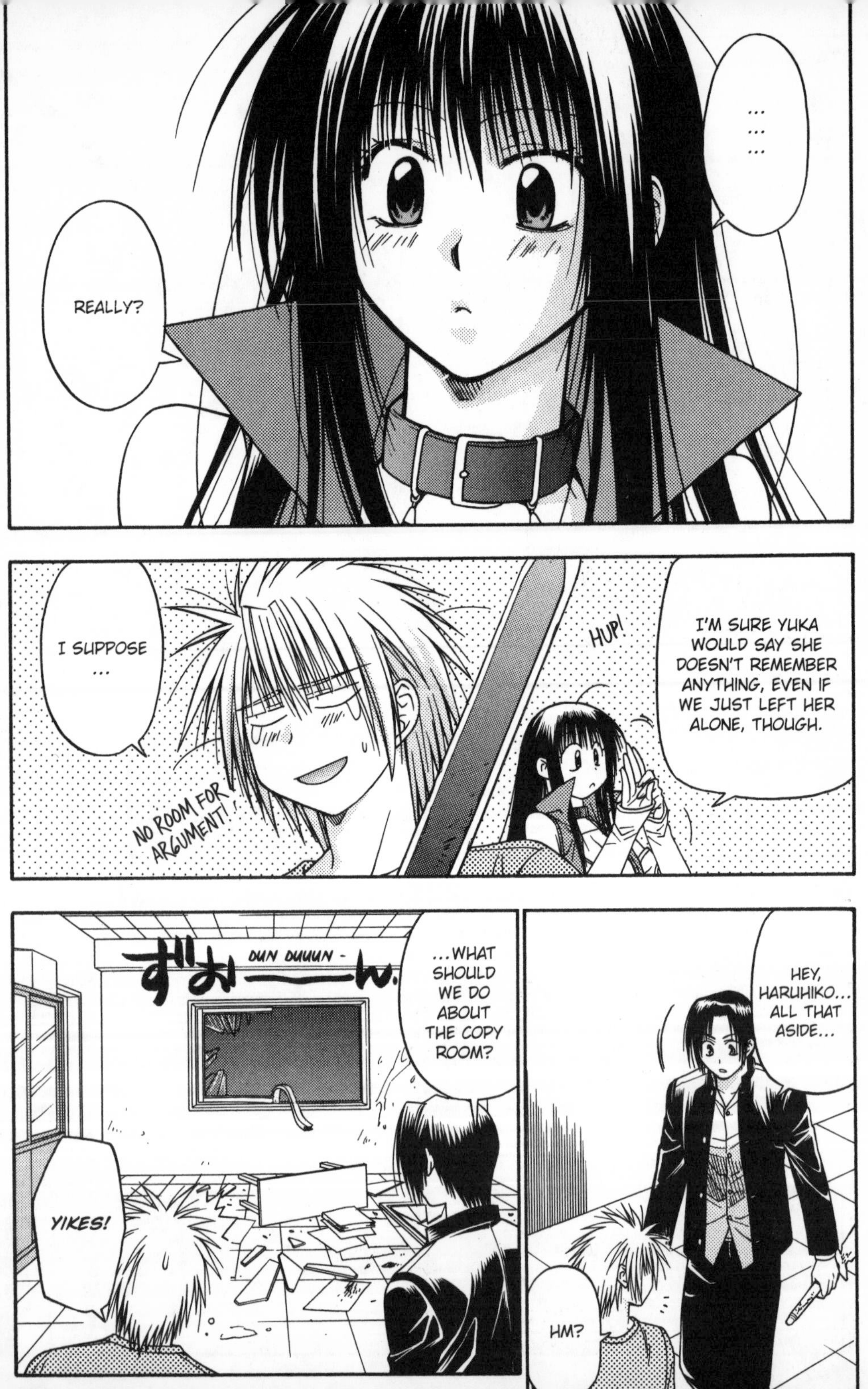
...
...
...
REALLY?
I'M SURE YUKA WOULD SAY SHE DOESN'T REMEMBER ANYTHING, EVEN IF WE JUST LEFT HER ALONE, THOUGH.
HUP!
I SUPPOSE ...
NO ROOM FOR ARGUMENT!
HEY, HARUHIKO... ALL THAT ASIDE...
HM?
...WHAT SHOULD WE DO ABOUT THE COPY ROOM?
ずお――ん
DUN DUUUN-
YIKES!

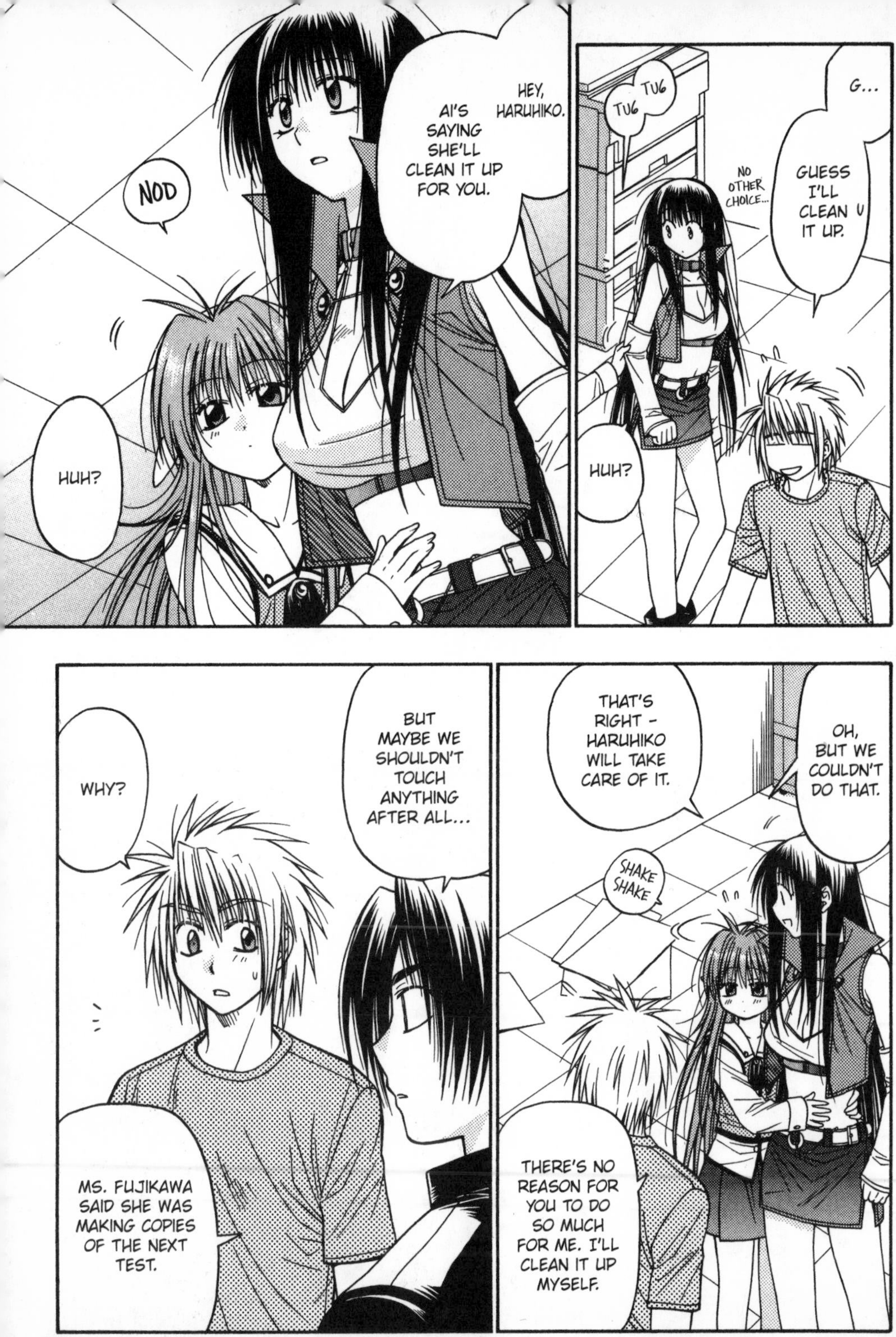
G...
GUESS I'LL CLEAN U IT UP.
TUG TUG
NO OTHER CHOICE...
HUH?
HEY, HARUHIKO.
AI'S SAYING SHE'LL CLEAN IT UP FOR YOU.
NOD
HUH?
OH, BUT WE COULDN'T DO THAT.
THAT'S RIGHT - HARUHIKO WILL TAKE CARE OF IT.
SHAKE SHAKE
THERE'S NO REASON FOR YOU TO DO SO MUCH FOR ME. I'LL CLEAN IT UP MYSELF.
BUT MAYBE WE SHOULDN'T TOUCH ANYTHING AFTER ALL...
WHY?
MS. FUJIKAWA SAID SHE WAS MAKING COPIES OF THE NEXT TEST.

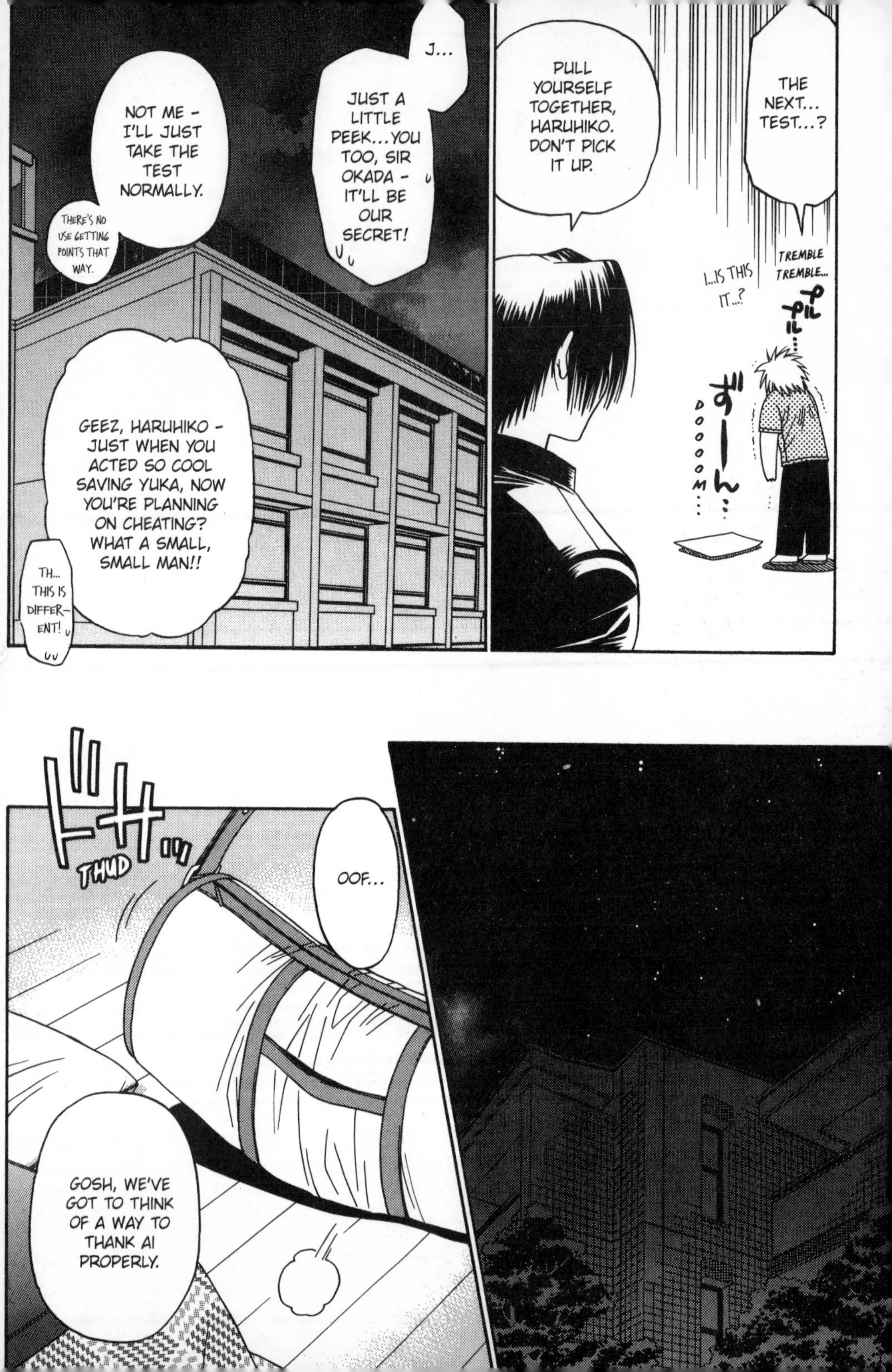
THE NEXT... TEST...?
PULL YOURSELF TOGETHER, HARUHIKO. DON'T PICK IT UP.
I...IS THIS IT...?
TREMBLE TREMBLE...
プルプル…
ずーん…
DOOOOOM...
J...
JUST A LITTLE PEEK...YOU TOO, SIR OKADA - IT'LL BE OUR SECRET!
NOT ME - I'LL JUST TAKE THE TEST NORMALLY.
THERE'S NO USE GETTING POINTS THAT WAY.
GEEZ, HARUHIKO - JUST WHEN YOU ACTED SO COOL SAVING YUKA, NOW YOU'RE PLANNING ON CHEATING? WHAT A SMALL, SMALL MAN!!
TH... THIS IS DIFFERENT!
ドサ
THUD
OOF...
GOSH, WE'VE GOT TO THINK OF A WAY TO THANK AI PROPERLY.

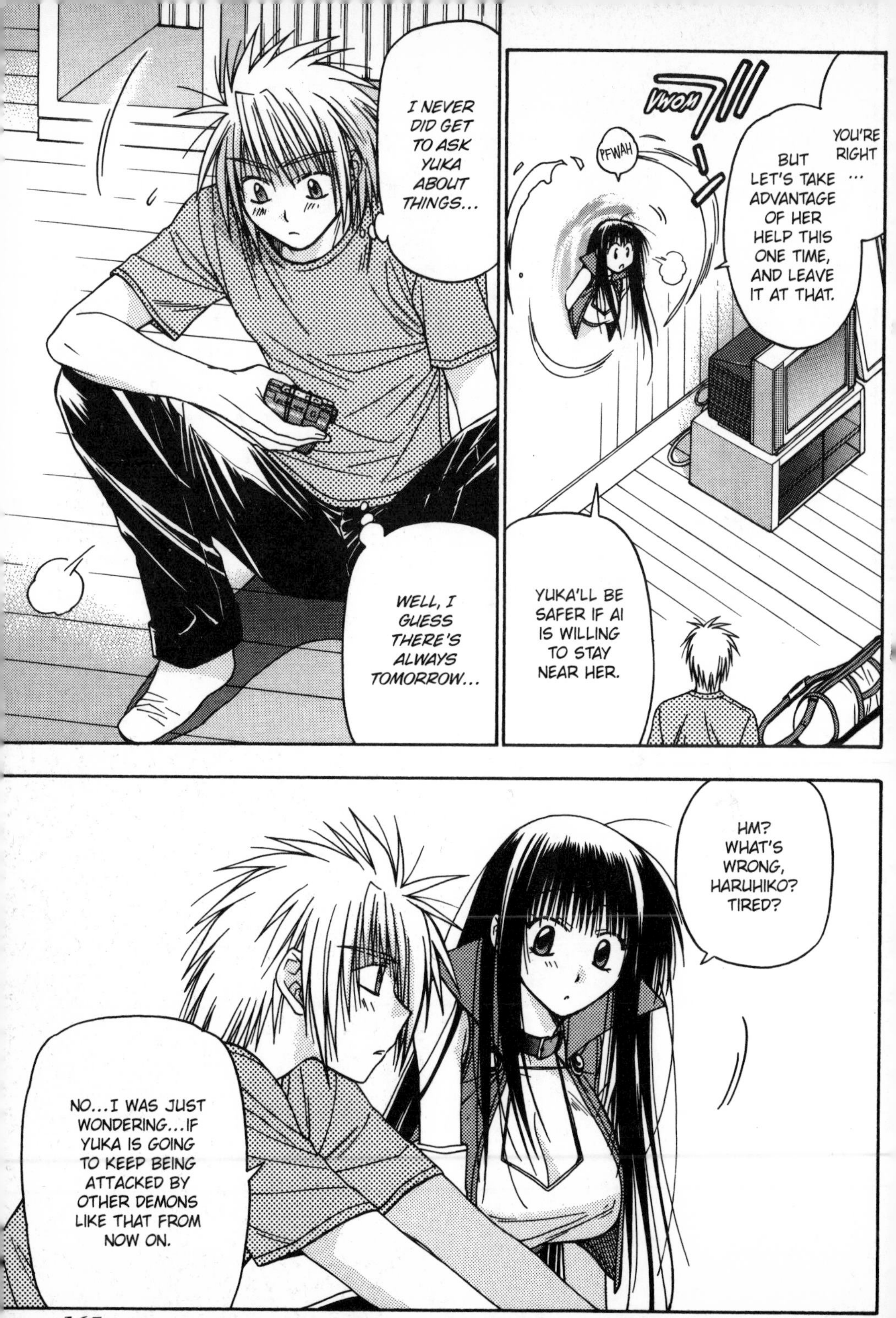
YOU'RE RIGHT...
BUT LET'S TAKE ADVANTAGE OF HER HELP THIS ONE TIME, AND LEAVE IT AT THAT.
VWOM
PFWAH
YUKA'LL BE SAFER IF AI IS WILLING TO STAY NEAR HER.
I NEVER DID GET TO ASK YUKA ABOUT THINGS...
WELL, I GUESS THERE'S ALWAYS TOMORROW...
HM? WHAT'S WRONG, HARUHIKO? TIRED?
NO...I WAS JUST WONDERING...IF YUKA IS GOING TO KEEP BEING ATTACKED BY OTHER DEMONS LIKE THAT FROM NOW ON.

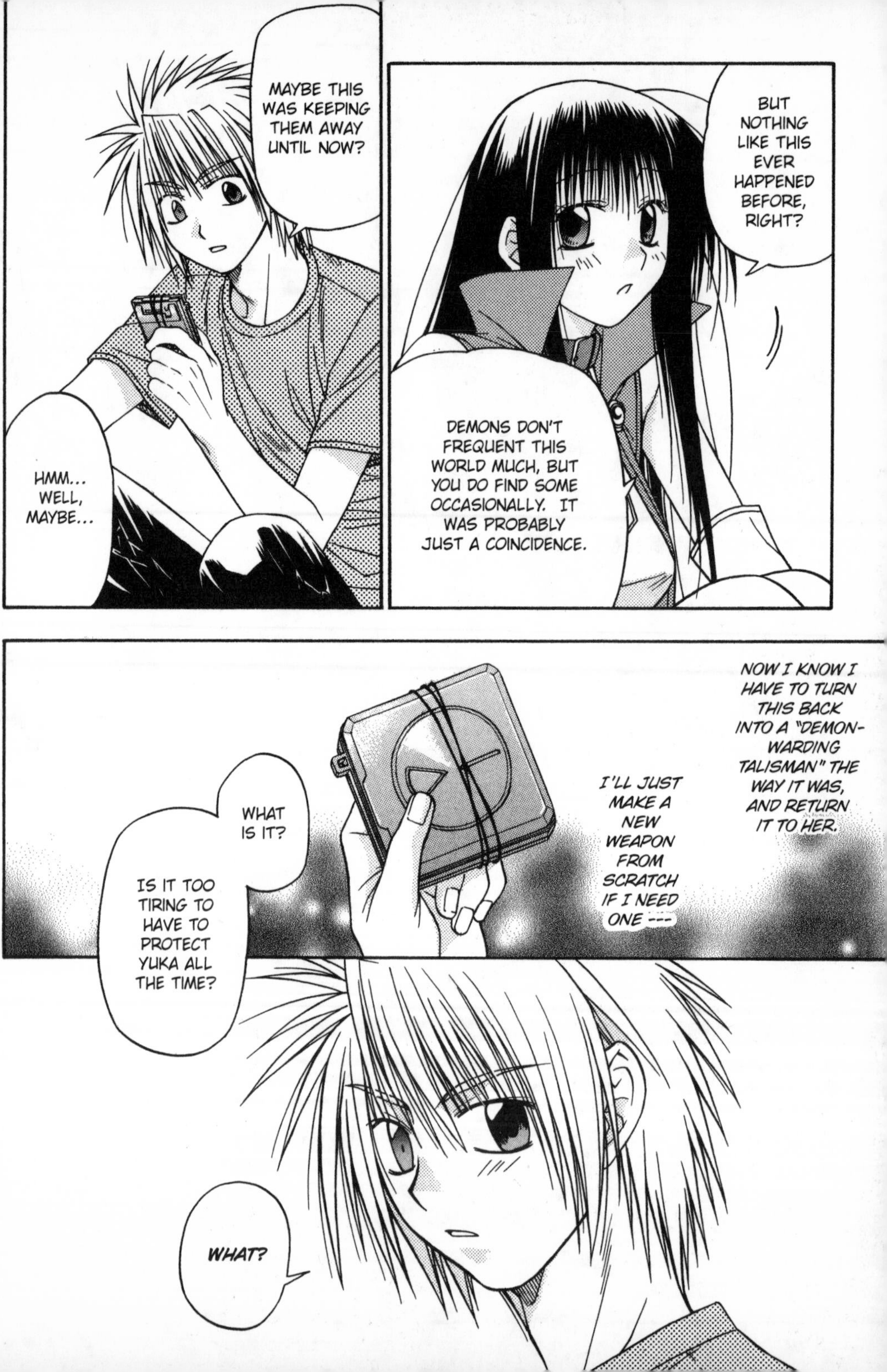
BUT NOTHING LIKE THIS EVER HAPPENED BEFORE, RIGHT?
DEMONS DON'T FREQUENT THIS WORLD MUCH, BUT YOU DO FIND SOME OCCASIONALLY. IT WAS PROBABLY JUST A COINCIDENCE.
MAYBE THIS WAS KEEPING THEM AWAY UNTIL NOW?
HMM... WELL, MAYBE...
NOW I KNOW I HAVE TO TURN THIS BACK INTO A "DEMON-WARDING TALISMAN" THE WAY IT WAS, AND RETURN IT TO HER.
I'LL JUST MAKE A NEW WEAPON FROM SCRATCH IF I NEED ONE ---
WHAT IS IT?
IS IT TOO TIRING TO HAVE TO PROTECT YUKA ALL THE TIME?
WHAT?

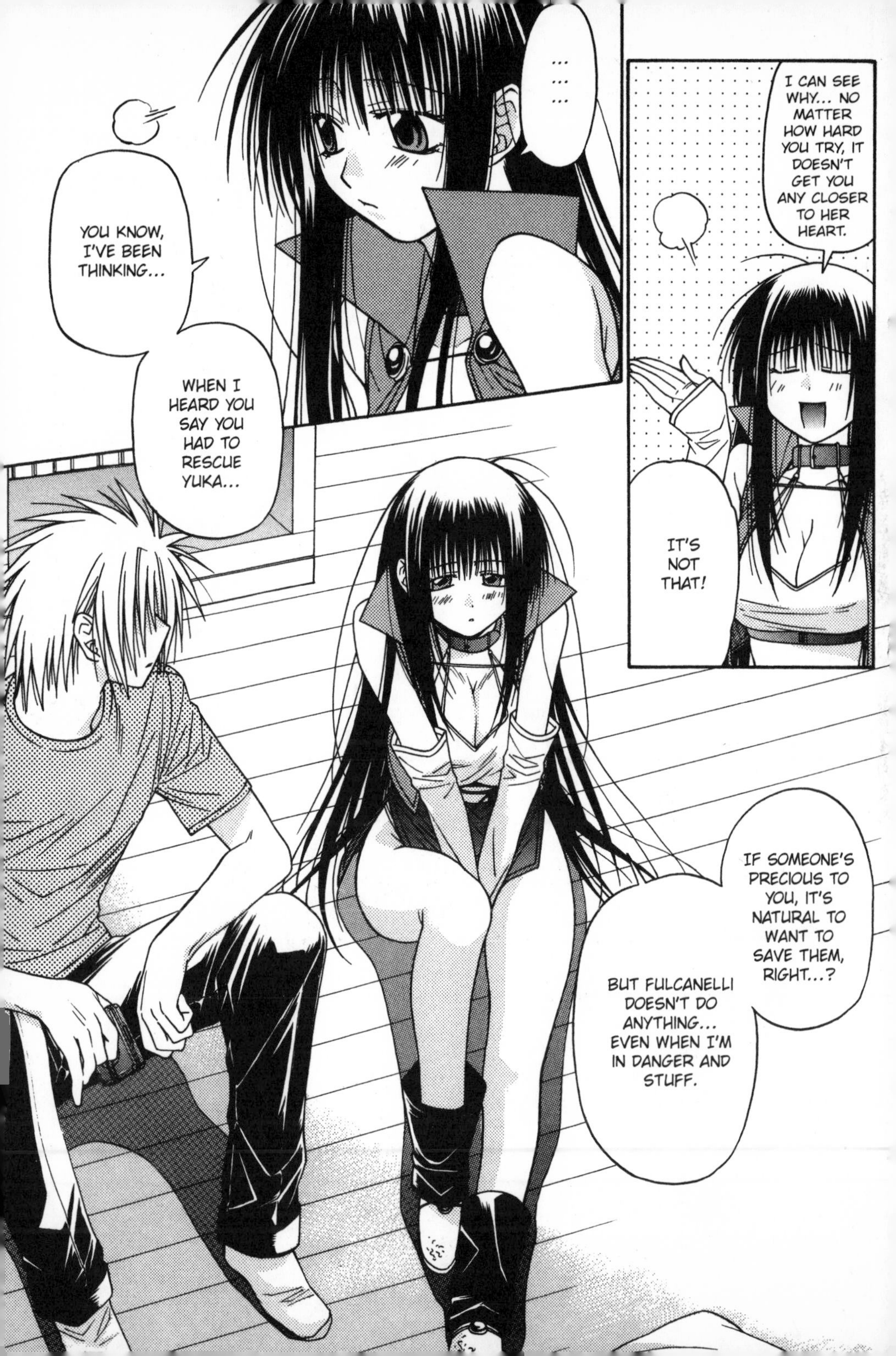
I CAN SEE WHY... NO MATTER HOW HARD YOU TRY, IT DOESN'T GET YOU ANY CLOSER TO HER HEART.
IT'S NOT THAT!
....
YOU KNOW, I'VE BEEN THINKING...
WHEN I HEARD YOU SAY YOU HAD TO RESCUE YUKA...
IF SOMEONE'S PRECIOUS TO YOU, IT'S NATURAL TO WANT TO SAVE THEM, RIGHT...?
BUT FULCANELLI DOESN'T DO ANYTHING... EVEN WHEN I'M IN DANGER AND STUFF.

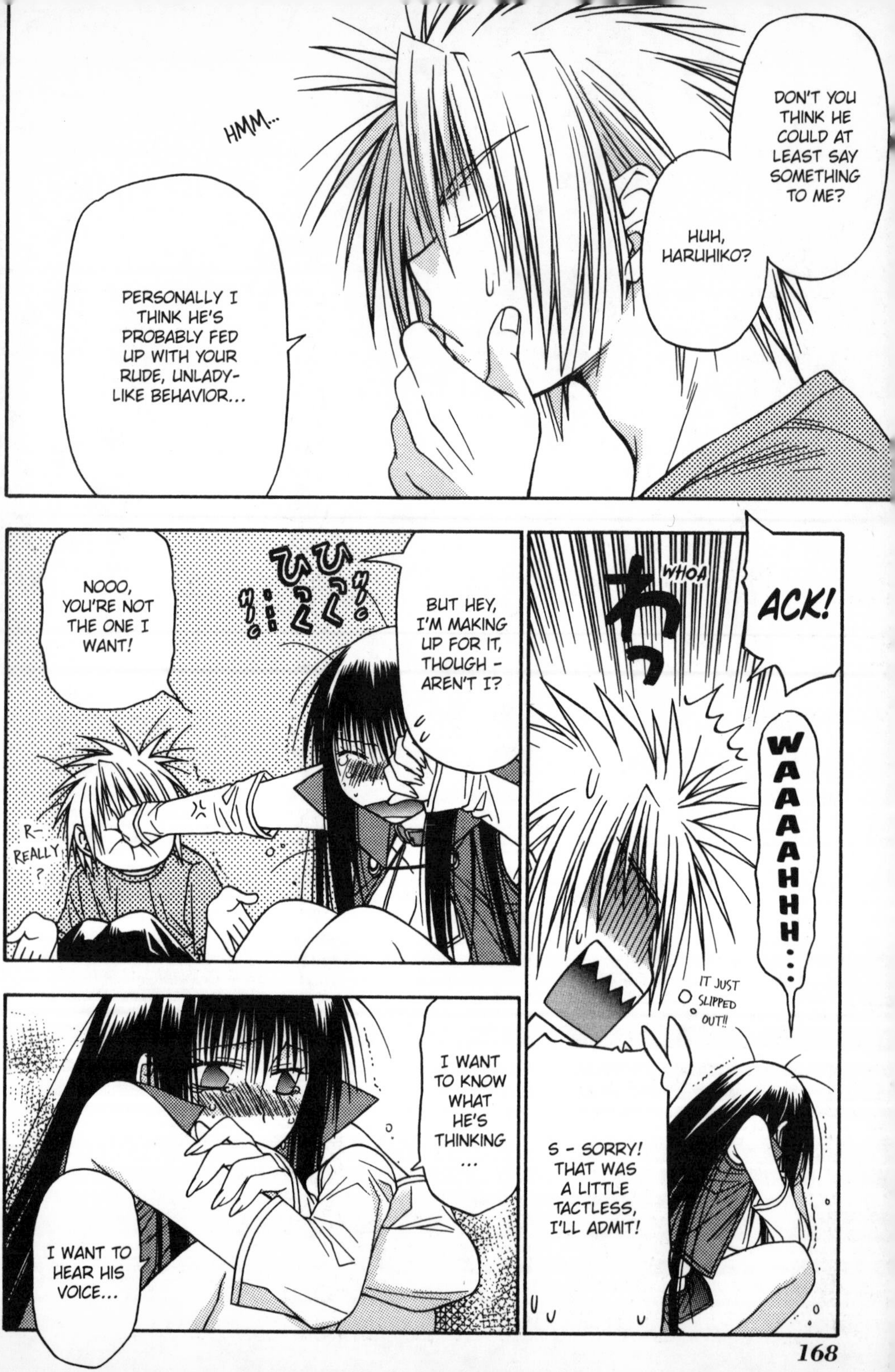
DON'T YOU THINK HE COULD AT LEAST SAY SOMETHING TO ME?
HUH, HARUHIKO?
HMM...
PERSONALLY I THINK HE'S PROBABLY FED UP WITH YOUR RUDE, UNLADY-LIKE BEHAVIOR...
わっ
WHOA
ACK!
WAAAAAHHH...
IT JUST SLIPPED OUT!!
S - SORRY! THAT WAS A LITTLE TACTLESS, I'LL ADMIT!
BUT HEY, I'M MAKING UP FOR IT, THOUGH - AREN'T I?
ひっく ひっく
NOOO, YOU'RE NOT THE ONE I WANT!
R-REALLY?
I WANT TO KNOW WHAT HE'S THINKING...
I WANT TO HEAR HIS VOICE...

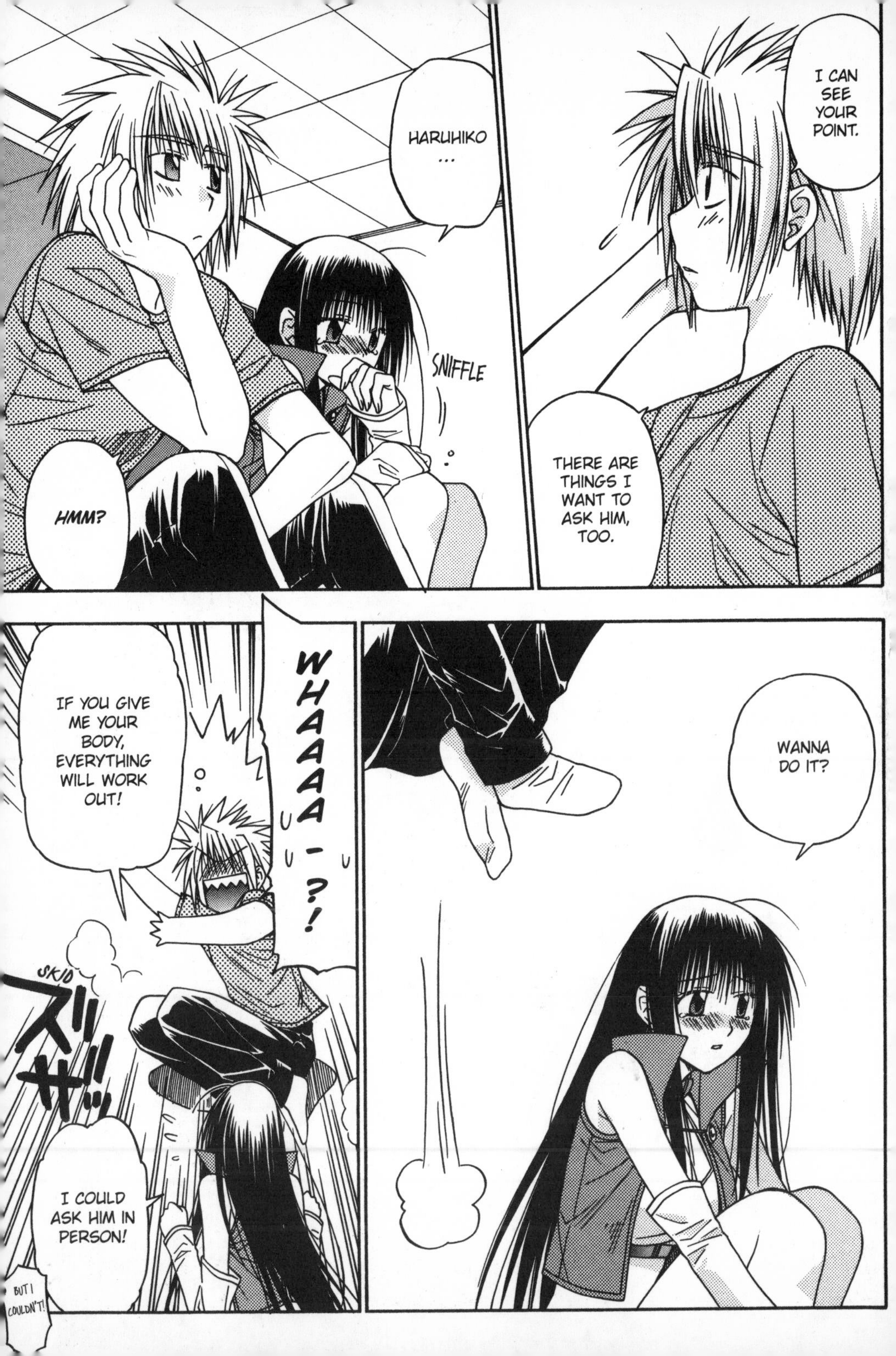
I CAN SEE YOUR POINT.
THERE ARE THINGS I WANT TO ASK HIM, TOO.
HARUHIKO ...
SNIFFLE
HMM?
WANNA DO IT?
WHAAAAA-?!
IF YOU GIVE ME YOUR BODY, EVERYTHING WILL WORK OUT!
SKID
I COULD ASK HIM IN PERSON!
BUT I COULDN'T!

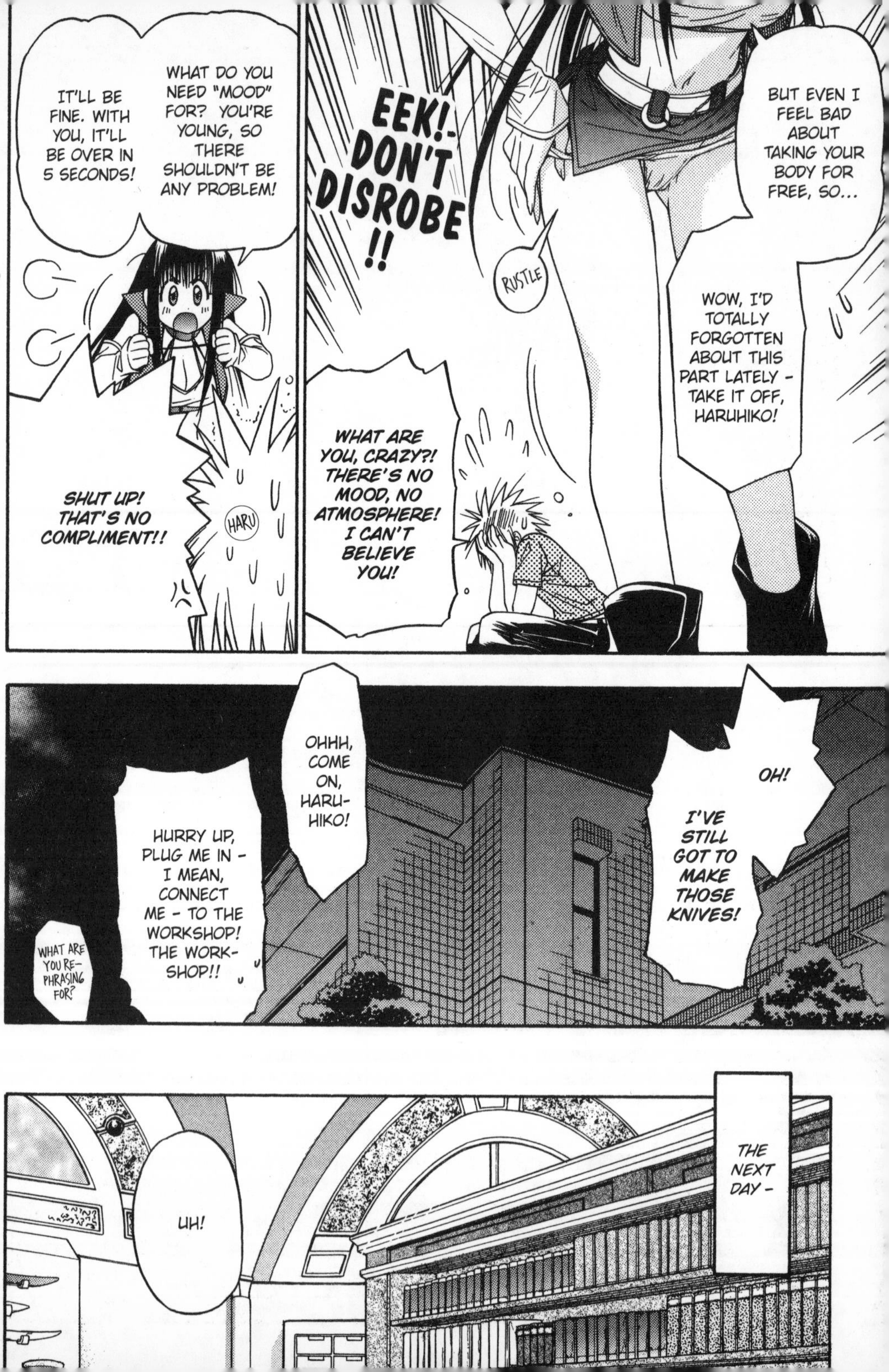
BUT EVEN I FEEL BAD ABOUT TAKING YOUR BODY FOR FREE, SO...
WOW, I'D TOTALLY FORGOTTEN ABOUT THIS PART LATELY - TAKE IT OFF, HARUHIKO!
EEK!- DON'T DISROBE!!
RUSTLE
WHAT ARE YOU, CRAZY?! THERE'S NO MOOD, NO ATMOSPHERE! I CAN'T BELIEVE YOU!
WHAT DO YOU NEED "MOOD" FOR? YOU'RE YOUNG, SO THERE SHOULDN'T BE ANY PROBLEM!
IT'LL BE FINE. WITH YOU, IT'LL BE OVER IN 5 SECONDS!
SHUT UP! THAT'S NO COMPLIMENT!!
HARU
OH!
I'VE STILL GOT TO MAKE THOSE KNIVES!
OHHH, COME ON, HARU-HIKO!
HURRY UP, PLUG ME IN - I MEAN, CONNECT ME - TO THE WORKSHOP! THE WORK-SHOP!!
WHAT ARE YOU RE-PHRASING FOR?
THE NEXT DAY -
UH!

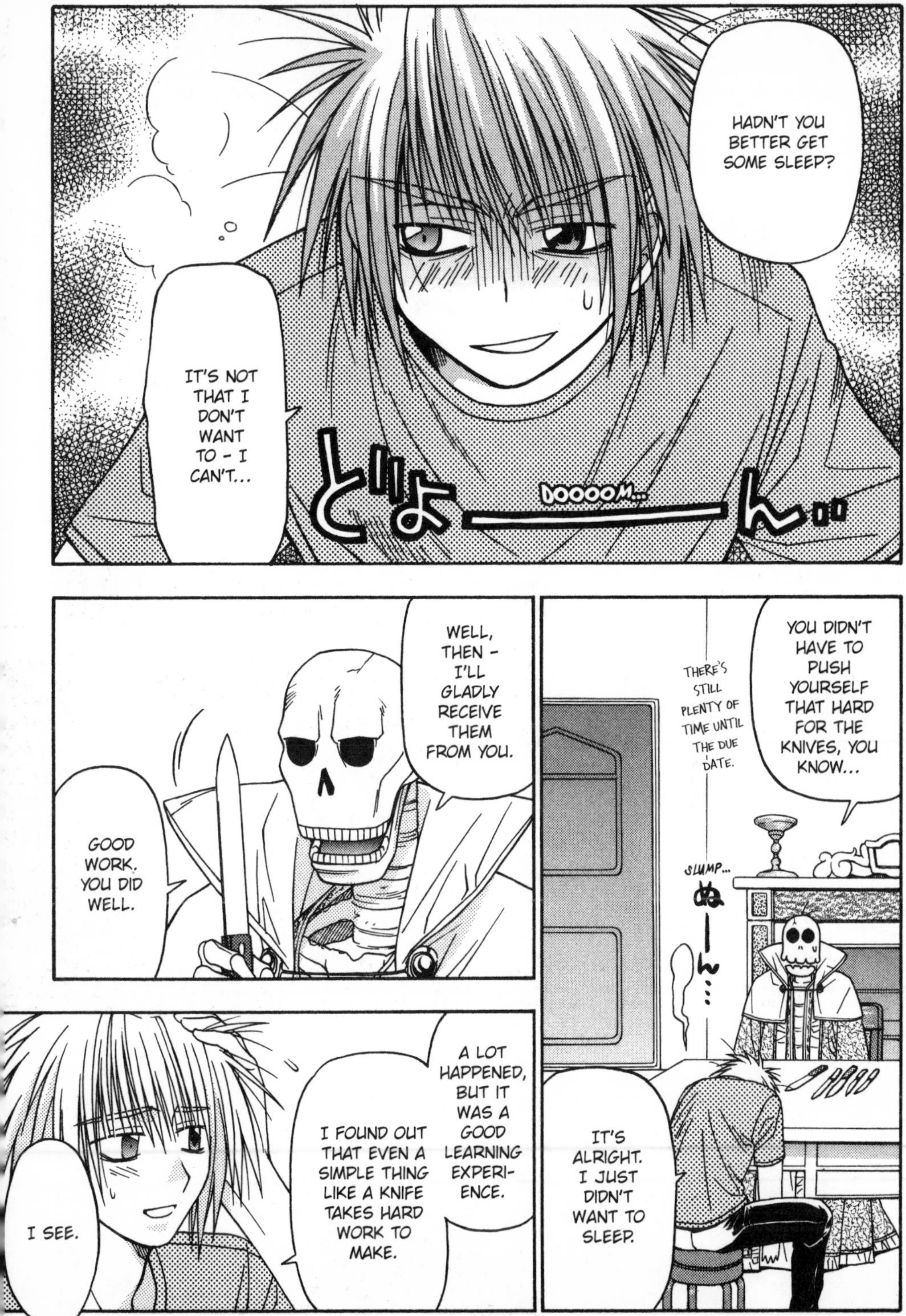
HADN'T YOU BETTER GET SOME SLEEP?
IT'S NOT THAT I DON'T WANT TO - I CAN'T...
どよーーーん
DOOOOM...
YOU DIDN'T HAVE TO PUSH YOURSELF THAT HARD FOR THE KNIVES, YOU KNOW...
THERE'S STILL PLENTY OF TIME UNTIL THE DUE DATE.
SLUMP...
ぬーん...
IT'S ALRIGHT. I JUST DIDN'T WANT TO SLEEP.
WELL, THEN - I'LL GLADLY RECEIVE THEM FROM YOU.
GOOD WORK. YOU DID WELL.
A LOT HAPPENED, BUT IT WAS A GOOD LEARNING EXPERI-ENCE.
I FOUND OUT THAT EVEN A SIMPLE THING LIKE A KNIFE TAKES HARD WORK TO MAKE.
I SEE.

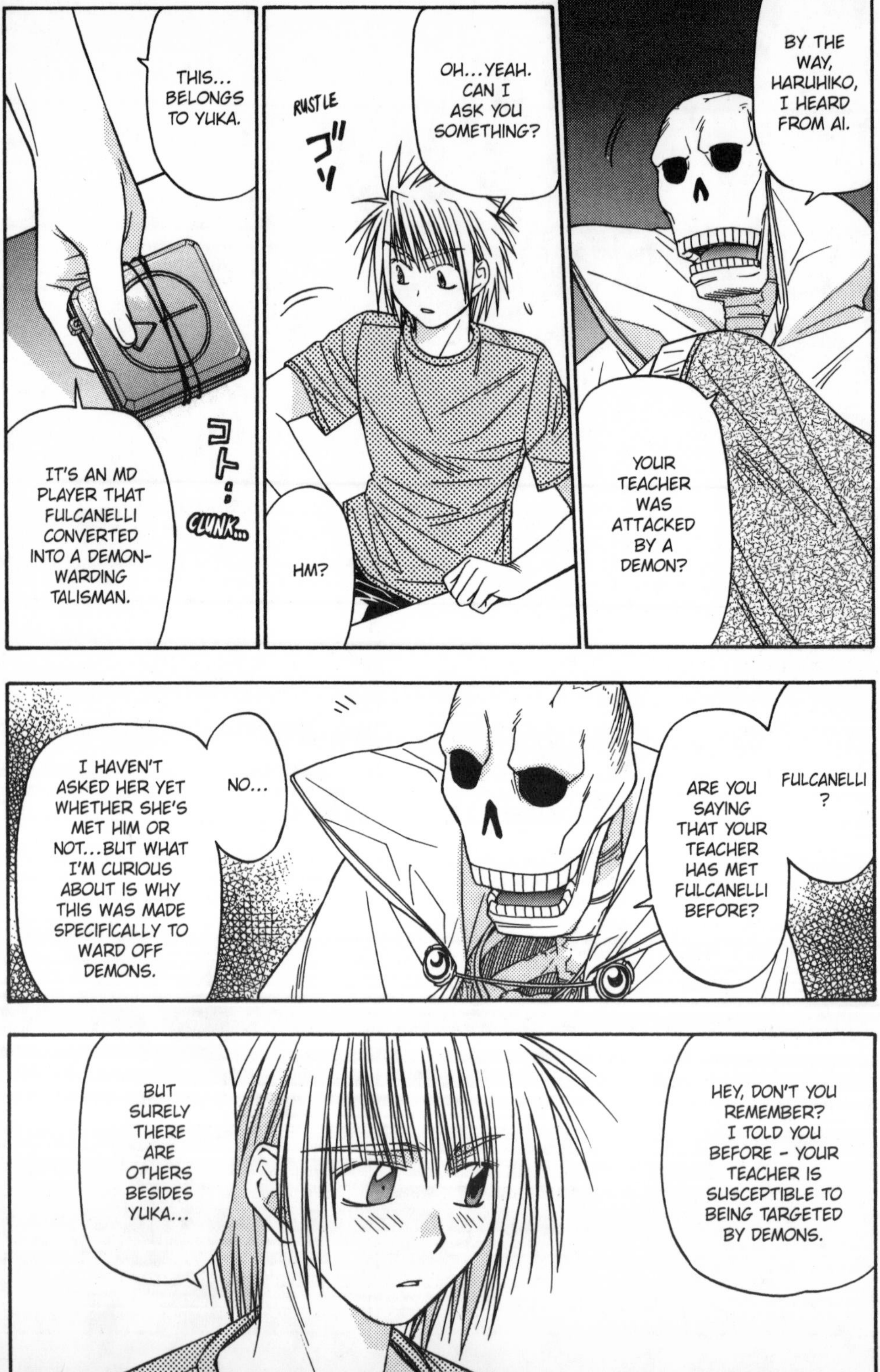
BY THE WAY, HARUHIKO, I HEARD FROM AI.
YOUR TEACHER WAS ATTACKED BY A DEMON?
OH...YEAH. CAN I ASK YOU SOMETHING?
RUSTLE
ゴソ
HM?
THIS... BELONGS TO YUKA.
コト
CLUNK...
IT'S AN MD PLAYER THAT FULCANELLI CONVERTED INTO A DEMON-WARDING TALISMAN.
FULCANELLI?
ARE YOU SAYING THAT YOUR TEACHER HAS MET FULCANELLI BEFORE?
NO...
I HAVEN'T ASKED HER YET WHETHER SHE'S MET HIM OR NOT...BUT WHAT I'M CURIOUS ABOUT IS WHY THIS WAS MADE SPECIFICALLY TO WARD OFF DEMONS.
HEY, DON'T YOU REMEMBER? I TOLD YOU BEFORE - YOUR TEACHER IS SUSCEPTIBLE TO BEING TARGETED BY DEMONS.
BUT SURELY THERE ARE OTHERS BESIDES YUKA...

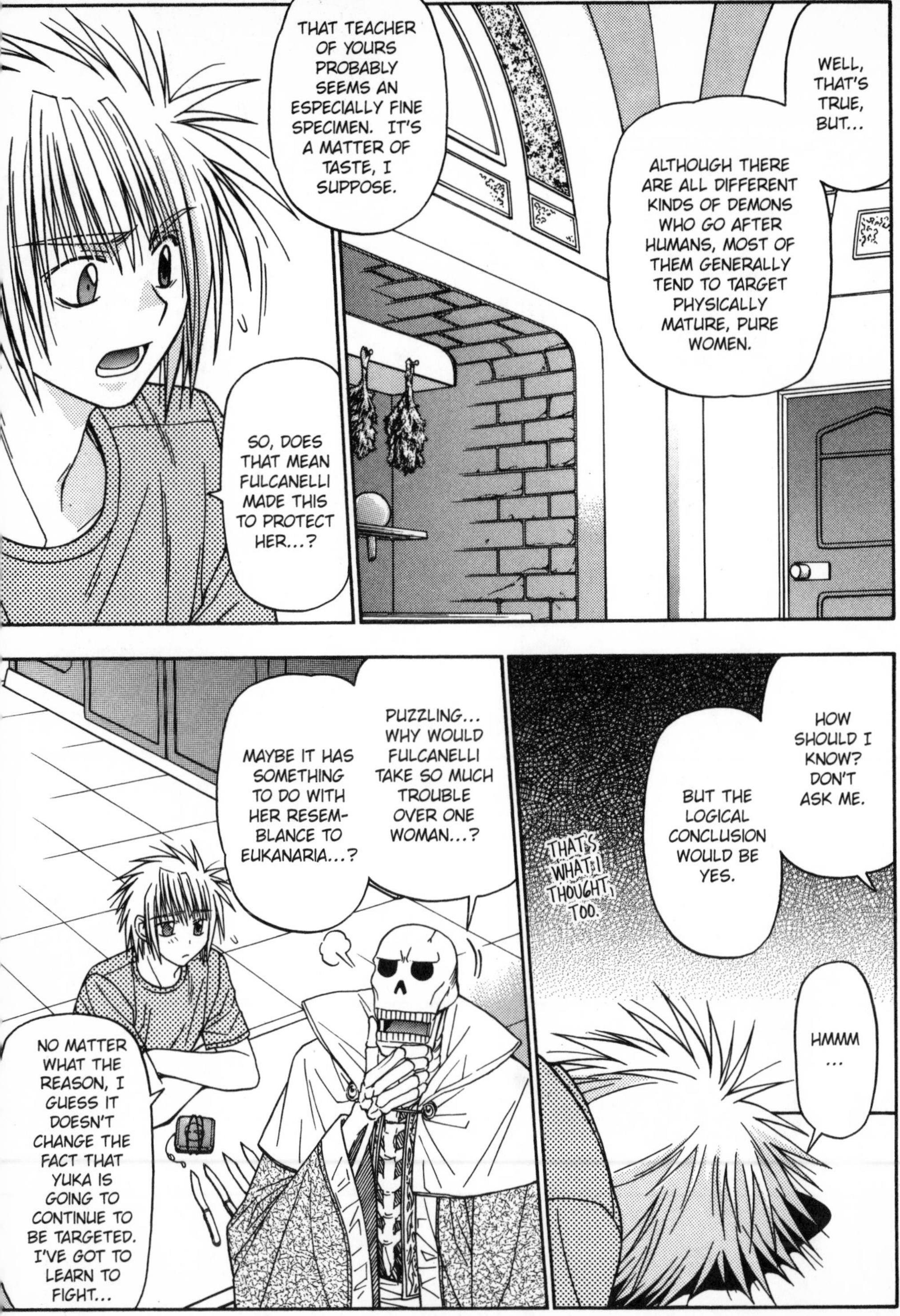
WELL, THAT'S TRUE, BUT...
ALTHOUGH THERE ARE ALL DIFFERENT KINDS OF DEMONS WHO GO AFTER HUMANS, MOST OF THEM GENERALLY TEND TO TARGET PHYSICALLY MATURE, PURE WOMEN.
THAT TEACHER OF YOURS PROBABLY SEEMS AN ESPECIALLY FINE SPECIMEN. IT'S A MATTER OF TASTE, I SUPPOSE.
SO, DOES THAT MEAN FULCANELLI MADE THIS TO PROTECT HER...?
HOW SHOULD I KNOW? DON'T ASK ME.
BUT THE LOGICAL CONCLUSION WOULD BE YES.
THAT'S WHAT I THOUGHT, TOO.
HMMM...
PUZZLING... WHY WOULD FULCANELLI TAKE SO MUCH TROUBLE OVER ONE WOMAN...?
MAYBE IT HAS SOMETHING TO DO WITH HER RESEMBLANCE TO EUKANARIA...?
NO MATTER WHAT THE REASON, I GUESS IT DOESN'T CHANGE THE FACT THAT YUKA IS GOING TO CONTINUE TO BE TARGETED. I'VE GOT TO LEARN TO FIGHT...

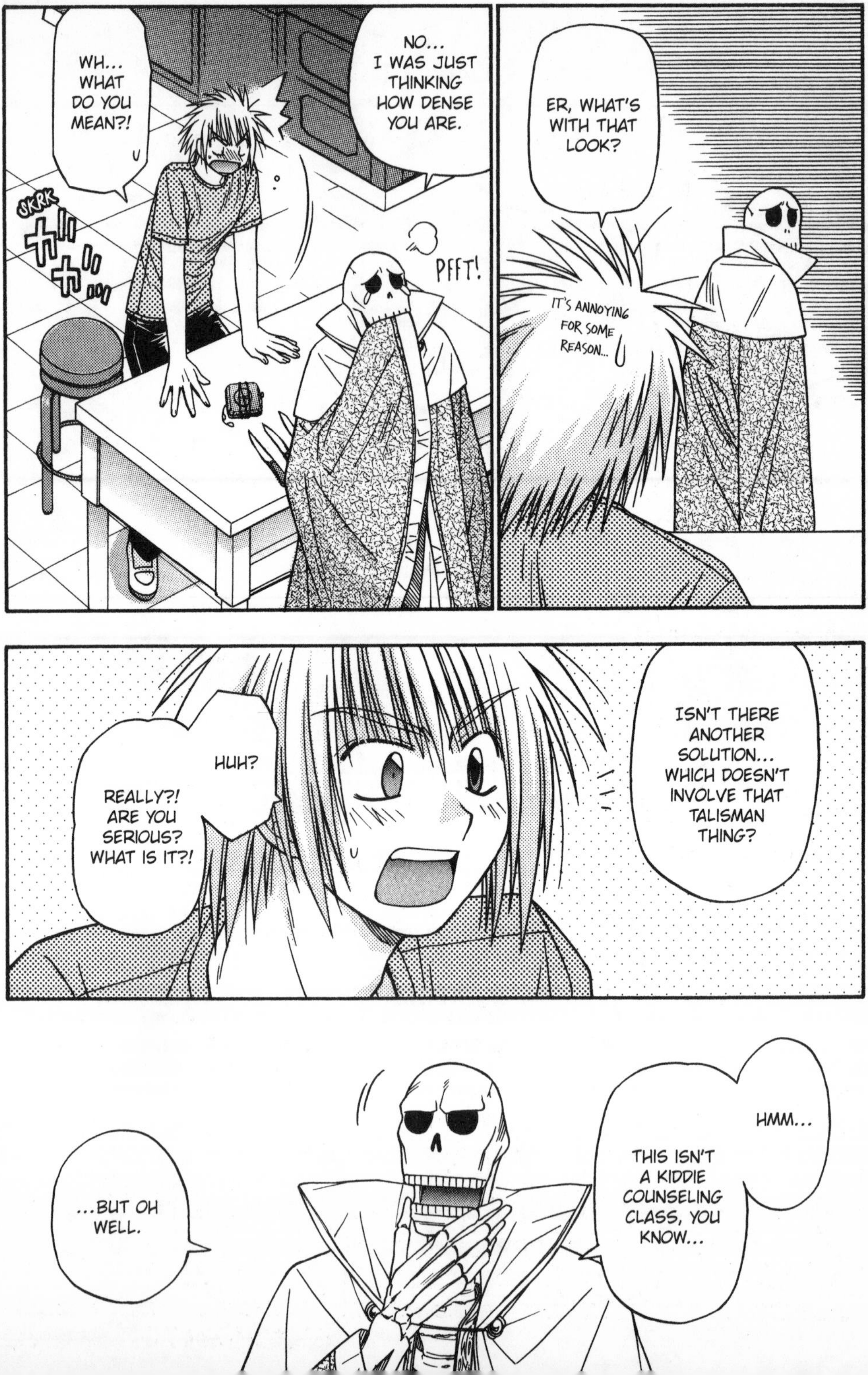
ER, WHAT'S WITH THAT LOOK?
IT'S ANNOYING FOR SOME REASON...
NO... I WAS JUST THINKING HOW DENSE YOU ARE.
PFFT!
WH... WHAT DO YOU MEAN?!
SKRK
ISN'T THERE ANOTHER SOLUTION... WHICH DOESN'T INVOLVE THAT TALISMAN THING?
HUH?
REALLY?! ARE YOU SERIOUS? WHAT IS IT?!
HMM...
THIS ISN'T A KIDDIE COUNSELING CLASS, YOU KNOW...
...BUT OH WELL.

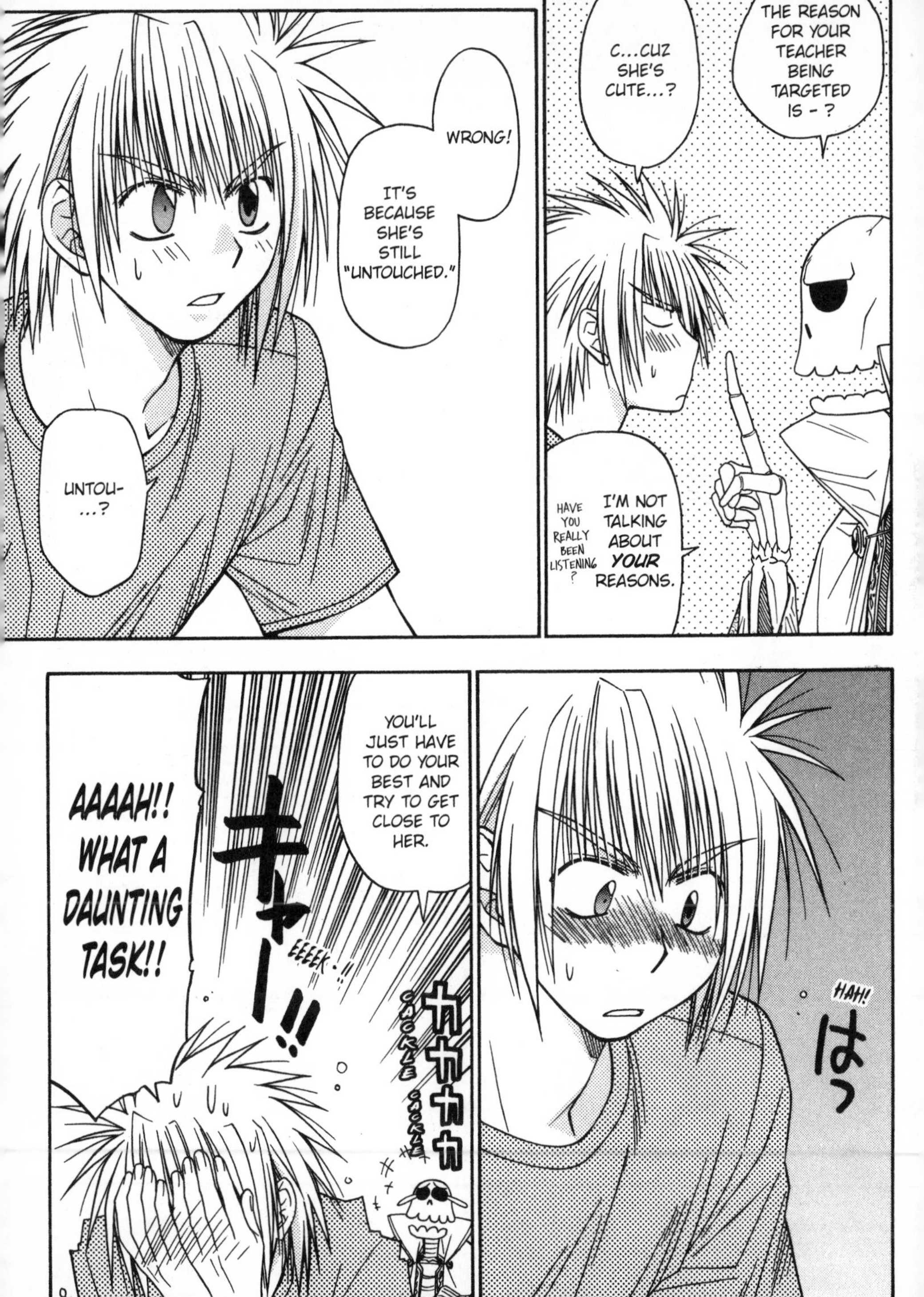
THE REASON FOR YOUR TEACHER BEING TARGETED IS - ?
C...CUZ SHE'S CUTE...?
I'M NOT TALKING ABOUT YOUR REASONS.
HAVE YOU REALLY BEEN LISTENING?
WRONG!
IT'S BECAUSE SHE'S STILL "UNTOUCHED."
UNTOU-...?
HAH!
はっ
YOU'LL JUST HAVE TO DO YOUR BEST AND TRY TO GET CLOSE TO HER.
キャー!!
EEEEK!!
カカカカ
CACKLE CACKLE
AAAAH!! WHAT A DAUNTING TASK!!

ENCHANTER 3 END

NANIWA-JIN BATTLE DIARY

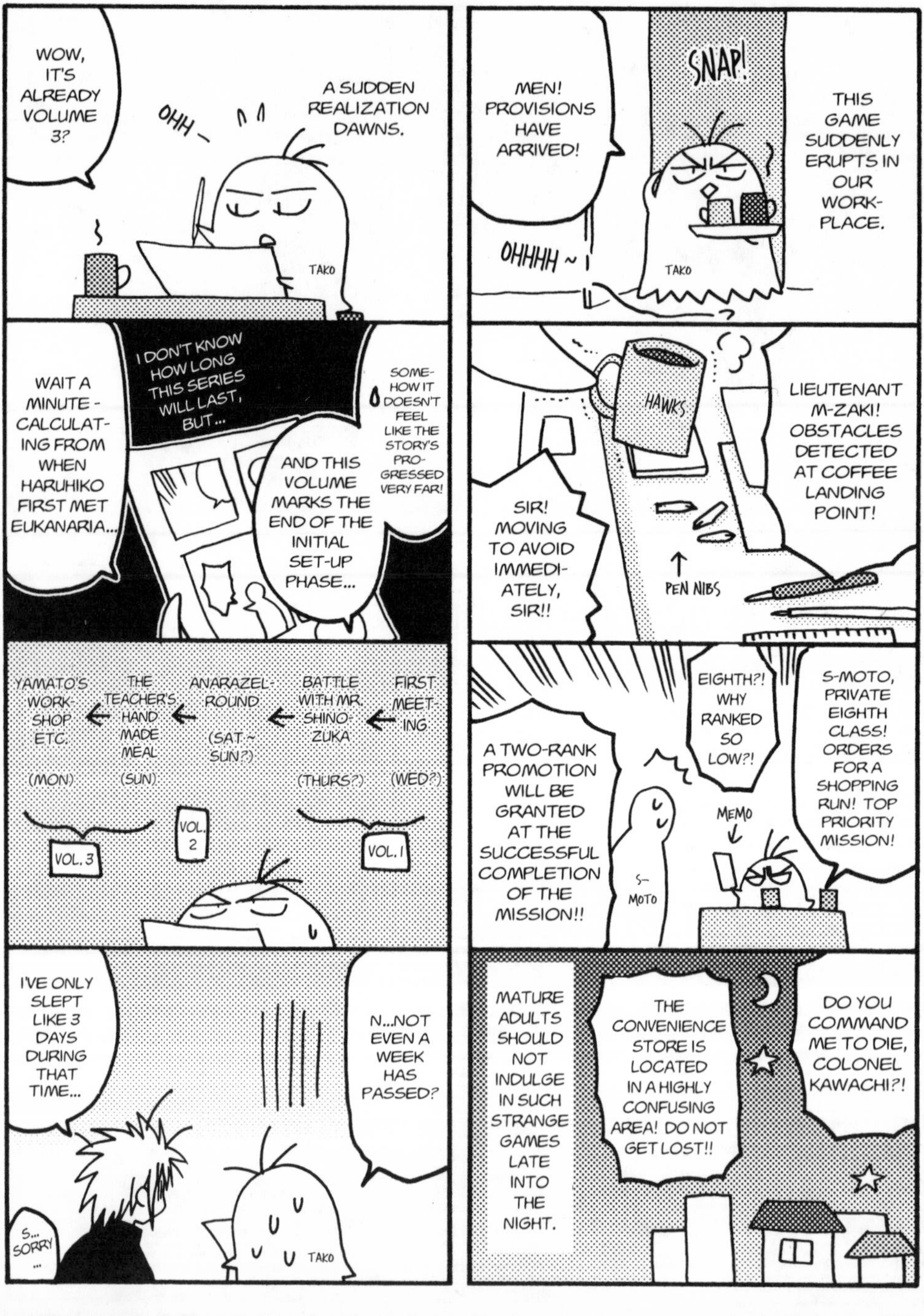
THIS GAME SUDDENLY ERUPTS IN OUR WORK-PLACE.
SNAP!
MEN! PROVISIONS HAVE ARRIVED!
TAKO
OHHHH ~ !
LIEUTENANT M-ZAKI! OBSTACLES DETECTED AT COFFEE LANDING POINT!
HAWKS
SIR! MOVING TO AVOID IMMEDI-ATELY, SIR!!
PEN NIBS
S-MOTO, PRIVATE EIGHTH CLASS! ORDERS FOR A SHOPPING RUN! TOP PRIORITY MISSION!
EIGHTH?! WHY RANKED SO LOW?!
MEMO
A TWO-RANK PROMOTION WILL BE GRANTED AT THE SUCCESSFUL COMPLETION OF THE MISSION!!
S-MOTO
DO YOU COMMAND ME TO DIE, COLONEL KAWACHI?!
THE CONVENIENCE STORE IS LOCATED IN A HIGHLY CONFUSING AREA! DO NOT GET LOST!!
MATURE ADULTS SHOULD NOT INDULGE IN SUCH STRANGE GAMES LATE INTO THE NIGHT.
A SUDDEN REALIZATION DAWNS.
WOW, IT'S ALREADY VOLUME 3?
OHH ~
TAKO
SOME-HOW IT DOESN'T FEEL LIKE THE STORY'S PRO-GRESSED VERY FAR!
I DON'T KNOW HOW LONG THIS SERIES WILL LAST, BUT...
AND THIS VOLUME MARKS THE END OF THE INITIAL SET-UP PHASE...
WAIT A MINUTE - CALCULAT-ING FROM WHEN HARUHIKO FIRST MET EUKANARIA...
FIRST MEET-ING (WED?)
BATTLE WITH MR. SHINO-ZUKA (THURS?)
ANARAZEL-ROUND (SAT ~ SUN?)
THE TEACHER'S HAND MADE MEAL (SUN)
YAMATO'S WORK-SHOP ETC. (MON)
VOL. 1
VOL. 2
VOL. 3
N...NOT EVEN A WEEK HAS PASSED?
I'VE ONLY SLEPT LIKE 3 DAYS DURING THAT TIME...
TAKO
S... SORRY ...

BONUS PAGE!!

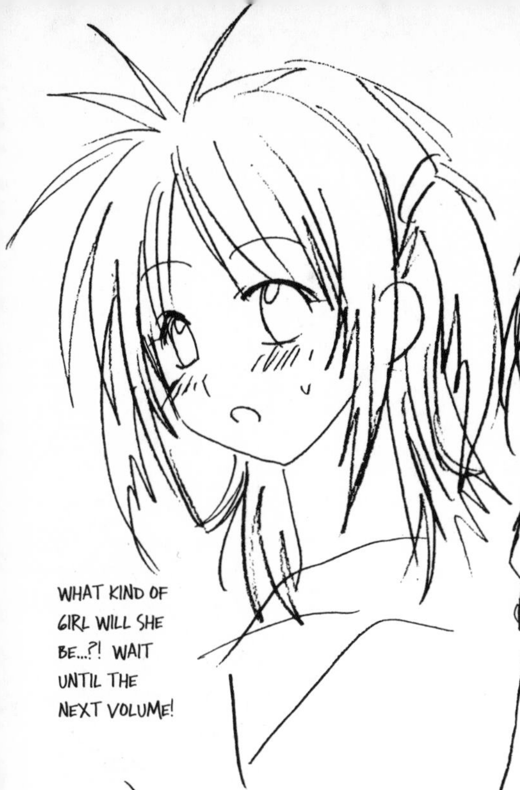

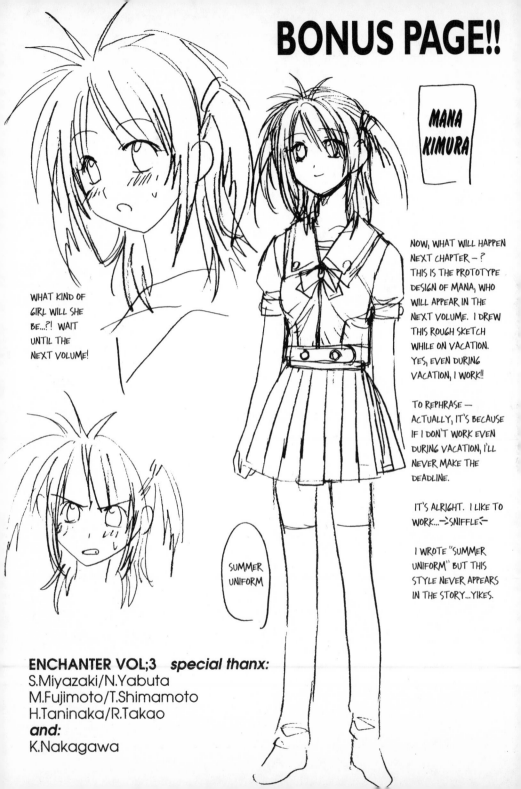

WHAT KIND OF GIRL WILL SHE BE...?! WAIT UNTIL THE NEXT VOLUME!

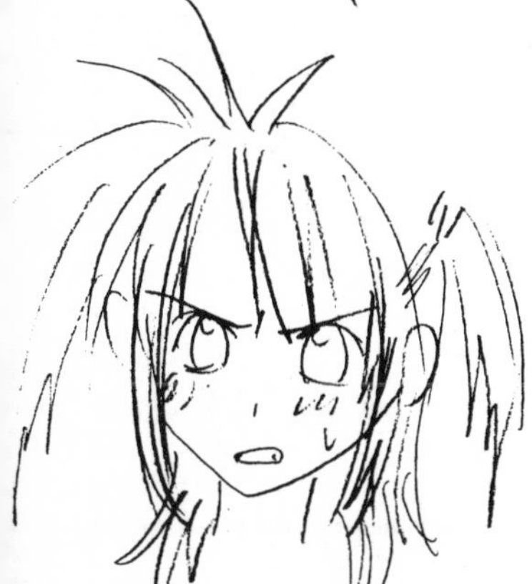

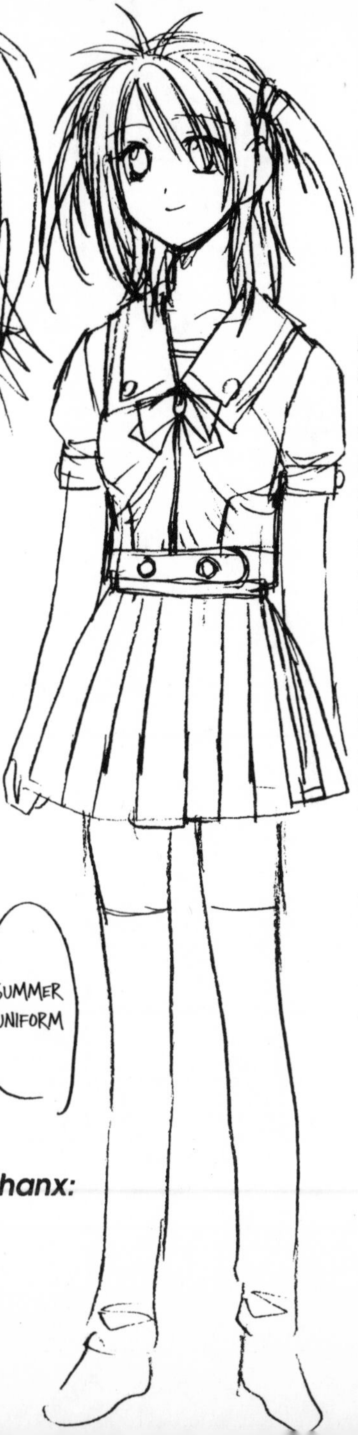
SUMMER UNIFORM

MANA KIMURA

NOW, WHAT WILL HAPPEN NEXT CHAPTER – ? THIS IS THE PROTOTYPE DESIGN OF MANA, WHO WILL APPEAR IN THE NEXT VOLUME. I DREW THIS ROUGH SKETCH WHILE ON VACATION. YES, EVEN DURING VACATION, I WORK!!

TO REPHRASE — ACTUALLY, IT'S BECAUSE IF I DON'T WORK EVEN DURING VACATION, I'LL NEVER MAKE THE DEADLINE.

IT'S ALRIGHT. I LIKE TO WORK... ⇀SNIFFLE↽

I WROTE "SUMMER UNIFORM" BUT THIS STYLE NEVER APPEARS IN THE STORY...YIKES.

ENCHANTER VOL;3 ***special thanx:***
S.Miyazaki/N.Yabuta
M.Fujimoto/T.Shimamoto
H.Taninaka/R.Takao
and:
K.Nakagawa

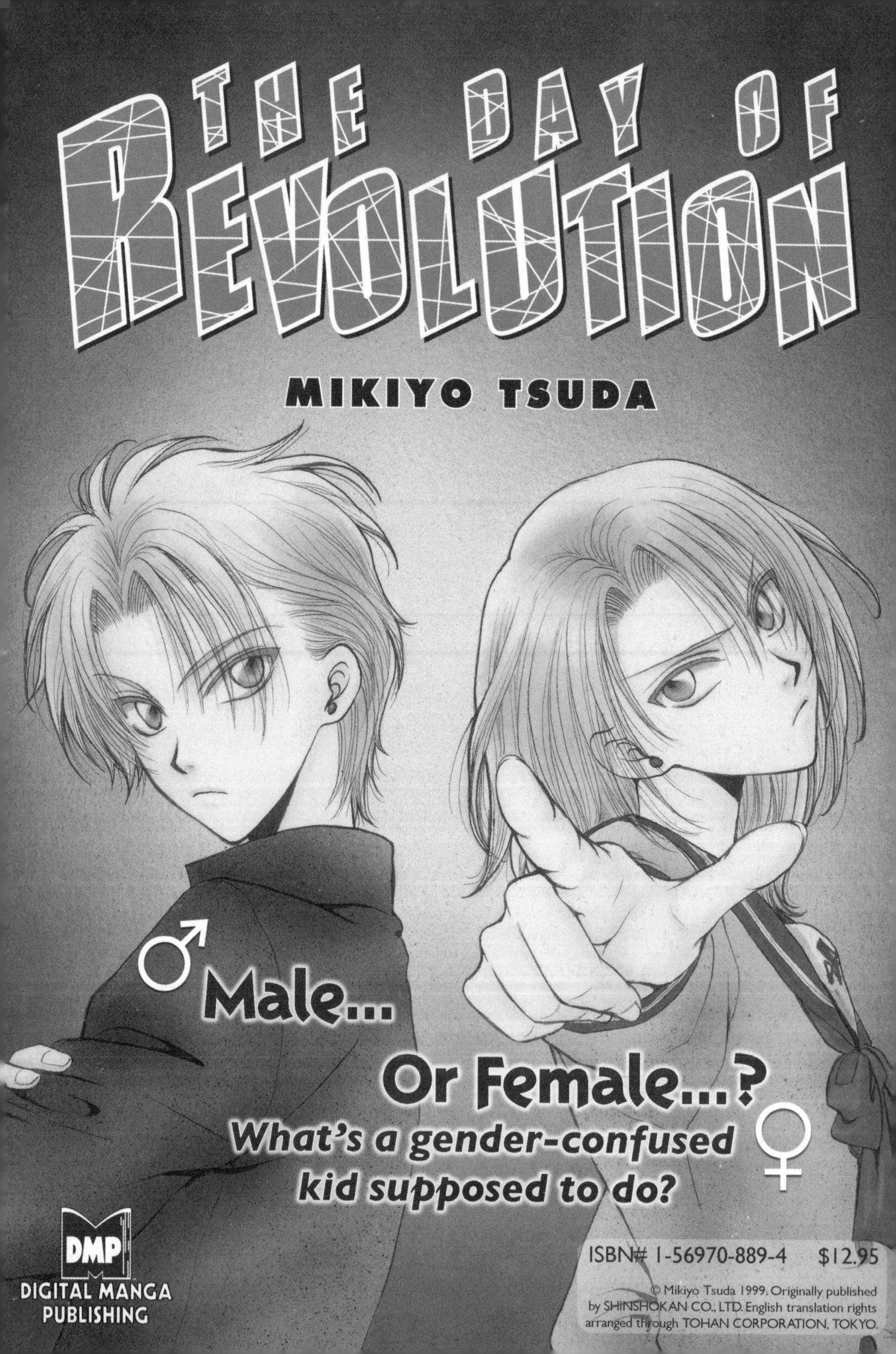
THE DAY OF
REVOLUTION
MIKIYO TSUDA
♂ Male...
Or Female...?
What's a gender-confused
kid supposed to do? ♀
DMP
DIGITAL MANGA
PUBLISHING
ISBN# 1-56970-889-4 $12.95
© Mikiyo Tsuda 1999. Originally published
by SHINSHOKAN CO., LTD. English translation rights
arranged through TOHAN CORPORATION, TOKYO.

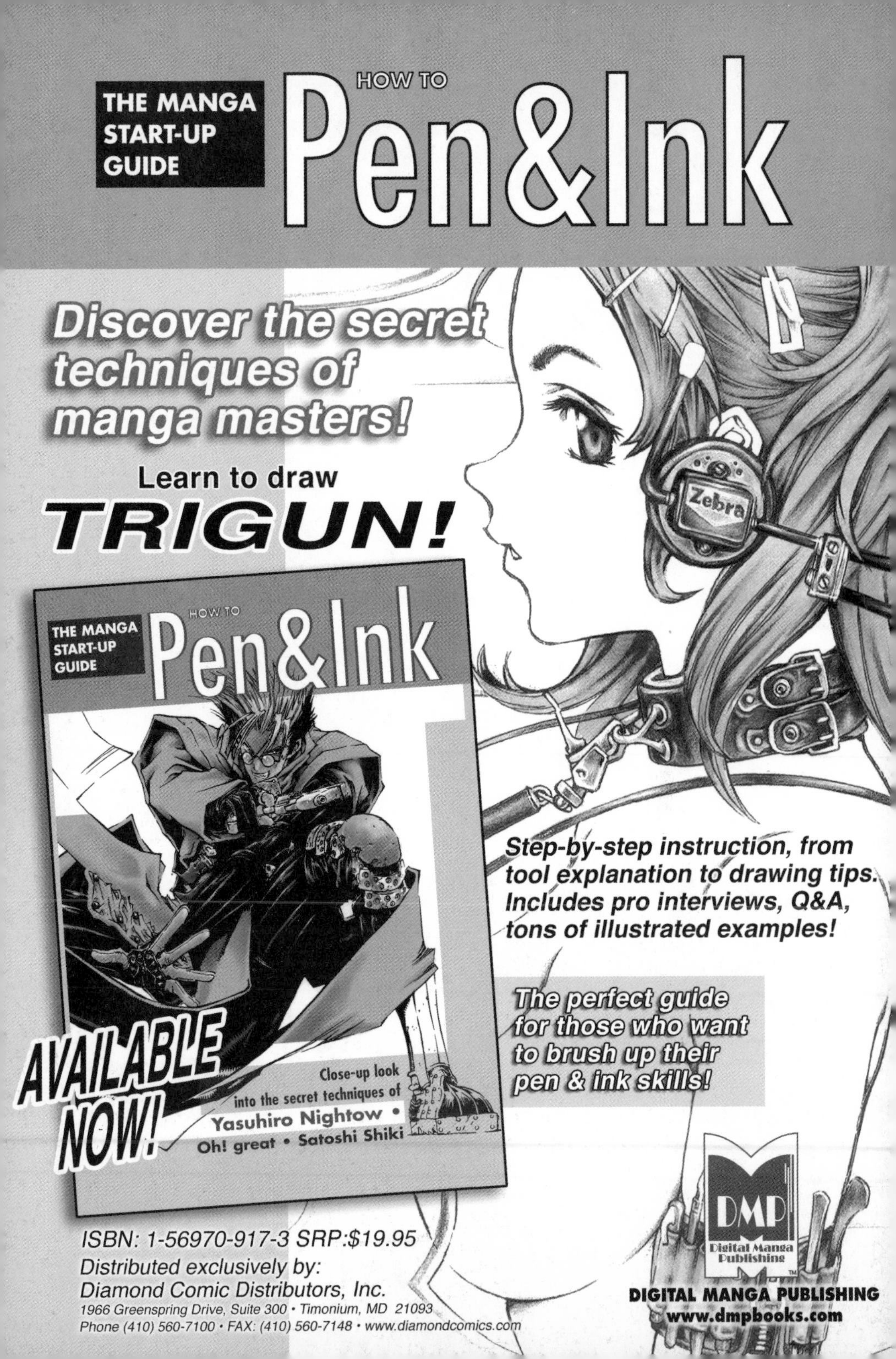

THE MANGA START-UP GUIDE
HOW TO
Pen&Ink
Discover the secret techniques of manga masters!
Learn to draw
TRIGUN!
THE MANGA START-UP GUIDE
HOW TO
Pen&Ink
Close-up look into the secret techniques of
Yasuhiro Nightow • Oh! great • Satoshi Shiki
AVAILABLE NOW!
Zebra
Step-by-step instruction, from tool explanation to drawing tips. Includes pro interviews, Q&A, tons of illustrated examples!
The perfect guide for those who want to brush up their pen & ink skills!
ISBN: 1-56970-917-3 SRP:$19.95
Distributed exclusively by:
Diamond Comic Distributors, Inc.
1966 Greenspring Drive, Suite 300 • Timonium, MD 21093
Phone (410) 560-7100 • FAX: (410) 560-7148 • www.diamondcomics.com
DMP
Digital Manga Publishing
TM
DIGITAL MANGA PUBLISHING
www.dmpbooks.com

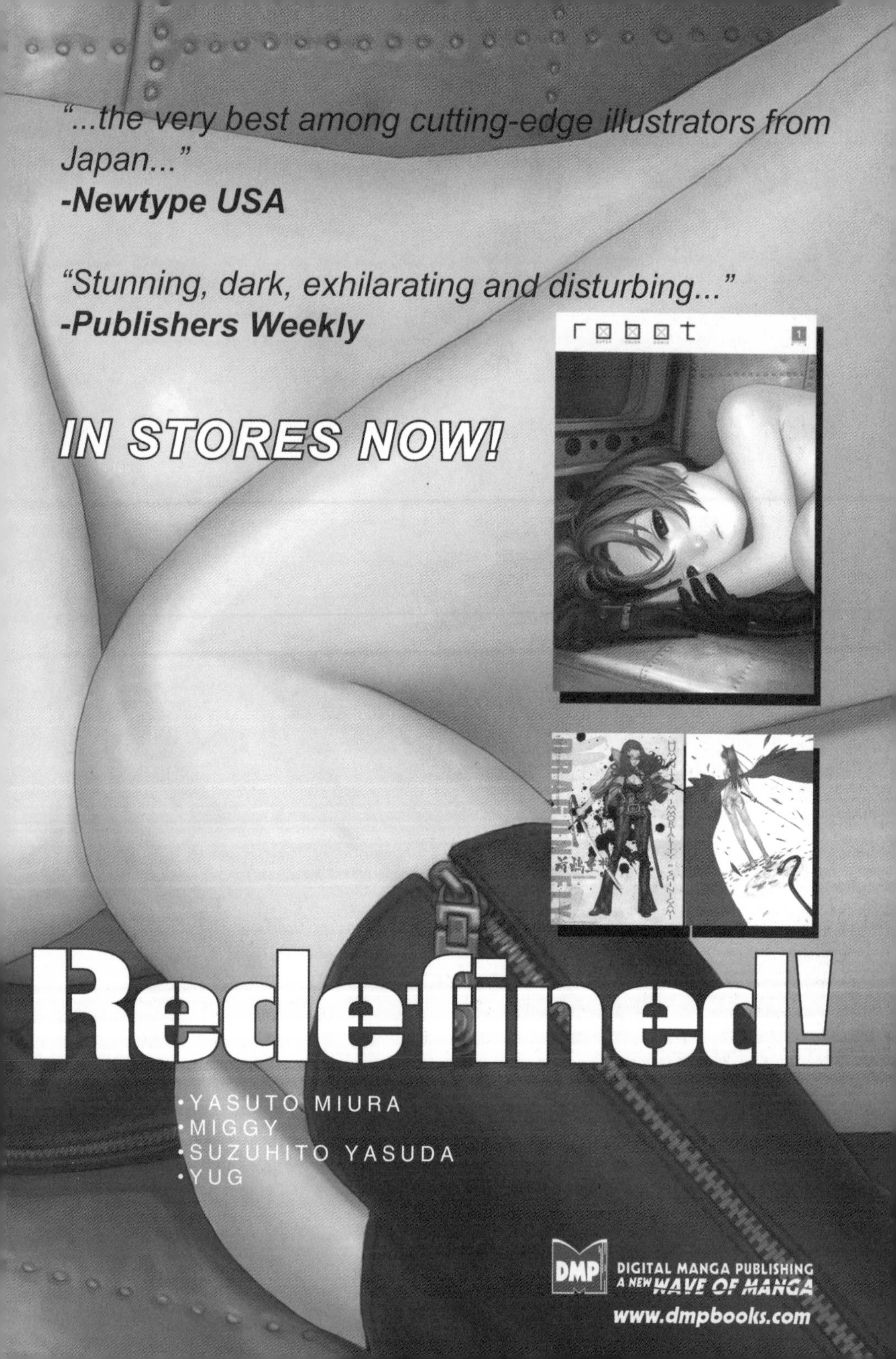
"...the very best among cutting-edge illustrators from Japan..."
-Newtype USA
"Stunning, dark, exhilarating and disturbing..."
-Publishers Weekly
robot
IN STORES NOW!
Redefined!
•YASUTO MIURA
•MIGGY
•SUZUHITO YASUDA
•YUG
DMP
DIGITAL MANGA PUBLISHING
A NEW WAVE OF MANGA
www.dmpbooks.com

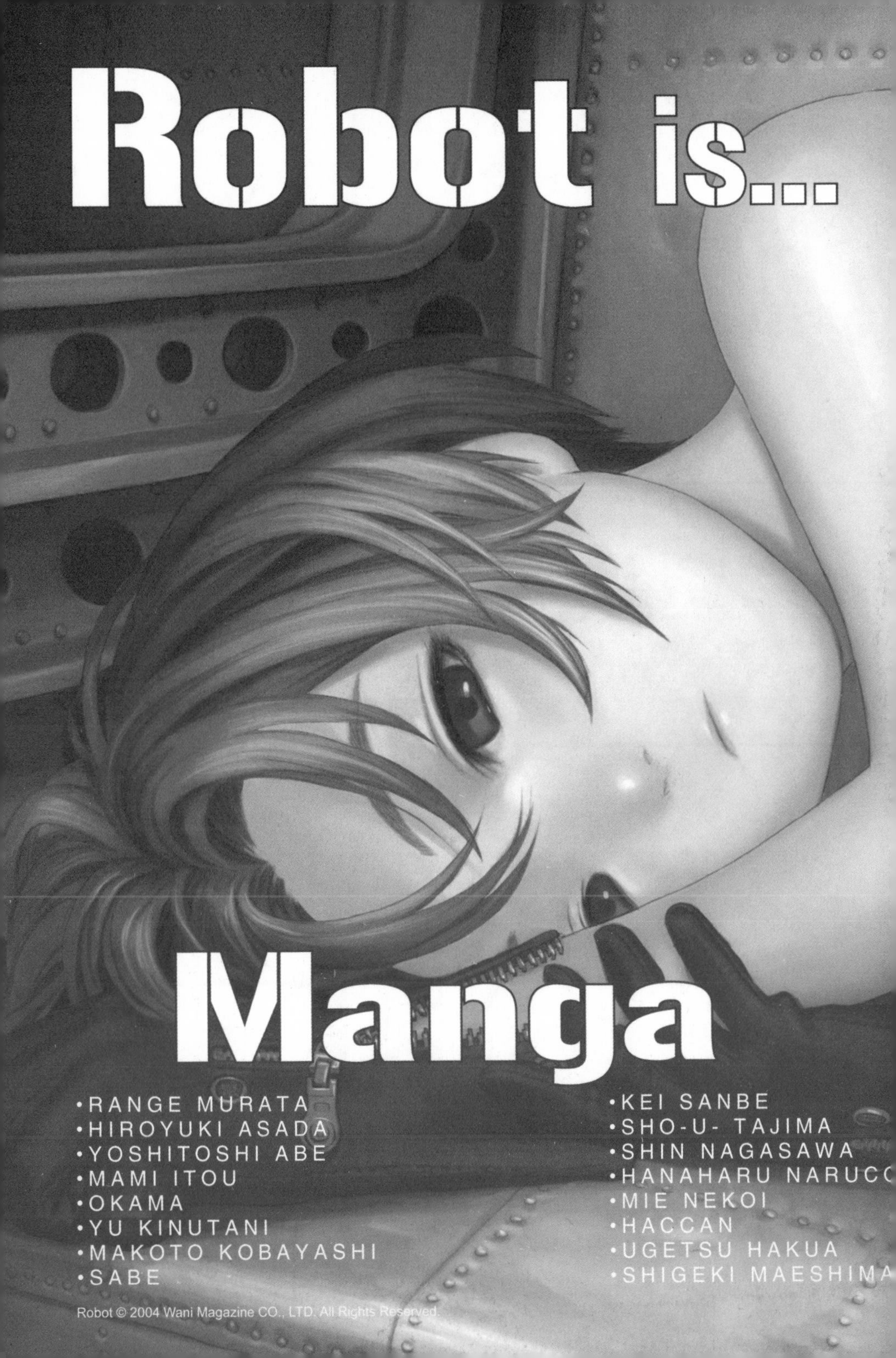
Robot is...
Manga
•RANGE MURATA
•HIROYUKI ASADA
•YOSHITOSHI ABE
•MAMI ITOU
•OKAMA
•YU KINUTANI
•MAKOTO KOBAYASHI
•SABE
•KEI SANBE
•SHO-U- TAJIMA
•SHIN NAGASAWA
•HANAHARU NARUC
•MIE NEKOI
•HACCAN
•UGETSU HAKUA
•SHIGEKI MAESHIMA
Robot © 2004 Wani Magazine CO., LTD. All Rights Reserved.

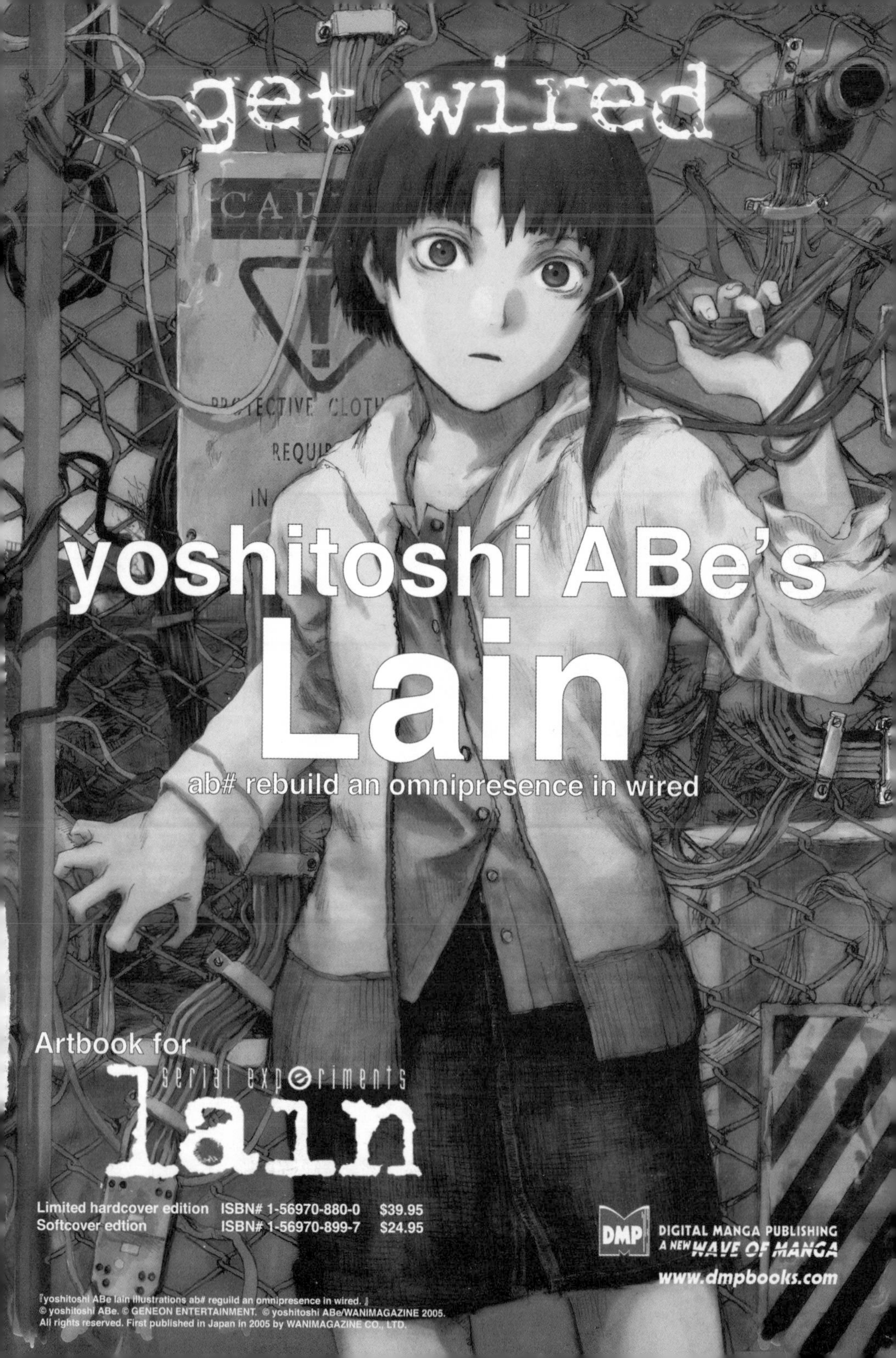

get wired
CAU
PROTECTIVE CLOTH
REQUIR
IN
yoshitoshi ABe's
Lain
ab# rebuild an omnipresence in wired
Artbook for
serial experiments
lain
Limited hardcover edition ISBN# 1-56970-880-0 $39.95
Softcover edtion ISBN# 1-56970-899-7 $24.95
DMP
DIGITAL MANGA PUBLISHING
A NEW WAVE OF MANGA
www.dmpbooks.com
『yoshitoshi ABe lain illustrations ab# reguild an omnipresence in wired.』
© yoshitoshi ABe. © GENEON ENTERTAINMENT. © yoshitoshi ABe/WANIMAGAZINE 2005.
All rights reserved. First published in Japan in 2005 by WANIMAGAZINE CO., LTD.

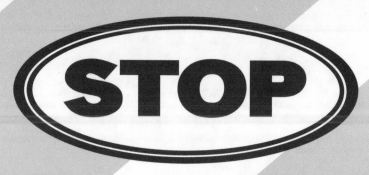

STOP

This is the back of the book! Start from the other side.

NATIVE MANGA readers read manga from *right to left*.

1
2
1
3
2
3
5
4
4
6
5
8
7
6

If you run into our ***Native Manga*** *logo on any of our books... you'll know that this manga is published in it's true original native Japanese right to left reading format, as it was intended. Turn to the other side of the book and start reading from right to left, top to bottom.*

Follow the diagram to see how its done.
Surf's Up!

NATIVE MANGA
READ RIGHT TO LEFT

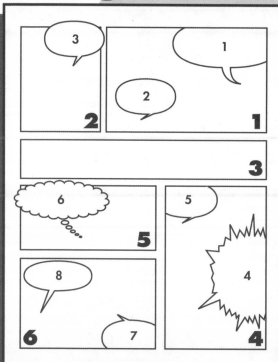

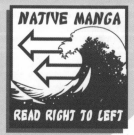